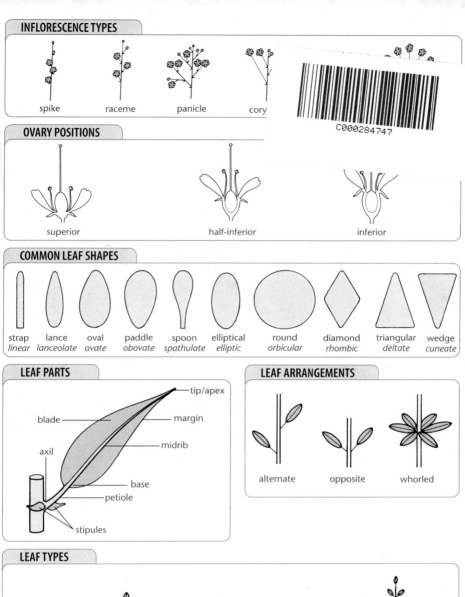

## INFLORESCENCE TYPES

spike  raceme  panicle  cory...

## OVARY POSITIONS

superior  half-inferior  inferior

## COMMON LEAF SHAPES

strap *linear* | lance *lanceolate* | oval *ovate* | paddle *obovate* | spoon *spathulate* | elliptical *elliptic* | round *orbicular* | diamond *rhombic* | triangular *deltate* | wedge *cuneate*

## LEAF PARTS

tip/apex
blade
margin
axil
midrib
base
petiole
stipules

## LEAF ARRANGEMENTS

alternate  opposite  whorled

## LEAF TYPES

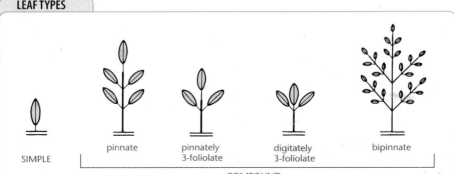

SIMPLE  pinnate  pinnately 3-foliolate  digitately 3-foliolate  bipinnate

COMPOUND

# FIELD GUIDE TO
# FYNBOS

## John Manning

Photography by
**Colin Paterson-Jones**
and **John Manning**

Struik Nature
(an imprint of Random House Struik (Pty) Ltd)
Reg. No. 1966/003153/07
80 McKenzie Street, Cape Town, 8001 South Africa
PO Box 1144, Cape Town 8000, South Africa

Visit us at **www.randomstruik.co.za**
Log on to our photographic website **www.imagesofafrica.co.za**
for an African experience.

First published 2007
3 5 7 9 10 8 6 4

**Publishing manager:** Pippa Parker
**Editor:** Helen de Villiers
**Design director:** Janice Evans
**Designer:** Louise Topping
**Illustrator:** John Manning
**Proofreader:** Tessa Kennedy

Reproduction by Hirt & Carter Cape (Pty) Ltd
Printed and bound by Craft Print International Ltd

**ISBN 978 1 77007 265 7**
**Barcode 9781770072657**

### Photographs:
FRONT COVER: *Erica longifolia*
PREVIOUS PAGE: *Nebelia sphaerocephala* (left),
Chincherinchee, *Ornithogalum thyrsoides* (middle),
Featherbush, *Aulax cancellata* (right)
THIS PAGE: Autumn Star, *Empodium flexile* (top),
*Bulbinella nutans* (middle), *Endonema retziodes* (bottom)
FOLLOWING PAGE: *Mimetes fimbriifolius* and *Leucadendron laureolum*
P32: *Agapanthus africanus* and *Hermas villosa* in mountain fynbos

The author and publisher are grateful to the Parker family of
Elandsberg Nature Reserve for their generous sponsorship.

# ACKNOWLEDGEMENTS

The idea for this guide was conceived by my long-time field companion and co-author Colin Paterson-Jones and brought to fruition by the Natural History team at Struik under Pippa Parker, editor Helen de Villiers and designer Louise Topping, with the help of proofreader Tessa Kennedy. I hope that they are pleased with the result. The distribution maps that are such an important part of the guide were generated from specimen data held in the PRECIS data base of the South African National Biodiversity Institute, under the auspices of Liesl Mostert, Hannelie Snyman and Hester Steyn. I am extremely grateful to them. My colleague from the same institute, Les Powrie, produced the excellent and detailed vegetation map. I also thank my fellow taxonomists at the Compton Herbarium for their help, especially Dee Snijman and Ted Oliver. Fritz Volk very kindly provided a suggested shortlist of *Erica* species from that enormous genus and Colin Paterson-Jones did the same for the Proteaceae. Advice on the Khoisan languages, the original source of the current vernacular names of several Western Cape plants, was freely given by Nigel Crawhall of the Indigenous Peoples of Africa Co-ordinating Committee. Ross Turner and Ernst van Jaarsveld provided the photographs of *Aloe haemanthifolia* and *Freylinia undulata*. Finally, my grateful thanks to Elizabeth Parker for her ongoing commitment to conservation and education, and to the South African National Biodiversity Institute for additional sponsorship from the Mia Karsten bequest to the Compton Herbarium.

# ABOUT THIS BOOK

*Field Guide to Fynbos* is the result of several decades of intensive fieldwork and study. It features a wide cross-section of the plants that characterise fynbos plant communities of the southwestern Cape. For the first time non-botanists have a chance of identifying a significant proportion of the bewildering diversity of fynbos species from the region. Over 1 150 species of wild flower are illustrated and described, with distribution maps, comparisons with similar species where applicable, and notes on traditional uses. These species are a selection from the almost 9 000 different flowering plants that occur in the Cape Floristic Region (see map on p.9), some three-quarters of which are fynbos species. A simple-to-use system, developed especially for this book, aids identification at all levels.

From among the estimated 7 000 species of true Cape fynbos, we have selected the most common and conspicuous to showcase its diversity, with an emphasis on those with showy, or at least evident, flowers. Only a few representatives of the Cape reeds (restios), which require microscopic study for their identification, are included, and other small-flowered genera, such as *Phylica* and *Thesium,* are similarly treated.

Fynbos is easily the most diverse and conspicuous vegetation type found in the southwestern Cape, and in the eyes of many people it is synonymous with the flora of the region. This is not strictly true, however, and other vegetation types, including forest, strandveld thicket, karroid shrubland and renosterveld, add to the beauty and diversity of the region. Although often important in garden cultivation, they contribute a meagre 20–30 per cent of the wild species in the southwestern Cape, and fall outside the scope of this book.

# CONTENTS

# THE WORLD OF FYNBOS

Fynbos is famous not only for the diversity and unusual composition of its plant species but also for the sheer beauty of many of its wildflowers. This unique vegetation is synonymous with the southern tip of Africa, where it occupies a crescent of country at the toe of the continent, reaching from the plateau above Vanrhynsdorp in the northwest to the city of Port Elizabeth in the southeast. Long recognised as the smallest of the six floral kingdoms of the world, this region is now more properly known as the Cape Floristic Region and is home to one of the world's richest floras. Gathered within an area of 90 000 km² are almost 9 000 species of flowering plants, two-thirds of which are found nowhere else on Earth. It is small wonder that Conservation International (a United States-based organisation concerned with conserving the Earth's living heritage) has identified the Cape Floristic Region as one of the ±30 critical biological hotspots on Earth. Pre-eminent among the botanical riches of the region is fynbos.

## History of fynbos

The first inkling of this extraordinary flora from Africa to reach scientists arrived in the form of a dried flowerhead of *Protea neriifolia*, gathered from the slopes above False Bay by the crew of a passing Dutch East Indiaman. European botanists were understandably baffled by its resemblance to a thistle, but this first tentative harbinger was soon followed by the arrival of bulbs of several species of Amaryllis, Hyacinth and Iris. The flowering of these bulbs in Holland in the first years of the 17th century ignited a passion for fynbos flowers that has shown no sign of abating.

Early botanical visitors to Cape Town were overwhelmed by the local flora. Swedish naturalist Andrew Sparrman, who visited the region in the latter half of the 18th century, was among the first to experience its wonders. His journal entry for April 1772 records his excitement: 'At first almost every day was a rich harvest of the rarest and most beautiful plants; … at every step we made one or more new discoveries' – and this was written in autumn, when relatively few species are in flower. Other early botanical visitors to Cape Town were similarly entranced. 'All that I had pictured to myself of the riches of the Cape in botany, was

*Erica nana* (Erica family)

far surpassed by what I saw in this day's walk. At every step a different plant appeared; and it is not an exaggerated description, if it should be compared to a botanic garden … so great was the variety everywhere to be met with,' enthused the English explorer William Burchell in his journal entry for the last week of November 1810.

By contrast, the early Dutch residents at the Cape were too preoccupied with more mundane matters to take much interest in the local vegetation, surprising Burchell with their indiscriminate and rather dismissive reference to the 'glorious heaths' of the area as mere *bosjes* (bushes).

The term *fynbos* (or *fynbosch*), recorded in the Tsitsikamma area by John Noble in 1868, was first formally used only in the early 20th century, when ecologist John Bews cited it as 'applied by the inhabitants of the Cape to any sort of small woodland growth that does not include timber trees'. Well into the 20th century, Cape botanists continued to describe the vegetation either as *macchia* (borrowing the term from the Mediterranean basin), or as *sclerophyll* bush or shrub. It was only in the latter half of the century that the term *fynbos* gained international currency as the appropriate name for the distinctive vegetation of the southwestern Cape, taking its place alongside *kwongan*, *matorral*, *chaparral* and *maquis* (*macchia*), the locally derived names for analogous heathland communities in southwestern Australia, Chile, California and the Mediterranean basin respectively.

Fynbos is one of the more distinctive of the many vegetation types that occur in southern Africa, an observation that amateur South African botanist Harry Bolus made as early as 1874. 'I believe that there exist few botanical boundaries as rigid [as that which separates the Cape flora from that of the interior],' he wrote to Sir Joseph Hooker, President of the Royal Society. His suggested boundary for the Cape flora conforms closely to that still used today to delimit the Cape Floristic Region.

# Fynbos distribution

As the dominant vegetation of the southwestern Cape, fynbos occurs in several bands along the west and southern Cape coasts, from north of Clanwilliam in the west to Port Elizabeth in the east (see map below). These bands, or belts, conform largely to the parallel sandstone and quartzite formations of the Cape Fold Mountains, and also clothe more or less extensive exposures of sand and limestone along the coastal shelves. By far the greatest portion of fynbos vegetation is contained within the boundaries of the Cape Floristic Region but suitable soils support smaller enclaves of fynbos well beyond its borders.

Along the West Coast, coastal sands and their associated communities of sand-plain fynbos extend for some distance northwards, almost to the Namibian border, and outcrops of quartzitic rock along the southern Cape coast allow grassy

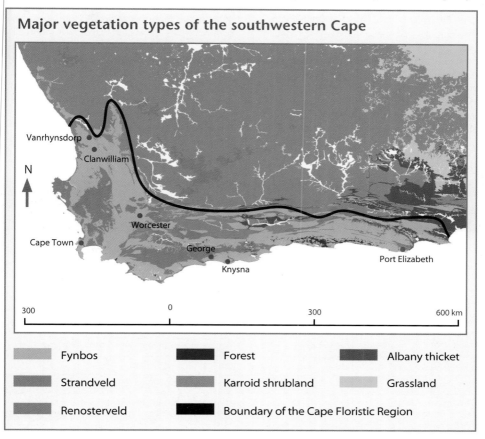

## Major vegetation types of the southwestern Cape

Vanrhynsdorp
Clanwilliam
N
Worcester
Cape Town
George
Knysna
Port Elizabeth

300    0    300    600 km

| Fynbos | Forest | Albany thicket |
| Strandveld | Karroid shrubland | Grassland |
| Renosterveld | Boundary of the Cape Floristic Region | |

fynbos to thrive as far east as Grahamstown. Beyond this, outlying fynbos communities occur on sandstone outcrops in southern KwaZulu-Natal near Port Edward, and scattered patches can be found on outcrops of sandstone, quartzite and basalt along the edge of the Drakensberg Mountains and eastern Escarpment, northwards into eastern Zimbabwe. The fynbos communities of the eastern seaboard, although structurally similar to the true Cape fynbos of the Cape Floristic Region and Namaqualand, differ from it floristically and are distinguished from it as Afro-montane and Afro-alpine fynbos. In this book we consider only Cape fynbos.

## Defining fynbos

Much of the distinctive character of fynbos is the result of the predominance of a relatively small number of plant groups. Indeed, almost half of the total species are accounted for by just 33 Cape floral elements, or lineages – defined as those groups that appear to have originated in the Cape and most of whose descendants are still there. The remaining species derive from groups that are more widespread outside of the Cape.

Although generally easy to recognise, fynbos is not as readily defined. Not only does it contain a diversity of plant communities itself, but fynbos also shares the Cape Floristic Region with several other vegetation types, including renosterveld, karroid shrubland, various thicket types and

forest. In addition, fynbos-like communities occur outside of the boundaries of the Cape Floristic Region, most especially along the edge of the interior escarpment to the north and northeast.

As a whole, fynbos is most inclusively defined as an evergreen, hard-leafed shrubland occurring on nutrient-poor soils, especially those derived from heavily leached sandstones or limestones; dominated by small- and leathery-leafed shrubs associated with evergreen, grass-like perennials; and comprising essentially members of plant groups that are characteristic of the Cape Floristic Region. This definition includes both true Cape fynbos, recognised particularly by the presence of restios, as well as the outlying Afro-montane fynbos communities, which lack restios.

Fynbos mostly occurs on acidic (pH 4.4–7.0), coarse-grained soils that are poor in nutrients, especially nitrogen and phosphorus. It rarely develops where the annual rainfall is less than 400 mm per annum or where droughts are common. In its adaptation to relatively infertile soils, fynbos is analogous to the heathlands of other Mediterranean regions.

The fynbos definition excludes renoster shrubland – another evergreen, fine-leafed vegetation type, dominated by the shrubby, granular-leafed renosterbos, *Elytropappus rhinocerotis* (Asteraceae), that once covered large tracts of the more fertile clay soils of the coastal forelands and intermontane valleys in the southwestern

| FAMILIES ENDEMIC OR NEAR-ENDEMIC TO CAPE FYNBOS | | | |
|---|---|---|---|
| | NUMBER OF SPECIES | | |
| Family | Cape Fynbos | Other | Total |
| BRUNIA | 63 | 1 | 64 |
| PENAEA | 23 | – | 23 |
| GRUBBIA | 3 | – | 3 |
| RORIDULA | 2 | – | 2 |
| GEISSOLOMA | 1 | – | 1 |
| LANARIA | 1 | 1 | 1 |
| PRIONIUM | 1 | 1 | 1 |

| FIVE LARGEST FYNBOS FAMILIES (Defined as those families with >90% species endemism in the Cape Floristic Region) | | |
|---|---|---|
| | NUMBER OF SPECIES | |
| Family | Cape Floristic Region | Worldwide |
| ERICA | 670 | 4 500 |
| PROTEA | 330 | 1 350 |
| RESTIO | 320 | 400 |
| CITRUS | 273 | 1 650 |
| PHYLICA | 137 | 900 |

| FIVE LARGEST FYNBOS GENERA | | |
|---|---|---|
| | NUMBER OF SPECIES | |
| Genus | Cape Floristic Region | Worldwide |
| ERICA | 670 | 860 |
| ASPALATHUS | 272 | 278 |
| PELARGONIUM | 148 | 270 |
| AGATHOSMA | 143 | 150 |
| PHYLICA | 133 | 180 |

## CAPE FYNBOS COMMUNITIES

| Fynbos type | Characteristics | Environment |
|---|---|---|
| GRASSY | High grass cover plus many small-leafed shrubs and resprouting perennials | Fine-textured, deep, fertile soils with significant summer rain |
| ASTERACEOUS | Sparse cover, comprising grasses and small-leafed shrubs, notably daisies, buchus and cliffortias but not ericas | Dry sites, often transitional to renosterveld and karroid shrublands; widespread on calcareous or shallow soils |
| RESTIOID | Dominant cover (>60%) of restios; low cover (<30%) of shrubs with few tall shrubs | Waterlogged sites or deep, well-drained soils, or shallow, stony slopes at high altitude, where shrubs cannot establish |
| ERICACEOUS | High cover of restios and small-leafed shrubs, mainly ericas | Cool, damp, south-facing slopes in acidic, humic soils with high winter rainfall |
| PROTEOID | Mainly tall, single-stemmed proteas (>10% cover) | Wide variety of soils with moderate winter rainfall |
| CLOSED-SCRUB | Mostly soft, broad-leafed shrubs plus significant cover (>10%) of restios and ericas | Well-drained streamsides on sandstone in the mountains |

Cape, but has now largely disappeared under the plough. Renosterveld is especially rich in bulbs but otherwise poor in typical fynbos plant groups – most significantly proteas, ericas and restios. It replaces fynbos on richer soils with a higher pH and a rainfall of around 600 mm per annum, but both give way to karroid shrublands under conditions of lower winter rainfall, around 250–300 mm per annum. With increasing summer rainfall, fynbos is supplanted by other vegetation types, including thicket, savanna and grassland, except on nutrient-poor soils.

Fynbos is not strictly a Mediterranean vegetation, in that it is not confined to regions of winter rainfall. The real determinants of fynbos vegetation appear to be limitations both on growth and on the annual replacement of leaves. These are most obviously the result of an absolute shortage of nutrients in intrinsically poor soils, such as the sandstones of the Cape Fold Mountains. Nutrient deficiencies also occur in richer soils where nutrients have either been leached out of the surface layers by heavy rains or are just not available to the plants for other reasons, such as low temperatures or soil acidity. This explains why patches of fynbos vegetation occur on nutrient-poor soils in subtropical southern KwaZulu-Natal, as well as on the highly leached basalt soils in the high Drakensberg. The dominance of fynbos in the southwestern Cape, in both strictly Mediterranean as well as temperate maritime climates, is primarily the result of the extensive exposures of nutrient-poor soils in the region.

## Recognising fynbos

Fynbos is characteristically a hard-leafed, relatively open shrubland, about 1–3 m tall, often with scattered taller bushes protruding above the canopy. Fynbos shrubs vary greatly in height and density but are mostly richly branched, with twisted trunks. True trees are virtually absent. The

Flypaper Bush, *Roridula gorgonias* (Roridula family)

*Geissoloma marginata* (Geissoloma family)

understorey of smaller shrubs always contains a conspicuous mix of restios, which may become dominant in some communities. Grasses are uncommon in most fynbos communities. Bulbs are normally plentiful but annuals are conspicuous only in the drier fynbos types. Most stands of fynbos contain a diversity of species, in some cases up to 121 different species in a single 100 m² quadrant, and it is only rarely that the vegetation is dominated by a single species, except over very small areas.

Fynbos is unique in its high proportion of members of the Erica, Protea, Restio, Citrus and Iris families. These five families, of the 100 or so families represented in fynbos, account for between 20 and 25 per cent of all fynbos species. This extraordinary imbalance in the composition of fynbos applies also to the genera, with relatively few but very large genera, such as *Erica* (670 species), *Aspalathus* (272 species), *Agathosma* (143 species) and *Phylica* (133 species), contributing a disproportionate number of species.

Fynbos is also distinguished by the presence of four endemic families, that is, all of their species grow only in fynbos. These are the Penaea, Grubbia, Roridula and Geissoloma families. Three others, the Brunia, Lanaria and Prionium families, are almost restricted to Cape fynbos. The Stilbe family, long thought to be a fynbos endemic, is now understood to include some forest species as well.

Within Cape fynbos, botanists recognise several different plant communities, whose distribution is determined primarily by the amount of available moisture, relative proportion of summer rainfall, intensity of summer drought and fertility of the soil. These communities are readily distinguished by their dominant plants (see the table of Cape Fynbos Communities, p.11). Most fynbos communities occur widely throughout the southwestern Cape, wherever appropriate conditions occur. The exceptions are grassy fynbos, which is mainly developed in the eastern half of the region, where the proportion of summer rainfall becomes significant, and ericaceous fynbos, which is concentrated in the extreme southwest, where conditions are mildest.

## Climate

The climate in the southwestern Cape is moderated by its proximity to the ocean, and is predominantly maritime, with mild winters and moderate summers. The West Coast, from the Cape Peninsula northwards, is cooled by the Benguela Current, which carries cold waters up from the Antarctic, while the southern Cape coast to the east falls under the influence of the warmer waters of the Agulhas Current sweeping down from the equator. The average midwinter temperature throughout the region varies between 7 and 15 °C in July, increasing to midsummer highs between 15 and 25 °C in January, except for the inland valleys where temperatures can soar into the late 30s or early

*Staavia brownii* (Brunia family)     *Grubbia rosmarinifolia* (Grubbia family)     *Glischrocolla formosa* (Penaea family)

40s in summer. There is little chance of frost in winter except in the interior valleys and, although the flanking mountains are usually dusted with snow in winter, this is of short duration.

Rainfall is highest in the mountains of the southwest and southern Cape, where it averages more than 1 000 mm per year, but varies between 250 and 650 mm over most of the region, except in the interior valleys where it drops to less than 250 mm per year. Persistent, strong southeasterly winds in summer are important not only in cooling the coastal areas, which consequently experience a difference of less than 10 °C between summer and winter temperatures, but also in bringing moisture, in the form of clouds, to the tops of the coastal mountain ranges along the southwest and southern coasts. The famous 'tablecloth' that spills over Table Mountain in the dry season may precipitate as much as 500 mm of moisture on the summit during the summer.

A true Mediterranean climate, in which most of the rain falls during the winter months, is restricted to the extreme southwest of the Cape Floristic Region, west of Mossel Bay. Rainfall along the southern coast between Mossel Bay and Port Elizabeth is nonseasonal, with almost no month in the year in which rain cannot be expected. Here, the climate is essentially temperate maritime, becoming progressively more subtropical east of Port Elizabeth, as average temperatures rise and the amount of summer rainfall increases.

## Topography and soils

The landscape in the southwestern Cape is dominated by the Cape Fold Mountains, in several more or less parallel series along the coastlines, averaging 1 000–1 500 m, with individual peaks exceeding 2 000 m. The major ranges are formed from layers of Table Mountain sandstone, often extravagantly folded; the minor ranges comprise smaller folds of sandstone and Witteberg quartzite.

These erosion-resistant sandstones and quartzites are acidic and poor in nutrients, especially nitrogen and phosphorus. In the west and southwest, outcrops of Cape granite are visible as characteristically rounded or domed hills. The coastal forelands are formed from Malmesbury shale, and the intermontane valleys cut into Bokkeveld shales and sandstones. Recent deposits of neutral sands, conglomerates and limestones overlie the coastal fringe.

Fynbos communities are mostly restricted to the nutrient-poor, sandy and calcareous soils of the mountains and coastal plains, with renosterveld occupying the more gentle exposures of richer, shale soils. The littoral fringe supports a coastal thicket, termed strandveld. Small pockets of forest are limited to sheltered gorges on the mountainsides, with the exception of the extensive expanse of the Tsitsikamma forest on the southern Cape coast around Knysna. In the drier intermontane valleys, fynbos and renosterveld give way to succulent karoo shrubland, dominated by succulent-leafed shrubs.

# Fynbos diversity

Cape fynbos plant communities cover over 41 000 km², or a little under half the total area of the Cape Floristic Region, but are estimated to contribute 70–80 per cent of the region's flora, making fynbos easily the most diverse vegetation type in this part of the world.

The entire Cape Floristic Region averages 94 unique species per 1 000 km², making it much more diverse than many other parts of the world. California and southwestern Australia, two other Mediterranean regions, have respective average diversities of 14 and just under 12 unique species per 1 000 km², and southern Africa as a whole averages just 8 unique species per 1 000 km². Within the Cape Floristic Region, fynbos alone may contain between 150 and 170 unique species per 1 000 km², an astonishing two or three times that measured for tropical rainforests. How is this extraordinary diversity possible? The secret lies in the scale at which it is measured.

At the local scale, the number of species occurring in a single plot of, say, one square kilometre, can be counted and compared with counts from similar plots in other vegetation types. This gives us a measure of local diversity (known technically as alpha diversity), which averages around 65 species per km² for Cape fynbos. This is slightly lower than available figures for renoster shrublands (84 species per km²) but compares well with figures for Australian *kwongan* heathlands; Californian *chaparral* communities, at 30 species per km², are much less diverse. At this scale, tropical rainforests are easily the most diverse habitats on Earth, with a local richness ranging between 130 and 190 species per km². On this basis, fynbos, although diverse, is not extraordinarily so. How then do we explain the enormous diversity for the vegetation type as a whole?

Botanists have now established that the main source of fynbos diversity lies not in the absolute number of species found at any particular site but in the proportion of species that is shared between sites, either nearby but with a different ecology, or distant and with a similar ecology (measures known respectively as beta and gamma diversity). Measured in this way, the diversity of Cape fynbos is far higher than other vegetation types – the result of the high rate at which species give way to others across environmental and geographical gradients. Put another way, Cape fynbos is characterised by exceptionally high numbers of highly localised species – those that are restricted to a single, small area, sometimes less than one square kilometre. In sites that are as little as 25 km apart, for instance, between half and two-thirds of the species have been replaced by different ones. This is in sharp contrast to tropical forests, where individual species are widely scattered, and is one of the reasons it is so difficult to identify fynbos species: each locality is likely to have a large proportion of different species.

This fynbos characteristic was already evident to the indefatigable Lady Anne Barnard, wife of the Secretary to the First British Administration of the Cape, soon after her arrival. In her diary entry for 10 October 1799, she notes '… I was more than ever confirmed in the opinion that a botanist here must live a year or two in the country … for he must be in many places at once as the plains, the marshy or dry soils, the tops of mountains or the gullies all produce very different flowers from each other in the same season'.

Quite why nutrient-poor soils should foster such a high diversity of species is not clear. One suggestion is that even slightly differing ratios of limiting soil nutrients constitute

Marsh rose, *Orothamnus zeyheri* (Protea family)

Fynbos is a fire-adapted vegetation, although too-frequent fires can be detrimental

microenvironments that are sufficiently different to permit a greater variety of plant species to occupy a given area than is the case in more fertile soils, where minor differences in nutrient ratios are not significant. While this is an attractive explanation for the relatively high levels of local diversity in fynbos, it does not explain the rapidity with which many species give way to others over short distances, or the high proportion of local species. Certainly, the diversity of microclimates that characterises the Cape Floristic Region as a result of its varied topography, soils and rainfall patterns is important in stimulating the evolution of different species. The role of fire in disrupting the succession of species and in providing opportunities for different survival strategies must also not be overlooked (see below). In addition, the particular distribution of nutrient-poor and nutrient-richer soils relative to one another is probably important in fostering the evolution of new species. It is likely that one of the key factors in the floristic diversity of the Cape is that bands of these soils, each bearing their own distinctive fynbos or renosterveld communities, alternate so regularly with one another. The relative isolation of the deposits or outcrops of sandstone within a surrounding sea of shale is likely to have encouraged the evolution of different species on each of the sandstone islands.

## Fire and fynbos

Fynbos is a fire-adapted vegetation and evidence suggests that, in the absence of regular fires, all but the drier fynbos types would become dominated by trees. Fynbos can thus be viewed as a fire-dependent vegetation type, along with grasslands and savannas.

The infertility of fynbos soils means that the recycling of soil nutrients is essential for fynbos survival. Fire is the motor that drives this cycle, and fires at appropriate intervals are not only an integral, but also an essential part of fynbos ecology. Fires are more common in fynbos than in any of the other heathlands around the world. This is a result of the extreme flammability of the dried, often intricately branched shrubs and restioids, and it is rare to find stands of fynbos vegetation that are more than 20 years old. Fires rejuvenate the vegetation by removing moribund growth and recycling precious nutrients back into the soil. They also remove the choking canopy that has grown up during the intervening years, allowing light to reach the soil surface.

Whether they re-establish by sprouting from a woody rootstock or through the germination of seed, fynbos shrubs that have been burned take several years to reach their former size. In the meantime the space that has been created promotes the luxuriant growth of herbaceous plants. Sunlight that reaches the soil surface after a fire stimulates the germination of a flush of annuals and short-lived perennials, whose seeds have often been primed by chemicals in the smoke itself. These plants take advantage of the flush of newly released nutrients and favourable growing conditions to complete short life cycles, returning to the soil as seeds once the larger shrubs overwhelm them, and remaining dormant until the next fire.

Fynbos regrowth is largely through the germination of seeds, either dropped from the canopy or stored in the soil. Plants with this strategy are known as 'reseeders', and their prevalence in fynbos distinguishes it from other fire-regulated vegetation types. Relatively few fynbos species are resprouters, regenerating by sprouting from the stump after a fire. Resprouters are able to regrow more rapidly than reseeders, using the reserves stored in their buried stems. Some resprouters, including several of the larger proteas, protect their trunks with a thick, insulating layer of corky bark and resprout from buds buried in the trunk, thereby gaining a height advantage over plants that are burned to the ground.

Fires in fynbos occur optimally every 10–14 years. Whereas bulbs and those short-lived species that make their appearance only after fires may flourish with more frequent burns, many shrubs reach reproductive maturity only after several years. Fires that occur too frequently, usually as a result of human intervention, destroy the adult plants of such slow-growing species and exhaust their seed banks, eventually bringing about their local extinction.

## Fynbos adaptations

Visitors to the Cape from southwestern Australia, in particular, will be struck by the similarity between the vegetation of the two regions – low, open shrublands with many of the same plant families represented. Members of the Pea, Protea, Citrus and Erica families will all seem familiar, although the individual species represent quite different genera. The most striking difference between *kwongan* and fynbos is the relative abundance of annual species in *kwongan* and the extraordinary wealth of bulbs in fynbos.

The structural similarity between fynbos and *kwongan* has been attributed primarily to the nutrient-poor soils of both subcontinents. The low levels of soil nutrients are thought to militate against growing new, replacement leaves each season, making it necessary for shrubs to remain evergreen and suitably constructed to weather the moisture stress of the dry, and often windy, summers. The preponderance of deciduous shrubs on richer soils in the southwestern Cape provides support for this hypothesis.

Paradoxically, the poor soils of the southwestern Cape may contribute to the floristic diversity of fynbos vegetation. Neither fynbos nor *kwongan* is as dense as *chaparral* or *maquis*, and their relatively open structure may favour the growth of a diversity of low-growing species that is only possible in more dense plant communities for a brief period after fire. Perhaps, too, small differences in the proportions of minerals assume a greater significance in poor soils than in richer ones, thereby providing more niches for plant species to occupy.

*Erica inflata* (Erica family) colours the Kliphuisvlakte above Porterville

# Roots

Fynbos plants exhibit several adaptations to enhance the uptake of minerals from the soil. The most common, found in plants throughout the world, relies on a symbiotic relationship with a soil fungus known as a 'mycorrhiza'. This fungus, which forms an intimate association with the roots of the plant and may account for as much as 40 per cent of the weight of its root system, reaches into the soil well beyond the roots to extract poorly soluble forms of nutrients, such as phosphorus and nitrogen, releasing them to the plant as required in exchange for carbohydrates. Mycorrhizal associations are especially common in ericas.

Members of the Protea family have developed an unusual form of root growth as an adaptation to nutrient-poor soils and periodic drought. Tufts of hundreds of fine rootlets, resembling cotton, sprout from the surface roots of the plants after the first rains of the season, rapidly absorbing surface moisture and minerals released by the decomposition of leaf litter. These 'proteoid' roots are short-lived, withering after two or three months to leave only the subsurface roots. Similar temporary root systems are also produced by restios.

Plants of the Pea family have developed a unique symbiotic association with nitrogen-fixing bacteria, which take up residence in specialised nodules on the roots. The bacteria convert gaseous nitrogen from the air into soluble forms that can be used by the plants, allowing them to thrive in nitrogen-poor soils.

Carnivorous plants, such as sundews and bladderworts, derive minerals, especially nitrogen, directly from the digestion of insects and other small animals that they trap with highly modified leaves.

*Erica blenna* (Erica family)

*Leucospermum mundii* (Protea family)

# Leaves

The foliage of fynbos shrubs is mostly brownish green or greyish in colour. Fynbos leaves are typically small, stiff and leathery, with thick cuticles and internal struts of woody tissue to prevent them from collapsing under moisture stress. The lower surface, at least, is often protected by hairs. Many fynbos shrubs are rich in bitter tannins or aromatic oils, which may serve to deter predators. The sticky surface of the floral bracts of certain shrubs may also act as a varnish, reducing water loss, as has been demonstrated to be the case in the flowers of many ericas, which are especially long-lived and are often produced in the heat of summer.

Two leaf shapes are especially prevalent among fynbos shrubs. Ericoid leaves are small and narrow or needle-like, with the margins rolled under to form one or two narrow grooves on the leaf underside. The

*Elegia mucronata* (Restio family)

stomata, or breathing pores, are restricted to these grooves, where they are relatively protected from water loss, and are often also covered with hairs as additional insulation. Ericoid leaves are developed in many unrelated, often smaller fynbos shrubs, including members of the Erica, Brunia, Polygala, Phylica, Pea, Daphne and Daisy families.

Proteoid leaves, in contrast, are associated with taller, less branched shrubs, notably members of the Protea family. These leaves are leathery, mostly elliptical and up to 15 cm long, with both surfaces anatomically similar, and are typically held with the edges facing upwards, mitigating the desiccating power of the midday sun.

Several herbaceous perennials, including restios and some fynbos grasses, have reduced their leaves to sheaths or done away with them entirely, transferring the function of photosynthesis to the stems instead.

Although proteoids (shrubs with proteoid leaves) are absent from certain fynbos communities, including the drier and high-altitude types, ericoids (shrublets with ericoid leaves) and restioids (slender perennials with reduced leaves) are always present.

## Flowers

Flowering in fynbos is concentrated in spring, between September and October, when pollinating insects are most in evidence. At this time of the year, some 60 per cent of the species are in bloom, but at least a fifth of fynbos species can be found in flower in any month of the year, and flowering never drops to the low summer levels recorded in Chile and southwestern Australia.

Several fynbos bulbs have separated their growth and flowering phases, enabling them to flower in the dry season, in midsummer or autumn, when competition for the available pollinators is relatively low.

Autumn flowering is especially marked among the members of the Amaryllis family. The seeds of many amaryllids do not enter a dormant phase like those of most plants, but continue to grow and germinate. By flowering at the end of the dry season, amaryllids ensure that their seeds are shed at the beginning of the wet winter, when conditions for their survival are optimal.

## Pollination

The flowers of many fynbos plants are unusual in appearance, sometimes strikingly beautiful. This is the result of the wide variety of strategies that they have evolved for attracting pollinators, many of which are not commonly employed in this role in other parts of the world. This unusual range of pollination systems is probably a result of the relative shortage of insects in the Cape, both in variety and number of individuals.

Plants specialised for butterfly pollination are rare in southern Africa but several spectacular scarlet-flowered fynbos species rely on the Mountain Pride butterfly for their pollination. Moth pollination is much more common across the subcontinent, but even here fynbos is unusual in the type of moths employed. Settling

Namaqua rock mouse, *Aethomys namaquensis*, with *Protea humiflora* (Protea family)

Mountain Pride butterfly, *Meneris tulbaghia*, on *Brunsvigia marginata* (Amaryllis Family)

moths pollinate several fynbos plants, notably members of the Daphne family, but almost no fynbos flowers are pollinated by hawkmoths, evidently because the larval foodplants of these moths are largely members of tropical plant families and thus rare in fynbos.

The southwestern Cape boasts an unusually high number of species of large horseflies and tangle-veined flies that are specialised for extracting nectar from tubular flowers. The long, needle-like mouthparts of these agile insects are adapted for siphoning nectar from the bottom of slender floral tubes, and more than 80 plant species rely on them for pollination.

Other important insect pollinators of fynbos and associated renosterveld communities are the furry-bodied monkey beetles, which favour brightly coloured, bowl-shaped flowers. Many of these flowers have dark markings on their petals to mimic the appearance of particular species of beetle.

Some four per cent of fynbos plants (or about 430 species) are adapted for pollination by sunbirds and sugarbirds, as opposed to only two per cent of plant species across southern Africa as a whole. Different bird species often show a preference for particular fynbos species. Orange-breasted Sunbirds, which are endemic to fynbos, are especially fond of ericas and other smaller flowers, whereas Malachite Sunbirds prefer the larger flowers of many bulbs. Cape Sugarbirds, another fynbos endemic, rely on

Monkey beetle on *Ixia polystachya* (Iris family)

Horsefly, *Philoliche aethiopica*, pollinating *Pelargonium columbinum* (Geranium family)

Southern Double-collared Sunbird pollinating *Kniphofia uvaria* (Aloe family)

*Mimetes hottentoticus* (Protea family) on Kogelberg Peak

proteas and pincushions for both food and shelter. It has been suggested that one of the reasons why bird-pollinated flowers, which typically produce large quantities of nectar, are so common in fynbos (and in Australian *kwongan*) is that nectar production is relatively undemanding of soil nutrients, which are in short supply in these two regions. The synthesis of the sugars in nectar relies more heavily on carbon, which comes from the air in unlimited quantities, than on scarce minerals.

Pollination by rodents is also unusually well developed in fynbos compared to the rest of the subcontinent; they are the primary pollinators of 35 specialised species of proteas. These so-called 'rodent proteas' secrete quantities of energy-rich nectar in yeast-scented flowerheads borne on the stems close to the ground, where they can be easily reached by Striped, Namaqua rock and Verreaux's mice, which are attracted to the plants particularly when the seeds that constitute an important food source are scarce.

## Seeds

The low fertility of fynbos soils places a significant limitation on the production of seeds, which are rich in nitrogen and phosphorus, both of which are in short supply. Possibly this is why many of the characteristic fynbos shrubs, including all proteas, daphnes, daisies, *Phylica* and *Cliffortia* species, and many *Aspalathus* species, have few or just a single ovule per flower. Even so, seed production in *Protea* and *Leucospermum* species is low, averaging between six and nine per cent. In some species, seed maturation takes place over many months, allowing longer periods for the accumulation of nutrients. Mass flowering after fire, when the level of nutrients in the soil has been increased by falls of ash, is another way of overcoming this limitation.

Many of the larger proteoid shrubs ensure survival after fire by sophisticated seed dormancy mechanisms, whereby germination is possible only when the moistened seeds are exposed to the alternating high and low temperatures that are experienced on the surface of soils that have been burned clear of other insulating vegetation.

Several proteas and conebushes protect their seeds from predators during inter-fire periods by storing them in hard, woody fruits. These remain sealed on the plants until the heat from the flames stimulates the protective fruits to burst open, scattering the seeds onto the newly fertilised and cleared soil. Other fynbos plants protect their seeds from fire and predators by attracting the attention of harvester ants, which then bury the seeds. The seeds are provided with edible, oily appendages, or elaiosomes, which entice the ants to remove the seeds to their subterranean nests. Here the insects remove the oily appendages before discarding the otherwise intact seeds, which lie buried, safe from rodent predators, until stimulated to germinate by a passing fire. In addition, the ant nest provides more nutrients and improved soil texture for the seedlings. About 1 300 fynbos species in 24 families, representing some 20 per cent of the flora, have this mutually beneficial relationship with ants. Seed dispersal by ants is also common in Australian *kwongan* but not in other heathlands around the world.

Open *Protea repens* heads spilling seed after fire

# The origins of fynbos

Although the appearance of the first flowering plants dates back to around 150 million years ago or more, their real flowering began about 90 million years ago, and it took another 10 million years before they began to dominate the fossil pollen record. Until then, flowering plants appear to have eked out an existence in the understorey of temperate coniferous forests and among the fields of ferns that covered the Earth, where they were probably restricted to disturbed habitats.

Most of southern Africa until around 60 million years ago was blanketed by subtropical forest, although there are sure to have been pockets of arid-adapted vegetation in dry valleys and on shallow soils. More recent pollen samples from the West Coast and Cape Peninsula corroborate the occurrence of distinctly tropical vegetation here, including palms and other tropical trees and shrubs, as recently as 10 million years ago, and these warm, humid conditions appear to have extended into the central Karoo. However, the discovery of fossil pollen of fynbos families, such as restios, proteas and ericas, from deposits in Namaqualand that have been dated to between 71 and 64 million years ago, indicates that these typical Cape elements were already present at this early time, probably as part of the forest itself.

Around 30 million years ago, the climate in southern Africa became drier and more seasonal as a result of the establishment of the South Atlantic high-pressure cell, which drives our modern climate. The evolution of corms from rhizomes in the southern African members of the Iris family, as an obvious adaptation to seasonal climates, appears to date from this time. Prior to this, the climate around the world had been largely warm and humid. The elevation of the central southern African plateau around 10 million years ago and the more or less concomitant establishment of the Benguela Current along the West Coast further increased the aridity in the western half of the subcontinent, and initiated the establishment of present weather patterns in the subregion. The development of the modern winter-rainfall climate in southern Africa, which led to the current expansion of fynbos vegetation, is

*Autumn fog blankets Table Bay, at the foot of Table Mountain*

thus a relatively recent event dating back a mere three to five million years. More recently, the southern African climate has undergone several modest oscillations coinciding with the recurrent ice ages that devastated the flora and fauna of the northern hemisphere. Although relatively small, these oscillations have been enough to push the boundary of the winter-rainfall region far to the northwest at times, most recently as 17 000–15 000 years ago. This would have allowed temperate plant communities such as fynbos to expand their range considerably beyond their current limits.

Indirect dating of the start of the diversification of the Cape lineages for which sufficient data is available from DNA studies, gives dates ranging from 18 million years ago for *Pelargonium* to eight million years ago for *Phylica*. This evidence, although scant, suggests that climatic changes, especially increasing aridity, were instrumental in the evolution of fynbos. As for the ancestors of fynbos, it would appear that several of the earliest, dating to around 80 million years ago, were drawn from groups that are shared with Australasia. These include the Protea, Iris,

Restio and Geissoloma families. At this time, Antarctica and Australia were still more or less contiguous, forming a great southern landmass that could well have been the ancestral home of these families. Dispersal to southern Africa across the nascent Indian Ocean would not have posed the problems that it does today. Other fynbos families, such as the Penaea and Stilbe families, seem to have been derived from lineages that originated in tropical Africa, with only a few, such as Palmiet, having their nearest relatives in South America. Many of the Cape elements found today in the mountains of tropical Africa appear to have migrated northwards to their current location rather than southwards from there, as was originally postulated for the genus *Protea*. In summary, therefore, there is no single source from which the ancestors of Cape fynbos were drawn. Much of the richness at the species level must be of recent age, having evolved since the establishment of the modern climate in the past few million years, and arising in an 'orgy of speciation' that was almost certainly assisted by the periodic pulses that characterise our current climate.

# Fynbos conservation

The high diversity of fynbos and the large number of local endemics dramatically increase the danger of extinction for a substantial proportion of its plants. In general terms, small areas with a great diversity of plant species are most likely to have the greatest number of rare and endangered species. This is a consequence of the high proportion of very localised species in such regions. Fynbos is especially vulnerable, and the Cape Peninsula is a typical example, with 161 species of flowering plants endemic, or restricted, to it.

Worldwide, around 10 per cent of all plant species are rare or endangered. In the southwestern Cape, where two-thirds of the species are endemic, nearly one-third are rare or endangered. This amounts to more than 2 000 fynbos species.

The number of species threatened with extinction in South Africa has risen dramatically since the last survey of rare and threatened plant species was completed in 1997. In the Protea family, for instance, the number of threatened species has risen from 22 per cent to 60 per cent, or almost two-thirds of the species. Similar trends are evident in other families.

The greatest threat to the plants of the southwestern Cape is the transformation of habitat for urban development, agriculture and silviculture. While species from lowland habitats are most threatened, the increasing cultivation of crops such as rooibos is putting pressure on upland species as well. Urban sprawl around Cape Town has caused the extinction of several species in recent years. Another major threat to fynbos is the encroachment of alien vegetation, especially Australian wattles and hakea. Fires at too-frequent intervals pose a threat to the local survival of fynbos species that are unable to re-establish under such a regime. Still others are under threat from the collection of wild plants for traditional medicinal use.

The responsibility for conservation rests with the individual, and everyone can make a difference. Join local interest groups in your neighbourhood concerned with conservation, or adopt and protect a small site with threatened species on it. With so many species surviving precariously on tiny fragments, fynbos needs all the help it can get to survive.

## VERNACULAR NAMES

Vernacular, or common, names have been provided where possible, gleaned primarily from Christo Smith's incomparable *Common Names of South African Plants*, but with reference to the many popular guides produced over the past century. In many cases, a selection has been made from among several choices, discarding those names that are uncommonly used, or are not especially applicable. Where the names have been suggested by some obvious visible attribute of the plants their derivation has not been given, but in cases where their origin is more obscure, this is explained. Most of the common names are originally Dutch or Afrikaans, reflecting the language spoken by the early settlers in the Cape, but others are derived from indigenous Khoi terms, representing just a fraction of the original Khoi plant taxonomy. English translations or transliterations have been provided where suitable.

Common names were used by the early inhabitants of the Cape primarily to identify plants in terms of their particular attributes, often medicinal, and, for this reason, were sometimes applied indiscriminately to several different species with similar properties. In addition, various names may have been applied to the same plant by different people and in different regions. Given the diversity of species in the Cape, with new ones still being discovered each year, it is not possible to assign a unique common name to each species. Although rarely specific, the vernacular names are invariably colourful, usually intensely informative, and often as familiar to the local inhabitants as Latin binomials are to botanists. They represent a rich cultural heritage that deserves to prosper.

# WHERE TO BEGIN

The arrangement of plant families, genera and species in this guide is an artificial one devised to aid identification at each level. To identify a fynbos specimen, turn first to Finding the Right Group (p.26). All fynbos plants fall under one of two basic divisions – monocotyledons or dicotyledons. Once you have selected the division appropriate to your specimen, proceed along the 'branches' of the diagram, making selections based on the generalised descriptions provided at each stage in order to arrive at one of the eight plant 'groups' on the right-hand side of the page. Each group represents an assembly of plant families with selected characteristics in common. Once you have identified the group to which your specimen probably belongs, proceed to the pictorial Guide to Family Groups (p.27), where a short summary of the families within each of the various groups is given, along with a photograph of a species from each family. At this point you can select what appears to be the appropriate family and then turn to the Descriptions of Fynbos Families (p.32) to check all the family features. Only now turn to the relevant family in the main body of the book.

The book describes 61 families, 18 of them monocotyledons and 43 dicotyledons. Within the larger families, the genera are grouped into sections as a further aid to identification. Follow the leads to the appropriate group of genera in each family. Read the descriptions of each genus in the section, paying particular attention to the portions that are *italicised* – the critical characteristics that define each genus.

Within the larger genera, the species are also sometimes arranged in clusters, defined by some obvious characteristic. The descriptions have been drawn up to accentuate the distinguishing features of each species. Read the description carefully and check the accompanying distribution map and the numbered photograph on the opposite page before deciding on the identity of your plant. In some instances, additional similar species are mentioned at the end of the description. An illustrated glossary (see inside front cover) and a glossary of words (inside back cover) are supplied to help interpret botanical terms.

The circumscriptions of the families and genera used here reflect modern interpretations of plant relationships resulting from recent advances in DNA-based studies. In most cases they coincide with traditional usages but there are some significant exceptions. While these changes may be confusing for some they are evidence of the ongoing advances in our understanding of the natural world. Where a species' name has changed through its reclassification under a different genus, it is listed under its new name, with its old name given in brackets, e.g. *Ammocharis longifolia* (= *Cybistetes longifolia*). Where dimensions are given in the descriptions, the usual range is indicated, from the smallest to the largest; unusually small or large sizes are inserted in parentheses before or after the normal range as appropriate. Likely flowering months are indicated by a 'calendar bar' above each species description. Where there is space, extra images have sometimes been included (as in 2A, 2B), showing other colour forms or close-up shots.

Arid fynbos on Gamkaberg with the Outeniqua Mountains in the background

# AIZOACEAE  Ice plant family

**GROUP SEVEN**

▸ SEPALS COLOURED AND PETAL-LIKE; PETALOID STAMINODES LACKING
▸▸ LEAVES ALMOST FLAT AND COVERED WITH GLISTENING BLADDER CELLS

## *Tetragonia*  SEA CORAL, KLAPPERBRAK

Annual or perennial herbs or shrublets, often sprawling. Leaves alternate, semi-succulent, often rhomboidal and minutely warty. Flowers 1 to many, mainly axillary, green, cream to yellow or magenta, *with 5 (7) petal-like sepals; ovary inferior or half-inferior;* stamens few to many, often in bundles. Fruits *1-seeded, usually 4-winged, indehiscent.* Africa, South America and Australia: ±60 spp; ±10 fynbos spp.

▸ TUBEROUS HERBS

**❶ *Tetragonia chenopodioides***  J F M A M J J A S O N D
Tuberous perennial with sprawling branches to 40 cm with rhomboid leaves that are often reddish beneath; bears ±sessile, yellow-green flowers in axillary and terminal clusters, with styles twice as long as the tepals. The fruits are 8-ridged. Coastal sands along the West Coast.

**❷ *Tetragonia nigrescens***  J F M A M J J A S O N D
Tuberous perennial with sprawling stems to 50 cm, and paddle-shaped to ±orbicular leaves that are often red beneath; bears yellow or cream (rarely orange) flowers, 3–4 mm in diameter, that are often purple on the reverse on slender pedicels in axillary and terminal flower clusters. The fruits are winged. Sandy and clay slopes and flats, from Namaqualand to the southern Cape. *Tetragonia halimoides,* from the West Coast, has larger flowers, 4–5 mm in diameter, and fruits 20–25 mm long.

**❸ *Tetragonia herbacea***  J F M A M J J A S O N D
Tuberous perennial with sprawling stems to 50 cm and paddle-shaped leaves; bears bright yellow flowers, 4–6 mm in diameter, on long pedicels in terminal flower clusters and solitary in the upper axils. The fruits are pear-shaped and smooth but ridged when dry. Mostly clay and granite slopes in the southwestern Cape.

▸ SOFTLY WOODY SHRUBS OR SUBSHRUBS
▸▸ LEAF MARGINS ROLLED UNDER AND MOSTLY COVERING THE UNDERSIDE

**❹ *Carpobrotus quadrifidus***  J F M A M J J A S O N D
(= *Carpobrotus sauerae*) Succulent perennial with trailing stems to 3 m long; robust, scimitar-shaped leaves, 18–25 mm in diameter; bears purple or pink flowers, 120–150 mm in diameter; the receptacle is oblong or ± globular and curves abruptly into the pedicel. Coastal rocks from Namaqualand and the West Coast.

**❺ *Tetragonia fruticosa*  Kinkelbossie**  J F M A M J J A S O N D
Sprawling shrub with long branches, often trailing through scrub; oblong leaves with the margin rolled under; bears yellowish flowers, 3–4 mm in diameter, in terminal racemes or 1–few in the upper axils. The fruits are broadly winged with knobs between the wings. Granite and sandstone slopes, especially along the coast, from Namaqualand to the Eastern Cape. *Tetragonia spicata* is a stiffly erect shrub.

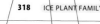

Numbers 11–19 across

1. Family group for identification
2. Family botanical name
3. First-tier lead to genus identification
4. Second-tier lead to genus identification
5. Genus botanical name
6. Genus vernacular name: English
7. Genus vernacular name: Afrikaans
8. Family common name
9. Species number: photograph
10. Species photograph
11. Species distribution map
12. First-tier lead to species identification
13. Second-tier lead to species identification
14. Species number
15. Species botanical name
16. Old name (following reclassification)
17. Species vernacular name
18. Similar species
19. Flowering months

# FINDING THE RIGHT GROUP

For purposes of this guide, plants have been assembled in eight 'groups' of plant families that have selected characteristics in common. Starting at the first level on the left, and working towards the right of the diagram, select the divisions that best describe your specimen, in order to reach the likely group in which it is featured. With the group selected, identify the appropriate family in the 'Guide to Family Groups' (opposite), before confirming details in 'Descriptions of Fynbos Families' (p.32). Finally, turn to the selected family in the section on species descriptions (starting on p. 40), where, with the help of photographs, you can identify the genus and then the species.

## MONOCOTYLEDONS

Herbs, rarely tree-like. Leaves with parallel venation, often strap-shaped. Flowers with sepals/petals and stamens in multiples of 3, usually with undifferentiated sepals and petals (= tepals).

| | |
|---|---|
| Grass-like plants with inconspicuous flowers | **GROUP ONE** |
| Wetland plants with reduced petals | **GROUP TWO** |
| Lily-like plants with conspicuous flowers | |
| Stamens 6. Flowers radially symmetrical | **GROUP THREE** |
| Stamens 3 or 1. Flowers often 2-lipped | **GROUP FOUR** |

## DICOTYLEDONS

Herbs, shrubs or trees. Leaves with netted or herring-bone venation, often toothed or lobed. Flowers with sepals/petals and stamens in multiples of 4 or 5, usually with differentiated sepals and petals.

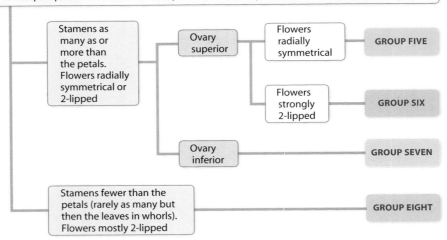

| | | | |
|---|---|---|---|
| Stamens as many as or more than the petals. Flowers radially symmetrical or 2-lipped | Ovary superior | Flowers radially symmetrical | **GROUP FIVE** |
| | | Flowers strongly 2-lipped | **GROUP SIX** |
| | Ovary inferior | | **GROUP SEVEN** |
| Stamens fewer than the petals (rarely as many but then the leaves in whorls). Flowers mostly 2-lipped | | | **GROUP EIGHT** |

# GUIDE TO FAMILY GROUPS

## GROUP ONE

**PALMIET FAMILY**
Tough, rush-like aquatic shrubs; leaves fibrous and saw-toothed.

**RESTIO FAMILY**
Hard, grass-like plants with leaves reduced to tubular sheaths; plants unisexual.

**SEDGE FAMILY**
Grass-like plants with 3-angled stems.

## GROUP TWO

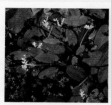 

**APONOGETON FAMILY**
Aquatic herbs with floating leaves; ovary of 3–6 separate carpels.

**ARUM FAMILY**
Leaves petiolate, arrowhead-shaped; flowers arum-like.

## GROUP THREE

**AGAPANTHUS FAMILY**
Flowers in umbels on leaf-less scapes, blue; ovary superior.

**AMARYLLIS FAMILY**
Flowers in umbels on leaf-less scapes; ovary inferior.

**ASPARAGUS FAMILY**
Shrubs or climbers, often spiny; leaves often needle-like; flowers in small axillary clusters; fruit a juicy berry.

**ANTHERICUM FAMILY**
Flowers on jointed pedicels, short-lived, several per bract.

**ALOE FAMILY**
Succulent perennials with yellow sap.

**HYACINTH FAMILY**
Bulbous perennials; flowers in spikes or racemes on leafless scapes.

**COLCHICUM FAMILY**
Cormous perennials; flowers usually opposite the bracts.

**LANARIA FAMILY**
Tough evergreen perennials; flowers densely hairy.

### STARGRASS FAMILY
Leaves 3-ranked; stamen filaments and style short; ovary inferior.

### CYANELLA FAMILY
Stamens clustered on short filaments, with apical pores; ovary half-inferior.

### BLOODROOT FAMILY
Rootstock bright orange; leaves oriented edgewise, often hairy; stamens 3, opposite the inner tepals.

### IRIS FAMILY
Leaves usually oriented edgewise; stamens 3, opposite the outer tepals; ovary inferior.

### ORCHID FAMILY
Flowers 2-lipped, often spurred; stamen 1, joined to the style.

### EUPHORBIA FAMILY
Sap milky; flowers unisexual, minute; fruit splitting into three, 1-seeded segments.

### CRASSULA FAMILY
Succulents with opposite leaves; ovary of 5 separate carpels.

### RANUNCULUS FAMILY
Leaves divided; stamens many; ovary of many separate carpels.

### SUNDEW FAMILY
Insectivorous, covered with reddish gland-tipped hairs; styles 3–5.

### CARNATION FAMILY
Leaves opposite, narrow; sepals joined into a tube; petals notched or fringed.

### MUSTARD FAMILY
Often with a sulphurous, cabbage-like smell; petals 4; stamens 6.

### TWINLEAF FAMILY
Stems jointed; leaves divided into 2 oblique leaflets, fleshy; stipules hard and sharp; stamens 8–10.

### GERANIUM FAMILY
Leaves often lobed; flowers in umbellate clusters; stamens 10 or 15; fruits beak-like.

### CITRUS FAMILY
Leaves gland-dotted and aromatic; ovary deeply lobed, often horned.

### FLAX FAMILY
Petals furled in bud, soon falling; stamens joined at the base; styles 3–5.

### HIBISCUS FAMILY
Leaves or stems scurfy, covered with star-shaped hairs; petals furled in bud; stamens often joined in a tube.

### MILKWEED FAMILY
Often succulent, with clear or milky sap; leaves opposite; flowers leathery; anthers fused to the style.

### OXALIS FAMILY
Rootstock a scaly bulb; leaves with 3(10) leaflets; stamens 10 in two unequal whorls; styles 5.

### CONVOLVULUS FAMILY
Twining climbers or creeping; leaves lobed; flowers furled like an umbrella in bud.

### PLUMBAGO FAMILY
Stems and leaves often scurfy; calyx papery and persistent; petals furled like an umbrella in bud; styles 5 or deeply 5-lobed.

### GENTIAN FAMILY
Leaves opposite; petals furled like an umbrella in bud.

### ERICA FAMILY
Heath-like shrubs; leaves whorled; flowers leathery; anthers 8, porose and tailed.

### PENAEA FAMILY
Leaves 4-ranked, overlapping; flowers tubular, leathery; sepals 4; petals 0.

### DAPHNE FAMILY
Heath-like shrubs with stringlike bark; sepals joined in a tube; petals 0; style lateral.

### PROTEA FAMILY
Flowers in heads or spikes; sepals 4, slender; petals 0; anthers arising directly on the sepals.

### POTATO FAMILY
Flowers often opposite the leaves; stamens sometimes opening by apical pores; ovary 2-chambered; fruit fleshy.

### FORGET-ME-NOT FAMILY
Leaves often bristly; inflorescence 1-sided and coiled; ovary 4-lobed.

### FUMITORY FAMILY
Twiners with lobed leaves; sepals 2, deciduous; petals 4, unequal.

### VIOLET FAMILY
Flowers violet-like, spurred or pouched; anthers joined around the ovary, with glands.

### MELIANTHUS FAMILY
Leaves regularly divided, with axillary stipules; calyx pouched; petals 4, unequal.

### POLYGALA FAMILY
Flowers sweet pea-shaped, with a fringed crest at the tip of the keel; sepals separate, often unequal; stamens 5–8.

### PEA FAMILY
Flowers sweet pea-shaped; stamens ±10; fruit a pod.

### ICE PLANT FAMILY
Succulents; leaves opposite, ±cylindrical; stamens and 'petals' numerous.

### MONTINIA FAMILY
Flowers unisexual; petals 4; ovary inferior.

### ROSE FAMILY
Leaf base sheathing; flowers unisexual; petals 0; stamens numerous; ovary inferior.

### DESERT PRIM-ROSE FAMILY
Hairy, mucilaginous annuals; flowers axillary, solitary; ovary inferior, styles 5–10.

### BELLFLOWER FAMILY
Anthers shedding pollen onto the style, either withered at maturity or joined into a ring.

### CARROT FAMILY
Plants with an aromatic, parsley-like smell; leaves often divided; flowers in umbels.

### GRUBBIA FAMILY
Leaves opposite, dull greyish; flowers in small axillary cones.

### PHYLICA FAMILY
Flowers small, in heads or clusters; petals insignificant; stamens opposite the petals.

### SANDALWOOD FAMILY
Leaves greyish and leathery; flowers small, without petals; anthers with a tuft of hairs.

### BRUNIA FAMILY
Heath-like shrubs; leaves with a minute black tip.

### DAISY FAMILY
Inflorescence a head surrounded by scale-like bracts; florets tubular; anthers joined in a collar.

### SCABIOUS FAMILY
Leaves opposite, lobed; flowers in heads, 2-lipped.

### STILBE FAMILY
Heath-like shrubs; leaves whorled, narrow or needle-like.

### MINT FAMILY
Leaves opposite on 4-angled stems; often aromatic; flowers 2-lipped; stamens 2 or 4; ovary 4-lobed.

### BLADDERWORT FAMILY
Delicate, apparently leafless insectivores; flowers 2-lipped and spurred; stamens 2.

### BROOMRAPE FAMILY
Plants turning black when damaged; leaves scale-like, fleshy, yellowish; flowers showy, 2-lipped; stamens 2 or 4.

### SUTERA FAMILY
Leaves opposite or tufted, often with aromatic, gland-tipped hairs; flowers irregular or 2-lipped; stamens 2 or 4, unequal.

# DESCRIPTIONS OF FYNBOS FAMILIES

## MONOCOTYLEDONS

### AGAPANTHUS FAMILY *Agapanthaceae* – p.56
Rhizomatous perennials with slimy sap. Leaves basal, in 2 ranks, strap-like and channelled with a thickened midrib. Inflorescence an umbel borne on a leafless scape, enclosed in bud by 2 large membranous or papery bracts. Flowers blue, spreading on slender pedicels, funnel-shaped with 6 tepals joined at the base in a short tube; stamens 6, arising at the top of the tube, unequal, flexed slightly downwards and arched up at the ends; ovary superior, the style slender and flexed downwards. Fruit 3-angled, dry at maturity, flexed sharply downwards on the pedicels. Restricted to temperate southern Africa: 10 spp.

### ALOE FAMILY *Asphodelaceae* – p.60
Rhizomatous perennials, often with swollen or tuberous roots, or single-stemmed to branched shrubs or trees, rarely annuals, the roots usually with yellow sap. Leaves usually succulent, in a spiral or in 2 ranks, channelled, flat or cylindrical, the margins often spiny. Inflorescence an unbranched or branched raceme or spike, sometimes crowded into a head. Flowers white, yellow, orange or red, star-like or tubular, with 6 tepals that are separate or joined into a tube; stamens 6, arising at the base of the ovary; ovary superior, style slender. Fruit mostly leathery or dry, rarely a fleshy berry. Africa and Eurasia, most diverse in southern Africa: ±750 spp.

### AMARYLLIS FAMILY *Amaryllidaceae* – p.50
Bulbous or rhizomatous perennials with slimy sap. Leaves basal, spirally arranged or more usually in 2 ranks, often strap-like, or slender to broad and usually without a midrib, sometimes spreading on the ground, rarely hairy. Inflorescence an umbel borne on a leafless scape, sometimes 1-flowered and borne at ground level, enclosed in bud by 2 or more large papery or leafy bracts. Flowers variously coloured, often red, pink or yellow, star- or funnel-shaped to tubular with 6 tepals that are separate or joined at the base in a short to long tube; stamens 6 (rarely more), arising at the top of the tube, equal or unequal, spreading or arching downwards; ovary inferior, the style slender and straight or arching downwards. Fruit dry or fleshy at maturity. Worldwide, mainly in the warm tropics and subtropics, most diverse in southern Africa; includes many horticultural species, among them the daffodil, narcissus, snowdrop and hippeastrum: ±850 spp.

### ANTHERICUM FAMILY *Anthericaceae* – p.60
Rhizomatous or tuberous perennials, sometimes with stiff or swollen roots, usually with leafy stems. Leaves in 2 ranks or in a basal rosette, narrow and channelled, fleshy or firm-textured, often fibrous at the base. Inflorescence a branched or simple raceme, with 1–few flowers at each node. Flowers on jointed pedicels, white, star-like, with 6 separate tepals; stamens 6, the filaments sometimes rough; ovary superior, the style slender. Fruit dry and usually 3-winged. Widespread, Africa, Eurasia and the Americas, mainly tropical: ±250 spp.

### APONOGETON FAMILY *Aponogetonaceae* – p.48
Rhizomatous or tuberous, aquatic perennials. Leaves basal, submerged or floating on long petioles, slender to oblong, mostly with a midrib. Inflorescence a small, unbranched or forked spike, often fleshy. Flowers usually whitish, sometimes unisexual, with 1 or 2 (rarely up to 6) separate tepals; stamens 6 (rarely more); ovary superior, of 3–6 separate carpels, the styles short and curved. Fruit membranous. African and Asian tropics, mainly in seasonal freshwater pools; the fruiting spikes of *Aponogeton distachyos* are used as a pot herb: 43 spp.

### ARUM FAMILY *Araceae* – p.48
Rhizomatous or tuberous perennial herbs or climbers, or minute floating aquatics. Leaves petiolate, the blades simple or variously divided, with watery sap. Inflorescence usually a fleshy column, surrounded by a large coloured or mottled bract. Flowers tiny, often unisexual, with 0–8 minute greenish tepals that are usually separate; stamens 1–7, separate or joined; ovary superior, style short. Fruit usually fleshy or leathery. Widespread and largely tropical or subtropical, mainly South and Central America; most species contain bundles of needle-like crystals of oxalic acid that make them unpalatable or toxic; the flower stems of *Zantedeschia aethiopica* are important as a cut-flower: ±3 300 spp.

### ASPARAGUS FAMILY *Asparagaceae* – p.58
Rhizomatous shrubs or climbers, often with swollen roots. Leaves reduced and scale-like, sometimes hooked, replaced by flattened or needle-like branchlets (cladodes) resembling leaves. Inflorescence a small axillary raceme or cluster, or 1-flowered. Flowers small, white or greenish, star-like or cup-shaped, with 6 tepals that are separate or joined at the base; stamens 6; ovary superior, style short. Fruit a fleshy berry. Africa and Eurasia, most diverse in southern Africa; the young shoots of *Asparagus officinalis* are used as a vegetable: ±120 spp.

**BLOODROOT FAMILY** *Haemodoraceae* – p.94

Rhizomatous or cormous perennials with bright orange sap. Leaves basal, oriented edgewise to the stem in 2 ranks forming a fan, flat or pleated, mostly hairy. Inflorescence a cylindrical or flat-topped panicle, often hairy or glandular. Flowers mauve or yellowish, irregular or star-like with 6 tepals that are separate (Cape species) or joined into a tube; stamens 3, opposite the inner whorl of tepals, equal or unequal; ovary superior or inferior, style slender and strongly flexed to one side. Fruit 3-lobed and dry. Southern Africa, Australia and tropical America: ±100 spp.

**COLCHICUM FAMILY** *Colchicaceae* – p.84

Cormous or tuberous perennials, sometimes twining. Leaves basal or in a loose spiral up the stem and then sometimes drawn into tendrils, usually thin-textured and mostly lance-shaped. Inflorescence a raceme or spike, or crowded into a head, sometimes 1-flowered. Flowers variously coloured, star-like or cup-shaped, with 6 tepals that are separate or joined at the base and often narrowed below and bearing a nectar gland; stamens 6; ovary superior, styles 3 or united below but forked above. Fruit dry or leathery. Africa, Eurasia and Australasia, most diverse in winter-rainfall southern Africa; most species contain the toxic alkaloid colchicine: ±170 spp.

**CYANELLA FAMILY** *Tecophilaeaceae* – p.90

Cormous or tuberous perennials, rarely climbing. Leaves basal or scattered along the stem, usually spirally arranged, lance-shaped, sometimes tendrilled. Inflorescence a raceme or panicle, or flowers solitary, mostly borne on leafy stems. Flowers white, mauve or yellow, star- or cup-shaped with 6 tepals that are separate or joined at the base; stamens 6, usually clustered together on short filaments, the anthers with apical pores; ovary half-inferior, style slender, central or flexed to one side. Fruit dry and globular. Tropical and temperate Africa, Chile and California: 25 spp.

**HYACINTH FAMILY** *Hyacinthaceae* – p.70

Bulbous perennials with slimy sap. Leaves basal, mostly channelled but without a midrib, fleshy, sometimes hairy. Inflorescence an unbranched raceme or spike borne on a leafless scape, sometimes the scape reduced and the flowers crowded between the leaves. Flowers variously coloured, star-like or funnel-shaped to tubular, with 6 tepals that are separate or united into a short or long tube; stamens 6, arising below the ovary or in the tube when present; ovary superior, style short or slender. Fruit 3-lobed and dry. Mainly subtropical and temperate Africa and Eurasia, most diverse in southern Africa; many species are important horticulturally, including bluebell, hyacinth and ornithogalum: ±900 spp.

**IRIS FAMILY** *Iridaceae* – p.96

Rhizomatous, cormous or bulbous perennials, rarely shrubs. Leaves mostly sword-shaped and oriented edgewise to the stem in 2 ranks forming a fan, sometimes leaves facing the stem and channelled, sometimes hairy. Inflorescence either a spike or the flowers clustered between leafy bracts, usually on leafy stems, sometimes the flowers borne at ground level. Flowers variously coloured, often irregular, star-like, *Iris*-like or funnel-shaped to tubular, with 6 tepals that are separate or joined into a short or long tube; stamens 3, opposite the outer whorl of tepals, arising at the mouth of the tube when present, sometimes joined at the base into a column; ovary inferior, style slender and usually divided above, sometimes the branches petal-like. Widespread but most diverse in southern Africa; many species are grown in gardens, and *Freesia*, *Gladiolus* and *Iris* are widely grown for the cut-flower trade: ±1 800 spp.

**LANARIA FAMILY** *Lanariaceae* – p.88

Rhizomatous, evergreen perennials. Leaves basal, tough and fibrous, strap-shaped and channelled, hairy below. Inflorescence a dense, flat-topped panicle, densely covered with white hairs. Flowers small, mauve, densely hairy on the outside, funnel-shaped with 6 tepals joined into a tube; stamens 6, unequal, arising at the mouth of the tube; ovary inferior, style slender. Fruit papery with 1 large, pea-like seed. Restricted to South Africa; mainly in grassy fynbos: 1 sp.

**ORCHID FAMILY** *Orchidaceae* – p.150

Tuberous or rhizomatous perennials, or epiphytes with fleshy roots. Leaves often in 2 ranks, sometimes spreading on the ground in terrestrial species. Inflorescence a spike, raceme or panicle. Flowers variously coloured, long-lasting, mostly 2-lipped, with 6 ±separate tepals, the lowermost often enlarged into a lip and spurred; stamen 1, united with the style to form a thick column, the pollen grains aggregated into pollinia; ovary inferior, often twisted. Fruit leathery or papery, containing numerous minute seeds. Worldwide, especially in the tropics, and second in number of species only to the Daisy family; many species are cultivated for their ornamental flowers: ±20 000 spp.

**PALMIET FAMILY *Prioniaceae* – p.42**
Tough, rush-like aquatic shrubs with fibrous stems. Leaves in apical rosettes, hard and fibrous, strap-like and channelled with saw-toothed margins. Inflorescence a large, bracteate panicle on a 3-angled stem. Flowers small and star-shaped, brown, with 6 separate, chaffy tepals; stamens 6; ovary superior, style short with 3 long branches. Fruit dry. Restricted to the southern shores of South Africa; on river banks and in streams: 1 sp.

**RESTIO FAMILY *Restionaceae* – p.42**
Rhizomatous, rush- or sedge-like perennials, the sexes usually on different plants. Leaves reduced to tubular sheaths scattered along the stems. Inflorescence a spike, raceme or panicle, frequently different in the sexes. Flowers minute, concealed among dry bracts, mostly with 6 dry, scale-like tepals; stamens 3; ovary superior, styles 1 or 3. Fruit a dry capsule or nutlet. Mainly southern hemisphere and most diverse in South Africa; essentially restricted to fynbos, where restios assume the place of grasses; often very common in seasonally waterlogged soils; used for thatching in the Western Cape: ±400 spp.

**SEDGE FAMILY *Cyperaceae* – p.46**
Rhizomatous or cormous, grass-like perennials or annuals, the stems mostly 3-angled. Leaves mostly basal, comprising a tubular sheath and narrow, channelled blade (rarely blade lacking). Inflorescence simple or branched, of 1 or more spike-like clusters. Flowers minute, in small spikes amongst papery bracts, with 3–6 scale-like tepals; stamens 3 (rarely 1); ovary superior, style simple or branched. Fruit a small nutlet. Worldwide, especially in moist places, in marshes or streams; widely used for basket-making and as ornamentals: ±5 000 spp.

**STARGRASS FAMILY *Hypoxidaceae* – p.88**
Rhizomatous or cormous perennials. Leaves basal, in 3 ranks, strap-shaped and channelled or pleated, often hairy, with fibrous bases. Inflorescence of 1 to several flowers on leafless, branched stalks in loose clusters arising from a common point, or the flower stalk reduced and flowers borne at ground level. Flowers white or yellow, occasionally pink to red, often green on the underside, star-shaped, with 6 tepals that are separate or joined into a tube; stamens 6, rarely 3, with short filaments; ovary inferior, sometimes drawn into a long, solid beak; style short, undivided. Fruit dry and opening from a lidded top, or a fleshy berry. Widespread in the tropics and subtropics, most diverse in southern Africa; species of *Hypoxis* are valued medicinally: ±130 spp.

## DICOTYLEDONS

**BELLFLOWER FAMILY *Campanulaceae* – p.340**
Mostly shrubs and perennials, sometimes annuals, often with milky sap. Leaves usually alternate, often toothed. Inflorescence usually a raceme, sometimes 1-flowered. Flowers mostly blue, cup-shaped or 2-lipped; sepals mostly 5; petals 4 or 5, united into a short or long tube that is sometimes split down the top or sides; stamens 4 or 5 (as many as the petals), either withered at maturity (cup-shaped flowers) or gathered into a tube (2-lipped flowers), shedding pollen directly onto the style; ovary mostly inferior, style slender, 2–10-lobed. Fruit dry, opening by apical valves. Worldwide, especially temperate: ±1 700 spp.

**BLADDERWORT FAMILY *Utriculariaceae* – p.466**
Delicate insectivorous perennials or annuals growing in wet places. Leaves inconspicuous, basal or scattered on creeping stems, some developed into insect traps. Inflorescence a raceme. Flowers white, mauve or yellow, 2-lipped; sepals 2 or 5; petals 5, joined into a 2-lipped corolla, the lower lip larger and spurred at the base; stamens 2, arising from the base of the tube on short, curved filaments; ovary superior, style slender, 2-lobed. Fruit dry, often opening by a lid. Worldwide in wet places: ±245 spp.

**BROOMRAPE FAMILY *Orobanchaceae* – p.466**
Parasitic or hemi-parasitic perennials or annuals, often fleshy and hairy, frequently turning black when drying. Leaves opposite, alternate or whorled, sometimes reduced and scale-like, often yellowish and lacking chlorophyll. Inflorescence a raceme or spike, rarely with solitary flowers in the upper axils. Flowers variously coloured, often conspicuous, irregular or 2-lipped; sepals 4 or 5, joined into a cup; petals 4 or 5 (rarely 3), joined into a 2-lipped corolla, the upper lip entirely or partially enclosed by the lower in bud; stamens 2 or 4, unequal, arising within the corolla tube; ovary superior, style slender. Fruit usually dry. Worldwide; complete or partial root-parasites on various shrubs and grasses; some, like witchweed (*Striga*) and broomrape (*Orobanche*), are pests of crops: ±600 spp.

**BRUNIA FAMILY *Bruniaceae* – p.374**
Shrubs, mostly heath-like. Leaves spirally arranged, small, more or less needle-like, always with a minute, dry black tip. Inflorescence often small, dense, rounded heads, sometimes spikes or panicles. Flowers mostly small, often cream or white, star- or cup-shaped; sepals 5, separate or joined at the base; petals 5, mostly separate but

sometimes joined below; stamens 5; ovary more or less inferior, styles 1 or 2, short. Fruit dry. South Africa, mostly Western Cape; near-endemic to Cape fynbos: ±64 spp.

## CARNATION FAMILY *Caryophyllaceae* – p.174
Annuals, perennials or small shrublets, the branches often evenly forked. Leaves mostly opposite, often narrow and untoothed. Inflorescence varied, more or less branched. Flowers mostly pink or white, star- or salver-shaped; sepals 4 or 5, mostly joined into a tube; petals 4 or 5, separate, sometimes narrowed below, often notched or fringed; stamens 4, 5 or 10, arising below the ovary; ovary superior, styles 2–5, slender. Fruit dry and splitting from the apex. Worldwide, mainly north temperate: ±2 200 spp.

## CARROT FAMILY *Apiaceae* – p.358
Tuberous perennials or annuals, occasionally shrubs or small trees, often aromatic (as of parsley or celery). Leaves alternate, the petioles sheathing at the base, mostly lobed or divided, often into fine segments and fennel- or parsley-like. Inflorescence simple or compound umbels. Flowers small, usually white to yellow, star-shaped, mostly on wiry pedicels; sepals 5; petals 5, separate, often keeled, soon falling; stamens 5; ovary inferior, styles 2, usually short. Fruit dividing into 2 segments, containing oil ducts. Worldwide, mainly in temperate regions; includes many culinary herbs and food plants such as carrot, parsnip, fennel, parsley and celery; some, such as hemlock, are deadly: ±3 500 spp.

## CITRUS FAMILY *Rutaceae* – p.190
Trees, shrubs or shrublets, often aromatic, rarely unisexual, frequently heath-like. Leaves opposite or alternate, often small and leathery or needle-like, sometimes divided, dotted with translucent oil glands and aromatic. Inflorescence terminal or axillary clusters or racemes, sometimes 1-flowered. Flowers mostly white to pink, star-shaped; sepals 5 (rarely 4), separate or joined at the base; petals 5 (rarely 4), separate, often narrowed below, very rarely 0; stamens 5 (rarely 10), arising at the base of the ovary or on the fleshy disc surrounding the ovary, sometimes alternating with petal- or gland-like staminodes; ovary superior, deeply lobed or divided into separate carpels, style slender. Fruit dry and splitting into segments, or fleshy. Worldwide, mostly tropical, but many in the Western Cape; includes several important fruits, among others, oranges, lemons and grapefruit; *Agathosma* species (buchu) are important flavorants and medicines: ±1 650 spp.

## CONVOLVULUS FAMILY *Convolvulaceae* – p.218
Herbs or shrubs, often twining, rarely parasitic. Leaves alternate, often arrowhead-shaped or lobed. Inflorescence mostly few-flowered and axillary. Flowers variously coloured, often showy, funnel-shaped, short-lived; sepals mostly 5, united below into a cup; petals 5, united into a narrow to wide tube, rolled like an umbrella when in bud, thin-textured; stamens 5, arising from the base of the corolla tube; ovary superior, styles 1 or 2, slender. Fruit dry. Worldwide, especially tropical: ±1 700 spp.

## CRASSULA FAMILY *Crassulaceae* – p.166
Mostly succulent shrubs, perennials or annuals. Leaves opposite or alternate, sometimes in rosettes, flat to cylindrical, succulent. Inflorescence usually branched, often flat-topped. Flowers variously coloured, mostly white or pink, star- or cup-shaped to tubular; sepals 3–5, separate or joined; petals 3–5, separate or joined into a tube; stamens as many as the petals or twice as many, arising at the base or on the petals; ovary superior, of 3–5 separate carpels, tapering into the styles. Fruit dry, of 3–5 separate segments. Worldwide, with centres of diversity in southern Africa and Central America; widely cultivated: ±1 500 spp.

## DAISY FAMILY *Asteraceae* – p.378
Small trees, shrubs, perennials or annuals, often aromatic. Leaves alternate or opposite, sometimes lobed or divided, hairless or variously hairy. Inflorescence a head surrounded by scale-like bracts. Flowers (florets) small, often yellow or purple, funnel-shaped or the outer series forming petal-like rays; sepals 0 or represented by minute scales or bristles; petals 4 or 5, joined into a narrow tube; stamens 4 or 5, with the anthers usually united into a tube around the style; ovary inferior, style slender, usually forked at the tip. Fruit a dry nutlet, often crowned with scales or bristles; rarely fleshy. Worldwide in all habitats; the largest plant family; numerous species are grown for food or as ornamentals: ±25 000 spp.

## DAPHNE FAMILY *Thymelaeaceae* – p.236
Small trees or shrubs, often heath-like, with tough bark stripping into strings. Leaves alternate or opposite, often narrow or needle-like and pressed to the stems, often covered with silvery hairs. Inflorescence a spike or head, rarely 1-flowered. Flowers usually white to yellow, or pinkish, tubular; sepals 4 or 5, joined into a slender or funnel-shaped tube, often coloured; petals absent but usually replaced by 4, 8 or 12 small, scale-like appendages inserted at the mouth of the tube; stamens 4, 8 or

10, arising in the tube and often hidden within it; ovary superior, style arising laterally, slender. Fruit enclosed within the calyx. Worldwide, especially Africa and Australia; many members are poisonous: ±600 spp.

### DESERT PRIMROSE FAMILY *Neuradaceae* – p.340
Prostrate, hairy annuals with a taproot and slimy or mucilaginous sap. Leaves alternate, toothed or deeply lobed, leathery and hairy. Inflorescence of solitary flowers in the leaf axils. Flowers yellow, cup-shaped; sepals 5, joined in a cup; petals 5, separate; stamens 10, arising on the calyx cup; ovary more or less inferior, styles 5–10, short. Fruit woody and disc-like, often spiny on top. Dry parts of Africa and western Asia to India: 9 spp.

### ERICA FAMILY *Ericaceae* – p.224
Ericoid shrubs, shrublets or small trees. Leaves mostly whorled, usually more or less needle-like, with the margins tightly rolled under, hard. Inflorescence a raceme or whorl, or small clusters on short-shoots. Flowers brightly coloured, often shades of pink, sometimes sticky, cup-shaped to tubular, leathery; sepals 4, joined below, sometimes coloured and larger than the petals; petals 4, joined into a short or long tube; stamens mostly 8, arising below the ovary, anthers often opening by basal pores and often tailed; ovary superior, style mostly slender. Fruit usually small and dry. Worldwide; in southern Africa represented essentially by the large genus *Erica*: ±4 500 spp.

### EUPHORBIA FAMILY *Euphorbiaceae* – p.164
Trees, shrubs or herbs, often succulent, with milky latex. Leaves usually alternate, undivided, sometimes rudimentary. Inflorescence varied, often surrounded by fleshy, petal-like bracts. Flowers often unisexual, tiny, greenish; sepals and/or petals small, sometimes absent; stamens 1–many; ovary superior. Fruit usually dry and 3-chambered with 1 seed per chamber, splitting between the lobes. Worldwide, mainly tropical and often in dry areas: ±7 000 spp.

### FLAX FAMILY *Linaceae* – p.202
Perennials or subshrubs, rarely shrublets or small trees. Leaves alternate, opposite or whorled, simple, stipules often present between the leaves as a gland. Inflorescence a panicle. Flowers mostly yellow or blue, star-shaped; sepals 4 or 5, separate or joined at the base, often glandular on the margins; petals 4 or 5, separate, narrowed below, soon falling, furled like an umbrella in bud; stamens as many as the petals or twice as many, with the filaments joined at the base into a cup; ovary superior, styles 3–5, sometimes joined at the base. Fruit dry, splitting between the lobes. Widespread; flax, *Linum usitatissimum*, is cultivated for both its stem fibres and its seeds, which are the source of linseed oil: ±250 spp.

### FORGET-ME-NOT FAMILY *Boraginaceae* – p.278
Trees, shrubs, perennials and annuals, often harshly hairy or bristly. Leaves mostly alternate, usually elliptical. Inflorescence usually a branched, 1-sided raceme coiling at the tip like a scorpion's tail. Flowers often shades of blue, cup-shaped; sepals 5, united below into a cup; petals 5, joined into a short tube, sometimes with scales or folds in the throat; stamens 5, arising in the floral tube; ovary superior, often deeply 4-lobed, style slender, sometimes forked above. Fruit fragmenting into several small, often bristly or barbed, nutlets, rarely fleshy. Worldwide, especially the Mediterranean: ±2 500 spp.

### FUMITORY FAMILY *Fumariaceae* – p.286
Bluish, brittle annuals or perennials, often sprawling or climbing, with watery, clear or yellow sap. Leaves divided into leaflets, often ending in a tendril. Inflorescence a raceme. Flowers mostly shades of pink or yellow, 2-lipped; sepals 2, often scale-like, soon falling; petals 4, in 2 dissimilar pairs, the outer 2 sometimes pouched or spurred at the base; stamens 2–6, usually joined in 2 bundles; ovary superior, style slender, 2-lobed. Fruit dry, sometimes bladdery. Mostly north temperate; closely related to and sometimes included in the Poppy family: ±530 spp.

### GENTIAN FAMILY *Gentianaceae* – p.222
Shrubs, perennials or annuals. Leaves mostly opposite or in a basal rosette, simple. Inflorescence mostly few-flowered. Flowers mostly pink or yellow, often showy, cup- or salver-shaped; sepals 4 or 5, joined into a cup; petals mostly 4 or 5, joined into a tube, furled like an umbrella in bud; stamens as many as the petals, arising in the tube; ovary superior, style short and thick. Fruit dry, rarely fleshy. Worldwide, mainly temperate and subtropical: ±1 200 spp.

### GERANIUM FAMILY *Geraniaceae* – p.180
Shrubs, perennials or annuals, often hairy and aromatic, sometimes succulent. Leaves alternate or opposite, usually lobed or divided. Inflorescence axillary, umbel-like. Flowers variously coloured, often pink to purple with darker veins, star-shaped or 2-lipped; sepals 5, separate or joined below; petals 5 (or fewer), separate, often notched at the

tips; stamens 10 or 15, sometimes not all fertile, filaments sometimes joined below; ovary superior, style dividing into 3–5 branches. Fruit with a long beak, fragmenting into segments and coiling from the base when ripe. Widespread in temperate and subtropical regions; includes many horticultural subjects in the genera *Geranium* and *Pelargonium*: ±800 spp.

## GRUBBIA FAMILY *Grubbiaceae* – p.368
Shrubs or subshrubs. Leaves opposite, with successive pairs at right angles to one another, narrow, dull and leathery. Inflorescence a small axillary, cone-like cluster. Flowers minute, reddish, star-shaped; sepals 4, separate; petals 0; stamens 8; ovary inferior, style slender. Fruit compound, fleshy. South Africa; endemic to Cape fynbos: 3 spp.

## HIBISCUS FAMILY *Malvaceae* – p.202
Trees, shrubs and perennials, with star-shaped hairs. Leaves alternate, often palmately lobed or divided, often with toothed margins, often conspicuously stipulate. Inflorescence an axillary cluster or 1-flowered. Flowers variously coloured, often yellow or pink, cup-shaped or furled, with or without a whorl of sepal-like bracts beneath the calyx; sepals 3–5, joined below in a cup; petals 5, separate but often joined to the base of the staminal column, furled like an umbrella in bud; stamens 5 to many, the filaments often joined into a tubular column; ovary superior, style often branched. Fruit dry, often fragmenting into segments. Worldwide, especially in the tropics; the family now includes the Sterculiaceae and Tiliaceae; many genera are cultivated, notably *Althaea* (hollyhock), *Abutilon* and *Hibiscus*; the tropical *Gossypium* is the source of cotton: ±3 500 spp.

## ICE PLANT FAMILY *Aizoaceae* – p.318
Succulent shrubs, perennials or annuals. Leaves mostly opposite, sometimes in rosettes, usually cylindrical or 3-sided. Inflorescence a small or large cluster, or flowers solitary. Flowers variously coloured, often brilliant red, purple or pink, symmetrical; sepals 4–6; petals absent, often represented by many narrow, colourful staminodes; stamens 4 to many, often numerous, sometimes with staminodes; ovary inferior, style often short or absent. Fruit a woody capsule, often opening by pointed flaps when damp, then star-shaped. More or less worldwide but mostly African and concentrated in the winter-rainfall region of western South Africa; characteristic plants of Succulent Karoo shrublands: ±2 000 spp.

## MELIANTHUS FAMILY *Melianthaceae* – p.284
Trees, shrubs or subshrubs, often foetid. Leaves alternate, divided into many-toothed leaflets, axis more or less winged, conspicuously stipulate, the stipules axillary. Inflorescence a raceme. Flowers greenish, brown or red, 2-lipped, twisting through 180° at flowering; sepals 5, unequal, joined into a cup, pouched below; petals 4 or 5, separate, narrowed below, unequal; stamens 4, separate or joined, arising below the ovary within a fleshy, nectar-secreting disc, short and often bent forwards; ovary superior, style slender, hairy at the base. Fruit leathery, 4-lobed or -winged. Sub-Saharan Africa: ±20 spp.

## MILKWEED FAMILY *Apocynaceae* – p.206
Trees, shrubs, perennials or annuals, sometimes vines, often succulents, with milky or clear sap. Leaves opposite with the pairs at right angles to one another, sometimes in whorls or occasionally reduced or absent. Inflorescence mostly a few-flowered, terminal or axillary cluster, often flat-topped. Flowers variously coloured, sometimes showy, cup-shaped to tubular, leathery; sepals 5, separate or joined below into a cup; petals 5, joined below in a narrow or wide tube, often with scales or hairs in the throat; stamens 5, sometimes united with the stigmas into a fleshy body; ovary superior, of 2 separate carpels, styles short, joined at the tips. Fruit consisting of paired, often horn-like segments, the seeds often plumed. Worldwide, mostly tropical; many contain poisonous alkaloids; the stapeliads, or carrion-flowers, are popular among succulent collectors: ±4 800 spp.

## MINT FAMILY *Lamiaceae* – p.462
Small trees, shrubs and perennials, sometimes annuals, mostly glandular and aromatic with essential oils; the stems often square in cross-section. Leaves opposite, sometimes in tufts, mostly toothed, broad or narrow. Inflorescence usually raceme- or spike-like with flowers in loose or tight whorls. Flowers variously coloured, often white or pink to blue, irregular, mostly 2-lipped; sepals 5, joined into a cup-like calyx, sometimes variously lipped; petals 5, joined into a 2-lipped corolla, the lower lip often larger, sometimes boat-shaped; stamens 2 or 4, arising in the tube; ovary superior, deeply 4-lobed above, style slender, often 2-lobed at the tip. Fruit of 4 nutlets. Worldwide, especially subtropical and Mediterranean; contains many culinary herbs, including basil, rosemary, sage and mint as well as several garden plants: ±7 000 spp.

## MONTINIA FAMILY *Montiniaceae* – p.338

Unisexual shrubs or small trees. Leaves alternate, simple, glaucous and leathery. Inflorescence a 1 to few-flowered terminal cluster. Flowers white, regular, star-shaped; sepals 4, joined in a cup with very short lobes; petals 4, separate, leathery; stamens 4 in male flowers, arising at the base of a fleshy, nectar-secreting disc or basin, short; ovary inferior, lacking in male flowers, style short, 2-branched. Fruit leathery, flask-shaped. Eastern and southern Africa and Madagascar: ±4 spp.

## MUSTARD FAMILY *Brassicaceae* – p.176

Perennials, annuals, shrubs or small trees, often tasting and smelling of mustard or sulphur. Leaves mostly alternate, often lobed or divided. Inflorescence usually a slender raceme, sometimes more or less flat-topped. Flowers often yellow, white or blue, cross-shaped; sepals 4 in 2 pairs, the inner often sac-like or spurred; petals 4 (rarely 0), separate, usually narrow at the base; stamens usually 6 with the outer 2 shorter (rarely many); ovary superior, sometimes stalked, style usually short. Fruit dry and papery, rounded to long and narrow, sometimes segmented or beaded, the outer wall splitting into 2 halves, leaving the seeds attached to a septum. Worldwide, mostly northern hemisphere; includes many ornamentals, and food plants such as cabbage, broccoli and mustard: ±3 000 spp.

## OXALIS FAMILY *Oxalidaceae* – p.212

Bulbous perennials, rarely annuals, often stemless, brittle and sour-tasting. Leaves alternate or basal, usually digitately divided into 3 to several leaflets that often fold closed at night. Inflorescence umbel-like, or 1-flowered. Flowers variously coloured, often pink or yellow, with a yellow centre, funnel-shaped; sepals 5, separate; petals 5, narrowed below and joined at the base, furled like an umbrella in bud; stamens 10 in 2 unequal whorls, joined at the base; ovary superior, styles 5, slender. Fruit fleshy, usually splitting explosively. Nearly cosmopolitan, mainly South America and southern Africa, especially Western Cape; the characteristic sour taste comes from oxalic acid crystals in the cells: ±900 spp.

## PEA FAMILY *Fabaceae* – p.290

Trees, shrubs, perennials or annuals. Leaves mostly alternate, usually compound, sometimes needle-like, often conspicuously stipulate. Inflorescence usually a raceme, sometimes tightly clustered. Flowers mostly yellow, or pink to purple, regular or irregular, often sweet pea-shaped; sepals mostly 5, often joined into a cup; petals mostly 5, the uppermost largest and forming a flag, the lower 2 joined into a keel hiding the stamens and style, and the 2 laterals forming wings; stamens mostly twice as many as the petals, frequently united into a split tube; ovary superior, style slender, usually hooked at the tip. Fruit a pod with seeds in 1 row. Worldwide; characterised by the presence of nitrogen-fixing bacteria in specialised root nodules; includes many important food plants, among them beans, peas and lentils: ±18 000 spp.

## PENAEA FAMILY *Penaeaceae* – p.232

Shrubs or shrublets, mostly hairless. Leaves opposite and in 4 ranks, simple and leathery, the whorls usually overlapping. Inflorescence a spike, small head-like cluster or sometimes 1-flowered. Flowers mostly yellow or pink, sometimes bicoloured, tubular or bell-shaped, leathery; sepals 4, brightly coloured and petal-like, joined into a fleshy tube; petals 0; stamens 4, with short fleshy filaments and anthers, arising in the throat of the tube; ovary superior, style slender, sometimes ridged or winged. Fruit dry. Endemic to Cape fynbos, often restricted to moist mountain tops: 23 spp.

## PHYLICA FAMILY *Rhamnaceae* – p.368

Trees or shrubs, sometimes spiny, often heath-like. Leaves usually alternate, simple and often glossy, often small and leathery or ericoid. Inflorescence of small clusters, spikes or heads, sometimes arranged in panicles. Flowers often cream-coloured or white, small, cup-shaped; sepals 4 or 5, joined below into a cup or tube; petals 4 or 5 and minute or absent, separate, arising in the mouth of the calyx tube; stamens 4 or 5, arising with the petals and opposite them; ovary superior or inferior, style short, sometimes divided above. Fruit hard and nutlike, or fleshy. Worldwide, mainly tropical and subtropical; several species are used medicinally and contain quinine-like compounds: ±900 spp.

## PLUMBAGO FAMILY *Plumbaginaceae* – p.220

Shrubs or perennials. Leaves alternate or in a basal rosette, stiff and leathery, sometimes reduced to scales, usually with scattered, scurfy chalk glands. Inflorescence a raceme or flat-topped panicle. Flowers mostly pink to blue, sometimes bicoloured, funnel- or salver-shaped; sepals 5, joined into a 5–15-ribbed tube, often papery and coloured, or with gland-tipped hairs; petals 5, joined below into a short or long tube, furled like an umbrella in bud; stamens 5, separate or arising at the base of the tube; ovary superior, styles 1 or 5, slender. Fruit dry, enclosed by the persistent calyx. Worldwide, especially the

Mediterranean and Near East, particularly maritime and arid areas in saline situations; excess calcium salts are excreted through the specialised chalk glands; Plumbago (*Plumbago auriculata*) is widely grown as an ornamental shrub in South Africa: ±650 spp.

## POLYGALA FAMILY *Polygalaceae* – p.286

Small trees, shrubs or perennials, often ericoid, sometimes thorny. Leaves mostly alternate, sometimes tufted, never lobed and often needle-like. Inflorescence usually 1-flowered, often raceme-like. Flowers mostly pink to purple, 2-lipped and sweet pea-shaped; sepals 5, separate, the lateral ones sometimes wing-like; petals 3 or 5, joined at the base to the stamens, the lowermost forming a keel with a fringe or crest at the end; stamens 5–8, the filaments usually joined into a split tube, curved at the ends; ovary superior, style slender, often flattened and lobed at the tip. Fruit dry, rarely fleshy. Nearly worldwide; some species of *Polygala* are popular garden plants: ±950 spp.

## POTATO FAMILY *Solanaceae* – p.274

Trees, shrubs, perennials, or annuals, erect or climbing, sometimes spiny. Leaves alternate or in tufts, often obscurely lobed. Inflorescence mostly a small, lateral cluster arising opposite or alongside the leaves, or 1-flowered. Flowers variously coloured but often shades of blue, star-shaped to funnel-shaped; sepals usually 4 or 5, joined below into a cup; petals 4 or 5, joined at the base or into a short or long tube; stamens 4 or 5, arising in the corolla tube, often clustered and opening by apical pores; ovary superior, 2-chambered, the cross-wall diagonally orientated relative to the stem, style slender or stout. Fruit often a fleshy berry. Worldwide, mainly tropical and subtropical; includes many important food plants, such as the tomato *(Lycopersicon esculentum)*, potato *(Solanum tuberosum)*, aubergine *(S. melongena)* and peppers *(Capsicum)*; ornamentals like petunia; and tobacco *(Nicotiana tabacum)*; many species contain poisonous alkaloids: ±2 600 spp.

## PROTEA FAMILY *Proteaceae* – p.246

Trees, shrubs or shrublets, erect or creeping, sometimes with the sexes on different plants. Leaves mostly alternate, or in whorls, sometimes divided into needle-like segments, flat or thread-like, leathery, often turned sideways. Inflorescence a raceme, panicle or a head and then often surrounded by coloured bracts. Flowers usually whitish, regular or irregular, slender, often hairy; sepals 4, separate or joined below into a tube, narrow or thread-like; petals 0; stamens 4, the anthers often stalkless and arising near the tips of the sepals; ovary superior, style stiff, often swollen or needle-like at the tip. Fruit a woody nutlet, often aggregated into a cone. Southern continents, mainly Australia and southern Africa; several species and hybrids of protea (*Protea*) and pincushion (*Leucospermum*) are grown as ornamentals or cut-flowers: ±1 350 spp.

## RANUNCULUS FAMILY *Ranunculaceae* – p.170

Annuals or perennials, sometimes shrubs or climbers, rarely aquatic. Leaves usually alternate or crowded at the base, often divided, usually sheathing at the base. Inflorescence a panicle, often flat-topped, or 1-flowered. Flowers variously coloured, often yellow or pink, star-shaped; sepals 3 to many, separate, often deciduous, sometimes petal-like; petals 0 to many, separate; stamens many, separate, arising at the base of the ovary; ovary usually of many separate carpels, styles slender or absent. Fruit of many nutlets, rarely fleshy. Worldwide, mainly temperate; many genera, including *Anemone*, *Delphinium* and *Ranunculus*, are cultivated in gardens and as cut-flowers: ±1 750 spp.

## ROSE FAMILY *Rosaceae* – p.338

Trees, shrubs or perennials, rarely annual, sometimes prickly or thorny. Leaves mostly alternate or in tufts, undivided or divided and often toothed, the petiole often clasping the stem, stipules often present. Inflorescence a raceme or panicle, or 1-flowered. Flowers often pink or white, sometimes unisexual, regular; sepals 3 or 5, joined into a cup-shaped tube; petals as many as the sepals or 0, separate, arising on the calyx tube; stamens 1 to many, usually arising on the calyx tube; ovary usually inferior, of 1 to many separate carpels, styles arising at the base of the carpels, slender. Fruit dry or fleshy, usually of separate fruitlets. Worldwide, mainly north temperate; includes many ornamentals, among them the rose, (*Rosa*), hawthorn (*Crataegus*), *Cotoneaster* and valuable fruits, such as apple (*Malus*), pear (*Pyrus*) and strawberry: ±3 000 spp.

## SANDALWOOD FAMILY *Santalaceae* – p.372

Trees , shrubs or herbs, sometimes spiny, often partially parasitic on the roots of other plants, mostly bluish or greyish green. Leaves alternate or opposite, leathery or fleshy, elliptical or sometimes reduced and scale-like. Inflorescence of small axillary clusters, spikes or heads, sometimes arranged in panicles. Flowers cream-coloured or white, small, cup-shaped; sepals 3–5, joined below into a cup or tube; petals absent; stamens 3–6, arising on the tube opposite the sepals, usually with a tuft of hairs behind; ovary inferior, style short. Fruit nutlike or fleshy. Worldwide, mainly tropical and subtropical; the sandalwood tree *(Santalum album)* yields a fine wood and sandal oil, which is used in perfume, soap and incense: ± 500 spp.

## SCABIOUS FAMILY *Dipsacaceae* – p.458
Shrublets, perennials or annuals. Leaves usually opposite, often lobed and divided. Inflorescence a small head surrounded by bracts. Flowers small, white or lilac, funnel-shaped and more or less 2-lipped; sepals 5–20 and bristle-like or united into a collar; petals 5, usually hairy, joined into a wide tube; stamens 4 (rarely 5), arising in the corolla tube; ovary inferior, style slender. Fruit an achene topped with bristles or a crown. Africa and Eurasia, mainly Mediterranean: 350–400 spp.

## STILBE FAMILY *Stilbaceae* – p.458
Trees, shrubs or shrublets, often heath-like. Leaves opposite or whorled, often narrow or needle-like and 2-grooved beneath, leathery. Inflorescence a spike, or axillary clusters. Flowers mostly small, often pink or cream to white, funnel-shaped or tubular, sometimes slightly irregular; sepals 5, mostly joined into a tube; petals 5, joined into a tube, nearly equal or weakly 2-lipped, often with a dense ring of hairs within; stamens usually 4 or 5, rarely 2, arising near the mouth of the tube; ovary superior, style slender. Fruit dry or fleshy. Africa; until recently the family was considered to comprise just 16 species of heath-like shrubs endemic to Cape fynbos but it is now clear that the forest trees *Halleria* and *Nuxia* also belong here: ±64 spp.

## SUNDEW FAMILY *Droseraceae* – p.172
Glandular, insectivorous perennials or annuals. Leaves basal and/or scattered along the stem, bearing sticky, reddish gland-tipped hairs and tentacles, narrow or broader. Inflorescence 1 to few-flowered. Flowers usually pink or white, star-shaped; sepals 5; petals 5, separate; stamens 5; ovary superior, styles 3–5, sometimes deeply divided. Worldwide, especially in moist, acidic soils: ±100 spp.

## SUTERA FAMILY *Scrophulariaceae* – p.470
Trees, shrubs, perennials or annuals. Leaves usually opposite, sometimes tufted, often toothed, frequently covered with gland-tipped hairs and foetid. Inflorescence a raceme, spike, head or panicle. Flowers variously coloured, often blue, mauve or white, usually irregular, often 2-lipped; sepals 4 or 5, joined into a short tube, sometimes unequal; petals 4 or 5, joined into a short or long tube; stamens usually 4, unequal, sometimes the anther lobes joined into 1; ovary superior, style slender. Fruit dry or fleshy. Worldwide, mainly Africa; has recently undergone a radical reclassification, whereby many northern hemisphere genera with 2-lipped flowers previously considered to belong here, such as foxglove *(Digitalis)*, snapdragon *(Antirrhinum)* and beardtongue *(Penstemon)*, are now classified in a separate family with the plantains *(Plantago)*; includes ornamentals such as *Nemesia* and *Sutera*: ±2 000 spp.

## TWINLEAF FAMILY *Zygophyllaceae* – p.178
Shrubs, perennials or annuals, often with jointed branches. Leaves usually opposite, often somewhat fleshy, frequently divided into 2 oblique leaflets, stipules often hard and sharp. Inflorescence 1–2-flowered in the axils. Flowers mostly yellow, star-shaped; sepals 5, separate or joined at the base; petals 4 or 5; stamens as many as the petals or twice as many, mostly unequal, arising at the base of the ovary and often with scales or appendages at the base; ovary superior, often surrounded by a fleshy, lobed disc at the base, styles 1–5, slender. Fruit dry and 5-lobed, rarely fleshy. Widespread in the tropics and subtropics, mostly deserts and arid regions: ±250 spp.

## VIOLET FAMILY *Violaceae* – p.284
Perennials, annuals, shrubs or trees. Leaves alternate, unlobed, often toothed. Inflorescence of solitary axillary flowers. Flowers often shades of blue or yellow, 2-lipped; sepals 5, usually separate; petals 5, separate, the lower often spurred or pouched; stamens 5, arising below the ovary, anthers joined in a ring around the ovary, bearing glands or nectaries on the back; ovary superior, style often swollen above. Fruit often splitting open explosively. Widespread in the tropics, with the genus *Viola* mainly temperate but widely cultivated: 830 spp.

# PRIONIACEAE

## Palmiet family

### *Prionium*  PALM RUSH, PALMIET

Tough, *rush-like aquatic shrubs with fibrous stems*. Leaves in apical rosettes, *hard and fibrous,* strap-like and channelled *with serrated margins*. Inflorescence a large panicle on a 3-angled stem. Flowers small and star-shaped, brown, with *6 dry tepals*; stamens 6, ovary superior, style with 3 long branches. South Africa, along the southern and southeastern seaboard, on river banks and in streams: 1 sp. The leaves were used in the manufacture of straw hats worn by slaves in early Cape Town.

**1** *Prionium serratum*

J F M A M J J A **S O N D**

Robust shrub to 2 m, with fibrous stems bearing terminal rosettes of hard, grey, strap-like leaves with sharply saw-toothed margins. River banks and streams on sandstone, often forming dense stands, in the Western and Eastern Cape and southern KwaZulu-Natal.

# RESTIONACEAE

## Restio family

▸ FLOWERS WITH 1 STYLE

### *Thamnochortus*  BESEMRIET

Tufted or tussock-forming perennials, mostly with simple stems and *often with clusters of sterile shoots at the nodes* in the year after flowering. *Male inflorescence* of many *nodding, cylindrical spikelets. Female inflorescence* of 1 to several *stiff, erect spikelets*; *ovary 1-chambered*, with *1 style.* Fruit a soft-walled nutlet. Winter-rainfall South Africa: ±33 spp, all fynbos. *Thamnochortus insignis* is of major importance for thatching in the southern Cape.

**2** *Thamnochortus insignis*  Dekriet

J F **M A M** J J A S O N D

Large, tufted perennial with simple, hairless stems to 2 m; the female spikelets are 15–25 mm long and the fruits are not longer than wide. Loamy soils between coastal dunes on the Agulhas Plain.

▸ FLOWERS WITH 2 OR 3 STYLES

### *Elegia*  ELEGIA, DEKRIET

*Tufted or rhizomatous perennials with simple or branched stems, often with shorter sterile stems.* Leaf sheaths usually deciduous. Male and female inflorescences similar, mostly aggregations of many spikelets, the bracts shorter than the flowers; *ovary 1- or 3-chambered, with 2 or 3 styles. Fruit a 1–3-seeded capsule or a hard, 1-seeded nutlet.* Winter-rainfall South Africa: ±45 spp, all fynbos. The genus has recently been enlarged to include both *Chondropetalum* and *Dovea*. *Elegia capensis* is a popular garden plant, and *E. tectorum* (better known as *Chondropetalum tectorum*) is used extensively for thatching.

**3** *Elegia capensis*  Fonteinriet

J F M A M J J A S O **N D**

Robust, brush-like perennial to 2 m, with stiffly erect stems bearing dense whorls of sterile branchlets. Seeps and streamsides on sandstone slopes in the Western and Eastern Cape.

### ❶ *Elegia filacea*

J **F** M A M J J A S O N D

Delicate, tufted perennial to 50 cm, with slender, unbranched stems, and deciduous leaf sheaths. The flowers are well exposed. Damp sandy flats and slopes to 2 100 m, often in large stands, in the Western and Eastern Cape.

### ❷ *Elegia tectorum* **Dekriet**

J F M **A** **M** J J **A** **S** **O** N D

(=*Chondropetalum tectorum*) Tufted perennial to 1 m, with deciduous leaf sheaths. The flowers are less than 3 mm long with petals that are smooth, or hairy only in the upper half. Seasonal marshes and seeps on deep sands in the Western and Eastern Cape.

### ❸ *Elegia mucronata* **Bergriet**

J F M A M J J A S **O** **N** D

(=*Chondropetalum mucronatum*) Robust tufted perennial with cane-like stems to 2 m. The floral spikes are subtended by large, pale spathes 5–10 cm long. Marshes and seeps, mainly montane, in the Western Cape.

## *Staberoha* **STABEROHA**

Tufted perennials with simple stems. Leaf sheaths persistent. *Male inflorescence* of 1–10 *nodding, top-shaped spikelets. Female inflorescence* of 1–6 stiff, *erect, cylindrical or spindle-shaped spikelets. Ovary 1-chambered*, usually with 2 or 3 styles. Fruit a flattened nutlet. A very distinctive genus, with its pendulous male spikes resembling diminutive pine cones. Winter-rainfall parts of the Western Cape: ±9 spp, all fynbos.

### ❹ *Staberoha aemula*

J F M A M **J** **J** **A** **S** O N D

Tufted perennial to 60 cm, with globular male spikelets and winged female flowers with blunt tepals. Seasonally moist sandy flats in the mountains of the Western Cape.

### ❺ *Staberoha distachya* **Cape grass**

J **F** **M** **A** **M** **J** **J** **A** **S** **O** **N** D

Tufted perennial to 60 cm, with top-shaped male spikelets and narrow female spikelets with sharp tepals. Mountain slopes in the Western Cape.

## *Willdenowia* **WILLDENOWIA**

Tufted, often untidy perennials, mostly with *branching stems*. Leaf sheaths persistent, *the apical portion membranous and soon decaying. Male inflorescence* of many florets in panicles, *not arranged in spikelets*, partially obscured by large bracts in bud. *Female inflorescence* of 1 to few *spikelets subtended by conspicuous spathes. Ovary 1-chambered*, with *2 styles. Fruit a large, woody nutlet*. Winter-rainfall South Africa: ±11 spp, all fynbos.

### ❻ *Willdenowia incurvata*

J F M A M **J** J A S O N D

Tufted perennial to 2 m, with finely ribbed, branching stems; the nutlets are pitted. Sandy coastal flats along the West Coast and near interior.

# CYPERACEAE

**Sedge family**

## *Ficinia* **FICINIA**

Tufted perennials. Leaves mostly basal, blades flat or keeled, usually with a *well-developed papery ligule* at the junction between blade and sheath. *Inflorescence a spike or head*, or panicle of heads, the spikelets roughly cylindrical with the glumes spirally arranged and closely overlapping, the *lower 1 or 2 glumes empty*, followed by several fertile bisexual florets, then by male florets or empty glumes; style 3-branched. *Nutlet carried on a short stalk.* Africa, mainly Western Cape: ±60 spp; 56 fynbos spp.

**1** *Ficinia radiata* **Stergras**

| J | F | M | A | M | J | J | A | S | O | N | D |

Tufted perennial, 5–25 cm with yellow spikelets in heads surrounded by radiating, chrome-yellow bracts. Sandy flats and lower slopes in moist places in the south-western Cape, often conspicuous after fire.

**2** *Ficinia truncata*

| J | F | M | A | M | J | J | A | S | O | N | D |

Grey-green, tufted perennial with blunt leaves and chestnut-brown spikelets. Limestone hills below 200 m along the southern coast. *Ficinia praemorsa* from the same area has narrow, quill-like leaves and yellowish spikelets.

## *Tetraria* **BERGPALMIET**

Wiry, tufted perennials, *sometimes very robust*. Leaves all basal or also cauline, blades usually keeled, sometimes lacking. Inflorescence a panicle or head of several to many spikelets, the *spikelets roughly cylindrical* with the glumes spirally arranged, the *lower 4–9 glumes empty*, followed by 1–4 with male florets, followed by 1 fertile bisexual floret; style 3–4-branched. Africa and Australasia, mainly Western Cape: ±50 spp; 38 fynbos spp.

**3** *Tetraria thermalis* **Bergpalmiet**

| J | F | M | A | M | J | J | A | S | O | N | D |

Robust, yellowish-green tufted perennial to over 2 m with arching, keeled leaves and dusky brown spikelets. Cooler sandstone slopes below 1 000 m in the south-western Cape. *Tetraria bromoides* has narrow, grass-like leaves.

47

# APONOGETONACEAE
## Aponogeton family

### *Aponogeton* PONDBLOSSOM, WATERBLOMMETJIE

Rhizomatous or tuberous, *aquatic perennials*. Leaves basal, submerged or floating on long petioles. *Inflorescence a small, simple or forked spike*, often fleshy. *Flowers with 1 or 2 tepals*; stamens 6 or more, *ovary of 3–6 separate carpels*. Old World tropics, mainly in seasonal freshwater pools: 43 spp. *Aponogeton distachyos* is cultivated in the Western Cape for its edible fruiting spikes, traditionally used to make *waterblommetjiebredie*, a mutton stew.

**1** *Aponogeton distachyos*

| J | F | M | A | M | J | J | A | S | O | N | D |

**Waterblommetjie** Rhizomatous aquatic with oblong, floating leaves 6–20 cm long; bears forked spikes with 2 rows of numerous fragrant white flowers, each with 1 petal up to 18 mm long. Pools and ditches in the southwestern Cape. *Aponogeton angustifolius* is a smaller plant with leaves 5–10 cm long and only 4–8 rather scattered, honey-scented flowers per spike, each flower with 2 petals 5–10 mm long.

# ARACEAE
## Arum family

### *Zantedeschia* ARUM LILY, VARKLELIE

Rhizomatous or tuberous perennials. Leaves basal, with a *spongy petiole* and an *assegai-* or *arrow-shaped blade*. Inflorescence *on a long scape*, surrounded by a conspicuous, *flaring spathe that has the edges overlapping at the base*. Flowers unisexual, without petals; female flowers at the base of the spike, male flowers above, with sessile anthers shedding pollen through apical pores. Fruits fleshy, green or orange when ripe. Southern Africa, mostly the eastern grasslands: 8 spp; 1 fynbos sp. *Zantedeschia aethiopica* is a popular garden plant that has become naturalised in California and elsewhere; the tubers, although rich in oxalic acid, are favoured by porcupines; the boiled leaves were used medicinally.

**2** *Zantedeschia aethiopica*

| J | F | M | A | M | J | J | A | S | O | N | D |

**Calla, varklelie** Rhizomatous geophyte, 60–100 cm with plain green, arrow-shaped leaves and a large, pure white, funnel-shaped spathe; the fruiting stems remain erect. Widespread through southern Africa in seasonally wet vleis and streams.

# AMARYLLIDACEAE     **Amaryllis family**

▸ FLOWERS USUALLY LONGER THAN THE PEDICELS; STAMEN FILAMENTS SEPARATE

## *Cyrtanthus*   FIRE LILY, VUURLELIE

Deciduous, bulbous perennials. Leaves *slender and strap-shaped*, sometimes twisted, *often with a midrib*. Flowers borne on a *hollow scape*, funnel-shaped to tubular and *often curved*, sometimes 2-lipped, variously coloured, spreading or nodding on very short pedicels, stamens arising in the tube in *2 series at different heights*. Fruits ellipsoid with *flattened, black seeds*. Southern Africa, mainly the eastern seaboard: ±50 spp; ±20 fynbos spp.

**❶ *Cyrtanthus elatus***

J F M A M J J A S O N D

**George** or **Knysna lily**   Bulbous perennial to 45 cm with bright green leaves present at flowering; bears 2–9 large, widely funnel-shaped, scarlet or rarely pink flowers. Forest margins and moist mountain slopes along the south coast, flowering well after fire.

**❷ *Cyrtanthus fergusoniae***

J F M A M J J A S O N D

Bulbous perennial to 20 cm with the leaves often dry at flowering; bears 4–8 tubular and 2-lipped bright red flowers. Shale or sand on sandstone or limestone ridges along the south coast.

**❸ *Cyrtanthus angustifolius***

J F M A M J J A S O N D

Bulbous perennial to 45 cm with the leaves usually green at flowering; bears 4–10 nodding, narrowly tubular scarlet flowers. Mountain slopes and flats in seasonal streams and vleis in the Western and Eastern Cape, flowering after fire.

**❹ *Cyrtanthus ventricosus* Vuurlelie**

J F M A M J J A S O N D

Bulbous perennial, 10–20 cm, with leaves usually dry at flowering; bears 2–12 nodding, vermilion to bright red flowers that are tubular but slightly swollen above, with the filaments arising at the base of the tube. Cool, south-facing sandstone slopes on coastal mountains of the southwestern Cape, flowering within 2 weeks after summer fires.

## *Gethyllis*   KUKUMAKRANKA

Deciduous, bulbous perennials. Leaves 1 to several, *often spirally twisted, sometimes hairy*. Flowers *solitary at ground level* (with the *ovary deeply buried* within the bulb), funnel- or star-shaped on a *long, solid tube*, white or pink, stamens sometimes numerous, on short filaments, separate or joined at the base. Fruit a *cylindrical or club-shaped* red to yellow berry, often fragrant. Arid areas of southern Africa, mainly winter rainfall: ±35 spp; 19 fynbos spp. The fragrant fruits appear in early winter and were traditionally used to flavour brandy and to perfume linen cupboards with their tropical fruit-like odour. The vernacular name *kukumakranka* is derived from the Khoisan name for the plants.

**❺ *Gethyllis afra***

J F M A M J J A S O N D

Bulbous perennial, 10–14 cm, with spiralled, smooth or hairy leaves that are dry at flowering; bears large, fragrant, cup-shaped flowers, white with red on the reverse, with more than 6 anthers. Sandy flats along the southwest Cape coast and near interior.

## *Haemanthus*  PAINTBRUSH LILY, KWASLELIE

Deciduous or evergreen, bulbous perennials. Leaves *mostly 2*, erect or prostrate, *tongue-shaped and leathery*, sometimes hairy, often *barred or spotted* with purple beneath. Flowers borne in *compact heads* surrounded by several *large, fleshy, red or pink bracts*, funnel-shaped, ±erect on very short pedicels, pink or red, rarely white; stamens ±erect. Fruit a soft, translucent berry. Southern Africa, most diverse in Namaqualand: 22 spp; 9 fynbos spp. The bulbs of *Haemanthus coccineus* were used as a diuretic and the fresh leaves as an antiseptic.

**①** *Haemanthus coccineus*  **Misryblom**    J F M A M J J A S O N D

Bulbous perennial, 6–20 cm, with spreading or ±erect leaves, sometimes fringed and usually speckled with red beneath and dry at flowering; bears scarlet flowers surrounded by numerous stiff and leathery bracts on a spotted scape. Widespread in coastal scrub and rocky slopes, from southern Namibia to the Eastern Cape, often in large clumps.

**②** *Haemanthus pubescens*    J F M A M J J A S O N D

Bulbous perennial, 7–12 cm, with prostrate, hairy leaves that are dry at flowering; bears scarlet flowers surrounded by 4 large, pointed, fleshy bracts on a smooth or hairy, often spotted, peduncle. Sandy flats along the West Coast.

**③** *Haemanthus sanguineus*    J F M A M J J A S O N D

**April fool, veldskoenblaar**  Bulbous perennial, 5–30 cm, with prostrate, leathery leaves, often outlined with red; bears red or pink flowers surrounded by leathery bracts on a plain red peduncle. Sandy and loamy slopes in the Western and Eastern Cape, flowering especially after fire.

## *Ammocharis*  MALGAS LILY, MALGASLELIE

Deciduous, bulbous perennials. Leaves *spreading or prostrate, in a fan*, strap-shaped, with a *blunt, often withered, tip*. Flowers funnel-shaped, white to red, borne on stout pedicels up to about as long as the flowers but elongating in fruit; stamens spreading. Fruit sometimes developing into a large tumbleweed with the peduncle remaining attached. Widespread through sub-Saharan Africa, mainly semi-arid areas: 6 spp; 2 fynbos spp.

**④** *Ammocharis longifolia*    J F M A M J J A S O N D

(=*Cybistetes longifolia*) **Malgaslelie**  Bulbous perennial, 25–35 cm with blunt, sickle-shaped leaves in a prostrate fan, green or dry at flowering; bears widely funnel-shaped, lily-scented cream to pink flowers; the 6-ribbed, spindle-shaped fruits mature into a large tumbleweed. Sandy and loamy flats in Namaqualand and the southwestern Cape.

▸ FLOWERS USUALLY SHORTER THAN THE PEDICELS; STAMEN FILAMENTS SOMETIMES JOINED TOGETHER AT THE BASE

## *Amaryllis*  BELLADONNA, MAARTBLOM

Robust, deciduous, bulbous perennials. Leaves *strap-shaped with a distinct midrib*, soft-textured. *Flowers large, funnel-shaped, pink*, borne on *short, stout pedicels*; stamens unequal, flexed downwards and arched up at the ends, joined at the base. Fruits globular, papery. Seeds large and fleshy, *pink*. Winter-rainfall South Africa: 2 spp; 1 fynbos sp.

**①** *Amaryllis belladonna*  **Maartblom**     J F M A M J J A S O N D

Bulbous perennial to 90 cm with erect tufts of strap-shaped leaves that are dry or absent at flowering; bears large, funnel-shaped, narcissus-scented pink flowers. Loamy soils in lowlands of the Western Cape, often in seasonal vleis, flowering best after fire.

## *Brunsvigia*  CHANDELIER LILY, KANDELAAR

Deciduous, bulbous perennials. Leaves erect or prostrate in 2 ranks, *broadly tongue-shaped, leathery*, often with reddish *cartilaginous margins*. Flowers funnel-shaped, *mostly irregular*, variously coloured, borne on stout pedicels as long as or much longer than the flowers; stamens equal or unequal, *flexed downwards* or rarely erect, joined at the base. Fruit developing into a large tumbleweed with the peduncle remaining attached. Widespread through southern Africa, mainly semi-arid areas: ±20 spp; 8 fynbos spp.

**②** *Brunsvigia bosmaniae*     J F M A M J J A S O N D

**Fragrant candelabra lily**  Bulbous perennial to 20 cm with 5 or 6 prostrate leaves that are dry at flowering; bears narcissus-scented, irregularly funnel-shaped pink flowers with flaring tepals in a large, rounded head; the stamens are flexed downwards and the outer stamens are about half as long as the inner; the fruits are 3-winged and heavily ribbed. Clay or gravelly soils along the West Coast and interior.

**③** *Brunsvigia marginata*  **False nerine**     J F M A M J J A S O N D

Bulbous perennial to 20 cm with 4 prostrate leaves that are dry at flowering; bears regular, funnel-shaped, bright scarlet flowers with spreading tepals in a compact head; the stamens are erect and prominent; the fruits are 3-winged. Rocky sandstone slopes in the mountains of the southwestern Cape.

**④** *Brunsvigia orientalis*     J F M A M J J A S O N D

**Koningskandelaar** Bulbous perennial, 40–50 cm, with 5 or 6 prostrate leaves that are dry at flowering; bears very irregular red flowers with unequally rolled tepals, on long red pedicels in a large, rounded head; the fruits are 3-winged and heavily ribbed. Sandy, mainly coastal, flats in the southwestern Cape. *Brunsvigia litoralis* from the southern Cape coast has 8 or more ±erect, somewhat twisted, leaves.

## *Crossyne*  PARASOL LILY, SAMBREELBLOM

Deciduous, bulbous perennials. Leaves prostrate in 2 ranks, broadly tongue-shaped, leathery, *fringed with stiff reddish bristles and speckled with red markings on the underside, especially towards the base*. Flowers small, widely funnel-shaped, dull maroon or yellow, borne on stout pedicels much longer than the flowers, stamens ±equal, spreading or flexed downwards, swollen below and joined at the base. Fruit developing into a large tumbleweed with the peduncle remaining attached. Western South Africa, mainly semi-arid parts: 2 spp; 1 fynbos sp.

**⑤** *Crossyne guttata*     J F M A M J J A S O N D

(=*Boophone guttata*) Bulbous perennial to 45 cm with 4–6 prostrate leaves that are dry at flowering; bears small maroon to dusty pink flowers 10–15 mm in diameter in a large, rounded head, with the tepals bent back; the stamens are spreading. Shale and granite flats and lower slopes in the southwestern Cape, flowering mainly after fire. *Crossyne flava* from Namaqualand has pale yellowish flowerheads of slightly larger flowers with the stamens flexed downwards.

55

## *Nerine*  NERINE, NERINA

Deciduous or evergreen, bulbous perennials. Leaves *thread-like to strap-shaped, succulent*. Flowers *mostly irregular*, pink or rarely white or red, with the tepals *narrow and more or less undulate or crinkly*, borne on pedicels a little longer than the flowers, stamens unequal, flexed downwards or rarely erect, joined at the base. Fruits globular, membranous. Southern Africa, most diverse in the grasslands of the eastern seaboard: ±23 spp; 4 fynbos spp.

**❶ *Nerine humilis***   J F **M A M** J J A S O N D

Bulbous perennial, 15–35 cm, with narrow leaves 4–10 mm wide, that are usually dry at flowering; bears spreading, irregularly flaring, pale to dark pink flowers with down-flexed stamens. Loamy or clay soil among rocks in the Western and Eastern Cape. *Nerine pudica* from the Riviersonderend Mountains has funnel-shaped flowers with broader, flat tepals.

**❷ *Nerine sarniensis*  Guernsey lily**   J F **M A M** J J A S O N D

Bulbous geophyte, 25–45 cm, with narrow leaves 8–20 mm wide, that are dry at flowering; bears upright, regularly flaring, red, rarely pink or white, flowers with erect stamens. Rocky mountain slopes in the southwestern Cape.

## *Strumaria*  CAPE SNOWFLAKE, SNEEUVLOKKIE

*Small*, deciduous, bulbous perennials. Leaves 2–6, thread-like to elliptical, erect or prostrate. Flowers borne in small heads on slender peduncles, spreading or nodding on pedicels as long as or longer than the flowers, *regular* and star-shaped to narrowly funnel-shaped, white or pink, rarely pale yellow, with *tepals usually separate, stamens joined below to the style*, which may be swollen or 3-winged. Fruits small, globular, papery. Southern Africa, mainly the semi-arid winter-rainfall region: 25 spp; 11 fynbos spp.

**❸ *Strumaria spiralis***   J F M **A M J J A** S O N D

Dainty, bulbous perennial, 5–15 cm, with 4–6 thread-like leaves; bears small, upright, funnel-shaped white or pink flowers on a wiry peduncle that is spirally twisted below. Seasonally wet flats and rock crevices especially along the south coast, sometimes in great numbers.

**❹ *Strumaria tenella***   J F M **A M J J** A S O N D

Dainty, bulbous perennial, 10–20 cm, with up to 6 thread-like leaves; bears small, spreading, star-shaped white or pinkish flowers on a slender peduncle. Seasonally damp, loamy flats along the West Coast and inland, often in large numbers.

# AGAPANTHACEAE                    Agapanthus family

## *Agapanthus*  AGAPANTHUS, BLOULELIE

Rhizomatous perennials. Leaves strap-shaped, keeled. *Inflorescence an umbel* borne on a stout, leafless peduncle. *Flowers blue*, funnel-shaped or cylindrical, spreading or nodding, thick-textured, the tepals joined below in a short tube; stamens 6, unequal, flexed slightly downwards and arched up at the ends, ovary superior. Seeds flattened, black. Southern Africa, mainly in montane grasslands: 10 spp; 3 fynbos spp. The evergreen *Agapanthus praecox*, from the southern coastal regions, is the widely grown agapanthus of horticulture.

**① *Agapanthus africanus*  Bloulelie**

`J F M A M J J A S O N D`

Evergreen perennial, 25–70 cm, with strap-shaped leaves; bears broadly funnel-shaped, deep blue flowers 25–40 mm long, in tight umbels on short pedicels. Rocky sandstone in cooler situations on the coastal mountains of the southwestern Cape, flowering mainly after fire. *Agapanthus praecox* from coastal scrub and forest margins in the southern Cape is a larger, evergreen species with mid-blue flowers 30–70 mm long.

# ASPARAGACEAE                          Asparagus family

## *Asparagus*  ASPARAGUS, KATDORING

Rhizomatous *shrubs or climbers*, often with swollen roots. *Leaves reduced and scale-like*, sometimes hooked, replaced by flattened or needle-like branchlets (cladodes or false leaves) resembling leaves, often on short spur-shoots. *Flowers axillary*, white, star-like or cup-shaped. Fruit a *fleshy berry*. Africa and Eurasia, most diverse in southern Africa: ±120 spp; 36 fynbos spp.

**② *Asparagus capensis***

`J F M A M J J A S O N D`

Erect, spiny shrub to 1 m, with the spines in 3s, the stems brush-like with whorls of short-shoots bearing needle-like false leaves mostly in clusters of 5; bears 1 or 2 star-shaped, tuberose-scented white flowers at the tip of each spur-shoot, the tepals and stamens spreading. Widespread on stony, often clay slopes from southern Namibia to the Eastern Cape.

**③ *Asparagus lignosus***

`J F M A M J J A S O N D`

Spiny shrublet to 80 cm, with pale, finely grooved stems and widely spreading branches bearing clusters of leathery, needle-like false leaves; bears 1–4 white flowers in the axils of the clusters, the tepals and stamens spreading. Rocky sandstone slopes and damp sandy flats in the southwestern Cape.

**④ *Asparagus rubicundus***

`J F M A M J J A S O N D`

Erect, spiny shrub to 1.5 m, with glossy, dark brown stems covered with spreading spines and bearing thread-like false leaves in clusters of ±10; bears 1 or 2 star-shaped white flowers in the axils of the tufts, with the tepals and stamens spreading. Sandy and granite slopes in the Kamiesberg of Namaqualand, and the Western and Eastern Cape.

**⑤ *Asparagus aethiopicus***

`J F M A M J J A S O N D`

Spiny climber to 3 m, with pale, ribbed stems covered with hooked spines and bearing stiff, peg-like false leaves in clusters of 4–6; bears racemes of fragrant, star-like white flowers, the tepals and stamens spreading. Widespread in dry bush from Namaqualand to the Eastern Cape.

**⑥ *Asparagus asparagoides***

`J F M A M J J A S O N D`

**Bridal creeper** Scrambler to 3 m, with many small, spindle-shaped tubers arising directly from the rhizome, and oval false leaves; bears solitary, nodding white flowers in the axils, the tepals joined below into a short tube and the stamens erect in the centre. Widespread in bush throughout southern and tropical Africa.

**1** *Asparagus ovatus*  ⬛ J F M A M J **J A** S O N D

Scrambler to 3 m, with spindle-shaped tubers on slender roots held well away from the rhizome, and glossy, oval false leaves; bears 1–3 nodding white flowers with brown midribs in the axils, and the tepals joined below into a short tube; the stamens are erect in the centre. In scrub, mostly coastal in the southwestern and Eastern Cape.

# ANTHERICACEAE                    Anthericum family

### *Chlorophytum*   GRASS LILY, GRASLELIE

Rhizomatous, tufted perennials, either with stiff, tapering roots or long, slender roots bearing tuberous swellings. Leaves narrow and channelled, *often fibrous at the base*. Flowers in leafy racemes or panicles, usually *with more than 1 at each node, on jointed pedicels*, star-shaped with separate tepals, *each lasting 1 day*. Fruits usually *3-winged*. Widespread in Africa, Eurasia and the Americas, mainly tropical: ±250 spp; 11 fynbos spp.

**2** *Chlorophytum rigidum*  J F M A **M J J A S O** N D

Rhizomatous perennial to 50 cm, with fleshy roots; bears white flowers in a slender, sparsely and widely branched raceme on pedicels that are jointed near the base; the fruits are roughly ribbed. Stony slopes and flats in the southwestern Cape.

**3** *Chlorophytum triflorum*  J F M A M J **J A S O** N D

Rhizomatous perennial to 1 m, with hard, dark and tapering roots, and leaves that are often minutely fringed on the margins; bears white flowers in unbranched racemes on pedicels that are jointed near the middle; the fruits are smooth. Sandy slopes and flats along the West Coast.

**4** *Chlorophytum undulatum*  J F M A M J **J A S O** N D

Rhizomatous perennial to 50 cm, with slender roots as well as short tubers, and leaves that are often minutely fringed on the margins; bears white flowers in unbranched racemes on pedicels that are jointed near the middle; the fruits are smooth. Widespread on stony flats and slopes in Namaqualand and the southwestern Cape. *Chlorophytum pauciphyllum* from the Cedarberg has a single, stiff leaf with fringed margins and a purple-spotted sheath.

# ASPHODELACEAE                         Aloe family

▸ FLOWERS STAR-SHAPED WITH SEPARATE TEPALS, USUALLY WHITE OR YELLOW

### *Bulbine*   BULBINE, KOPIEVA

Tufted, rhizomatous or tuberous perennials, rarely annuals or shrublets, with wiry or swollen roots. Leaves succulent or fleshy, channelled or cylindrical, sometimes coiled. Flowers in an unbranched, sometimes head-like raceme, *yellow to orange, star-like or the tepals bent back, each lasting 1 day*, the stamens densely *hairy or with fluffy filaments*. Fruits on horizontal pedicels or erect with the pedicels curved up at the end. Africa and Australia, mainly southern Africa: ±50 spp; 20 fynbos spp. The leaf sap of several species was widely used as an antiseptic and emollient.

**1 Bulbine annua**

`J F M A M J J A S O N D`

Tufted annual, 15–40 cm, with wiry roots and many quill-like leaves; bears a dense raceme of yellow flowers on long pedicels; the fruits are globular and ±erect on pedicels ±20 mm long. Sandy soils along the coast in the southwestern Cape.

**2 Bulbine lagopus**

`J F M A M J J A S O N D`

Tufted perennial to 40 cm with wiry roots and many quill-like leaves from an upright rhizome; bears a dense raceme of yellow flowers; the fruits are ±globular and carried erect on pedicels 10–15 mm long. Widespread on rocky and stony slopes from the Western Cape to Lesotho.

**3 Bulbine favosa**

`J F M A M J J A S O N D`

Slender perennial, 15–50 cm, with a tuber and a few, thread-like leaves that are dry at flowering; bears a loose raceme of fragrant yellow flowers; the fruits are globular and carried upright. Sandy and limestone flats and slopes in the southwestern Cape.

**4 Bulbine cepacea**

`J F M A M J J A S O N D`

Tufted perennial, 20–40 cm, often growing in clumps, with a large flat-based tuber and narrow, flattened leaves, usually dry at flowering, and surrounded at the base by a fibrous sheath; bears a dense raceme of yellow flowers; fruits are ellipsoidal and carried upright. Stony flats and lower slopes in the southwestern Cape.

**5 Bulbine praemorsa**

`J F M A M J J A S O N D`

Slender or stout perennial, 40–60 cm, with a small tuber and fleshy, channelled leaves surrounded at the base by a short, fibrous neck; bears a loose raceme of yellow to orange flowers; the fruits are ellipsoidal and carried upright. Common and widespread, mostly on rocky sandstone slopes in Namaqualand and the southwestern Cape. *Bulbine longifolia* is a smaller plant, to 20 cm, without persistent fibres around the base of the leaves.

## *Trachyandra*  TRACHYANDRA, VELDKOOL

Tufted, rhizomatous or tuberous perennials or shrublets, with wiry or swollen roots. Leaves succulent or fleshy, flat or channelled, often surrounded at the base by membranous or papery *tubular sheaths*. Flowers in a raceme or panicle, *white or pinkish, usually with paired yellow spots at the base of each tepal, star-like or the tepals bent back, each lasting 1 day*, the stamens with *rough filaments*. Fruits erect or pendulous. Africa, mainly winter-rainfall southern Africa: ±50 spp; 24 fynbos spp. The young flower spikes of some species, *Trachyandra ciliata* in particular, make a tasty vegetable.

▶ **LEAVES WITH PAPERY OR MEMBRANOUS SHEATHS AT THE BASE**

**6 *Trachyandra ciliata*  Veldkool**

`J F M A M J J A S O N D`

Sprawling perennial to 50 cm with fleshy, swollen roots and soft, spongy, straggling leaves that are channelled and usually hairy; bears white flowers in an elongate raceme, unbranched or sparsely branched, usually hairy; the fruits are pendent, hairless and 6–14 mm long. Damp sandy coastal flats from Namaqualand to the Eastern Cape.

**1** *Trachyandra falcata*

`J F M A M J J A S O N D`

Erect perennial to 1 m with thickened roots and few, sickle-shaped, leathery leaves; bears white flowers in a stout, unbranched or sparsely branched raceme with a large, encircling bract at the branch; the fruits are hairless and ±12 mm long. Sandy or clay flats and lower slopes from southern Namibia to the southwestern Cape.

**2** *Trachyandra muricata*

`J F M A M J J A S O N D`

Perennial to 90 cm with thickened roots and few, sickle-shaped, rough-haired leaves that are not individually sheathed at the base; bears many nodding white flowers in a widely branching panicle that is roughly hairy at the base; the fruits are hairless and 5 mm long. Stony clay or granite slopes in scrub and renosterveld from southern Namibia to the southwestern Cape. *Trachyandra revoluta* has many roughly-hairy, quill-like leaves that are individually wrapped with brown, papery sheaths at the base.

**3** *Trachyandra divaricata*

`J F M A M J J A S O N D`

Stout, tufted perennial to 90 cm with thickened roots and many fleshy, quill-like, hairless, bright green leaves that are individually wrapped with brown, papery sheaths at the base; bears many nodding white flowers in a widely branching panicle; the fruits are hairless and 10 mm long. Coastal dunes and sand flats from southern Namibia to the Eastern Cape.

▸ **LEAVES NOT ENCIRCLED BY PAPERY OR MEMBRANOUS SHEATHS AT THE BASE**

**4** *Trachyandra tabularis*

`J F M A M J J A S O N D`

Erect perennial to 1.2 m with wiry roots and stiff, narrow, often channelled leaves; bears white flowers in sparsely branched, ±erect racemes; the fruits are hairless and ±9 mm long. Sandy flats and lower slopes in lowland fynbos in the extreme southwestern Cape, flowering best after fire.

**5** *Trachyandra hirsutiflora*

`J F M A M J J A S O N D`

Erect perennial to 60 cm with fleshy roots and narrow, tough, rough-haired leaves; bears white flowers crowded in a head-like raceme on hairy pedicels; the fruits are densely hairy and ±15 mm long. Sandy flats and lower slopes in the southwestern Cape, flowering mainly after fire.

## *Bulbinella* **BULBINELLA, KATSTERT**

Tufted, rhizomatous perennials, with wiry or swollen roots. Leaves soft or firm-textured but *not succulent*, narrow and triangular in section or channelled, decaying into *prominent, often netted fibres at the base*, all equal or the inner ones smaller. Flowers in a *dense raceme*, white or pinkish, yellow or orange, star-like, each lasting several days. Fruits with *1 or 2 shield-shaped seeds* per chamber. Mainly winter-rainfall southern Africa with a few species in New Zealand: 22 spp; 14 fynbos spp.

▸ **PLANTS MOSTLY MORE THAN 50 CM; INNER LEAVES SHORTER AND SMALLER THAN THE OUTER**

**6** *Bulbinella latifolia*

`J F M A M J J A S O N D`

Robust perennial to 1 m with yellow roots and 5–10 unequal, broadly strap-shaped leaves to 65 mm wide; bears deep yellow or orange flowers in a cylindrical raceme. Seasonally damp sandstone or granite, rarely dolerite, from the Kamiesberg in Namaqualand to the Cedarberg Mountains.

### ❶ *Bulbinella nutans*

J F M A M J J A S O N D

Perennial to 1 m with yellow roots and 5–13 unequal, narrowly channelled leaves to 25 mm wide; bears yellow or cream flowers in a conical raceme. Damp, peaty soils or seasonal marshes in the southwestern Cape.

### ❷ *Bulbinella punctulata*

J F M A M J J A S O N D

Perennial to 1 m with conspicuously netted fibres at the base of the stem and 2–4 unequal, narrowly channelled leaves to 6 mm wide; bears yellow flowers in a cylindrical raceme. Rocky sandstone mountain slopes in the southwestern Cape, often in moist places.

### ❸ *Bulbinella caudafelis*

J F M A M J J A S O N D

Perennial to 80 cm with 5–11 unequal, narrowly channelled leaves to 9 mm wide that are sometimes finely toothed on the margins; bears white flowers with a pink tinge in a narrowly conical raceme. Widespread on damp sandstone, granite or clay slopes in the southwestern Cape. *Bulbinella graminifolia* has a more slender raceme, to 15 mm in diameter, of pure white flowers.

▶ **PLANTS MOSTLY LESS THAN 50 CM; ALL LEAVES ±EQUAL IN LENGTH**

### ❹ *Bulbinella triquetra*

J F M A M J J A S O N D

Dainty perennial to 35 cm with a tuft of 10–40 equal, thread-like leaves to 2 mm wide and finely toothed along the margins; bears yellow flowers in a rounded to narrowly conical raceme. Damp sand and granite in the southwestern Cape.

### ❺ *Bulbinella divaginata*

J F M A M J J A S O N D

Slender perennial to 45 cm, leafless at flowering, with a tuft of 4–40 equal, thread-like leaves to 2 mm wide, usually not fully formed at flowering, surrounded at the base by a membranous sheath; bears yellow flowers in a narrowly cylindrical raceme. Mainly clay soils in renosterveld in Namaqualand and the southwestern Cape.

### ❻ *Bulbinella trinervis*

J F M A M J J A S O N D

Slender perennial to 40 cm, leafless at flowering, with a tuft of 5–7 equal, thread-like leaves to 1 mm wide; bears white to pinkish flowers in a narrowly cylindrical raceme. Rocky sandstone slopes in the southwestern and Eastern Cape.

▶ **FLOWERS TUBULAR WITH THE TEPALS JOINED TOGETHER BELOW, MOSTLY ORANGE OR RED**

## *Kniphofia*  RED-HOT POKER, VUURPYL

Tufted, rhizomatous perennials, rarely with aerial stems. Leaves soft or fibrous, *not succulent*, narrow and channelled, *V-shaped* in cross-section, often with minutely toothed margins. Flowers in a loose or dense raceme, white, yellow or various shades of red, *tubular*, the *buds often differently coloured*, the stamens often protruding but later withdrawn. Africa and southern Arabia, with a few species in New Zealand. Mainly winter-rainfall and eastern parts of southern Africa: ±70 spp; 4 fynbos spp. Several species and hybirds are popular garden plants.

**1** *Kniphofia tabularis*

J F M A M J J A S O N D

Perennial, 60–120 cm, with channelled, somewhat fleshy leaves; bears reddish-orange flowers (tipped blackish in bud) in open, cylindrical racemes; the floral bracts are narrow and 7–11 mm long. Wet sandstone cliffs and seeps in the mountains of the extreme southwestern Cape.

**2** *Kniphofia uvaria*

J F M A M J J A S O N D

Perennial, 50–120 cm, often in small clumps, with channelled, fibrous leaves; bears orange to greenish-yellow flowers in dense, oblong to globular racemes; the floral bracts are oval and 3–9 mm long. Seeps, marshes and streams on sandstone slopes from Namaqualand to Eastern Cape. *Kniphofia praecox* from the southern Cape is a larger species with narrow, longer floral bracts and prominently protruding anthers.

## *Aloe*  ALOE, AALWYN

Stemless succulent perennials, shrubs or trees, with slender or swollen roots. Leaves *succulent*, narrow and channelled but *curved in cross-section* to broadly lance-shaped, usually with *sharp, horny teeth on the margins* and sometimes the surfaces as well, *plain or spotted*. Flowers in simple or branched, narrow to head-like racemes, white, yellow or, more usually, various shades of orange and red; *tubular*, rarely slightly 2-lipped, the stamens protruding or just included within the flower. Africa and Arabia; widely cultivated as ornamentals: ±500 spp; ±25 fynbos spp. The sap of the North African *Aloe vera* is an important cosmetic and medicine, and A. ferox fulfils the same role in southern Africa.

▸ **LEAVES WITHOUT MARGINAL TEETH**

**3** *Aloe haemanthifolia*

J F M A M J J A S O N D

Stemless perennial with tongue-shaped leaves in a 2-ranked fan, greenish grey with reddish margins, spineless; bears scarlet flowers in simple, head-like racemes. Sandstone ledges in sheltered river valleys in mountains of the southwestern Cape.

**4** *Aloe plicatilis*  Kaapse kokerboom

J F M A M J J A S O N D

Stout, dichotomously branched shrub or small tree to 5 m with tight fans of oblong, unarmed leaves at the branch tips; bears scarlet flowers in short, rather loose racemes. Sheltered sandstone slopes in valleys in the mountains of the southwestern Cape.

▸ **LEAVES WITH MARGINAL TEETH**

**5** *Aloe microstigma*

J F M A M J J A S O N D

Stemless or short-stemmed perennial with clusters of lance-shaped or triangular leaves to 50 cm, copiously spotted with white, and toothed on the margins; bears orange to yellow flowers in simple, conical racemes. Dry karroid slopes from Namaqualand to the Eastern Cape; especially common in the Little Karoo.

**6** *Aloe ferox*  Bitteraalwyn, bitter aloe

J F M A M J J A S O N D

Single-stemmed shrub to 3 m, the stems covered below with dry leaves, with large, broadly lance-shaped leaves that are toothed on the margins and often the undersurface; bears slightly upcurved orange to red flowers with protruding stamens in dense, cylindrical racemes on branched stems. Dry, rocky slopes in scrub and savanna along the south coast to KwaZulu-Natal.

### ❶ *Aloe perfoliata*  Mitre aloe

J F **M A M J J A** S O **N** **D**

(=*Aloe mitriformis*) Sprawling, often branched, shrublet with stems 1–2 m long, covered with narrowly oval leaves that are sparsely speckled with white and sharply toothed on the margins; bears scarlet flowers in branched, head-like racemes. Rocky slopes and cliffs in the southwestern Cape.

### ❷ *Aloe arborescens*  Kransaalwyn

J F M A **M J** J A S O N D

Many-branched shrub to 3 m with narrow leaves that are down-flexed above and sharply toothed on the margins; bears scarlet to orange or rarely yellow flowers in conical, mostly unbranched, racemes. Widespread throughout southeastern Africa in bush and forest.

### ❸ *Aloe succotrina*  Bergaalwyn

J F M A M **J J A S** O N D

Unbranched or branched shrub to 2 m, sometimes forming dense clumps, with dark green, lance-shaped leaves that have coarse white teeth on the margins; bears red flowers with green tips in conical racemes. Sandstone rocks and cliffs in the extreme southwestern Cape.

### ❹ *Aloe comosa*

**J** F M A M J J A S O N **D**

Single-stemmed shrub to 2 m with narrow, erect or spreading leaves finely toothed on the margins, old leaves persisting on the stem; bears ivory-coloured, ovoid flowers that are pink in bud, closely pressed against the stem in very long, slender racemes. Dry, rocky sandstone slopes in the Cedarberg and adjacent mountains.

# HYACINTHACEAE                    Hyacinth family

## *Drimia*   POISON SQUILL, BRANDUI

Deciduous, rarely evergreen, bulbous perennials. *Leaves often dry at flowering*, 1 to many, thread-like to elliptical, erect or prostrate, hairless or hairy. Flowers borne in heads or racemes, with at least the *lower bracts spurred at the base, each flower lasting only up to 1 day*, spreading or nodding, star-, funnel- or bell-shaped, white to pinkish, with tepals that are usually separate or sometimes joined below. Fruits ovoid or 3-winged with *flattened seeds*. Africa and Eurasia: ±100 spp; 11 fynbos spp. The bulbs of several species are highly poisonous and sometimes, as in *Drimia elata*, an irritant, and were used medicinally.

### ❺ *Drimia capensis*  Maerman

J F **M A M J J A** S O N **D**

Bulbous perennial to 2 m, flowering without the leaves, which are in basal tuft and are oblong to elliptical; bears almost stalkless, white or cream flowers in dense whorls on a slender spike, with the petals curled back and the stamens projecting together. Clay and lime soils in the Western and Eastern Cape.

### ❻ *Drimia elata*  Jeukbol

J F M A **M J J** A S O **N D**

Bulbous perennial to 1 m, flowering without the leaves, which are erect or spreading in a basal tuft and narrowly elliptical, often with crinkly, hairy margins; bears silvery white, green or dull purplish flowers in a raceme, with the petals curled back and the stamens projecting together. Widespread throughout southern Africa in sandy and clay soils. *Drimia media*, from the southwestern Cape coast, is an evergreen species with similar flowers but firm, quill-like leaves.

**1** *Drimia exuviata*   J F M A M J J A **S O** N D

Bulbous perennial to 1 m with a few erect, leathery, quill-like leaves 3–4 mm in diameter, that are wrapped below in a horizontally barred sheath; bears star-shaped, rose-scented, white flowers that are often flushed with purple and have dark keels. Clay and granite outcrops from Namaqualand to the Eastern Cape. *Drimia filifolia* from the southwestern Cape is smaller, with leaves ±1 mm in diameter.

## *Eucomis*   PINEAPPLE LILY, WILDEPYNAPPEL

Deciduous, bulbous perennials. Leaves few to several, flat or erect, elliptical and hairless, underside sometimes barred or spotted with purple towards the base. Flowers borne in dense racemes on plain or mottled stalks, *topped with a crown of long, leafy bracts*, spreading or nodding, star-shaped, white or greenish, sometimes speckled with purple, with tepals that are joined below. Fruits 3-winged with *rounded seeds*. Southern Africa and Zimbabwe, mainly in montane grassland: 10 spp; 1 fynbos sp. Several species and hybrids are cultivated.

**2** *Eucomis regia*    J F M A M J **J A** S O N D

Bulbous perennial, 8–15 cm, with broad, plain green leaves that usually spread on the ground; bears dense spikes of cream to greenish flowers on short pedicels to 2 mm long. Mostly cooler, south-facing clay slopes in renosterveld in Namaqualand and the southwestern Cape.

## *Lachenalia*   LACHENALIA, VIOOLTJIE

Deciduous, bulbous perennials. Leaves 1 to several, flat or erect, quill-like to flat and round, hairless or hairy, sometimes warty, *often barred or spotted with dark green or purple, surrounded at the base below ground level by a transparent, membranous sheath*. Flowers borne in dense clusters or racemes, sometimes at ground level between the leaves, *with the lower bracts often reduced, often with sterile upper flowers*, spreading or nodding, funnel-shaped to tubular with tepals that are joined below or for much of their length; variously coloured, the outer tepals *often with a swollen, darkly coloured tip; the stamens arising at 2 different* levels. Fruits 3-angled or -winged with *rounded seeds*. Southern Africa, mainly the winter-rainfall parts: ±110 spp; ±70 fynbos spp. Several of the larger species are cultivated. The vernacular name *viooltjie*, probably originally applied to species of *Ornithogalum*, derives from the squeaking sound produced when the stems are drawn across one another.

▸ FLOWERS 20–35 MM LONG, OFTEN ORANGE OR RED

**3** *Lachenalia aloides*   J F M A **M J J A S O** N D

**Cape cowslip, vierkleurtjie** Bulbous perennial, 5–31 cm, with 1 or 2 lance-shaped leaves that are plain green or spotted; bears nodding, cylindrical flowers 20–35 mm long, on long pedicels, in combinations of orange, red, yellow or greenish blue, with greenish markings, and the inner tepals much longer than the outer; the anthers are concealed within the flowers. Granite and sandstone outcrops in the southwestern Cape.

**4** *Lachenalia bulbifera* **Rooinaeltjie**   J F **M A M J J A S** O N D

Bulbous perennial, 8–30 cm, with 1 or 2 lance-shaped leaves that are plain green or blotched; bears nodding, cylindrical flowers 20–35 mm long, on fairly long pedicels, orange to red with darker red or brown markings and green tips, with the inner tepals only slightly longer than the outer; the anthers are concealed within the flowers. Sandy slopes and flats, mainly along the coast in the southwestern Cape.

**1** *Lachenalia rubida*  **Sandviooltjie**  | J | F | **M** | **A** | **M** | **J** | **J** | A | S | O | N | D |

Bulbous perennial, 6–25 mm, with 1 or 2 lance-shaped leaves that are plain green or spotted green or purple; bears nodding, cylindrical flowers 20–32 mm long, on short pedicels, plain or densely spotted with pink or red, the inner tepals much longer than the outer; the anthers are concealed within the flowers. Sandy flats and slopes, mainly along the coast, in southern Namaqualand and the southwestern Cape.

▶ **FLOWERS LESS THAN 20 MM LONG, ON PEDICELS GREATER THAN 5 MM LONG**

**2** *Lachenalia pustulata*  | J | F | M | A | M | J | **J** | **A** | **S** | **O** | N | D |

Bulbous perennial, 15–35 cm, with 1 or 2 plain green, lance-shaped leaves that are smooth or, more usually, densely warty; bears shortly cylindrical flowers 7–9 mm long, on long pedicels, shades of cream, blue or pink with green or brownish markings; the anthers are slightly or well exposed. Often in large colonies in clay soil in the southwestern Cape.

**3** *Lachenalia unifolia*  | J | F | M | A | M | J | **J** | **A** | **S** | **O** | N | D |

Bulbous perennial, 10–35 cm, with 1 narrow leaf that is banded with green and maroon; bears cylindrical flowers 8–15 mm long, on short or long pedicels, blue, pink or pale yellow, with white tips; the anthers are concealed within the flowers. Sandy granitic or sandstone soils in Namaqualand and the southwestern Cape. *Lachenalia hirta* has a leaf with stiff-haired margins.

▶ **FLOWERS LESS THAN 20 MM LONG, SESSILE OR ON SHORT PEDICELS UP TO 2 MM LONG**

**4** *Lachenalia pusilla*  | J | F | M | **A** | **M** | **J** | J | A | S | O | N | D |

Bulbous perennial, 1–4 cm, with 2–4 plain or spotted oblong leaves in a basal rosette; bears heads of heavily scented white flowers 8–10 mm long, at ground level between the leaves on obsolete pedicels; the anthers are well exposed. Common on sandy flats and slopes in the southwestern Cape.

**5** *Lachenalia contaminata*  | J | F | M | A | M | J | **J** | **A** | **S** | **O** | N | D |

Bulbous perennial, 6–25 cm, with several erect, quill-like leaves; bears bell-shaped white flowers 5–9 mm long, with brown or reddish markings, on short pedicels; the anthers are concealed within the flowers or exposed. Wet places, often common in the southwestern Cape.

**6** *Lachenalia pallida*  | J | F | M | A | M | J | **J** | **A** | **S** | **O** | N | D |

Bulbous perennial, 12–30 cm, with 1 or 2 lance-shaped leaves that are sometimes warty; bears cylidrical flowers 8–10 mm long, on short pedicels, cream to dark yellow with brown or green markings; the anthers are concealed within the flowers. Clay soils, often in large colonies, in the southwestern Cape.

**7** *Lachenalia longibracteata*  | J | F | M | A | M | J | **J** | **A** | S | O | N | D |

Bulbous perennial, 7–35 cm, with 1 or 2 lance-shaped leaves that are plain or spotted; bears a spike of cylindrical flowers 10–14 mm long, on short pedicels with long bracts, pale blue, or yellow with a blue base, with brown or green markings; the anthers are concealed within the flowers. Clay flats and slopes along the West Coast.

### ❶ *Lachenalia muirii*

J F M A M J J A S **O N D**

Bulbous perennial, 10–25 cm, with 1 or 2 narrow leaves that are withered at flowering time; bears a spike of sessile, urn-shaped to cylindrical flowers 10–12 mm long, pale blue and white with brown or maroon markings; the anthers are concealed within the flowers. Limestone hills and flats along the Agulhas coast.

### ❷ *Lachenalia mutabilis* Bontviooltjie

J F M A M J **J A S** O N D

Bulbous perennial, 10–45 cm, with 1 erect, lance-shaped leaf with crinkly margins; bears a spike of sessile, cylindrical to urn-shaped flowers 8–10 mm long, pale blue and white with yellow tips, or yellowish green, with brown markings, always with several lilac to bright purplish sterile upper flowers; the anthers are concealed within the flowers. Sandy and stony slopes in Namaqualand and the southwestern Cape.

## *Massonia*   HEDGEHOG LILY, KRIMPVARKIE

Deciduous, bulbous perennials. Leaves 2, *pressed flat against the ground*, rounded, hairless or hairy, sometimes warty, *surrounded at the base below ground level by a transparent, membranous sheath*. Flowers borne *at ground level* in a spike or dense cluster nested between the leaves, spreading or nodding, funnel-shaped to tubular, with petals that are joined below or for much of their length, green to whitish or pale yellowish, sometimes flushed pink, the petals *often bent sharply back and then forwards again at the base; the stamens arising at the mouth of the tube and joined at the base*. Fruits 3-angled or -winged with *rounded seeds*. Southern Africa, mainly the drier winter-rainfall parts: ±10 spp; 5 fynbos spp.

### ❸ *Massonia depressa* Bobbejaanboek

J F M A **M J J** A S O N D

Bulbous perennial to 5 cm with 2 flat leaves that are sometimes blotched with green or maroon; bears a cluster of green, white, yellowish or pinkish flowers that are deeply cup-shaped, with a tube that is 4–8 mm in diameter at the mouth and contains copious nectar; the fresh anthers are large, ±2.5 mm long. Sandy and clay flats from Namaqualand through the Karoo into the Eastern Cape.

### ❹ *Massonia pustulata*

J F M A M **J J A S** O N D

Bulbous perennial to 5 cm with 2 flat leaves that are smooth, hairy or warty; bears a cluster of rose-scented, white or cream flowers that fade to pink and have a narrow tube 1.5–2 mm in diameter at the mouth; the yellow anthers are ±1 mm long. Sandy and clay flats, often coastal, in the southern Cape. *Massonia echinata*, from the interior West Coast to the Eastern Cape, has purple or blue anthers.

## *Albuca*   SLIME-LILY, SLYMLELIE, TAMARAK

Bulbous perennials. Leaves 1 to several. Flowers in slender or flat-topped racemes, *often nodding*, with *thick-textured petals, white to yellowish with a green longitudinal band, the inner petals usually erect and differing from the outer in having a thickened, hooded or flap-like tip*. Fruit usually *with diverging crests on each side*. Africa: 110–140 spp; South Africa: 100–120 spp. One or two of the species, especially *A. nelsonii*, are grown horticulturally. The vernacular name *tamarak(ka)* is derived from the Khoisan name.

▶ **INNER TEPALS WITHOUT A HINGED TIP; OUTER STAMENS WITH SMALLER ANTHERS THAN THE INNER STAMENS**

**1 *Albuca clanwilliamae-gloria***

| J | F | M | A | M | J | J | A | S | O | N | D |

(*=Ornithogalum clanwilliamae-gloria*) Bulbous perennial to 2 m, with 3 or 4 slender, channelled leaves that are dry at flowering; bears a stiffly erect raceme of large, nodding, dull yellow flowers with dark yellow or green bands, 25–35 mm long; the outer anthers are slightly smaller. Deep, sandy soils in restioid fynbos in the Olifants River valley and towards Lamberts Bay.

**2 *Albuca fragrans***

| J | F | M | A | M | J | J | A | S | O | N | D |

(*=Ornithogalum fragrans*) Slender or sometimes stout, bulbous perennial to 1 m, with 2–4 narrow, channelled leaves that clasp the stem at the base; bears racemes that droop in bud, with nodding yellow flowers with broad green bands, 15–25 mm long; the outer anthers are slightly smaller. Sandy slopes and flats, often coastal, along the west and southwest coasts.

▶ **INNER TEPALS WITH A HINGED, FLESHY TIP; OUTER STAMENS ALL STERILE (WITHOUT ANTHERS)**

**3 *Albuca cooperi* Geldbeursie**

| J | F | M | A | M | J | J | A | S | O | N | D |

(*=Ornithogalum cooperi*) Bulbous perennial, 35–60 cm, with the outer bulb tunics decaying into fibres at the top, and 2 or 3 slender, channelled leaves that clasp the stem in the lower part and are warty towards the base; bears a raceme of fragrant, nodding yellow flowers with broad green bands, 15–25 mm long; the inner petals have a hinged flap at the tip and the outer stamens are sterile. Stony, mostly sandy slopes and flats, sometimes limestone, from Namaqualand to the Eastern Cape.

**4 *Albuca flaccida***

| J | F | M | A | M | J | J | A | S | O | N | D |

(*=Ornithogalum flaccidum*) **Slime lily, slymlelie** Bulbous perennial, 40–100 cm, with 3–5 fleshy, channelled leaves that clasp the stem below; bears a raceme of fragrant, nodding yellowish flowers, sometimes with broad green bands, 15–25 mm long; the inner petals have a hinged flap at the tip and the outer stamens are sterile. Mostly coastal in deep, sandy soils, in the southwestern Cape.

**5 *Albuca juncifolia***

| J | F | M | A | M | J | J | A | S | O | N | D |

(*=Ornithogalum imbricatum*) Bulbous perennial, 15–30 cm, with 4–10 slender, stiff leaves that are channelled below but often cylindrical above, and not clasping the stem below; bears racemes that droop at the tips, with fragrant, nodding yellow flowers that have broad green bands, 15–25 mm long; the inner petals have a hinged flap at the tip and the outer stamens are sterile. Sandy and calcareous flats from the interior West Coast to the southern Cape.

**❶ *Albuca canadensis***

| J | F | M | A | M | J | J | A | S | O | N | D |

(=*Albuca maxima*) **Wittamarak**  Bulbous perennial, 40–150 cm, with the outer bulb tunics slightly fibrous at the top, and 4–6 fleshy, channelled leaves that clasp the stem below; bears racemes of weakly nodding, white flowers with broad green bands, 15–25 mm long; the inner petals have a hinged flap at the tip and the outer stamens are sterile. Rocky sandstone or granitic soils from Namaqualand to the southern Cape.

## *Ornithogalum*   CHINCHERINCHEE, TJIENK

Bulbous perennials. Leaves usually lance-shaped. Flowers in slender or flat-topped racemes, star-, cup- or bell-shaped, *pale greenish, white, yellow or orange, sometimes with a dark eye*. Fruit egg- or spindle-shaped *with flattened or angled seeds*. Widespread through Africa and Eurasia into India: ±160 spp.; South Africa: ±80 spp. Several species are extremely poisonous and may cause stock losses; some of the larger-flowered species are important in horticulture. The vernacular name *tjienkerientjee* is an onomatopoeic rendering of the squeaking sound produced when the stems are drawn across one another.

▶ **FLORAL BRACTS SMALL, AWL-SHAPED AND FRINGED AT THE BASE; FLOWERS SMALL TO MEDIUM-SIZED**

**❷ *Ornithogalum graminifolium***

| J | F | M | A | M | J | J | A | S | O | N | D |

Bulbous perennial, 10–30 cm, with 2–5 leaves that are often dry at flowering, narrow and grass-like, sometimes hairy, reddish below and forming a papery neck around the base of the stem; bears white, dull yellow or pale pink flowers 5–10 mm long, mostly in a narrow, spike-like raceme, with only a few open at a time. Stony clay flats and slopes, often in seasonally moist sites, from the West Coast to KwaZulu-Natal and into the interior.

**❸ *Ornithogalum hispidum***

| J | F | M | A | M | J | J | A | S | O | N | D |

Bulbous perennial, 10–40 cm, with 3–6 leaves that are dry at flowering, lance-shaped and often hairy, clasping the stem with long, tubular bases that are often spotted; bears racemes of white flowers, 8–18 mm long, typically with a bright yellow ovary. Clay flats or rock outcrops from Namaqualand to the Little Karoo.

▶ **FLORAL BRACTS RELATIVELY LARGE AND BOAT-SHAPED; FLOWERS MEDIUM-SIZED TO LARGE**

**❹ *Ornithogalum strictum***

| J | F | M | A | M | J | J | A | S | O | N | D |

**Chincherinchee**  Bulbous perennial, 20–80 cm, with soft, whitish outer bulb tunics, and 6–12 leaves that are sometimes dry at flowering and ±erect and lance-shaped, without fringed margins; bears a narrowly cylindrical raceme of glossy white flowers 10–20 mm long; the inner stamen filaments are shortly winged at the base. Clay or loam flats, often in seasonally moist sites, along the interior West Coast.

**❺ *Ornithogalum thyrsoides***

| J | F | M | A | M | J | J | A | S | O | N | D |

**Chincherinchee**  Bulbous perennial, 20–80 cm, with the outer bulb tunics soft and whitish, and ±7 leaves that are sometimes dry at flowering, ±erect and lance-shaped, without fringed margins; bears a conical or rounded raceme of glossy white flowers, often with a blackish centre, 10–20 mm long; the inner stamen filaments have broad, membranous wings at the base that clasp the ovary. Sandy flats and lower slopes, often in vleis, from Namaqualand to the southern Cape.

### ① *Ornithogalum conicum*

**Summer chincherinchee**  Bulbous perennial, 30–90 cm, with a large bulb with whitish, papery outer bulb tunics, and 5–10 leaves that are dry at flowering, spreading and shortly lance-shaped, with fringed margins; bears a conical raceme of dull white flowers 10–20 mm long and lightly honey-scented; all 6 stamen filaments are thread-like, without wings at the base. Rocky slopes and sandy flats along the West Coast.

### ② *Ornithogalum dubium*  Geeltjienk

J F M A M J J A S O N D

Bulbous perennial, 10–50 cm, with the outer bulb tunics dark black, and 3–8 leaves that are sometimes dry at flowering, ±erect or spreading and lance-shaped, with minutely fringed margins; bears a rounded raceme of glossy white, yellow or orange flowers, often with a green or brown centre, 10–20 mm long; the inner stamen filaments are sometimes winged at the base and the style is sometimes very short. Clay flats and stony slopes from the interior West Coast to the Eastern Cape.

## *Spetaea*  CAPE BLUEBELL

Deciduous, bulbous perennial. Leaves several, erect, narrow, with the *margins rolled inwards*. Flowers borne in slender racemes, spreading, narrowly cup-shaped, with *bright blue petals* that are joined below; *the stamens are joined at the base*. Fruits top-shaped with globular seeds. Seasonally wet cliffs in the mountains of the southwestern Cape: 1 sp.

### ③ *Spetaea lachenaliiflora*

J F M A M J J A S O N D

Bulbous perennial, 20–40 cm, with narrow, deeply channelled leaves; bears a raceme of deeply cup-shaped purple-blue flowers 8–12 mm long. Sandstone cliffs on wet ledges or seepages in the mountains around Bainskloof.

## *Veltheimia*  VELTHEIMIA, SANDLELIE

Deciduous or almost evergreen bulbous perennials. Leaves several, elliptical or oblong, *often undulate or crinkly*. Flowers borne in a dense raceme, *nodding, tubular with petals that are joined for much of their length*, pinkish; *the stamens arise obliquely near the middle of the tube*. Fruits *large and 3-winged* with *2 rounded seeds per chamber*. Southern Africa: 2 spp; 1 fynbos spp. *Veltheimia bracteata* is a popular garden plant.

### ④ *Veltheimia capensis*

J F M A M J J A S O N D

Bulbous perennial, 20–40 cm, with matte greyish or bluish undulate or crinkly leaves; bears a dense raceme of nodding, tubular, finely pinkish speckled flowers 20–35 mm long. Rocky slopes from Namaqualand to the Little Karoo. *Veltheimia bracteata*, from coastal parts of the southern and Eastern Cape, has glossy green leaves and flowers in the spring.

# COLCHICACEAE        Colchicum family

## *Ornithoglossum*   SNAKE LILY, SLANGKOP

Cormous perennials. Leaves few, lance-shaped and channelled, clasping the stem at the base. *Flowers in leafy racemes on long pedicels, often nodding,* green or brownish, sometimes white and maroon, the tepals separate, *narrowed below and bearing a small, hollowed nectary near the base*; styles long and slender. The vernacular name alludes to the toxicity of many members of the family. Southern and tropical Africa: 8 spp; 1 fynbos sp.

**❶ *Ornithoglossum viride***   Eendtjies    J F M A M J **J A S O** N D
Cormous perennial, 5–30 cm, with 2 or 3 narrow leaves and green or purplish flowers 10–20 mm in diameter; the floral nectary is a small pocket or mouth-like structure much narrower than the tepal base. Mostly deep sandy soils in the southwestern Cape, often coastal.

## *Colchicum*   MEN-IN-A-BOAT, PATRYSBLOM

Cormous perennials, mostly with the stem *underground* or very short. Leaves 2 to few, lance-shaped to oval, often *spreading on the ground*. Flowers clustered in a *head-like raceme between the leaves among enlarged, often coloured, bracts that conceal the flowers*, white to pale greenish, the tepals separate and narrowed into a claw at the base and *often cupped above*, the stamens arising in the cup, *with a swollen, nectar-secreting base*, the styles slender. Africa and the Mediterranean, mostly winter-rainfall southern Africa: ±40 spp; ±6 fynbos spp. The vernacular name *patrysblom* possibly refers to the belief that the corms were scratched out by francolins, although they have been recorded as being toxic to crows; another possibility is that the attractively marked bracts of some species suggest the speckling on the breasts of the birds. Recent DNA studies have led to the inclusion of all species of *Androcymbium* within the genus *Colchicum*.

**❷ *Colchicum eucomoides***    J F M A M J **J A** S O N D
(=*Androcymbium eucomoides*) Stemless perennial with narrow, often tapered leaves that grade into the green, leaf-like bracts. Damp clay and gravelly soils in open places from Namaqualand to the Eastern Cape.

**❸ *Colchicum capense***   Patrysblom    J F M A M **J J A** S O N D
(=*Androcymbium capense*) Stemless perennial with lance-shaped leaves that have fine hairs along the margins, and are sharply differentiated from the white bracts, which are sometimes striped or flushed with green. Damp clay and loamy soils in Namaqualand and the southwestern Cape.

## *Baeometra*   BEETLE LILY, KEWERLELIE

Cormous perennial with a *stiffly erect stem bearing several narrow leaves* that clasp the stem below. Flowers *in a spike* with just the *lower flowers subtended by narrow bracts*, yellow to orange with reddish reverse, the tepals separate, the *styles very short and hooked*. Winter-rainfall Western Cape; reported to be poisonous to cattle: 1 sp.

**❹ *Baeometra uniflora***    J F M A M J J **A S O** N D
Erect perennial to 25 cm with several narrow leaves; bears yellow to orange flowers, 15–20 mm in diameter, in a spike. Mainly damp sandstone and granite slopes in the southwestern Cape.

85

## *Wurmbea*   SPIKE LILY, WITKOPPIE

Cormous perennials. *Leaves 3*, lance-shaped and channelled or rarely quill-like, clasping the stem at the base. Flowers *sessile in spikes without bracts*, white or pink to cream, sometimes dark red-purple, the *tepals separate or joined into a short to long tube*, spreading above, with *paired nectar-bearing areas at the base of the blades*; styles short and hooked or slender and thread-like. Africa and Australia, mainly Western Cape: 40 spp; 15 fynbos spp. The circumscription of the genus has recently been enlarged to include the 2 species of *Onixotis*.

▸ **TEPALS SEPARATE FROM THE BASE**

**❶ *Wurmbea punctata***            | J | F | M | A | M | J | **J** | **A** | **S** | O | N | D |

(=*Onixotis punctata*) **Hanekammetjie**  Short perennial, 10–20 cm, with 3 lance-shaped leaves, the uppermost set about halfway up the stem; bears white to pink flowers in short spikes; the styles are completely separate. Moist, rocky and clay slopes and seeps in the southwestern Cape.

**❷ *Wurmbea stricta***            | J | F | M | A | M | J | J | **A** | **S** | **O** | N | D |

(=*Onixotis stricta*) **Rysblommetjie, waterphlox, dipidax**  Slender perennial, 20–50 cm, with 3 quill-like leaves that are triangular in section, the upper 2 set just below the flower spike; bears pale pink flowers, darkly marked in the centre, in elongate spikes; the styles are joined together near the base. Marshes and seasonal pools in Namaqualand and the southwestern Cape.

▸ **TEPALS JOINED BELOW INTO A SHORT OR LONG TUBE**

**❸ *Wurmbea spicata***            | J | F | M | A | M | J | **J** | **A** | **S** | **O** | **N** | D |

Cormous perennial, 5–20 cm, with narrowly lance-shaped leaves; bears white to cream flowers, sometimes with dark margins; the flower tube is shorter than the tepals. Mostly clay and granite slopes in renosterveld in the southwestern Cape. *Wurmbea elongata* has flowers with narrow tepals to 1 mm wide, in a slender spike about 1 cm in diameter.

**❹ *Wurmbea inusta***            | J | F | M | A | M | J | J | A | **S** | **O** | **N** | D |

Cormous perennial, 5–20 cm, with narrow leaves; bears fragrant, greenish or cream flowers with purple margins, marked with a single large spot on the tepals; the flower tube is slightly longer than the tepals. Damp flats in the southwestern Cape.

**❺ *Wurmbea marginata* Swartkoppie**     | J | F | M | A | M | J | J | A | **S** | **O** | N | D |

Cormous perennial, 6–22 cm, with lance-shaped leaves; bears foetid-smelling red or purple flowers with darker margins; the flower tube is shorter than the tepals, and the stamens are very short. Mostly clay or loam flats in the southwestern Cape. *Wurmbea recurva*, also with maroon flowers, has smaller tepals, less than 5 mm long, that are curved backwards.

# LANARIACEAE

# Lanaria family

## *Lanaria*  KAPOK LILY, PERDEKAPOK

Rhizomatous, evergreen perennial. Leaves *strap-shaped and channelled with coarse hairs at the base*, the margins finely toothed. Flowers small, in a tight, *flat-topped panicle*, mauve, funnel-shaped, densely white-haired on the outside. Winter-rainfall South Africa: 1 sp, fynbos.

**1** *Lanaria lanata*

| J | F | M | A | M | J | J | A | S | O | N | D |

Tufted, evergreen perennial, 30–80 cm, with fibrous, grass-like leaves that are finely toothed along the margins; bears small mauve flowers in a dense, white-woolly panicle. Clay and sandstone slopes in the southwestern and Eastern Cape.


# HYPOXIDACEAE

# Stargrass family

## *Empodium*  AUTUMN STAR, PLOEGTYDBLOMMETJIE

Cormous perennials. *Leaves usually pleated* and hairless, often developing after flowering. *Flowers solitary*, sometimes the peduncle shortened and *the flowers at ground level*, yellow, star-shaped, with a well-developed *solid flower tube above the ovary. Fruits fleshy, 1-chambered*. Southern Africa, mainly winter-rainfall parts: ±9 spp; 4 fynbos spp. The vernacular name *ploegtydblommetjie* is a colourful reminder of the importance to early farmers of natural signs of the changing seasons, the appearance of the flowers coinciding with the onset of the winter rains.

**2** *Empodium plicatum*

| J | F | M | A | M | J | J | A | S | O | N | D |

**Ploegtydblommetjie** Dwarf perennial, 10–30 cm, with narrow leaves surrounded at the base by pale sheaths, sometimes absent or just emerging at flowering; bears flowers at ground level, with the ovary enclosed by the sheaths and drawn into an elongate beak more than 50 mm long. Damp clay and granite flats and lower slopes in the southwestern Cape. *Empodium gloriosum* from the southern Cape has the ovary mostly protruding from the leaf sheaths.

**3** *Empodium veratrifolium*

| J | F | M | A | M | J | J | A | S | O | N | D |

Perennial, often clumped, to 30 cm with broad leaves surrounded at the base by a dark brown sheath; bears flowers on long peduncles, with the ovary just below the tepals and separated from them by a short beak to 10 mm long. Crevices in granite rock outcrops around St Helena Bay.


## *Spiloxene*  CAPE STAR, STERRETJIE

Cormous perennials. Leaves broad to thread-like, *usually channelled* and hairless. Flowers 1–6 in a *cluster on a slender peduncle subtended by 1 or 2 bracts*, white, yellow or orange, star-shaped with separate tepals. Fruit a dry capsule *opening from a lidded top*. Winter-rainfall southern Africa: ±25 spp; 18 fynbos spp.

▸ **FLOWER OR FLOWERS SUBTENDED BY 2 BRACTS**

**4** *Spiloxene aquatica*  **Watersterretjie**

| J | F | M | A | M | J | J | A | S | O | N | D |

Aquatic perennial, 10–30 cm, with firm, needle-like leaves; bears clusters of 2–7 white flowers with green reverse subtended by 2 broad, leaf-like bracts. Seasonal pools and marshes in Namaqualand and the southwestern Cape.

89

**1** *Spiloxene schlechteri*

J F M A M **J J A** S O N D

Perennial to 10 cm with ±erect, firm, quill-like leaves; bears 1 or 2 yellow flowers with reddish or green reverse, subtended by 2 firm-textured, leaf-like bracts. Marshy flats in the southwestern Cape. *Spiloxene flaccida* has channelled leaves, V-shaped in section, and softer bracts.

**2** *Spiloxene serrata*

J F M **A M J J A S O** N D

Perennial, 6–20 cm, with narrow, channelled, grass-like leaves that are minutely toothed along the margins; bears solitary yellow, orange or white flowers with green reverse, subtended by 2 narrow bracts. Seasonally damp flats and lower slopes in Namaqualand and the southwestern Cape.

▶ **FLOWER SUBTENDED BY 1 BRACT**

**3** *Spiloxene ovata*

J F M A M J **J A S O** N D

Perennial, 6–20 cm, with broad, elliptical leaves; bears solitary yellow or white flowers with reddish reverse and broadly elliptical tepals, subtended by a single, narrow bract. Seasonally wet rocks and depressions in Namaqualand and the southwestern Cape.

**4** *Spiloxene canaliculata*

J F M A M J **J A S O** N D

Perennial, 10–30 cm, with narrow, grass-like leaves, U-shaped in section; bears solitary, large yellow or orange flowers striped on the reverse and with a dull black centre, subtended by a single, large, leaf-like bract; the seeds are uniquely J-shaped. Seasonally wet granite flats on the West Coast, mainly around Darling.

**5** *Spiloxene capensis*  **Peacock flower**

J F M A M J **J A S O** N D

Perennial, 10–30 cm, with narrow, grass-like leaves, V-shaped in section; bears solitary, often large, yellow or white to pink flowers striped on the reverse and usually with an iridescent green or dull black centre, subtended by a single, large, leaf-like bract. Seasonally wet clay or granite flats in the southwestern Cape. *Spiloxene curculigoides* has a long sheath surrounding the base of the leaves, and smaller flowers.

91

# TECOPHILAEACEAE
## Cyanella family

### *Cyanella*   LADY'S HAND, RAAPTOL

Cormous perennials. Leaves several, mostly in a basal rosette, lance-shaped to thread-like. Flowers in simple or branched racemes, rarely with shortened axis and the flowers apparently solitary, on *slender pedicels bearing a small bract near the middle*, white, yellow, pink or blue, the *stamens in 2 groups with the upper anthers smaller, and the style directed to one side*. Southern Africa, mainly winter rainfall: 7 spp; 4 fynbos spp. The roasted corms are edible and the vernacular name *raaptol* derives from their resemblance either to a turnip (*raap*) or a top (*tol*).

**❶ *Cyanella alba*  Toe-toe uintjie**

| J | F | M | A | M | J | J | A | S | O | N | D |

Perennial, 12–25 cm, with thread-like leaves; bears fragrant, yellow or white to pink flowers on long pedicels arising directly among the leaves, with 5 upper and 1 lower, larger stamen. Stony clay soils in renosterveld along the mountains inland of the West Coast.

**❷ *Cyanella hyacinthoides***

| J | F | M | A | M | J | J | A | S | O | N | D |

Perennial, 25–40 cm, with narrowly lance-shaped leaves that are sometimes velvety; bears unscented or fragrant mauve or white flowers on spreading pedicels in branched racemes, with 5 upper and 1 lower, larger stamen. Mostly clay and granite slopes, often in renosterveld, in Namaqualand and the southwestern Cape.

**❸ *Cyanella lutea*  Geelraaptol**

| J | F | M | A | M | J | J | A | S | O | N | D |

Perennial, 12–25 cm, with lance-shaped leaves; bears racemes of fragrant yellow, or rarely pink, flowers on spreading pedicels that are bent up at the end, with 5 upper and 1 lower, larger stamen, the anthers minutely spotted. Mostly clay, or limestone flats, throughout southwestern South Africa.

**❹ *Cyanella orchidiformis***

| J | F | M | A | M | J | J | A | S | O | N | D |

Perennial, 30–40 cm, with soft, often wavy, lance-shaped leaves; bears fragrant mauve flowers with a darker centre on ±erect pedicels in branched racemes, with 3 upper and 3 lower, larger stamens. Rocky flats and lower slopes, often in damper places, from southern Namibia to Clanwilliam.

# HAEMODORACEAE    **Bloodroot family**

## *Dilatris*  BLOODROOT, BLOEDWORTEL

*Rhizomatous perennials. Leaves in a dense fan, oriented edgewise to the stem,* flat and fibrous. Flowers in *a dense, rounded or flat-topped panicle, on a stem with greyish hairs or with reddish, gland-tipped hairs,* mauve or yellowish, mostly regular, long-lasting, *1 stamen shorter than the others and with a larger anther,* ovary inferior. Winter-rainfall Western Cape: 4 spp, all fynbos.

**❶ *Dilatris corymbosa*  Rooiwortel**     J F M A M J J A S O N D

Rhizomatous perennial, 40–60 cm, with grey-haired stems and narrowly sword-shaped leaves; bears mauve flowers in a flat-topped panicle, the long stamens about the length of the oval tepals, and with the anthers half as long as the anther of the short stamen. Damp sandstone slopes in the mountains of the extreme southwestern Cape. *Dilatris pillansii* has all the stamens shorter than the tepals.

**❷ *Dilatris ixioides***     J F M A M J J A S O N D

Rhizomatous perennial, 20–40 cm, with grey-haired stems and narrow, grass-like leaves; bears mauve flowers in a flat-topped or rounded panicle, the long stamens twice as long as the oval tepals, and with the anthers a quarter as long as the anther of the short stamen. Rocky sandstone slopes in the southwestern Cape.

**❸ *Dilatris viscosa***     J F M A M J J A S O N D

Rhizomatous perennial, 45–60 cm, with sword-shaped leaves and with stems covered in red, gland-tipped hairs; bears dull orange or yellow flowers in a rounded or flat-topped panicle, the long stamens slightly longer than the narrowly oblong tepals, with anthers less than half as long as the anther of the short stamen. Montane marshes and seeps in the southwestern Cape.

## *Wachendorfia*  BUTTERFLY LILY, ROOIKANOL

Rhizomatous perennials. *Leaves in a loose fan, oriented edgewise to the stem, pleated.* Flowers in a cylindrical or open panicle on a mostly hairy stem, yellow to brownish with dark markings at the base of the upper 3 tepals, *irregular, lasting 1 day or less,* stamens equal, ovary superior. Winter rainfall South Africa: 4 spp, all fynbos.

**❹ *Wachendorfia paniculata***     J F M A M J J A S O N D

Rhizomatous perennial, mostly 20–70 cm, with narrow, usually hairy leaves; bears pale apricot to yellow flowers in an open panicle subtended by papery bracts. Mainly damp sandstone soils in the southwestern and southern Cape, flowering best after fire. *Wachendorfia multiflora* has a short spike of yellow to brownish flowers with narrow tepals, and green bracts.

**❺ *Wachendorfia thyrsiflora***     J F M A M J J A S O N D

Robust, rhizomatous perennial, 1–2 m, with broad, hairless leaves; bears golden-yellow flowers crowded in a dense, cylindrical panicle subtended by papery bracts. Permanent marshes and streambanks in the southwestern and southern Cape.

# IRIDACEAE
# Iris family

▶ WOODY SHRUBS

## *Klattia*  KLATTIA, KAMMETJIESBOS

*Evergreen shrubs* with a woody underground rootstock. Leaves *crowded at the tips of the stems in tight fans*, sword-shaped and *fibrous, without a midrib*. Flowers in tight clusters at the branch tips, subtended by *large, firm, often coloured bracts*, red, white or yellow with purple tips, radially symmetrical, the tepals *long and thread-like* with slightly widened tips, joined at the base into a short tube; the style is 3-notched at the tip. Sheltered mountainsides at high altitudes in the southwestern Cape: 3 spp, all fynbos.

**❶ *Klattia stokoei***    J F **M** A M J J A S O N D **D**

Evergreen shrub, 60–120 cm, with fans of tough, sword-shaped leaves at the branch tips; bears brush-like clusters of red flowers between bright red bracts. Mountain slopes and seeps in the Kogelberg Mountains. *Klattia flava* has yellow flowers and *K. partita* purplish-black flowers.

## *Witsenia*  WITSENIA, BOKMAKIERIESTERT

*Evergreen shrub* with a woody underground rootstock. Leaves *crowded towards the end of the stems in tight fans*, sword-shaped and *fibrous, without a midrib*. Flowers *in pairs*, enclosed at the base by firm, yellowish bracts, yellowish green flushed blackish green in the outer part and with velvety yellow tepals, radially symmetrical, the *tepals united into a long tube and remaining closed*; the *stamens are completely enclosed within the tepals* and the style is 3-notched at the tip. Marshes in the southwestern Cape: 1 sp, fynbos. The vernacular name *bokmakieriestert* derives from the resemblance of the yellow and black inflorescence to the tail of the shrike-like Bokmakierie.

**❷ *Witsenia maura*  Waaiertjie**    J F M A M J J A S O **N** D **D**

Slender, woody shrub to 2 m with fans of tough, narrowly sword-shaped leaves; bears pairs of tubular, blackish-green flowers in clusters at the branch tips, with bright yellow, velvety tepals. Marshes and seeps on the coast and mountains of the southwestern Cape.

## *Nivenia*  BUSH IRIS

*Evergreen shrub* with a woody underground rootstock. Leaves *crowded towards the end of the stems in tight fans*, sword-shaped and *fibrous, without a midrib*. Flowers *solitary or in pairs*, enclosed at the base by firm, dry or papery bracts, arranged in *flat-topped panicles or clusters*, bright blue to mauve, radially symmetrical and *salver-shaped*, the tepals united into a tube, sometimes heterostylous with short- and long-styled morphs; the style is divided into 3 short branches. Mountains in the southwestern Cape: 10 spp, all fynbos.

**❸ *Nivenia corymbosa***    J F **M** A M J J A S O N D **D**

Evergreen shrub, 50–200 cm, with sword-shaped leaves in fans; bears clusters of small, deep blue flowers with a tube 11–13 mm long, each branch terminating in a single flower. Rocky sandstone slopes along streams and drainage lines in the mountains between Tulbagh and Wellington. *Nivenia dispar* from the Swartberg Mountains has a floral tube 16–20 mm long and *N. binata* from the same mountains has 2 flowers per ultimate branch.

**1** *Nivenia stokoei*

J F M A M J J A S O N D

Evergreen shrub, 40–60 cm, with sword-shaped leaves in fans; bears clusters of large, pale to deep blue or mauve flowers with a tube 27–37 mm long, each branch terminating in a single flower. Rocky sandstone ridges in fynbos in the Kogelberg Mountains.

▶ **EVERGREEN, RHIZOMATOUS PERENNIALS; LEAVES WITHOUT A RAISED MIDRIB**

## *Aristea*  ARISTEA, BLOUSUURKANOL

Rhizomatous, *evergreen* perennials. Leaves in loose fans, often *tough and fibrous, without a midrib*. Flowers in clusters enclosed by bracts, or spathes, often many clusters collected into large compound inflorescences, *blue to mauve, lasting less than a day and shrivelling in the early afternoon, the tepals almost separate*; style curving away from the centre and either minutely notched or 3-lobed at the tip, the lobes fringed. Fruits cylindrical or *3-winged*. Sub-Saharan Africa and Madagascar, mainly southern Africa: 52 spp; 33 fynbos spp.

**2** *Aristea biflora*

J F M A M J J A S O N D

Unbranched perennial, 20–40 cm, with narrow leaves, lateral flower clusters sessile or lacking; bears large lilac flowers that have transparent to translucent bronze windows on the lower margins of the inner 3 tepals, with 3 fringed stigma lobes. Fruits long and cylindrical. Loamy clay in renosterveld around Caledon, flowering only after fire.

**3** *Aristea spiralis*

J F M A M J J A S O N D

Usually unbranched perennial, 20–50 cm, with flattened, 2-winged stems and fairly broad, soft leaves, lateral flower clusters sessile and spathes green with transparent margins; bears large white or pale-blue flowers with a small dark eye, facing to the side, with long stamens and style and 3 fringed stigma lobes. Fruits long and cylindrical. Rocky sandstone and granite slopes to 600 m in the southwestern and southern Cape, flowering after fire.

**4** *Aristea africana*  **Maagbossie**

J F M A M J J A S O N D

Small, usually branched perennial, mostly 10–15 cm, with flattened stems and narrow leaves, the spathes translucent with dark keels, finely fringed and sometimes rusty brown at the tips; bears blue flowers with 3 fringed stigma lobes. Fruits short and 3-winged. Sandy flats and mountain slopes in the southwestern Cape.

**5** *Aristea dichotoma*

J F M A M J J A S O N D

Highly branched, cushion-forming perennial, 15–30 cm, with stems flattened below and narrow greyish leaves, the spathes narrow, translucent with dark keels; bears blue flowers with 3 fringed stigma lobes. Fruits short and 3-winged, translucent with dark ribs. Sandy flats and lower slopes in Namaqualand and along the West Coast. *Aristea glauca* has flattened, 2-winged stems that are not as highly branched.

**6** *Aristea bakeri*  **Klatt**

J F M A M J J A S O N D

Robust perennial to 1 m with rounded, usually well-branched stems and narrow, fibrous leaves, the spathes dry and rusty brown with transparent margins, usually minutely hairy towards the base; bears blue flowers with an unlobed style. Fruits oblong and 3-winged, woody. Stony sandstone slopes from the southwestern to the Eastern Cape, flowering mainly after fire.

**①** *Aristea capitata*

J F M A M J J A S **O N D**

Robust, often clump-forming perennial to 1.5 m with strap-like, fibrous leaves, and cylindrical stems that are closely branched at the tip so that the flower clusters are crowded and overlapping, the spathes dry, membranous and translucent with dark keels; bears blue flowers with an unlobed style. Fruits short and 3-winged. Mountain slopes in moist places, 100–900 m, in the southwestern and southern Cape.

## *Bobartia* RUSH IRIS, BLOMBIESIE

Rhizomatous, evergreen perennials. Leaves in a basal tuft, tough and fibrous, *mostly long and cylindrical*. Flowers on a long, leafless stem in a *terminal head enclosed by a leaf-like or dry spathe*, rarely in a branched inflorescence, *on hairy pedicels*, yellow (rarely bluish), *lasting less than a day*, the tepals separate or united into a short tube; the *style divided into 3 thread-like branches that extend between the stamens*. Winter-rainfall South Africa: 14 spp, all fynbos.

**②** *Bobartia indica*

J F M A M J J A S O N D

Tufted perennial to 1 m or more with trailing, cylindrical leaves that are longer than the stems; bears yellow, star-shaped flowers in a dense head comprising 6–40 individual clusters subtended by a green spathe with a long, needle-like tip. Sandy flats and sandstone slopes in the extreme southwestern Cape, flowering mainly after fire.

**③** *Bobartia orientalis*

J F M A M J J A S O N D

Tufted perennial, 40–130 cm, with ±erect, cylindrical leaves about as long as the stems; bears yellow, star-shaped flowers in a dense head comprising 10–100 short, individual clusters subtended by a green spathe. Fruits ±globular, 4–8 mm long. Mainly dry, stony, sandstone slopes, often in large colonies, in the southwestern Cape and the southern to the Eastern Cape.

▸ **FLOWERS IN CLUSTERS WITH EACH CLUSTER ENCLOSED BY A PAIR OF LEAFY BRACTS; STYLE BRANCHES OFTEN PETAL-LIKE OR FRINGED; LEAVES SOMETIMES CHANNELLED**

## *Moraea* MORAEA, TULP

Deciduous, cormous perennials, sometimes stemless. Leaves usually grass-like and *channelled without a midrib*, sometimes broader and rarely quill-like. Flowers in clusters enclosed by leathery, leaf-like spathes, variously coloured and marked, often yellow or blue, lasting several days or less than 1, usually *Iris-like but sometimes cup-shaped* with the tepals separate or rarely joined into a short tube, the outer tepals often larger than the inner, which may be reduced or claw-like; the stamen filaments are separate or joined into a cylindrical column; the style branches are *sometimes flattened and petal-like* and conceal the anthers. Widespread throughout sub-Saharan Africa and extending into the Middle East but concentrated in the winter-rainfall parts of South Africa.

The genus has recently been redefined to include all of the species with channelled leaves, including those previously recognised as the separate genera *Galaxia* and *Homeria*: 195 spp; 116 fynbos spp. The corms of certain species, such as *Moraea fugax*, formed an important part of the diet of hunter-gatherers in the past but several others, notably the *tulps* (previously placed in *Homeria*), such as *M. miniata*, are poisonous to stock.

## ▶ FLOWERS CUP-SHAPED WITH ALL THE TEPALS SIMILAR

### ❶ *Moraea versicolor*

`J F M A M J J A S O N D`

Stemless perennial, 2–5 cm, with oblong to lance-shaped leaves that have undulating margins; bears cup-shaped flowers, pink to purple, often with a yellow centre; the stamen filaments are joined for most of their length and the stigmas are lobed; the flowers last from ±12h00 to 16h30. Moist clay and granite flats in the southwestern Cape. *Moraea variabilis* from around Ceres has the stamen filaments joined throughout their length.

### ❷ *Moraea fugacissima*  Clockflower

`J F M A M J J A S O N D`

Stemless perennial, 3–6 cm, with narrow or needle-like leaves; bears cup-shaped flowers, bright yellow, and the stigmas are fringed; the flowers last from ±10h30 to 16h00. Wet sand and clay flats in Namaqualand and the southwestern Cape.

### ❸ *Moraea galaxia*  Clockflower

`J F M A M J J A S O N D`

Stemless perennial, 2–4 cm, with oblong to lance-shaped leaves that have thickened, fringed margins; bears cup-shaped flowers, yellow, and the stigmas are fringed; the flowers last from ±10h30 to 16h00. Damp flats, mainly on sandstone soils in the southwestern Cape. *Moraea luteoalba* from the Cedarberg Mountains usually has the tepals paler towards the edge, and the stamen filaments only joined near the base.

### ❹ *Moraea lewisiae*  Volstruisuintjie

`J F M A M J J A S O N D`

Slender perennial, 20–90 cm, with 1–3, long, narrow, trailing leaves; bears star-shaped flowers, yellow, with the tepals all similar; the style is divided into 6 thread-like stigmatic arms that spread between the anthers; the fruits are narrowly ellipsoid and project out of the floral bracts; the flowers last from ±15h30 to 19h00. Various soils and habitats, mostly in dry sites, from Namaqualand to the Eastern Cape.

### ❺ *Moraea miniata*  Tulp

`J F M A M J J A S O N D`

Perennial, 15–60 cm, with 2 or 3 narrow trailing leaves; bears flowers that are star-shaped and usually salmon-orange, sometimes yellow or white, and minutely speckled in the centre, with the tepals all similar and not forming a cup, such that the anthers are prominently displayed; the stamen filaments are joined into a column 6–8 mm long that is hairy at the base and the anthers are 2 mm long. Mainly clay slopes in renosterveld and karroid scrub in Namaqualand and the southwestern Cape.

### ❻ *Moraea collina*  Tulp

`J F M A M J J A S O N D`

Perennial, 20–50 cm, with 1 trailing leaf and the stem flexed outwards above the leaf sheath; bears yellow or salmon flowers, lightly scented, with the tepals all similar and forming a deep cup that encloses the stamens; the stamen filaments are joined into a column 6–7 mm long that is hairy at the base and the anthers are 5–6 mm long. Lower mountain slopes and flats on sand or clay in the extreme southwestern Cape, flowering commonly after fire.

**1** *Moraea flaccida* **Groottulp**

J F M A M J J A S O N D

Perennial, 35–60 cm, with 1 trailing leaf and the stem flexed outwards above the leaf sheath; bears salmon flowers with a yellow centre or entirely yellow; the tepals are all similar and form a wide, shallow cup that does not completely enclose the anthers; the stamen filaments are joined into a column 7–8 mm long that is smooth or minutely haired at the base and the anthers are 8–11 mm long. Seasonally wet or marshy sandstone and granitic soils in the southwestern Cape.

**2** *Moraea ochroleuca* **Aas-uintjie**

J F M A M J J A S O N D

Perennial, 35–75 cm, with 1, rarely 2, trailing leaves and a straight stem; bears yellow or orange flowers with a yellow cup, scented, with the tepals all similar and forming a wide cup that does not completely enclose the anthers; the stamen filaments are joined into a smooth, slender column 7–10 mm long and the anthers are 5–8 mm long. Rocky sandstone slopes in the southwestern Cape, flowering only after fire.

## ▶ FLOWERS IRIS-LIKE WITH THE INNER TEPALS LANCE- OR SPEAR-SHAPED

**3** *Moraea ciliata*

J F M A M J J A S O N D

Stemless perennial, 5–10(20) cm, with 3–5 sparsely to densely haired, usually grey leaves, sometimes with crinkly margins; bears blue or yellow flowers, rarely white, and strongly vanilla-scented, with narrow ±erect inner tepals and lance-shaped style crests; the flowers last from midday to late afternoon. Sandy and clay slopes in Namaqualand and the southwestern Cape.

**4** *Moraea gawleri*

J F M A M J J A S O N D

Slender, wiry-stemmed, branching perennial, 15–45 cm, with 2 or 3 leaves that have crinkly margins; bears yellow, cream or brick-red flowers, sometimes bicoloured, with short floral bracts and spreading, spear-shaped inner tepals; the flowers last from late morning to late afternoon. Sandy or clay slopes, usually in renosterveld, from Namaqualand to the Eastern Cape.

**5** *Moraea inconspicua* **Taai-uintjie**

J F M A M J J A S O N D

Slender, branched perennial with conspicuously sticky stems 20–45 cm, with 2 or 3 narrow, trailing or loosely coiled leaves; bears small flowers, yellow to brown or cream, with the tepals all similar and usually bent sharply backwards; the flowers last 1 day. Sandy and clay slopes from Namaqualand to the Eastern Cape.

**6** *Moraea lugubris* **Kersblakertjie**

J F M A M J J A S O N D

Short perennial, 6–16 cm, with 2 or 3 leaves; bears deep blue flowers with the tepals all similar and spreading, and with conspicuous, feathery style branches; the flowers last 1 day. Usually in damp or seasonally wet sandstone soils in the southwestern Cape, flowering best after fire.

**7** *Moraea tricolor*

J F M A M J J A S O N D

Stemless perennial, 5–15 cm, with 3–5 hairy or hairless leaves; bears yellow, red or purple flowers, fragrant, with spear-shaped, spreading inner tepals and short, broad style crests; the flowers last from mid-morning to late afternoon. Seasonally wet sandy flats in the extreme southwestern Cape.

### ❶ *Moraea papilionacea*

Tufted perennial, 10–20 cm, with short or sparsely hairy stems branching from the base, with 3 or 4 often hairy leaves; bears yellow or salmon flowers with lance-shaped inner tepals; the flowers last 1 day. Mostly seasonally wet sandstone soils, sometimes clay, in renosterveld and transitional fynbos in the southwestern Cape.

### ❷ *Moraea ramosissima* **Vlei-uintjie**

Robust, well-branched perennial, 50–120 cm, with several to many leaves in a fan; bears bright yellow flowers with red anthers; the tepals are all similar; the flowers last from mid-morning to late afternoon. Damp sandstone flats and slopes, often along streams and in seeps, in the southwestern and southern Cape, flowering only after fire.

### ❸ *Moraea angusta*

Erect perennial, 20–40 cm, with a rod-like stem that is sometimes sticky at the nodes, and a solitary, quill-like leaf; bears large flowers that are pale yellow, often flushed with brown or grey, with clear yellow nectar guides; the inner tepals are narrow; the stamen filaments are joined only at the base for less than 2 mm and the style crests are longer than the style branches. Rocky sandstone flats and slopes in the southwestern Cape.

### ❹ *Moraea anomala*

Erect perennial, 20–40 cm, with a rod-like stem and a solitary, quill-like leaf; the flowers are large and yellow with yellow nectar guides outlined in grey; the inner tepals are narrow; the stamen filaments are joined for up to half their length; the flowers last from midday to sunset. Mountains and flats, often on clay, in the southwestern Cape.

### ❺ *Moraea neglecta*

Erect perennial, 20–50 cm, with rod-like stem, sticky at the nodes, and a solitary, quill-like leaf; bears large yellow flowers, the nectar guide streaked with dots; inner tepals are narrow; the stamen filaments are joined only at the base for less than 2 mm and the style crests are shorter than the style branches; the flowers last from early afternoon to sunset. Usually deep, sandy soils, in the southwestern Cape.

### ❻ *Moraea fugax*

**Soetuintjie, Hottentotsuintjie** Perennial with short, crowded branches, 12–80 cm, with 1 or 2 narrow trailing leaves inserted on the stem well above ground, just below the branches; bears large, strongly vanilla-scented flowers, blue, white or yellow; the inner tepals are lance-shaped; the fruits are characteristically pointed; the flowers last from early afternoon to sunset. Deep sands and rocky sandstone and granitic soils from Namaqualand to the southwestern Cape.

▸ **FLOWERS IRIS-LIKE WITH THE INNER TEPALS SMALL AND 3-LOBED OR THREAD-LIKE**

### ❼ *Moraea bellendenii* **Patrysuintjie**

Willowy-stemmed perennial, 50–100 cm, with a single, trailing leaf; bears pale yellow flowers speckled in the centre; the outer tepals are ±erect and cupped and the inner tepals are small and 3-lobed with a short, obliquely twisted central cusp; the flowers last several days. Granitic, sandy or clay slopes in the southwestern and southern Cape. *Moraea tricuspidata* has white flowers.

**❶ *Moraea tripetala* Blou-uintjie**  J F M A M J J **A S** O N D

Slender perennial, 20–45 cm, with a single, narrow leaf that is occasionally hairy below; bears blue to violet flowers, rarely white; the outer tepals are bent backwards and the inner tepals are minute and cusp-like; the stamens are separate almost to the base and tightly pressed against the stalk-like bases of the outer tepals; the flowers last several days. Common and widespread in rocky sandstone and clay soils from the West Coast into the southwestern and southern Cape.

**❷ *Moraea unguiculata* Wituintjie**  J F M A M J J **A S O N** D

Slender perennial, 20–50 cm, with a single, narrow leaf; bears small flowers that are white to cream or brownish, rarely violet; the outer tepals are bent sharply backwards and the inner tepals are small and 3-lobed with an inrolled central cusp; the flowers last several days. Mostly shale slopes in renosterveld from Namaqualand to the Eastern Cape.

**❸ *Moraea villosa***  J F M A M J J **A S** O N D

**Peacock moraea, uiltjie**  Perennial, 30–40 cm, with soft-haired stems and a solitary, hairy leaf; bears large flowers, purple, blue or pale orange, with conspicuous iridescent nectar guides on the broad, spreading outer tepals; the inner tepals are small and 3-lobed with a long, slender central cusp; the flowers last several days. Stony granite and clay slopes and flats in renosterveld in the southwestern Cape. *Moraea tulbaghensis* has bright orange flowers.

## *Ferraria*  SPIDER LILY, SPINNEKOPBLOM

Cormous perennials with disc-like corms lacking papery or fibrous coverings. Leaves leathery and sword- or lance-shaped, usually with a raised midrib. Flowers in clusters enclosed by large, leathery, leaf-like spathes, *yellowish or grey to brown, irregularly speckled, mostly lasting less than a day, cup-shaped with separate tepals* that are *crinkly or ruffed on the margins*; the *stamen filaments are united into a cylindrical column* and the *style branches are deeply fringed and conceal the anthers*. Southern and south tropical Africa, mainly winter-rainfall South Africa: 13 spp; 7 fynbos spp.

**❹ *Ferraria crispa* Inkpotjie, krulletjie**  J F M A M J J **A S O** N D

Robust, often densely branched perennial, 40–100 cm, with narrow leaves; bears shallowly cup-shaped, cream to yellowish flowers sparsely to densely speckled with brown, sometimes plain brown, cocoa-scented; anther lobes parallel to one another. Mainly coastal in deep sands or granite outcrops in the southwestern Cape.

**❺ *Ferraria uncinata***  J F M A M J J **A S O** N D

Tufted perennial, 10–40 cm, with a tight fan of rather blunt, lance-shaped leaves that are thickened and crinkly on the margins; bears deeply cup-shaped, blue to purple flowers with yellowish or brown margins and tepals that are drawn into long, coiled tips; the anther lobes diverge from one another in a 'V'. Mainly sandstone outcrops along the West Coast.

**❻ *Ferraria variabilis***  J F M A M J J **A S O** N D

Tufted perennial, 6–20 cm, with sword-shaped leaves sheathing the stem; bears shallowly cup-shaped, yellowish to brown flowers banded or speckled with brown; the anther lobes diverge from one another in a 'V'. Sandy and shale flats and rock outcrops from southern Namibia to the Little Karoo.

▸ **FLOWERS IN SPIKES OR SOLITARY, WITH EACH FLOWER SUBTENDED BY AN INNER AND OUTER BRACT; LEAVES ALMOST ALWAYS WITH A RAISED MIDRIB; STYLE BRANCHES THREAD-LIKE**

▸ ▸ **FLORAL BRACTS MEMBRANOUS OR PAPERY AND MORE OR LESS TRANSLUCENT, WITH THE OUTER BRACT OFTEN 3-TOOTHED, OR FRINGED**

## *Ixia*  IXIA, KALOSSIE

Cormous perennials with slender, *wiry stems*. Leaves sword-shaped, often rather short. Flowers in a spike, spirally arranged, *subtended by short, pale or translucent membranous bracts, often 3-toothed at the tips*; variously coloured, *often dark in the centre; radially symmetrical* with the tepals joined into a short or long tube; the stamens erect in the centre of the flower, the *style dividing into 3 short branches below the top of the anthers*. Winter-rainfall South Africa: ±50 spp; 46 fynbos spp. Hybrids of several species are cultivated as spring bulbs but the flowers close at night or in inclement weather. The vernacular name derives from the Afrikaans *kalotjie*, originally a skull-cap but applied to the headdress worn by Malay slaves in early Cape Town, which the flowers were thought to resemble.

▸ **FLORAL TUBE CYLINDRICAL OR FUNNEL-SHAPED WITH THE STAMEN FILAMENTS ARISING BELOW THE MOUTH**

**❶ *Ixia paniculata*  Pypkalossie**     J F M A M J J A **S O N D**

Perennial, 40–100 cm, with several sword-shaped leaves; bears a spike of cream to buff-coloured flowers with a cylindrical tube 35–70 mm long that partially encloses the purple anthers. Seeps and stream banks in the southwestern Cape.

**❷ *Ixia odorata*  Soetkalossie**     J F M A M J J A **S O N** D

Perennial, 20–50 cm, with several narrow or sword-shaped leaves that are often slightly coiled at the tips; bears a compact spike of small, fragrant, pale-yellow flowers with a funnel-shaped tube 5–15 mm long. Sandstone and granite slopes in the southwestern Cape. *Ixia esterhuyseniae* from high altitudes is a smaller plant with bright yellow flowers.

**❸ *Ixia rapunculoides*  Bloukalossie**     J F M A M J J **A** S O N D

Perennial, 15–70 cm, usually branched, with sword-shaped leaves; bears a spike of blue, mauve or pink flowers with a funnel-shaped tube 6–15 mm long that partially encloses the anthers. Mostly clay soils in renosterveld in Namaqualand and the interior of the southwestern Cape.

▸ **FLORAL TUBE THREAD-LIKE WITH THE STAMEN FILAMENTS ARISING AT THE MOUTH**

**❹ *Ixia micrandra***     J F M A M J **J A** S O N D

Slender perennial, 25–50 cm, usually unbranched, with narrow or thread-like leaves; bears a short, compact spike of pink to mauve flowers with a thread-like tube 3–5 mm long and very short, almost round anthers. Sandstone slopes in the southwestern Cape.

**❺ *Ixia scillaris***     J F M A M J J A **S O N** D

Perennial, 25–50 cm, with sword-shaped leaves; bears a slender, loose spike of pink to mauve flowers with a thread-like tube 3–4 mm long and short, asymmetrically flexed anthers. Sand and clay flats and slopes in Namaqualand and the southwestern Cape. *Ixia erubescens* has crinkly leaf margins.

### ❶ *Ixia dubia*

J F M A M J J A **S O N D**

Perennial, 25–60 cm, with sword-shaped to narrow leaves; bears a compact spike of orange to yellow flowers with a small dark centre, flushed reddish on the reverse, with a thread-like tube 5–15 mm long and partly or entirely black filaments; the bracts are translucent pink. Sandstone and granite flats and slopes in the southwestern Cape.

### ❷ *Ixia maculata*

J F M A M J J A **S** O N D

Perennial, 20–50 cm, with sword-shaped leaves; bears a compact spike of yellow to orange flowers with a large dark centre that often has a yellowish, star-like marking in the middle, with a thread-like tube 5–20 mm long and filaments that are partially or wholly joined together; the bracts are rather papery and rusty brown. Granite and sandstone flats and slopes, mostly in fynbos, along the West Coast.

### ❸ *Ixia lutea*  Geelkalossie

J F M A M J J **A S** O N D

Perennial, 15–35 cm, with sword-shaped leaves; bears a compact spike of cream to yellow, or red to purple, flowers with a dark centre, and with a thread-like tube 6–12 mm long; the bracts are flushed brownish or red. Clay flats and slopes in renosterveld along the West Coast.

### ❹ *Ixia polystachya*  Koringblommetjie

J F M A M J J A **S O N D**

Wiry perennial, 40–80 cm, often branched, with narrow leaves; bears a loose, or sometimes compact, spike of white or pink to mauve flowers, sometimes with a small dark centre, and with a thread-like tube 5–15 mm long. Granitic and sandstone slopes and flats in the southwestern Cape.

## *Sparaxis*  SPARAXIS, FLUWEELTJIE

Cormous perennials. Leaves sword-shaped in a closely set fan and *finely veined*, with a prominent midrib. Flowers few to many in a 1-sided or spiral spike, subtended by *dry, papery or crinkly bracts that are irregularly fringed and streaked with brown*, variously coloured and marked, 2-lipped or bowl-shaped, with the tepals joined into a short to long tube; the stamens either arched together under the upper tepal or erect, the style dividing into 3 short branches. Winter-rainfall South Africa, mainly in clay soils: 15 spp; 14 fynbos spp. Hybrids between a few of the colourfully marked, symmetrically flowered species are popularly cultivated as spring bulbs.

### ❺ *Sparaxis bulbifera*

J F M A M J J A **S** O N D

Branching perennial, 15–45 cm, developing axillary cormlets after blooming, with sword-shaped leaves; bears nearly symmetrical white to cream flowers that are often purplish on the reverse, the tube 14–16 mm long. Seasonally wet, sandy or clay flats, often in roadside ditches in the extreme southwestern Cape.

### ❻ *Sparaxis grandiflora*  Botterblom

J F M A M J J **A S** O N D

Perennial, 10–25 cm, with sword-shaped, sometimes prostrate leaves; bears almost symmetrical white or yellow to plum-red flowers, the tube 10–14 mm long. Clay flats and slopes in renosterveld in the southwestern Cape.

### ❼ *Sparaxis metelerkampiae*

J F M A M J J **A S** O N D

Perennial, 15–30 cm, with sword-shaped leaves; bears long-tubed, 2-lipped, purple flowers marked with white on the lower tepals, the tube 45–50 mm long, the style branches very short. Rocky sandstone slopes along the interior of the West Coast.

**1** *Sparaxis variegata*

J F M A M J J **A S** O N D

Perennial, 25–40 cm, with blunt, sword-shaped leaves; bears long-tubed, 2-lipped, yellow and violet flowers streaked with purple at the throat, the tube 42–45 mm long, the style branches long. Rocky sandstone slopes in the Olifants River valley.

**2** *Sparaxis villosa*

J F M A M J J **A S** O N D

Perennial, 12–35 cm, with sword-shaped, often blunt leaves; bears small, 2-lipped, yellow flowers with purple upper tepals, the tube ±16 mm long. Clay and granite slopes along the West Coast. *Sparaxis caryophyllacea* from the northern Cedarberg Mountains has larger flowers and purple-spotted leaf sheaths.

## *Tritonia*   TRITONIA, AGRETJIE

Cormous perennials. Leaves often sword-shaped in a closely set fan, with a prominent midrib, sometimes quill-like or H-shaped in cross-section with winged, often crinkly, margins, rarely U-shaped in cross-section. Flowers 1 to many in a 1-sided or spiral spike, subtended by *dry, firm-textured or papery bracts that are often 3-toothed*, variously coloured and marked, 2-lipped or bowl-shaped, with the tepals joined into a short to long tube; the stamens either arched together under the upper tepal or erect, the style dividing into 3 short branches. Eastern and southern Africa, mainly winter-rainfall South Africa: 28 spp; 16 fynbos spp. Hybrids between a few of the colourfully marked, symmetrically flowered species are popularly cultivated as spring bulbs. The vernacular name derives from the French *aigrette*, an allusion to the plume-like appearance of the flower spikes of some species.

**3** *Tritonia crocata*

J F M A M J J A **S O N** D

**Mosselbaaikalkoentjie** Perennial, 25–50 cm, with sword-shaped leaves; bears large, bowl-shaped orange flowers with translucent, window-like patches on the lower margins of the tepals, the tube 8–15 mm long. Clay slopes in renosterveld in the southern Cape. *Tritonia squalida* from limestone soils in the southern Cape has dull pink or mauve flowers; *T. deusta* from the southwestern Cape lacks translucent windows on the tepals and often has dark markings.

**4** *Tritonia undulata*  (=*Tritonia crispa*)

J F M A M J J A S **O N D**

Perennial, 18–35 cm, with the leaves crinkly along the margins; bears a horizontal, 1-sided spike of tubular cream-coloured flowers with red markings on the lower tepals and flushed pink on the reverse, the tube 30–70 mm long, with small blunt bracts with brown tips. Rocky sandstone slopes in fynbos in the southwestern Cape, flowering after fire. *Tritonia cooperi* has the leaf margins raised into wings.

**5** *Tritonia pallida*  **Katjietee**

J F M A M J J A **S O** N D

Perennial, 20–40 cm, with sword-shaped leaves; bears an erect spike of tubular cream or pink to pale lilac flowers with a small, yellowish-green tooth on each of the lower tepals, the tube 30–70 mm long, with fairly short, acute bracts. Sandstone and clay slopes, often in large communities, in the Little Karoo. *Tritonia flabellifolia*, from the southwestern Cape, has long, tapering floral bracts.

▶ ▶ FLORAL BRACTS GREEN OR BROWN AND FIRM-TEXTURED ALTHOUGH SOMETIMES WITH MEMBRANOUS MARGINS; STYLE 3-BRANCHED WITH EACH OF THE BRANCHES DEEPLY FORKED AND THE STYLE THUS WITH 6 BRANCHES

## *Lapeirousia*  PAINTED PETALS, CABONG

Cormous perennials with *bell-shaped corms that have woody corm coats*. Leaves sword-shaped and often conspicuously *ridged or ribbed*. Flowers in a simple or branched spike, spirally arranged, subtended by firm *green bracts*, variously coloured and marked, sometimes scented, mostly 2-lipped with the tepals joined into a short to long tube; the stamens mostly arched together under the upper tepal, rarely erect, the style dividing into *3 branches that are in turn forked for half their length*. Widespread across sub-Saharan Africa, mainly in semi-arid regions: 41 spp; 14 fynbos spp. The corms of several species were important sources of food for early hunter-gatherers. The vernacular names *cabong* or *chabi* are derived from Khoisan names for the plants.

▶ FLORAL TUBE LESS THAN 15 MM LONG

**①** *Lapeirousia azurea*

| J | F | M | A | M | J | J | A | **S** | **O** | N | D |

Perennial, 6–12 cm, with sickle-shaped leaves that have a midrib and often undulating margins; bears a flat-topped cluster of funnel-shaped, deep blue flowers with blackish markings on the lower tepals and a floral tube 8–12 mm long. Granitic soils in renosterveld around Malmesbury. *Lapeirousia neglecta* from the southwestern mountains, flowering only after fire, is a taller plant with open panicles of white or lilac flowers.

**②** *Lapeirousia corymbosa*

| J | F | M | A | M | J | J | **A** | **S** | **O** | **N** | D |

**Koringblommetjie**  Perennial, 5–15 cm, with sickle-shaped leaves that have a midrib and often undulating margins; bears a flat-topped cluster of radially symmetrical, pale to deep blue flowers with a white central star and a floral tube 4–7 mm long. Sandy and granitic soils in the southwestern Cape.

**③** *Lapeirousia divaricata*

| J | F | M | A | M | J | J | **A** | **S** | **O** | N | D |

Perennial, 7–25 cm, with ribbed leaves; bears a spike of strongly 2-lipped, white to pale pink flowers marked with red on the lower tepals and a floral tube 10–12 mm long; the bracts are marked with white windows. Damp, sandy places in the inland mountains of the West Coast.

▶ FLORAL TUBE MORE THAN 20 MM LONG

**④** *Lapeirousia anceps*

| J | F | M | A | M | J | J | A | **S** | **O** | N | **D** |

Slender perennial, 10–30 cm, with ribbed leaves; bears a short spike of tubular, cream to pink flowers marked with red on the lower tepals, the floral tube (25)40–80 mm long; the bracts are very short. Deep sand or stony slopes in fynbos from southern Namaqualand and the southwestern Cape.

**⑤** *Lapeirousia fabricii*

| J | F | M | A | M | J | J | A | **S** | **O** | N | D |

Perennial, 15–25 cm, with ribbed leaves; bears spikes of tubular, cream to pink flowers with red markings on the lower tepals, each with a curved, claw-like appendage near the base, the floral tube 30–50 mm long. Stony sandstone slopes in fynbos from Namaqualand to the West Coast.

**1 *Lapeirousia jacquinii***  | J | F | M | A | M | J | J | **A** | **S** | O | N | D |

Perennial, 8–12 cm, with ribbed leaves; bears a spike of tubular, dark purple flowers, with cream and reddish streaks on the lower tepals, the floral tube 30–40 mm long; the bracts are 2-keeled towards the base and blunt with white windows. Seasonally moist sand in the southwestern Cape.

**2 *Lapeirousia pyramidalis***  | J | F | M | A | M | J | **J** | **A** | **S** | O | N | D |

Short perennial, 5–10 cm, with ribbed leaves; bears a pyramidal spike of tubular, cream to bluish or dark purplish to magenta flowers marked with cream or white on the lower tepals, the floral tube 20–40 mm long; the broad, rather spreading bracts are notched. Shale and sandstone soils in fynbos and renosterveld in the southwestern Cape.

## *Micranthus*   COMBFLOWER, BLOUVLEIPYPIE

Cormous perennials. Leaves flat and sword-shaped with a midrib, or quill-like, or hollow and cylindrical. Flowers *small, crowded in a dense, 2-ranked spike*, subtended by *dry, brownish bracts with broad, transparent, membranous margins, blue*, 2-lipped with the tepals united into a short tube; the stamens arching together under the upper tepal, the style dividing into *3 branches that are in turn forked for half their length*. Winter-rainfall Western Cape, often in damp places: 3 spp, all fynbos.

**3 *Micranthus junceus* Blouvleipypie**  | **J** | F | M | A | M | J | J | A | **S** | **O** | **N** | **D** |

Perennial, 25–45 cm, with slender, quill-like leaves; bears small blue flowers in a dense, 2-ranked spike. Seeps and other damp sites on granite or sandstone soils in the southwestern Cape. The other 2 species are distinguished only by their leaves: flat in *Micranthus alopecuroides* and swollen and tubular in *M. tubulosus*.

## *Thereianthus*   THEREIANTHUS, BLOUBERGPYPIE

Cormous perennials. Leaves flat and sword-shaped, or narrow and ribbed. Flowers *crowded in dense, spirally twisted spikes,* subtended by *dry, brownish bracts, blue or white,* mostly 2-lipped with the tepals united into a short or long, more or less straight tube; the stamens arching together under the upper tepal, the style dividing into *3 branches that are in turn forked for half their length*. Winter-rainfall Western Cape, mostly on sandstone soils: 8 spp, all fynbos.

**4 *Thereianthus minutus***  | J | F | M | A | M | J | J | A | S | O | **N** | **D** |

Perennial, 10–20 cm, with sickle-shaped leaves that have a definite midrib; bears tubular magenta flowers with a tube 20–30 mm long, which is longer than the tepals. Seeps and wet sandstone rocks in the southwestern Cape.

**5 *Thereianthus bracteolatus***  | **J** | F | M | A | M | J | J | A | S | O | **N** | **D** |

Perennial, 15–25 cm, with narrow leaves without prominent veins; bears deep blue or purple flowers with prominently veined tepals, the tube 10–12 mm long and the anthers prominently displayed on filaments 8–10 mm long. Dry, sandstone slopes in the southwestern Cape, flowering after fire.

**6 *Thereianthus spicatus***  | J | F | M | A | M | J | J | A | S | **O** | **N** | D |

Perennial, 18–30 cm, with narrow or quill-like leaves that have prominent veins; bears blue to mauve flowers, the tube 12–20 mm long and the anthers on short filaments ±4 mm long. Sandstone slopes in the southwestern Cape, flowering after fire.

## *Watsonia*  WATSONIA, SUURKANOL

Robust, deciduous or sometimes evergreen, cormous perennials. Leaves tough and fibrous, sword-shaped with a prominent midrib and margins. Flowers in a 2-sided spirally twisted spike, subtended by *dry, firm-textured or leathery bracts*, usually *pink, orange or red*, rarely white or pale yellow, usually 2-lipped, with the tepals joined into a short to long tube; the stamens usually arched together under the upper tepal, the style dividing into *3 branches that are in turn forked for half their length*. Eastern parts of southern Africa, mainly winter-rainfall South Africa: 52 spp; 32 fynbos spp. The white form of *Watsonia borbonica* (long known as *W. arderneii*), along with various hybrids, are popular as roadside plantings and in larger gardens around Cape Town. The vernacular name alludes to the rather sour taste of the corms.

▶ **FLOWERS FUNNEL-SHAPED OR CYLINDRICAL, OFTEN PINK**

**❶ *Watsonia marginata***

| J | F | M | A | M | J | J | A | S | O | N | D |

Branched perennial, 50–200 cm, with broadly sword-shaped leaves that have thick, translucent margins; bears a wand-like spike of bowl-shaped, pink, white or purple flowers with a gradually flared tube 13–20 mm long, the stamens erect in the centre, the filaments ±10 mm long; the fruits are rounded. Sandy and granitic soils, often damper sites, in the mountains of the southwestern Cape.

**❷ *Watsonia laccata***

| J | F | M | A | M | J | J | A | S | O | N | D |

Dwarf perennial, 30–40 cm, with short, sword-shaped leaves; bears pink to orange, funnel-shaped flowers with a flared tube ±20 mm long, the stamens lying on the lower tepals, with filaments to 18 mm long; the fruits are narrow and tapering. Lower stony slopes in fynbos and renosterveld in the southern Cape.

**❸ *Watsonia borbonica***

| J | F | M | A | M | J | J | A | S | O | N | D |

Robust, branched perennial, 50–200 cm, often with purple stems, and bright apple-green, sword-shaped leaves; bears funnel-shaped magenta, or rarely white, flowers with a flared tube 20–40 mm long, the stamens usually lying on the lower tepals, with filaments 13–20 mm long; the fruits are blunt. Mainly rocky sandstone slopes, also granite and clay, in the southwestern Cape, flowering well after fire.

**❹ *Watsonia aletroides***

| J | F | M | A | M | J | J | A | S | O | N | D |

Dwarf perennial to 45 cm with short, sword-shaped leaves; bears nodding, red to pinkish cylindrical flowers with very small tepals, often tipped white, with a tube 35–45 mm long, the filaments 30–35 mm long; the fruits are narrow and tapered. May hybridise with *Watsonia laccata*. Clay slopes, mainly in renosterveld, in the southern Cape.

▶ **FLOWERS TRUMPET-SHAPED, USUALLY RED OR ORANGE**

**❺ *Watsonia stokoei***

| J | F | M | A | M | J | J | A | S | O | N | D |

Perennial to 1 m with sword-shaped leaves; bears relatively small, pale reddish flowers with a cylindrical tube 20–30 mm long, the filaments 22–30 mm long; the fruits are elliptical. Marshes and seeps in the mountains along the West Coast.

**❻ *Watsonia fourcadei***

| J | F | M | A | M | J | J | A | S | O | N | D |

Perennial to 2 m, with sword-shaped leaves; bears mostly orange to red, sometimes pink or purple, flowers with a cylindrical tube 40–50 mm long, the filaments 38–45 mm long; the inner bracts are deeply forked and the fruits are tapered. Rocky sandstone slopes in the southwestern and southern Cape.

### ❶ *Watsonia knysnana*

`J F M A M J J A S O N D`

Robust perennial to 1.6 m with sword-shaped leaves; bears mostly pink to purple flowers with a cylindrical tube 30–45 mm long, the filaments 16–28 mm long; the fruits are blunt. Sandstone slopes in fynbos in the southern and Eastern Cape.

### ❷ *Watsonia tabularis*

`J F M A M J J A S O N D`

Perennial to 1.5 m with sword-shaped leaves, the stem leaves conspicuously inflated; bears salmon-pink flowers with a cylindrical tube 40–50 mm long, the filaments 35–40 mm long; the fruits are blunt. Rocky sandstone slopes on the Cape Peninsula.

### ❸ *Watsonia coccinea*

`J F M A M J J A S O N D`

Short perennial, 14–40 cm, with sword-shaped leaves; bears purple, pink or scarlet flowers with a cylindrical tube 38–45 mm long, the filaments 25–30 mm long; the inner bracts are as long as or longer than the outer; the fruits are rather large and blunt. Seasonally moist sandstone flats and seeps in the southwestern Cape.

### ❹ *Watsonia meriana*  Waspypie

`J F M A M J J A S O N D`

Robust perennial, 60–200 cm, sometimes with cormlets up the stems, and with sword-shaped leaves; bears dull orange, pink or mauve flowers with a cylindrical tube 42–50 mm long, the filaments 35–45 mm long; the inner bracts are as long as or longer than the outer and the fruits are blunt. Sandy or granitic soils, often in vleis and streambanks, from Namaqualand to the southwestern Cape, sometimes forming dense colonies through vegetative reproduction from cormlets produced on the stems.

### ❺ *Watsonia schlechteri*

`J F M A M J J A S O N D`

Perennial, 40–100 cm, with sword-shaped leaves that have very thick margins; bears scarlet flowers with a cylindrical tube 40–50 mm long, the filaments 35–45 mm long; the fruits are short and blunt. Rocky sandstone slopes in fynbos in the southwestern and southern Cape, flowering mainly after fire.

### ❻ *Watsonia spectabilis*

`J F M A M J J A S O N D`

Short perennial, 25–50 cm, with sword-shaped leaves; bears large scarlet flowers with a cylindrical tube 38–48 mm long and pointed tepals 30–35 mm long, the filaments 30–40 mm long; the fruits are blunt. Sandy flats and plateaus, often near water, in the southwestern Cape.

## *Freesia*  FREESIA, FLISSIE

Cormous perennials. Leaves in an erect or prostrate fan, sword-shaped with a raised midrib and often with *blunt or rounded tips*, soft-textured. *Flowers in a 1-ranked, horizontal and scalloped spike*, subtended by green or dry papery bracts, mostly cream to yellow flushed dull purple and strongly scented, rarely green or red, 2-lipped with the tepals united into a long tube that is either narrow throughout or abruptly expanded into a broadly cylindrical upper portion; the stamens arching together and the *style divided into 3 deeply forked branches*. Eastern parts of southern and tropical Africa: 17 spp; 14 fynbos spp. Commercial hybrid freesias are enormously popular worldwide for their glorious fragrance.

### 1 *Freesia caryophyllacea*

J F M **A M J** J A S O N D

Dwarf perennial, 5–10 cm, with blunt leaves often spreading on the ground; bears fragrant, funnel-shaped white flowers with yellow markings on the lower tepals. Clay soils and limestone in renosterveld and coastal bush in southwestern Cape.

### 2 *Freesia alba*

J F M A M J **J A S O** N D

Erect perennial, 12–40 cm, with sharply pointed leaves that develop small corms in the axils along the stem underground; bears fragrant, funnel-shaped white flowers flushed dull purple, usually with yellow markings only on the median lower tepal. Sandy or stony soils in coastal fynbos and scrub in the southern Cape.

### 3 *Freesia leichtlinii*

J F M A M J J **A S** O N D

Perennial, 8–20 cm, with sword-shaped leaves that develop small corms in the axils underground; bears fragrant, funnel-shaped, creamy yellow flowers with orange markings on the lower tepals. Deep coastal sands and limestone in fynbos and scrub on the Agulhas plain. *Freesia fergusoniae* from clay flats around Riversdale has short, blunt leaves that lack axillary corms.

### 4 *Freesia viridis*  Groenagretjie

J F M A M **J** J **A S** O N D

Erect perennial, 10–35 cm, with sharply pointed leaves that are sometimes crinkly along the margins and greyish; bears small, tubular, green to dull brown flowers that are fragrant only at night, with narrow tepals that are curled at the tips and a slender tube that is sharply bent at the top. Stony clay and limestone outcrops in Namaqualand and the West Coast.

▸ ▸ **FLORAL BRACTS GREEN OR BROWN AND FIRM-TEXTURED, SOMETIMES WITH MEMBRANOUS MARGINS; STYLE BRANCHES LOBED BUT NOT DEEPLY FORKED**

## *Pillansia*  PILLANSIA

Robust, evergreen, cormous perennial. Leaves fibrous, *strap-like and loosely twisted, without a midrib*. Flowers in a *branched panicle*, subtended by *firm, leathery bracts, orange, radially symmetrical* with the tepals united into a short tube; the style dividing into *3 slender branches*. Southwestern Cape in fynbos: 1 sp.

### 5 *Pillansia templemannii*

J F M A M J J A S **O** N D

Robust, evergreen perennial, 60–90 cm, with strap-like, loosely twisted, fibrous leaves without a midrib; bears large, bowl-shaped, orange flowers in a branched panicle. Sandstone slopes around the Kogelberg, flowering after fire, sometimes in large numbers.

## *Romulea*  ROMULEA, FROETANG

Cormous perennials, *the corms mostly asymmetric, with woody coats*. Leaves thread-like, with *narrow longitudinal grooves*. Flowers *solitary at the tip of each branch, often borne at ground level*, subtended by firm green bracts, often with transparent margins, variously coloured and marked but *usually white or yellow in the centre, radially symmetrical and cup-shaped* with the tepals joined into a short tube; the stamens erect in the centre of the flower, the style *dividing into several short branches below the top of the anthers*. Southern Africa to southern Europe and Middle East, mainly the winter-rainfall region: ±85 spp; 54 fynbos spp. Accurate species identification requires careful examination of the corm and is best left to an expert. The young fruits are juicy and were eaten by children. The vernacular name *froetang* is a Malay corruption of the Portuguese *fruta*.

**1** *Romulea hirsuta*

J F M A M J J **A S** O N D

Perennial, usually branching above ground, 6–10 cm, with a bell-shaped corm and 2 basal leaves; bears pink to rose or coppery orange flowers with dark marks at the edge of a yellow cup. Sandstone or clay slopes and flats in the southwestern Cape.

**2** *Romulea cruciata*

J F M A M J **J A S** O N D

Stemless perennial, 5–12 cm, with a pointed corm and 2 to several basal leaves; bears magenta to lilac flowers with dark blotches at the edges of a yellow cup. Sandstone and granite slopes and rocks in the southwestern Cape.

**3** *Romulea rosea* **Knikkertjie**

J F M A M J **J A S** O N D

Stemless perennial, 10–40 cm, with a rounded corm and several basal leaves; bears pink to purple or sometimes white flowers with a yellow cup and purple feathering on the reverse of the tepals. Sandy and clay slopes and flats from the southwestern to the Eastern Cape.

**4** *Romulea flava*

J F M A M **J J A S** O N D

Perennial, 10–40 cm, usually branching above the ground, with an oblique corm and 1 or 2 basal leaves that are often rather swollen and clasping at the base; bears white or yellow, rarely blue or pinkish, flowers with a yellow cup and pale green reverse; the inner bract is entirely membranous or papery. Moist sand and clay in fynbos and renosterveld in the southwestern and southern Cape.

**5** *Romulea leipoldtii*

J F M A M J J A **S O** N D

Perennial to 20 cm, branching above the ground, with an oblique corm and 2 basal leaves; bears cream flowers with a wide yellow cup, not blotched on the reverse. Damp sandy sites along the West Coast.

**6** *Romulea tabularis*

J F M A M J **J A S** O N D

Perennial to 10 cm, branching above the ground, with an oblique corm and 1 or 2 basal leaves; bears blue to white flowers with a wide yellow cup, often blotched on the reverse and sometimes fragrant. Damp or marshy sandy or limestone flats along the western and southwestern Cape coasts.

## *Geissorhiza* SATINFLOWER, SYBLOM

Cormous perennials with *woody corm coats* that either overlap one another as if tiled, or are stacked in concentric layers. Leaves mostly narrow with a raised midrib, sometimes ridged or rounded in cross-section. Flowers few to many in a spike, spirally arranged and subtended by *soft-textured green bracts*, blue, purple, pink, white or yellow, usually *salver-shaped*, with tepals joined in a short to long tube; the stamens either erect or flexed downwards, sometimes 1 shorter than the remaining 2, the style divided into 3 short branches, sometimes curving downwards. Winter-rainfall parts of South Africa, mainly Western Cape: 85 spp; 80 fynbos spp.

▶ **LEAVES FLAT OR WITH THE MARGINS ONLY LIGHTLY THICKENED**

**7** *Geissorhiza aspera* **Sysie**

J F M A M J J **A S** O N D

Perennial, 10–35 cm, with a finely velvety stem and sword-shaped leaves that have the margins and midrib lightly thickened; bears blue to violet, rarely white, flowers with a very short tube 1–2 mm long and 1 stamen slightly shorter than the others; the bracts are dry and brown in the upper half. Widespread and common, mostly in sandy soils, in the southwestern Cape.

### 1 *Geissorhiza monanthos* Bloukelkie

J F M A M J J **A S O** N D

Perennial, 6–20 cm, with velvety stems and narrow, flat leaves; bears large, glossy, dark blue flowers that are paler in the centre with a dark ring, and with a short tube 2 mm long and stamens that arch downwards. Sandy slopes and granite outcrops along the West Coast.

### 2 *Geissorhiza ovata*

J F M A M J J **A S O** N D

Perennial, 6–15 cm, with oval, leathery leaves that spread on the ground; bears a few moderately large white flowers, flushed pink or reddish on the outside with a well-developed tube, usually 10–20 mm long. Sandstone slopes and flats in the southwestern Cape, flowering mainly after fire.

### 3 *Geissorhiza ornithogaloides*

J F M A M J J **A S O** N D

Small perennial, 4–10 cm, with narrow, flat leaves; bears 1 or 2 small, bright yellow flowers with a short tube 2–3 mm long; the bracts are rather round. Mostly damp clay flats and lower slopes in the southwestern and southern Cape.

## ▶ LEAVES NEEDLE-LIKE, RIBBED, OR WITH THE MARGINS THICKENED OR WINGED

### 4 *Geissorhiza juncea*

J F M A M J J **A S O N** D

Slender perennial, 20–40 cm, the base of the plant sticky and covered with adhering sand grains, with thin needle-like leaves; bears small, cream to yellow flowers with a short tube 2–3 mm long. Sandy flats and lower slopes, often in wet or marshy sites in the southwestern Cape.

### 5 *Geissorhiza inflexa*

J F M A M J J **A S** O N D

Perennial, 12–35 cm, with sword-shaped leaves that have the margins and midrib raised into narrow, minutely haired wings; bears moderately sized white flowers (rarely red or purple around Tulbagh and Stellenbosch) with a very short tube 1–2.5 mm long; the bracts are conspicuously dry and reddish brown in the upper half. Moist clay flats and slopes in renosterveld in the southwestern Cape.

### 6 *Geissorhiza radians* Wynkelkie

J F M A M J J A **S O** N D

Perennial, 8–16 cm, with narrow, ridged leaves that have the margins and midribs thickened and raised, the uppermost leaf with a swollen, ribbed sheath; bears large, rather cupped, deep blue flowers with a red centre outlined with a white ring, and with a tube 6–8 mm long and stamens that arch downwards and are bent up at the ends. Damp, sandy soils along the West Coast.

### 7 *Geissorhiza schinzii*

J F M A M J J **A S O N** D

Perennial, 10–20 cm, with narrow, sticky leaves that have the margins and midrib raised into narrow wings; bears large pink flowers with dark veins, and with a long tube 25–35 mm long and protruding stamens; the bracts are almost as long as the tube. Stony sandstone slopes in extreme southwestern Cape, flowering after fire.

### 8 *Geissorhiza exscapa*

J F M A M J J A **S O** N D

Perennial, 18–30 cm, with narrow or needle-like, sticky leaves that have the margins rolled over the surface; bears large, creamy white flowers with darker veins, flushed reddish on the outside with a very long tube 40–80 mm long, and protruding stems; the bracts are about half as long as the tube. Deep, sandy soils along the coast and sandstone slopes in Namaqualand and the West Coast.

**❶ *Geissorhiza imbricata***

J F M A M J J A S O N D

Perennial, 6–25 cm, with narrow, ridged leaves that have the margins and midribs thickened and raised, the uppermost leaf with a swollen, ribbed sheath; bears large white to pale yellow flowers, often flushed red on the outside, with a tube 2–8 mm long. Damp, poorly drained flats in the southwestern Cape.

## *Hesperantha* HESPERANTHA, AANDBLOM

Cormous perennials with *woody corm coats*. Leaves mostly narrow or sword-shaped. Flowers few to many in a spike, spirally arranged and subtended by green, soft-textured bracts, mostly pink or white, rarely lilac, yellow or red, usually *salver-shaped*, with the tepals joined in a short to long tube; the stamens either erect or flexed downwards, the *style dividing at the top of the tube into 3 long, spreading, thread-like branches*. Sub-Saharan Africa, mainly winter-rainfall South Africa: ±80 spp; 27 fynbos spp. The majority of the white-flowered species open only in the evening, when they become highly fragrant, whereas the colourful species open in the day and are mostly unscented.

**❷ *Hesperantha bachmannii***

J F M A M J J A S O N D

Slender perennial, 15–30 cm, with narrow leaves; bears nodding, white flowers with a curved tube 10 mm long and tepals that are bent sharply backwards, opening in the afternoon and sweetly scented. Widespread, usually on clay slopes in renosterveld, from Namaqualand to the Eastern Cape.

**❸ *Hesperantha falcata* Bontrokkie**

J F M A M J J A S O N D

Perennial, 6–30 cm, with sword- or sickle-shaped leaves; bears white (or yellow, only between Caledon and George) flowers that are red to brown on the outside, with a straight tube 4–9 mm long, the yellow form opening in the afternoon but the white form opening in the early evening, becoming fragrant. Widespread on sandstone and shale slopes in the southwestern and southern Cape.

**❹ *Hesperantha radiata***

J F M A M J J A S O N D

Slender perennial, 20–40 cm, with short, very narrow leaves that are often withered at flowering; bears a stiffly erect spike of nodding, white to cream flowers that are red to brown on the outside, with a curved tube 10–18 mm long and tepals that bend backwards, opening in the early evening, becoming fragrant; the bracts have their lower margins joined around the spike axis, and are thus somewhat tubular. Widespread on sandstone, granite and clay soils in fynbos and renosterveld, from Namaqualand to Swaziland.

## *Babiana* BABIANA, BOBBEJAANTJIE

Cormous perennials, often with *hairy stems*. Leaves sword- or wedge-shaped, *pleated and usually hairy*. Flowers in a 2-ranked or spiral spike, subtended by *green, usually hairy bracts with dry tips* (rarely dry and papery), often partially or completely blue, less commonly white, yellow, pink or red, bowl-shaped or 2-lipped, the tepals united into a short or long tube; the stamens either arched together or symmetrically arranged, the style dividing into 3 short branches. Southern Africa, mainly winter-rainfall parts: 86 spp; 50 fynbos spp. The corms are favoured by baboons and porcupines, hence the allusion in the vernacular name *bobbejaantjie*.

## ▶ OVARY DENSELY HAIRY

### ❶ *Babiana fragrans*

| J | F | M | A | M | J | **J** | **A** | S | O | N | D |

Perennial, 7–20 cm, with lance-shaped, thin-textured, soft-haired leaves; bears fragrant, 2-lipped, violet to pale blue flowers with yellow markings on the lower tepals, with a moderately long tube 18–22 mm long; the inner bracts are split into 2 and the ovary is densely hairy. Sandstone and granite slopes along the West Coast.

### ❷ *Babiana rubrocyanea*

| J | F | M | A | M | J | J | **A** | **S** | O | N | D |

**Blue-and-red babiana** Dwarf perennial, 5–15 cm, with stiff, hairy leaves; bears bowl-shaped, deep blue flowers with a red centre, and a tube 15–20 mm long; the inner bracts are split into 2 and the ovary is densely hairy. Granitic sand in renosterveld around Darling.

### ❸ *Babiana stricta*

| J | F | M | A | M | J | J | **A** | **S** | **O** | N | D |

Slender, erect perennial, 10–20 cm, with narrow, stiff, short-haired leaves; bears almost salver-shaped, mauve to violet or white to pale yellow flowers, often with darker markings at the base of the lower tepals, with a tube 8–18 mm long and dark blue or black, arrow-shaped anthers; the inner bracts are split into 2 and the ovary is hairy. Clay soils in renosterveld in the southwestern Cape.

### ❹ *Babiana angustifolia*

| J | F | M | A | M | J | J | **A** | **S** | O | N | D |

Perennial, 10–20 cm, with stiff, short-haired leaves; bears cup-shaped, weakly 2-lipped, dark blue to violet flowers with red or black markings and dark anthers, and with a tube 11–17 mm long that is curved so that the flowers face the bottom of the stem; the inner bracts are split into 2 and the ovary is densely hairy. Damp clay flats and lower slopes in renosterveld along the West Coast.

### ❺ *Babiana odorata*

| J | F | M | A | M | J | **J** | **A** | S | O | N | D |

Perennial to 15 cm with lance-shaped, soft-haired leaves; bears fragrant, 2-lipped, pale yellow flowers with darker markings on the lower tepals and a short tube 10–14 mm long; the inner bracts are split into 2 and the ovary is densely hairy. Damp clay and granitic soils in renosterveld along the West Coast.

### ❻ *Babiana mucronata*

| J | F | M | A | M | J | **J** | **A** | S | O | N | D |

Perennial, 5–15 cm, with lance-shaped, short-haired leaves; bears acrid-scented, 2-lipped, pale blue flowers with yellow markings on the lower tepals, which are conspicuously narrowed at the base, with a tube mostly 12–20 mm long; the inner bracts are split into 2 and the ovary is densely hairy. Rocky sandstone slopes, mainly in the Olifants River valley.

## ▶ OVARY HAIRLESS OR SCARCELY HAIRY

### ❼ *Babiana ambigua*

| J | F | M | A | M | J | J | **A** | **S** | O | N | D |

Dwarf perennial, 5–8 cm, with narrow, soft-haired leaves that are often longer than the stem; bears fragrant, 2-lipped, blue to mauve flowers with white to cream markings on the lower tepals, and with a short tube 10–19 mm long; the inner bracts are split into 2 and the ovary is hairless. Sandy or gravelly flats and lower slopes in the southwestern Cape.

### ❶ *Babiana scabrifolia*

Short perennial, 5–9 cm, with soft-textured, lance-shaped, short-haired leaves that are longer than the stem and twisted or coiled when young; bears sweet-scented, 2-lipped, blue to lilac flowers with yellow and purple markings on the lower tepals, with a tube 12–18 mm long; the inner bracts are split in 2 and the ovary is sparsely hairy. Sandy soils in dry fynbos in the Olifants River valley.

### ❷ *Babiana nana*

Dwarf perennial, 3–10 cm, with soft-textured, soft-haired leaves, often short and broad; bears large, fragrant, 2-lipped, blue or violet flowers with white markings on lower tepals, with a tube 12–17 mm long; the inner bracts are forked at the tip and the ovary is hairless. Sandy coastal flats and dunes in the southwestern Cape.

### ❸ *Babiana tubiflora*

Perennial, 7–15 cm, with narrow, soft-haired leaves that are longer than the stem; bears unscented, tubular, white to cream flowers, sometimes with red markings, with a tube 50–100 mm long; the inner bracts are forked at the tip and the ovary is hairless. Deep, sandy flats and lower slopes, mostly along the coast in the southwestern Cape.

### ❹ *Babiana thunbergii*

**Rooibobbejaantjie, strandlelie**   Robust perennial with short, horizontal branches, 40–70 cm, with stiff, minutely haired leaves; bears strongly 2-lipped, red flowers that face the tip of the spike, with a curved tube 30–40 mm long; the inner bracts are deeply forked and the ovary is hairless. Sandy coastal flats and dunes in Namaqualand and on the West Coast.

### ❺ *Babiana ringens*  Rotstert

Perennial with the main stem sterile and forming a perch and the flowers borne on a short side branch at ground level, 15–40 cm, with narrow, very stiff, hairless or minutely haired leaves; bears strongly 2-lipped, red flowers with a curved tube 30–45 mm long; the inner bracts are forked and the ovary is hairless. Sandy flats, often coastal, in the southwestern Cape.

## *Chasmanthe*   COBRA LILY, PIEMPIEMPIE

Cormous perennials. Leaves in a basal fan, sword-shaped with a raised midrib, soft-textured. Flowers in a 1- or 2-ranked spike, subtended by *small, leathery green bracts with dry tips, orange,* very *unequally 2-lipped* with the tepals joined into a long tube that is very *narrow and usually twisted below* and *cylindrical above;* the stamens arched together beneath the *spoon-shaped dorsal tepal,* the style dividing into 3 short branches. Seeds *globular, almost smooth,* orange or reddish brown. Mainly winter-rainfall South Africa: 3 spp, all fynbos. *Chasmanthe floribunda* is a popular garden plant in Cape Town. The vernacular name is possibly an onomatopoeic rendition of the squeaking sound produced by rubbing the stems together.

### ❻ *Chasmanthe aethiopica*

Perennial, 40–65 cm, with soft-textured leaves; bears several orange flowers in 1 rank in an unbranched spike, the tube flaring abruptly and almost pouched above the twisted lower portion; fruits large and reddish purple within, containing pea-sized, thinly fleshy, orange seeds. Mainly coastal in bush and on forest margins, spreading by runners and often forming large colonies, in the southwestern and Eastern Cape.

**1** *Chasmanthe floribunda*

J F M A M J **J A S** O N D

Robust perennial, 45–100 cm, with soft-textured leaves; bears several to many orange (rarely watery yellow) flowers in 2 ranks in a branched spike, the tube flaring gradually above the almost straight lower portion; fruits small and brown, containing small, hard, reddish-brown seeds. Coastal and inland on sandstone and granite in scrub in the southwestern Cape.

## *Tritoniopsis*  TRITONIOPSIS, RIETPYPIE

Evergreen or deciduous, cormous perennials. Leaves green or dry at flowering, sword-shaped with *more than 1 equally strong main vein* unless very narrow, sometimes narrowed into a wire-like petiole. Flowers in a spirally twisted spike, *subtended by dry, firm-textured or leathery bracts, with the inner bract longer than the outer*, variously coloured and marked, usually 2-lipped, with the tepals joined into a short to long tube; the stamens usually arched together under the upper tepal, the style dividing into 3 short branches. Winter-rainfall South Africa, mainly on sandstone soils and flowering best after fire: 24 spp, all fynbos.

▸ **FLORAL TUBE LESS THAN 20 MM LONG**

**2** *Tritoniopsis parviflora*

J **F M A M J J A S** O **N D**

**Pepersouskousie** Perennial, 15–40 cm, with narrow, 1- or 2-veined leaves; bears pepper-scented, strongly 2-lipped, yellow and maroon flowers with a short tube ±4 mm long. Rocky sandstone slopes in the southwestern Cape, flowering only after fire.

**3** *Tritoniopsis ramosa*

J F M **A M J J A** S O N D

Slender, branched perennial, 15–50 cm, with narrow, 1–3-veined leaves; bears a loose spike of pink flowers with very narrow tepals marked with red, with a tube 8–20 mm long; the fruits are small with pale windows. Sandstone slopes in the southwestern and southern Cape, flowering mostly after fire.

**4** *Tritoniopsis dodii*

J **F M A M J J A** S O N D

Slender perennial, 15–50 cm, with narrow, 1–3-veined leaves; bears mostly a short, dense spike of greyish pink flowers with very narrow tepals marked with red, with a tube 5–8 mm long. Sandstone slopes in the extreme southwestern Cape.

**5** *Tritoniopsis lata*

J F **M A M J J A** S O N D

Perennial, 25–50 cm, with narrow, 1–3-veined leaves; bears pink flowers with the upper tepal noticeably longer and broader, 7–12 mm wide, with a tube 7–10 mm long. Sandstone slopes in seasonal seeps or drainage lines in the extreme southwestern Cape.

▸ **FLORAL TUBE MORE THAN 20 MM LONG**

**6** *Tritoniopsis antholyza*  **Karkarblom**

J **F M A M J J A** S O **N D**

Robust perennial to 90 cm, with 3–6-veined, lance-shaped leaves; bears tubular, yellowish pink to red flowers with a tube 25–30 mm long. Rocky sandstone slopes in the southwestern and southern Cape.

### ① *Tritoniopsis caffra*

J F M A M J J A **S O N D**

Perennial, 20–80 cm, with 2–4-veined, sword-shaped leaves; bears very asymmetrical red flowers with the upper tepal long and spoon-shaped with a tube 20–30 mm long. Sandstone slopes in the southern and Eastern Cape.

### ② *Tritoniopsis burchellii*

J **F M A** M J J A S O N D

Stiffly erect perennial, 50–90 cm, with 3-veined, lance-shaped basal leaves that are narrowed below into a petiole and brown stem leaves that are drawn into long cusps; bears tubular, scarlet flowers with a tube 30–40 mm long. Rocky sandstone slopes in the southwestern Cape.

### ③ *Tritoniopsis triticea*  Rooibergpypie

J F M **A** M J J A S O N D

Stiffly erect perennial, 50–90 cm, with 3-veined, lance-shaped basal leaves that are narrowed below into a petiole and brown stem leaves that are drawn into long cusps; bears tubular, scarlet flowers with small tepals and a tube 25–30 mm. Rocky granite and sandstone slopes in the southwestern and southern Cape.

### ④ *Tritoniopsis nervosa*

J **F M A M J J A** S O N **D**

Erect perennial, 50–100 cm, with 2- or 3-veined, sword-shaped leaves; bears fragrant, long-tubed, 2-lipped, pale yellow to white flowers with a slender tube 30–40 mm long. Rocky mountain slopes in the Cedarberg and Ceres mountains.

## *Melaspherula*   FAIRY BELLS, BAARDMANNETJIE

Cormous perennial with a slender, *wiry, often branched stem* and a *bell-shaped corm with a woody coat*. Leaves soft-textured and sword-shaped. Flowers in loose spikes, *subtended by short, blunt, green bracts*, pale yellow to cream coloured with dark streaks on the lower tepals, 2-lipped with the tepals tapering into slender points and joined into a very short tube; the stamens are arched together beneath the upper tepal and the style divides into 3 short branches. *Fruits top-shaped* and 3-winged. Sheltered places throughout winter-rainfall southern Africa: 1 sp.

### ⑤ *Melaspherula ramosa*

J F M A M J **J A S** O N D

Diffusely branching perennial, 30–60 cm, with soft-textured leaves; bears small, sour-smelling, cream to pale yellow flowers in a loose, wiry spike with the lower tepals streaked with red-brown in the midline. Mostly sheltered sites on sandstone or limestone slopes from southern Namibia to the Eastern Cape.

## *Gladiolus*   GLADIOLUS, PYPIE

Cormous perennials. Leaves sword-shaped, sometimes with the margins and midrib variously thickened or raised, or round in cross-section and longitudinally grooved, narrow or broad, rarely ribbed, sometimes hairy. Flowers few to many in a 1- (rarely 2-) ranked spike, subtended by *soft-textured green bracts*, variously coloured and marked, sometimes scented, *mostly 2-lipped* but sometimes salver-shaped, with the tepals joined into a short to long tube; the stamens mostly arched together under the upper tepal, rarely erect; the style dividing into 3 short branches, *the seeds flattened, with a broad, papery wing*. Africa and Madagascar into Eurasia, mainly southern Africa: ±250 spp; ±105 fynbos spp. Hybrids between a few of the summer-rainfall species are widely grown as cut-flowers.

139

### ▶ LEAVES REDUCED, BRACT-LIKE AND CLASPING THE STEM, WITHOUT BLADES

**❶ *Gladiolus martleyi***    J **F M A M** J J A S O N D

Slender perennial, 20–35 cm, with reduced leaves sheathing the stem, the true foliage leaves dry at flowering, 1 or 2 and needle-like with 4 longitudinal grooves; bears several fragrant, 2-lipped, white to mauve flowers with red and yellow markings on the lower tepals, with a short tube 10–12 mm long. Sandy and rocky flats and lower slopes in the southwestern Cape.

**❷ *Gladiolus brevifolius***   Herfspypie    J F **M A M** J J A S O N D

Slender perennial, 15–50 cm, with reduced leaves sheathing the stem, the lowermost often purple, the true foliage leaves dry at flowering, 1–3, narrowly sword-shaped and hairy; bears several unscented, 2-lipped, pink to grey flowers with yellow and red markings on the lower tepals, with a short tube 11–13 mm long. Stony sandstone and shale slopes in the southwestern Cape.

**❸ *Gladiolus monticola***   Bergpypie    **J F** M A M J J A S O N **D**

Slender perennial, 30–45 cm, with reduced leaves sheathing the stem, the lowermost often purple, the true foliage leaves dry at flowering, 1–3, narrowly sword-shaped and hairy; bears several unscented, long-tubed, pale pink or apricot flowers with red markings on the lower tepals, with a tube 22–30 mm long. Rocky sandstone slopes on the Cape Peninsula.

**❹ *Gladiolus carmineus***   Cliff gladiolus    J **F M A** M J J A S O N D

Perennial to 35 cm with reduced leaves sheathing the stem, rarely with a short, sword-shaped blade; bears a few large, funnel-shaped, deep pink flowers with white streaks on the lower tepals, with a tube 30–35 mm long. Coastal sandstone cliffs and rocks around Hermanus.

### ▶ LEAVES HAIRY, SWORD-SHAPED

**❺ *Gladiolus hirsutus***   Lapmuis    J F M A **M J J A S** O N D

Perennial, 30–60 cm, with hairy, often short, sword-shaped leaves and a hairy stem; bears mostly unscented, 2-lipped, pink to purple or white flowers streaked with red on the lower tepals, with a tube usually 15–25 mm long. Rocky sandstone slopes, flowering best after a fire, in the southwestern Cape.

**❻ *Gladiolus caryophyllaceus***    J F M A M J J **A S** O N D

**Sandpypie** Robust perennial, 18–75 cm, with hairy, sword-shaped leaves that have thickened, often reddish margins and a hairy stem; bears large, fragrant, funnel-shaped, pink to mauve flowers streaked and speckled with red, with a tube 30–40 mm long. Sandy flats and slopes, usually growing in clumps of restios, in Namaqualand, the West Coast and the Swartberg.

**❼ *Gladiolus bonaspei***   Vlamme    J F M **A M J J A** S O N D

Slender perennial, 30–50 cm, with hairy, rather short, narrowly sword-shaped leaves and a hairy stem; bears few trumpet-shaped, orange (rarely yellow) flowers with rounded tepals, with a cylindrical tube 35–45 mm long that is narrowed in the lower part. Sandy flats and lower slopes in the southern Cape Peninsula.

▶ **LEAVES HAIRLESS AND SWORD-SHAPED OR NARROW AND ±FLAT**

**1** *Gladiolus carinatus* **Blou Afrikaner** | J | F | M | A | M | J | J | **A** | **S** | O | N | D |
Perennial, 30–60 cm, with base of stem purple and mottled white and narrow leaves with thickened midrib; bears fragrant, 2-lipped, blue or yellow, occasionally pink, flowers marked with yellow and blue on lower tepals, with a short tube 6–10 mm long. Deep coastal sands, lower slopes from Namaqualand to the southern Cape.

**2** *Gladiolus rogersii* **Riversdale bell** | J | F | M | A | **M** | **J** | **J** | **A** | **S** | **O** | N | D |
Slender perennial, 30–60 cm, with narrow, leathery, almost thread-like leaves without strongly thickened margins; bears fragrant, bell-like, blue to purple flowers with yellow or white markings on the lower tepals, with a tube 12–19 mm long. Sandstone and limestone flats and slopes to 1 000 m in the southern Cape.

**3** *Gladiolus venustus* **Perskalkoentjie** | J | F | M | A | M | J | **J** | **A** | **S** | O | N | D |
Perennial, 20–60 cm, with narrow, grass-like leaves; bears fragrant, 2-lipped, pink to purple flowers with greenish tips to the lower tepals, which are strongly pinched at the base and sharply flexed downwards, with a tube 12–17 mm long. Clay and sandstone slopes in the interior southwestern Cape.

**4** *Gladiolus orchidiflorus* | J | F | M | A | M | J | J | **A** | **S** | **O** | N | D |
**Groenkalkoentjie** Perennial, 30–80 cm, with narrow, often grass-like leaves; bears fragrant, strongly 2-lipped, greenish to purple flowers, with the upper tepal narrow and strongly arched and the lower tepals with yellowish markings tipped with purple, with a short tube 9–14 mm long. Clay and sandstone soils, widespread in western South Africa.

**5** *Gladiolus grandiflorus* | J | F | M | A | M | J | J | A | **S** | O | N | D |
Stout perennial, 25–50 cm, with leathery, sword-shaped leaves; bears funnel-shaped, cream to greenish flowers, sometimes with a darker median streak on the lower or all the tepals, with a tube 25–50 mm long. Clay slopes in renosterveld in the southern Cape. *Gladiolus floribundus* has a tube 40–70 mm long.

**6** *Gladiolus carneus* | J | F | M | A | M | J | J | A | S | **O** | **N** | **D** |
**White Afrikaner, painted lady** Perennial, 25–60 cm, with narrowly sword-shaped leaves; bears funnel-shaped, pink or white flowers, often with dark pink markings on the lower tepals, with a tube 20–40 mm long that is about as long as the upper tepal. Sandstone slopes, often in damp sites in the southwestern and southern Cape.

**7** *Gladiolus pappei* | J | F | M | A | M | J | J | A | S | **O** | **N** | D |
Slender perennial, 20–35 cm with narrow leaves; bears 1–3, long-tubed, funnel-shaped, dark pink flowers with red and white markings on the lower tepals, with a tube 30–35 mm long. Marshes on sandstone slopes, mostly on the Cape Peninsula, flowering after fire.

**8** *Gladiolus angustus* | J | F | M | A | M | J | J | A | S | **O** | **N** | D |
Robust perennial, 60–120 cm, with narrowly sword-shaped leaves; bears long-tubed, cream-coloured flowers that have red, arrow-shaped markings on the lower tepals, with a slender tube 50–110 mm long that is much longer than the tepals. Streams and marshes on sandstone soils, mainly along the West Coast.

**142** IRIS FAMILY

**1** *Gladiolus undulatus* **Vleipypie**   J F M A M J J A S O N D

Robust perennial, 30–150 cm, with sword-shaped leaves; bears long-tubed, greenish-white to cream flowers with long, tapering, often crinkly tepals, the lower usually with red, lozenge-shaped markings, with a slender tube 50–75 mm long that is slightly longer than the tepals. Montane marshes and streamsides on sandstone and granite slopes in the Kamiesberg and southwestern Cape.

**2** *Gladiolus cardinalis* **New year lily**   J F M A M J J A S O N D

Perennial, 60–120 cm, with narrowly sword-shaped leaves and an inclined or drooping stem; bears several large, funnel-shaped red flowers with white splashes on the lower tepals, with a tube 30–40 mm long. Waterfalls and wet cliffs in the extreme southwestern Cape.

**3** *Gladiolus cunonius* **Lepelblom**   J F M A M J J A S O N D

Perennial, 20–45 cm, with soft-textured, narrowly sword-shaped leaves; bears several strongly asymmetrical, tubular, bright red flowers with the upper tepal long and spoon-shaped and the lower 3 tepals minute and greenish, with a cylindrical tube 12–15 mm long that is narrowed below. Coastal in sandy soils in the southwestern and southern Cape.

**4** *Gladiolus priorii*   J F M A M J J A S O N D

Slender perennial, 30–40 cm, with rather short, slender leaves and a zigzag stem; bears few trumpet-shaped, dull red flowers with lance-shaped tepals, with a cylindrical tube 40–45 mm long that is narrowed in the lower part. Sandstone and granite slopes along the coast in the southwestern Cape.

**5** *Gladiolus maculatus*   J F M A M J J A S O N D

**Brown Afrikaner**   Slender perennial, 30–60 cm, with narrow, leathery, short-bladed leaves; bears fragrant, long-tubed, funnel-shaped, brownish flowers with dark speckling, with a tube 25–45 mm long. Mainly clay slopes in renosterveld in the southwestern and Eastern Cape.

▶ **LEAVES X- OR H-SHAPED IN CROSS-SECTION, OR RIBBED, OR NEEDLE-LIKE WITH HEAVILY THICKENED MARGINS**

**6** *Gladiolus inflatus*   J F M A M J J A S O N D

**Tulbagh bell, Blouklokkie**   Slender perennial, 25–60 cm, the lowermost leaf needle-like with 4 longitudinal grooves; bears nodding, unscented, bell- or funnel-shaped, mauve, pink or white flowers with red markings on the lower tepals, with a curved tube 12–25(30) mm long. Rocky sandstone slopes in the southwestern Cape.

**7** *Gladiolus patersoniae* **Karoo bell**   J F M A M J J A S O N D

Slender perennial, 30–50 cm, the lowermost leaf needle-like with 4 longitudinal grooves; bears nodding, fragrant, bell-like, blue to pearly grey flowers with yellow markings on the lower tepals, with a short, sharply bent tube 10–12 mm long. Rocky sandstone slopes in the southern Cape and Little Karoo.

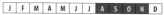

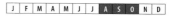

### ❶ *Gladiolus bullatus*  Caledon bell

`J F M A M J J A S O N D`

Slender perennial, 50–80 cm, with narrow, short-bladed leaves; bears 1 or 2 large, bell-like blue flowers marked with yellow on the lower tepals, with a short, bent tube 10–16 mm long and tapering, prominently ribbed bracts. Sandstone slopes in fynbos around Hermanus and Bredasdorp.

### ❷ *Gladiolus trichonemifolius*

`J F M A M J J A S O N D`

**Geelkalkoentjie**  Slender perennial, 10–25 cm, with needle-like leaves that have 4 longitudinal grooves; bears funnel-shaped, often fragrant, yellow to whitish flowers with dark streaks on the lower tepals or occasionally with a dark centre, with a tube 16–20 mm long. Seasonally wet, sandy flats in the southwestern Cape.

### ❸ *Gladiolus debilis*  Little painted lady

`J F M A M J J A S O N D`

Slender perennial, 35–50 cm, with narrow, almost thread-like leaves that have thickened margins and midrib; bears long-tubed, white flowers with widely spreading tepals, the lower 3 spotted or blotched with red markings, with a cylindrical tube 15–22 mm long and short, ridged bracts. Rocky sandstone slopes in the extreme southwestern Cape.

### ❹ *Gladiolus gracilis*  Bloupypie

`J F M A M J J A S O N D`

Sender perennial, 30–60 cm, with a flexed stem and stiff, narrow leaves that are H-shaped in cross-section with the winged margins curved over; bears fragrant, 2-lipped, blue to grey or occasionally pink or yellow flowers with dark streaks on the lower tepals, with a tube 12–18 mm long. Mostly clay slopes or sometimes on granite, rarely in sand, in the southwestern Cape.

### ❺ *Gladiolus caeruleus*  Saldanha pypie

`J F M A M J J A S O N D`

Perennial, 40–60 cm, with rather soft-textured leaves that are H-shaped in cross-section with winged margins; bears fragrant, 2-lipped, pale blue flowers with dark spotting on the lower tepals, with a tube ±15 mm long. Limestone outcrops and chalky sands around Saldanha Bay.

### ❻ *Gladiolus hyalinus*

`J F M A M J J A S O N D`

**Small brown Afrikaner**  Slender perennial, 25–50 cm, with the lowermost leaf long and slender with thickened margins and midrib; bears long-tubed, dull brownish to cream flowers with dark speckles, the upper tepal usually with transparent edges, with a tube 25–35 mm long. Shale, granite and sandstone slopes in fynbos and renosterveld, in Namaqualand and the southwestern Cape.

### ❼ *Gladiolus liliaceus*

`J F M A M J J A S O N D`

**Large brown Afrikaner, ribbokblom**  Perennial, 35–70 cm, with the lowermost leaf long and narrow, with thickened margins and midrib; bears long-tubed, funnel-shaped, brown to russet or beige flowers that turn mauve in the evening and become strongly clove-scented, with a tube 40–55 mm long and long, tapering bracts drawn into a slender point. Clay slopes, mainly in renosterveld in the southwestern and southern Cape.

### ① *Gladiolus tristis*

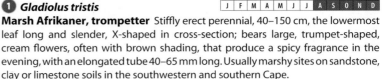

J | F | M | A | M | J | J | A | S | O | N | D

**Marsh Afrikaner, trompetter** Stiffly erect perennial, 40–150 cm, the lowermost leaf long and slender, X-shaped in cross-section; bears large, trumpet-shaped, cream flowers, often with brown shading, that produce a spicy fragrance in the evening, with an elongated tube 40–65 mm long. Usually marshy sites on sandstone, clay or limestone soils in the southwestern and southern Cape.

### ② *Gladiolus watsonius*  **Rooi Afrikaner**

J | F | M | A | M | J | J | A | S | O | N | D

Stiffly erect perennial, 30–50 cm, with the lowermost leaf narrow and H-shaped in cross-section, with a heavily thickened midrib and margins; bears trumpet-shaped, red to orange flowers, with a cylindrical tube 45–55 mm long that is narrowed in the lower part. Clay and granite slopes in renosterveld in the southwestern Cape.

### ③ *Gladiolus alatus*  **Kalkoentjie**

J | F | M | A | M | J | J | A | S | O | N | D

Compact perennial, 8–25 cm, with longitudinally ribbed, sickle-shaped leaves and a ridged or winged stem; bears fragrant, strongly 2-lipped, orange flowers with the upper tepal held upright and the lower 3 tepals greenish yellow towards the base, with a short tube 10–14 mm long. Mostly sandy flats, slopes and plateaus in the southwestern Cape. One of 3 similar fynbos species: *Gladiolus pulcherrimus* has smooth leaves and an erect dorsal tepal; *G. speciosus* has smooth leaves and an arched dorsal tepal, and produces small corms on long, thread-like stolons.

### ④ *Gladiolus meliusculus*

J | F | M | A | M | J | J | A | S | O | N | D

**Pienkkalkoentjie** Stout perennial, 12–25 cm, with sickle-shaped, strongly ribbed leaves and a ridged stem; bears fragrant, strongly 2-lipped, pink to orange flowers with the upper tepal held upright and the lower tepals with black and greenish markings at the base, with a short tube ±11 mm long. Damp sandstone and granite slopes and flats along the West Coast.

### ⑤ *Gladiolus virescens*

J | F | M | A | M | J | J | A | S | O | N | D

Perennial, 10–25 cm, with narrow, strongly ribbed or quill-like leaves; bears very fragrant, strongly 2-lipped, yellow to pink flowers with darker feathering and an upright upper tepal, with a short tube 9–15 mm long. Sandstone or clay slopes in the southwestern and southern Cape.

### ⑥ *Gladiolus watermeyeri*

J | F | M | A | M | J | J | A | S | O | N | D

**Soetkalkoentjie** Perennial, 10–30 cm, with narrow, strongly ribbed leaves; bears highly fragrant, strongly 2-lipped, pearly grey flowers with chocolate brown feathering and yellowish-green lower tepals, with the upper tepal arched and hooded and with a tube 14–16 mm long. Sandstone rock sheets and slopes around Nieuwoudtville and the northern Cedarberg.

# ORCHIDACEAE         Orchid family

▶ LIP DIVIDED OR FRINGED, AND SPURRED; ANTHER ERECT

## *Bonatea*   WOOD ORCHID

Tuberous perennials. Leaves oblong or elliptical, often crowded towards the base and sometimes withered at flowering. Flowers few to many in a dense or loose spike, green and white, the upper 3 tepals cohering to form a hood, the *petals deeply forked* and the *lip deeply 3-lobed and spurred* with a *small tooth or peg in the mouth of the spur; the stigmas on 2 slender stalks joined to the lip, with a hood-like rostellum above.* Africa and Arabia, mainly subtropical: 20 spp; 2 fynbos spp.

**① *Bonatea speciosa***     J F M A M J J A S O N D

**Green wood orchid, Oktoberlelie** Robust perennial to 1 m with oblong leaves; bears green and white flowers in a cylindrical spike, highly fragrant at night, the petals deeply forked and the lip with a spur 25–47 mm long. Coastal scrub and forest margins from the Cape Peninsula to tropical Africa.

## *Bartholina*   SPIDER ORCHID

Small, tuberous perennials with *hairy stems.* Leaf *1, hairy,* rounded and *pressed against the ground.* Flowers *large, solitary,* white to mauve, with a *deeply fringed lip bearing a slender spur at the base.* Winter-rainfall southern Africa: 2 spp, both fynbos.

**② *Bartholina burmanniana***     J F M A M J J A S O N D

Slender perennial to 20 cm with a hairy stem and single, rounded, hairy leaf pressed to the ground; bears a solitary white flower with the lip deeply divided into thread-like, pointed lobes. Clay slopes and flats, from the southwestern to Eastern Cape, flowering mostly after fire. *Bartholina etheliae* has lip lobes with spoon-shaped tips.

## *Holothrix*   THREAD ORCHID, TRYPHIA

Small, tuberous perennials, mostly with *hairy stems.* Leaves *2, in a basal pair,* rounded and *pressed against the ground.* Flowers small, many, usually in a *1-sided spike,* white or greenish, with a *deeply lobed or fringed lip bearing a slender spur at the base.* Africa, Arabia and Madagascar, mainly southern Africa: ±55 spp; 13 fynbos spp. The vernacular name *tryphia* is an older generic name for the plants.

**③ *Holothrix villosa***     J F M A M J J A S O N D

Slender perennial to 36 cm with a silky-haired stem and leaves; bears small, green flowers, with the lip divided into 3–5 lobes. Sandstone and granite slopes and pavements from Namaqualand to the Eastern Cape.

**④ *Holothrix aspera***     J F M A M J J A S O N D

Slender perennial to 25 cm with a sparsely haired stem but hairless leaves; bears white flowers streaked with purple and with the lip divided into 7 unequal, rounded lobes. Sandy slopes or rock pavements in Namaqualand and the south-western Cape.

▶ LIP NOT DIVIDED NOR SPURRED; ANTHER HORIZONTAL OR PENDENT
▶ ▶ PETALS JOINED TO THE MARGINS OF THE MIDDLE SEPAL TO FORM A HOOD

## *Ceratandra* SHIELD ORCHID

Tuberous perennials with clusters of thickened, furry roots. Leaves numerous, *narrow and scattered on the stem*, sometimes with an additional basal cluster of narrow leaves. Flowers many in a loose or dense spike, yellow or pink and white, the median sepal united with the petals and mostly *bent back*, the *lip united to the column and anchor- or kidney-shaped*. Western and Eastern Cape, mainly winter rainfall: 6 spp, all fynbos.

**❶ *Ceratandra atrata***

| J | F | M | A | M | J | J | A | S | O | N | D |

Perennial to 35 cm with narrow leaves; bears many greenish-yellow flowers in a loose spike, with an anchor-shaped lip and with horn-like rostellum arms 7–8 mm long. Marshes or rock flushes and streambanks in the southwestern and southern Cape, flowering after fire.

**❷ *Ceratandra grandiflora***

| J | F | M | A | M | J | J | A | S | O | N | D |

Perennial to 35 cm with narrow leaves; bears many orange-yellow flowers in a rounded or flat-topped raceme, with a spoon- or spade-shaped lip and with horn-like rostellum arms ±6 mm long. Damp sandstone flats along the southern Cape coast, flowering after fire.

## *Corycium* MONKSHOOD ORCHID

Tuberous perennials. Leaves *numerous*, narrow and scattered up the stem but clustered towards the base. Flowers many in a dense spike, yellow to greenish or maroon to brown, with the *3 upper tepals cohering to form a deep hood, the lateral sepals almost joined together* and *the lip united to the column and bearing a shield-shaped appendage that spreads over the anther*. East tropical and southern Africa, mainly Western Cape: 14 spp; 10 fynbos spp.

**❸ *Corycium crispum***

| J | F | M | A | M | J | J | A | S | O | N | D |

Perennial to 40 cm with the leaves crinkly along the margins; bears numerous yellow flowers with a green lip appendage, the lateral sepals joined for three-quarters of their length and the lip appendage with 2 down-flexed lobes. Sandy flats in Namaqualand and the southwestern Cape.

**❹ *Corycium orobanchoides***

| J | F | M | A | M | J | J | A | S | O | N | D |

Perennial to 42 cm with the lower leaves barred with red towards the base; bears numerous yellow-green flowers with purple or black tips to the petals, the lateral sepals almost completely joined and the lip appendage shield-like with long, horizontal lobes pointing backwards. Sandy flats in the southwestern Cape.

## *Pterygodium* BONNET ORCHID, MOEDERKAPPIE

Tuberous perennials. Leaves *few*, elliptical to lance-shaped. Flowers mostly in a loose spike, yellow to cream or greenish, the *upper 3 tepals cohering to form a shallow hood, with the lip united to the column at the base and with a tall, conical or funnel-shaped appendage*. East and southern Africa, mainly winter rainfall: 18 spp; 13 fynbos spp.

### ❶ *Pterygodium hallii*

J F M A M J J A S O N D

Robust tuberous perennial to 55 cm with overlapping, lance-shaped leaves up the stem; bears many pale-green flowers in a dense spike with the lip uppermost and with an oval-oblong appendage. Short, dry scrub in Namaqualand and the West Coast as far south as Langebaan. *Pterygodium inversum* from coastal regions in the southwestern Cape has a deeply 2-lobed lip appendage.

### ❷ *Pterygodium alatum*

J F M A M J J A S O N D

Perennial to 20 cm with narrowly elliptical leaves clustered towards the base; bears 2 to many, pale greenish-yellow flowers, the lip with 2 broad spreading side-lobes on either side of a small, pointed midlobe and with a spoon-shaped appendage. Sandy flats and slopes in the southwestern and southern Cape.

### ❸ *Pterygodium catholicum*

J F M A M J J A S O N D

**Cowled friar** Perennial to 35 cm with oblong leaves; bears a few yellowish-green flowers, often flushed reddish, in a moderately loose spike with the lip appendage minutely toothed at the tip. Clay vleis in renosterveld in the southwestern and southern Cape, flowering mostly after fire.

## *Disperis* WITCH ORCHID, MOEDERKAPPIE

Small, tuberous perennials, sometimes with hairy stems. Leaves few, lance- to heart-shaped. Flowers 1 to several in a loose spike, yellow to greenish or pink to purple, with the upper 3 tepals cohering to form a deep hood, *the lateral sepals each with a conical or club-shaped spur, the lip united to the column at the base and flexed back over it, often concave and bearing a slender, often hairy, tail-like appendage.* Sub-Saharan Africa and Old World tropics: ±84 spp; 12 fynbos spp.

### ❹ *Disperis circumflexa*

J F M A M J J A S O N D

Perennial to 20 cm with 2 narrowly lance-shaped leaves; bears 2–10 greenish and white flowers with a horizontal, boat-shaped lip. Sand, clay or granite soils in Namaqualand and the southwestern Cape.

### ❺ *Disperis capensis*

J F M A M J J A S O N D

Perennial with a soft-haired stem to 50 cm with 2 lance-shaped leaves; bears a solitary green and magenta or cream flower with conspicuously tailed sepals and a narrow lip that is curled forwards at the tip. Sandstone seeps in the southwestern and Eastern Cape.

### ❻ *Disperis villosa*

J F M A M J J A S O N D

Small perennial with a short-haired stem to 10 cm (rarely more) with 2 elliptical leaves, the lower petiolate; bears 1–4 yellowish-green flowers with a slipper-shaped lip. Clay and granite slopes in the southwestern Cape.

▶ ▶ PETALS NOT JOINED TO THE MIDDLE SEPAL (ALTHOUGH SOMETIMES ENCLOSED WITHIN IT)

## *Satyrium*  SATYR ORCHID, TREWWA

Tuberous perennials. Leaves scattered along the stem and sheathing it or crowded towards the base, sometimes pressed to the ground. Flowers in a dense, sometimes head-like raceme, *often with leafy, down-flexed bracts*, mostly white to greenish or pink, the *ovary not twisted*, the *lip uppermost and hooded, with 2 long or short spurs, the remaining tepals smaller and roughly similar, the column long and slender*. Africa and Madagascar, extending into Asia, mainly southern Africa: ±88 spp; 29 fynbos spp.

### ▶ FLORAL SPURS SHORTER THAN THE OVARY

**①** *Satyrium pumilum*  **Aasblom**

J F M A M J J A **S O** N D

Dwarf, mostly stemless perennial to 5 cm with 3–5 lance-shaped leaves; bears a cluster of 2–4 relatively large flowers that are dull green outside, the lip boldly marked with transverse bars of dark maroon, the sepals and petals joined for most of their length and the lip with 2 short, sac-like spurs. Damp flats and rock pavements or ledges in Namaqualand and the southwestern Cape.

**②** *Satyrium coriifolium*  **Rooitrewwa**

J F M A M J J **A S O** N D

Stout perennial to 80 cm with 2–4 elliptical to oval leaves clustered at the base of the stem, leathery in texture and purple-spotted towards the base; bears several bright yellow to orange flowers in a dense spike with bracts sharply down-flexed, the lip crested and with slender spurs 9–12 mm long that are shorter than the ovary. Moist clay and sand in the southwestern and southern Cape.

**③** *Satyrium erectum*

J F M A M J **J A S O** N D

Perennial to 60 cm with 2 fleshy, oval or elliptical leaves pressed to the ground; bears many fragrant, pale to deep pink flowers with darker tinges and spots on the petals in a dense spike with the bracts sharply down-flexed, the lip with slender spurs 5–11 mm long that are shorter than the ovary. Dry sandstone and clay flats from Namaqualand to the southern Cape.

**④** *Satyrium ligulatum*

J F M A M J J A **S O N** D

Perennial to 55 cm with 1–4 oval to narrowly oval leaves that are clustered towards the base of the stem; bears yellowish green to dull creamy white flowers in a narrow spike with the bracts sharply down-flexed, the sepals erect alongside the lip and tapering with dry, brownish tips, the lip sac-like with a narrow mouth and slender spurs 5–10 mm long that are shorter than the ovary. Scrub, forest and grassland from Namaqualand to KwaZulu-Natal.

### ▶ FLORAL SPURS LONGER THAN THE OVARY

**⑤** *Satyrium carneum*  **Rooikappie**

J F M A M J J A **S O** N D

Stout perennial to 80 cm with 2–4 thick and fleshy leaves, the lowest 2 somewhat spreading; bears many pale pink to rose or sometimes white flowers in a dense spike with the bracts sharply down-flexed, the lip somewhat keeled and with slender spurs 14–20 mm long that are longer than the ovary. Sandy, coastal flats and slopes in the southwestern and southern Cape.

**① _Satyrium humile_**

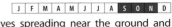

Slender perennial to 40 cm with 2 oval leaves spreading near the ground and conspicuous tubular sheaths on the stem; bears many cream flowers tinged green, pink or brownish in a dense spike with the bracts sharply down-flexed, the lip with slender, diverging or spreading spurs 12–26 mm long that are longer than the ovary. Stony sandstone slopes in the southwestern and southern Cape, flowering especially after fire. _Satyrium bicorne_ has descending spurs and a small, beak-like lip apex.

**② _Satyrium odorum_ Ruiktrewwa**

Perennial to 55 cm with 2–6 oval to narrowly oval leaves; bears few to many yellowish-green flowers, sometimes with a purple tinge, in a moderately dense spike, highly fragrant at night, the lip sac-like with a narrow entrance and with slender spurs 13–18 mm long that are longer than the ovary. Rocky slopes in scrub in the southwestern and southern Cape.

## _Disa_ DISA

Tuberous perennials. Leaves scattered up the stem or basal, sometimes on a separate shoot, green or dry at flowering. Flowers in a loose or dense, cylindrical or flat-topped spike, variously coloured, with the _upper, or median, sepal hooded and bearing a spur, the petals usually smaller and enclosed within the dorsal sepal_, the lip small or large, sometimes fringed. Africa and the Arabian Peninsula, mainly southern Africa; now includes the species previously placed in _Herschelia_, _Monadenia_ and _Schizodium_: ±170 spp; ±100 fynbos spp.

▶ **FLORAL SPUR UP TO 10 MM LONG**

**③ _Disa atricapilla_**

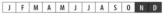

Perennial to 30 cm with narrow leaves in a basal tuft; bears bicoloured flowers in a flat-topped cluster, the median sepal white, with an obsolete spur, the lateral sepals sharply keeled and red or black and white and the petals and lip maroon. Seeps and moist sandstone slopes in the southwestern Cape, flowering mostly after fire.

**④ _Disa bivalvata_**

Perennial to 30 cm with narrow leaves in a basal tuft; bears bicoloured flowers in a flat-topped cluster, the sepals white, with an obsolete spur, and the petals and lip maroon. Moist sandstone slopes and seeps in the southwestern and southern Cape, flowering mostly after fire.

**⑤ _Disa bracteata_**

(=_Monadenia bracteata_) Erect perennial to 30 cm with leafy stems; bears numerous small, greenish flowers tinged with maroon in a dense spike, the spur pendent and 3–4.5 mm long, and both pollen masses attached to a single gland. Coastal fynbos, especially along roadsides and other disturbed places, from the southwestern to the Eastern Cape.

**⑥ _Disa racemosa_ Vlei disa**

Slender perennial to 1 m with narrow leaves in a basal tuft; bears a few pale pink flowers with darker veins in a loose spike, the median sepal dish-shaped with an obsolete spur. Sandstone seeps and marshes from the southwestern to the Eastern Cape, flowering mainly after fire.

159

### ❶ *Disa tenuifolia*

J | **F** | M | A | M | J | J | A | S | **O** | N | **D**

Slender perennial to 30 cm with narrow, grass-like leaves in a basal tuft and broader stem leaves; bears a few bright yellow flowers in a loose spike, the dorsal sepal with an obsolete spur. Mountain seeps in the southwestern Cape, flowering mostly after fire.

### ❷ *Disa tripetaloides*

J | F | M | A | M | J | J | A | S | **O** | **N** | D

Slender perennial to 60 cm with narrowly lance-shaped leaves in a basal tuft; bears a few white to pink flowers in a loose spike, the dorsal sepal with a conical to cylindrical spur 2–3 mm long. Stream banks and mountain seeps in the southwestern and southern Cape, and southern KwaZulu-Natal.

### ❸ *Disa graminifolia*  Blue disa

J | **F** | **M** | A | M | J | J | A | S | O | N | D

(=*Herschelia graminifolia*) Slender perennial to 60 cm with a basal tuft of grass-like leaves that are dry at flowering; bears a few blue to violet flowers in a loose spike, the tips of the petals lime green and the lip elliptical, flat and mostly purple, the spur club-shaped and 2–4 mm long. Sandstone mountains among rocks in the southwestern and southern Cape. *Disa purpurascens* has a tapering spur and the margins of the lip are curved upwards.

### ❹ *Disa lugens*  Green-bearded disa

J | F | M | A | M | J | J | A | **S** | **O** | **N** | D

(=*Herschelia lugens*) Slender perennial to 60 cm with a basal tuft of grass-like leaves that are dry at flowering; bears a few greenish-cream or sometimes almost black flowers with mauve lateral sepals, the lip deeply fringed and green to grey-green and the spur cylindrical and 1–5 mm long. Sandy soils from the southwestern to the Eastern Cape.

### ❺ *Disa spathulata*

J | F | M | A | M | J | J | A | **S** | **O** | N | D

(=*Herschelia spathulata*) **Oupa-pyp, begging hand** Slender perennial to 30 cm with a basal tuft of narrow leaves that are dry at flowering; bears a few maroon to pale lime or green and blue flowers with a long, stalked lip that is arrow-shaped or forked at the tip, the spur club-shaped and 1.5–3 mm long. Seasonally wet sandstone and shale, mainly in the southwestern and southern Cape.

### ❻ *Disa flexuosa*  Fried egg orchid

J | F | M | A | M | J | J | A | **S** | **O** | N | D

(=*Schizodium flexuosum*) Slender perennial to 30 cm, with the leaves clustered at the base of the wiry, flexed stem; bears a few white flowers with bright yellow petals and lip spotted with black, the oval sepals 7–11 mm long and the spur curved upwards and 2–4 mm long. Seasonally moist, sandy flats in the southwestern Cape.

### ❼ *Disa obliqua*

J | F | M | A | M | J | J | **A** | **S** | **O** | N | D

(=*Schizodium obliquum*) Slender perennial to 30 cm with the leaves clustered at the base of the wiry, flexed stem; bears a few pale pinkish flowers with the tip of the lip greenish to purple; the lance-shaped sepals are 8–10 mm long and the spur is straight or curved downwards and constricted at the base. Sandstone slopes in the southwestern Cape. One of 3 similar species: *Disa bifida* has sepals 10–15 mm long and an upcurved spur; *D. inflexa* does not have the spur constricted at the base.

### ▶ FLORAL SPUR 10–20 MM LONG

**1** *Disa ferruginea*  **Cluster disa**    J **F** M A M J J A S O N D

Slender perennial to 45 cm with narrow leaves in a basal cluster, dry at flowering; bears many bright red to orange flowers crowded in a head-like spike among dry bracts, the dorsal sepal narrowing gradually into a slender spur 7–20 mm long. Sandstone mountain slopes in the southwestern and southern Cape.

**2** *Disa uniflora*  **Red disa**    J F **M** A **M** J J A S O N D

Erect or flexible perennial to 60 cm with narrowly lance-shaped leaves clustered towards the base; bears 1 to few large, carmine red to orange flowers, the dorsal sepal paler and streaked with red and bearing a wedge-shaped spur 10–15 mm long. Wet cliffs, streamsides and seeps in the mountains of the southwestern Cape.

**3** *Disa cornuta*    J **F** M A M J J A **S O N D**

Robust perennial to 60 cm with overlapping, lance-shaped leaves covering the stem; bears many purple and silvery green flowers in a dense spike, the dorsal sepal with a spur 10–20 mm long. Sandstone slopes and grassland from the southwestern Cape to tropical Africa.

### ▶ FLORAL SPUR MORE THAN 20 MM LONG

**4** *Disa draconis*  **White disa**    J F M A M J J A S **O** N D

Slender or robust perennial to 60 cm with tongue-shaped leaves in a basal tuft, dry at flowering; bears few to many cream or white flowers with purple streaks, the paddle-shaped dorsal sepal completely enclosing the petals and drawn into a slender spur 35–45 mm long. Sandy coastal flats along the West Coast.

**5** *Disa harveiana*  **Lilac disa**    J F M A M J J A S **O N D**

Perennial to 30 cm with narrow leaves in a basal tuft, dry at flowering; bears few to many cream or mauve flowers with purple or red streaks, the oblong dorsal sepal not completely enclosing the petals and drawn into a slender spur 20–90 mm long. Sandstone mountain slopes mainly in the southwestern Cape.

**6** *Disa longicornu*  **Drip disa**    J F M A M J J A S O N **D**

Slender perennial with a somewhat flexible stem to 20 cm with narrowly elliptical leaves in a basal tuft; bears a solitary, large, pale greyish-blue flower with a down-curved, horn-like spur 20–35 mm long. Wet cliffs on Table Mountain and the Jonkershoek Mountains.

# EUPHORBIACEAE — Euphorbia family

## *Euphorbia* EUPHORBIA, MELKBOS

Trees, shrubs or herbs, often succulent and sometimes spiny, *usually with milky latex*. Leaves often reduced or soon lost. Flowers *unisexual*, minute, arranged in a *small, cup-like, 'false flower' (cyathium) surrounded by 5 fleshy, petal-like glands, sometimes the upper leaves coloured*. Worldwide, predominantly succulent in drier areas: ±2 000 spp; ±20 fynbos spp. The milky sap of several species is highly irritant and toxic.

**① *Euphorbia tuberosa***

| J | F | M | A | M | J | J | A | S | O | N | D |

**Melkbol, wilderamenas** Stemless, tuberous-rooted perennial to 5 cm with oblong to paddle-shaped leaves, narrowed below into a long petiole and usually minutely haired with undulate or crisped margins, exuding a milky latex when damaged; bears clusters of false flowers on trailing stems, each one 4–6 mm in diameter and surrounded by 5 fleshy yellowish to greenish lobes. Sandy and stony flats and slopes in Namaqualand and the southwestern Cape. *Euphorbia ecklonii* has broadly elliptical leaves pressed to the ground; *E. mira* has thread-like leaves; *E. silenifolia* has narrow, tapering leaves.

**② *Euphorbia caput-medusae***

| J | F | M | A | M | J | J | A | S | O | N | D |

**Medusa's head, vingerpol** Sprawling shrublet with a rosette of warty, more or less club-shaped branches, 10–30 mm in diameter, arising from a short, thick stem and with small, narrow, rapidly deciduous leaves at the branch tips; bears large false flowers 10–18 mm in diameter, each surrounded by deeply fringed, pale yellow or cream and green lobes. Sandy flats and stony slopes in Namaqualand and the southwestern Cape.

**③ *Euphorbia burmannii***

| J | F | M | A | M | J | J | A | S | O | N | D |

**Steenbokmelkbos, soetmelkbos** Many branched shrublet, 15–100 cm, with smooth, greyish-green to dark green stems 3–5 mm in diameter and rapidly deciduous leaves 2–3 mm long; bears clusters of false flowers, each 2–4 mm in diameter and surrounded by 5 fleshy, pale green lobes. Sandy and stony flats and slopes from Namaqualand to the Eastern Cape.

**④ *Euphorbia mauritanica***

| J | F | M | A | M | J | J | A | S | O | N | D |

**Beesmelkbos, geelmelkbos** Many branched shrub to 2 m with smooth, bright green stems 3–6 mm in diameter and rapidly deciduous leaves 8–15 mm long; bears clusters comprising a central male false flower surrounded by 5–7 bisexual false flowers, each 7–15 mm in diameter and surrounded by fleshy, bright yellow glands. Common on sandy flats along the coast and on stony slopes in the drier interior.

165

# CRASSULACEAE Crassula family

▶ LEAVES SPIRALLY ARRANGED OR OPPOSITE; STAMENS 10, TWICE AS MANY AS THE PETALS

## *Cotyledon*  COTYLEDON, VARKOOR

Shrubs, mostly succulent. *Leaves opposite*, large and fleshy, persistent. Flowers usually nodding on a stout peduncle, red to yellowish, with *5 petals that are joined in an urn-shaped or cylindrical tube longer than the lobes; stamens 10*. Africa and Arabia, mainly southern Africa: 9 spp; ±4 fynbos spp. Although toxic, the juice is used medicinally.

**1** *Cotyledon orbiculata* **Kouterie**    `J F M A M J J A S O N D`

Succulent shrublet with brittle stems to 1 m and fleshy, hairless or velvety leaves, broadly paddle- to spindle-shaped with a grey bloom; bears clusters of nodding, tubular, dull reddish flowers on stout stems. Widespread through western southern Africa in sandy or stony soils in scrub.

## *Tylecodon*  TYLECODON, BANDJIESBOS

Shrublets or shrubs, sometimes tree-like with a thick, fleshy trunk, the branches covered with knobbly leaf scars. *Leaves spirally arranged, deciduous or dry at flowering.* Flowers on simple or branched peduncles, variously coloured, often nodding, with 5 *petals that are joined in an urn-shaped or cylindrical tube usually longer than the lobes; stamens 10*. Southern Africa, mainly the winter-rainfall region: 41 spp; 8 fynbos spp. The vernacular name derives from the fanciful resemblance of the tufted leaves to ribbons, or *bandjies*, tied to the end of a stick.

**2** *Tylecodon grandiflorus*    `J F M A M J J A S O N D`

**Rooisuikerblom**  Succulent, often sprawling, shrublet to 50 cm with leaves that are withered at flowering but not dropping off cleanly, bright green and narrowly paddle-shaped, the margins often rolled upwards; bears arching, somewhat 1-sided clusters of tubular, slightly irregular reddish flowers with a tube 30–40 mm long that curves gently upwards. Rocky outcrops, often granitic, along the West Coast.

**3** *Tylecodon paniculatus* **Botterboom**    `J F M A M J J A S O N D`

Succulent shrublet with stout, peeling stems to 1.5 m and paddle-shaped, bright green leaves that are absent at flowering, dropping off cleanly from the stem; bears branched stems of nodding, urn-shaped, yellowish to red flowers with a tube 12–16 mm long. Rocky slopes from Namibia through the Little Karoo.

**4** *Tylecodon wallichii*    `J F M A M J J A S O N D`

**Kandelaarbos, karkeibos**  Succulent shrublet with warty stems to 1 m and paddle-shaped leaves that are absent at flowering, dropping off cleanly; bears spreading clusters of nodding, urn-shaped, greenish-yellow flowers with a tube 7–12 mm long. Stony flats and slopes from Namaqualand to the Little Karoo.

▶ LEAVES OPPOSITE AND ± JOINED AT THE BASE; STAMENS USUALLY 5, AS MANY AS THE PETALS

## *Crassula*  CRASSULA, STONECROP

Shrubs, perennials or annuals, mostly succulent, sometimes tuberous. *Leaves opposite*, often crowded in rosettes, *each leaf pair more or less joined at the base around the stem*. Flowers 1 to many in simple or branched clusters, variously coloured, mostly white or pink, *usually with 5 petals that are separate or joined at the base into a cup- or urn-shaped tube; stamens usually 5*. Worldwide, but predominantly southern hemisphere and mainly drier areas of southern Africa: 300+ spp; ±100 fynbos spp. Popular among succulent collectors.

▶ ANNUAL HERBS

### ❶ *Crassula dichotoma*

| J | F | M | A | M | J | J | A | S | O | N | D |

Wiry-stemmed annual to 20 cm with leaves that are fleshy, lance-shaped and obscurely toothed; bears flat-topped clusters of salver-shaped, yellow to orange flowers, often marked red in the throat, the petals 8–15 mm long. Sandy flats in Namaqualand and the southwestern Cape.

### ❷ *Crassula natans*  Watergrass

| J | F | M | A | M | J | J | A | S | O | N | D |

Erect or floating annual, sometimes with perennial basal parts, 2–25 cm, with leaves that are fleshy and narrow to paddle-shaped; in submerged forms the upper, floating leaves are broader and form little rafts; bears 1–3 small, star-shaped, white to pinkish flowers in the upper axils, the petals 1.5–2.0 mm long. A variable species that is widespread throughout South Africa in moist depressions or pools.

▶ PERENNIALS OR SHRUBS WITH CUP-SHAPED OR TUBULAR FLOWERS TO 10 MM LONG

### ❸ *Crassula muscosa*

| J | F | M | A | M | J | J | A | S | O | N | D |

**Akkedisstert, skoenvetierbossie**  Sprawling, closely leafy perennial, 10–50 cm, with small, closely overlapping, scale-like leaves in 4 ranks; bears clusters of small, star-shaped, yellowish flowers in the axils of the upper leaves, the petals 1–2 mm long. Rocky outcrops and slopes throughout southern Africa.

### ❹ *Crassula saxifraga*

| J | F | M | A | M | J | J | A | S | O | N | D |

Tuberous perennial, 5–25 cm, with 1(2) pairs of rounded, thin-textured leaves with scalloped margins, sometimes not fully expanded at flowering; bears several nodding, tubular, white to pinkish flowers on a slender stalk, the petals 3.5–7.5 mm long. Sheltered stony slopes or crevices from Namaqualand to the Eastern Cape.

### ❺ *Crassula capensis*  Cape snowdrop

| J | F | M | A | M | J | J | A | S | O | N | D |

Tuberous perennial, 5–20 cm with 2 or 3(4) pairs of broadly paddle-shaped to rounded, thin-textured leaves with scalloped margins; bears several nodding, cupped, white to pinkish flowers on a slender stalk, the petals 3–8 mm long. Damp slopes in the southwestern and southern Cape.

### ❻ *Crassula atropurpurea*

| J | F | M | A | M | J | J | A | S | O | N | D |

Shrublet to 60 cm with fleshy, ovoid to paddle-shaped leaves, usually hairy and papillate with horny margins; bears globular clusters of tubular, cream-coloured flowers ±4 mm long, arranged in elongate panicles. Drier rocky slopes and rock pavements in southwestern South Africa.

**169**

### ❶ *Crassula dejecta*

Shrublet to 40 cm, the young branches covered with recurved hairs, with oblong to oval, bright green leaves that have rounded hairs on the margins; bears flat-topped or rounded clusters of tubular white flowers tinged reddish, the petals ±8 mm long. Rock outcrops in Namaqualand and the southwestern Cape.

### ❷ *Crassula rupestris*

**Concertina plant, sosaties** Shrublet to 50 cm with fleshy, oval to lance-shaped, greyish or pinkish leaves that have horny red or yellow margins; bears short-stalked, rounded clusters of whitish flowers tinged pink, the petals 4–6 mm long. Dry, stony slopes from Namibia to the Eastern Cape, often in large numbers.

▶ **SHRUBS WITH TUBULAR FLOWERS 20–40 MM LONG**

### ❸ *Crassula coccinea*

**Red crassula, keiserkroon** Shrublet to 60 cm with oval to elliptical leaves; bears flat-topped heads of tubular, bright scarlet flowers 30–45 mm long. Sandstone outcrops in the extreme southwestern Cape.

### ❹ *Crassula fascicularis* **Ruiksissie**

Shrublet to 40 cm with ±erect, narrow to lance-shaped leaves, usually with recurved hairs on the margins; bears flat-topped clusters of tubular, cream to yellow-green flowers 20–32 mm long that are fragrant at night. Sandstone slopes in the south-western Cape.

### ❺ *Crassula obtusa* **Klipblom**

Sprawling shrublet to 15 cm, the branches often rooting at the nodes, with oblong to paddle-shaped leaves that have hairy margins; bears clusters of 1–5 tubular, white flowers tinged pinkish, 30–40 mm long, and fragrant at night. Sandstone ledges in the southwestern and southern Cape.

# RANUNCULACEAE       Ranunculus family

### *Anemone*   ANEMONE, ANEMOON

Perennials. *Leaves basal* and usually much divided or lobed, the flowering stem with 1 or more *whorls of small leaves partially joined together to form a collar below the flowers*. Flowers 1–3, large and showy, with *4–20 deciduous, petal-like sepals* (true petals absent). Cosmopolitan, mainly temperate: ±120 spp; 1 fynbos sp.

### ❻ *Anemone tenuifolia* **Wild anemone**

Tufted perennial to 40 cm with leathery leaves that are twice- or thrice-divided into triangular, 3-toothed segments, the margins rolled under; bears solitary, large pinkish-white flowers on woolly peduncles, the sepals silky beneath. Moist sandstone slopes in the southwestern and southern Cape.

171

## *Knowltonia*  KNOWLTONIA, BRANDBLAAR

Perennials. *Leaves basal, leathery, once- to thrice-divided into toothed segments.* Flowers few to many, white or yellowish to green, sometimes tinged pink, with *8–23 deciduous, petal-like sepals* (true petals absent). *Fruits fleshy.* Central and southern Africa, mainly Western Cape, in sheltered or moister situations: 8 spp; 5 fynbos spp. The fresh leaves and roots are an irritant, causing blistering, and were used medicinally. Recent studies show that *Knowltonia* is a specialised, fleshy-fruited group within the genus *Anemone,* and is to be transferred to it. The appropriate names in *Anemone* are given in square brackets in anticipation of this.

### 1 *Knowltonia anemonoides*

J F M A M J J A S O N D

*[Anemone anemonoides]*  Thinly silky, tufted perennial to 30 cm with leathery leaves, twice- or thrice-divided into evenly toothed, oval segments that are more hairy beneath than above; bears clusters of greenish-white to purple flowers on peduncles that are usually much longer than the leaves; the fruits are usually hairy. Rocky slopes in the southwestern Cape, flowering after fire. *Knowltonia capensis [Anemone knowltonia]* from the extreme southwestern Cape is a shorter plant with the flower stalks ± as long as the leaves, which are more hairy on the upper surface, and outer sepals that are shorter and more hairy than the inner ones.

### 2 *Knowltonia vesicatoria*

J F M A M J J A S O N D

*[Anemone vesicatoria]* **Katjiedrieblaar, tandpynblare**  Hairless, tufted perennial to 1.2 m with leathery leaves, once- or twice-divided into finely toothed, oval segments; bears clusters of white to yellowish-green flowers on peduncles that are not much longer than the leaves; the fruits are hairless. Scrub or wooded ravines from the southwestern to the Eastern Cape.

# DROSERACEAE
## Sundew family

## *Drosera*  SUNDEW, DOUBLOM

*Glandular, insectivorous perennials or annuals.* Leaves basal and/or scattered along the stem, *covered with sticky glands and tentacles.* Flowers few to several on short or slender peduncles with the end drooping in bud, usually pink, mauve or white, closing at night. Worldwide, mainly southern hemisphere, especially Australia: ±80 spp; 14 fynbos spp.

### 3 *Drosera capensis*

J F M A M J J A S O N D

Rhizomatous perennial to 30 cm with a distinct, woody stem below the leaves, which are strap-shaped to elliptical and petiolate; bears several pink to magenta flowers 20–30 mm in diameter in a drooping, 1-sided raceme on a slender scape that curves outwards from the plant at the base; the stigmas are swollen. Marshy sandstone in the southwestern and southern Cape.

### 4 *Drosera aliciae*

J F M A M J J A S O N D

Stemless, tufted perennial to 40 cm with leaves in a basal rosette, spoon-shaped, hairy beneath; bears several small, pink flowers 15–20 mm in diameter in a drooping, 1-sided raceme on a wiry scape that curves outwards from the base of the plant; the stigmas are each divided into 2 or 3 branches. Peaty sandstone in the mountains in the southern and Eastern Cape.

**❶ *Drosera trinervia***    J F M A M J J **A S O N** D

Stemless, tufted perennial to 10 cm with wedge-shaped leaves in a basal rosette; bears a few small, white to mauve or red flowers 10–16 mm in diameter in a flat-topped raceme; the stigmas are each divided into many branches. Peaty sandstone slopes in Namaqualand and the southwestern Cape.

**❷ *Drosera acaulis***    J F M A M J J A S **O N D**

Dwarf, stemless perennial to 6 cm with wedge-shaped leaves in a basal rosette; bears a solitary pink to purple flower 15 mm in diameter on a very short stem; the stigmas are each divided into many branches. Damp sandstone slopes in the interior mountains along the West Coast.

**❸ *Drosera pauciflora***    J F M A M J J **A S O N** D

Stemless, tufted perennial to 20 cm with paddle-shaped leaves in a basal rosette; bears a few large, pink or mauve flowers 40–60 mm in diameter with a dark centre in a flat-topped raceme; the stigmas are each divided into many branches. Damp, loamy or sandy flats in the southwestern Cape.

**❹ *Drosera cistiflora* Snotrosie**    J F M A M J J **A S O** N D

Slender perennial to 40 cm with or without basal leaves but always with slender leaves scattered up the stem; bears a few large white, creamy yellow, pink, mauve, purple or red flowers 30–40 mm in diameter with a dark centre in a flat-topped raceme; the stigmas are each divided into many branches. Damp, sandy flats and seeps from Namaqualand to the southern Cape.

# CARYOPHYLLACEAE    **Carnation family**

## *Dianthus*   PINK, ANGELIER

Annuals, perennials or softly woody shrublets. Leaves opposite, *narrow and grass-like, hairless,* each pair *joined at the base into a short sheath.* Flowers 1 or few, white, pink or red, the sepals *joined into a long calyx tube surrounded at the base by several bracts,* enclosing the stalk-like bases of the petals, which are usually *fringed or toothed at the tips;* stamens 10, *usually hidden within the tube,* the style divided into 2 branches. Old World, especially the Mediterranean: ±300 spp; 5 fynbos spp. *Dianthus caryophyllaceus* from the Mediterranean is the florists' carnation.

**❺ *Dianthus albens***    J **F** M A M J J A S **O N D**

**Wild pink, wilde-angelier** Loosely tufted or sprawling perennial to 40 cm with narrow, grass-like leaves; bears several white to purple flowers on axillary scapes; the calyx is 12–18 mm long and the narrowly paddle-shaped petals are entire or toothed. Sandy flats and slopes, often coastal, from the southwestern to the Eastern Cape.

## *Silene*   CAMPION, WILDETABAK

Annuals, biennials or perennials. Leaves opposite, never toothed, often hairy. Flowers few to several in a panicle or 1-sided raceme, white, pink or red, often closing during the day, the *sepals joined into a long calyx tube without any bracts at the base,* enclosing the stalk-like bases of the petals, which are *often notched at the tips;* stamens 10, *usually hidden within the tube,* the ovary *stalked* and the style divided into *2–5 branches.* Worldwide, mainly Eurasia: ±700 spp; 6 fynbos spp.

175

**1** *Silene bellidioides*

J F M A M J J A S O N D

Soft perennial to 60 cm covered in short, gland-tipped hairs, with lance-shaped leaves; bears a few white or pink to crimson flowers with a calyx 18–22 mm long and notched petals, opening at night and then fragrant; the fruits have a short stalk ±2 mm long. Sandy flats and slopes from the southwestern Cape to Mpumalanga.

**2** *Silene undulata*

J F M A M J J A S O N D

Soft perennial to 60 cm covered in short, gland-tipped hairs, with lance-shaped leaves; bears a few white or pink flowers with a calyx 22–35 mm long and notched petals, opening at night and then fragrant; the fruits have a longer stalk 4–6 mm long. Slopes and flats through southern and tropical Africa.

# BRASSICACEAE                          Mustard family

## *Heliophila*   SUNFLAX, SPORRIE

Shrubs, perennials or annuals. Leaves narrow or broad, often lobed or divided, with or without minute stipules. Flowers in racemes or panicles, *mostly mauve or blue*, sometimes pink or white, closing at night and in cool weather. *Fruits often slender and beaded, tipped by the swollen style.* Southern Africa, mainly winter-rainfall parts: 85 spp; 55 fynbos spp. Following recent research the genus has been expanded to include several smaller genera that were distinguished by their differently shaped fruits, including the wild stock, *Brachycarpaea juncea*.

▸ **PERENNIALS OR SHRUBLETS**

**3** *Heliophila elata*

J F M A M J J A S O N D

Slender shrublet to 1 m with willowy stems that are minutely haired towards the base and thread-like, sometimes lobed, leaves, subtended by minute stipules; bears blue to mauve flowers with more or less hairless sepals; the lightly beaded fruits are 20–80 mm long. Sandy flats and slopes in arid fynbos in the south-western Cape.

**4** *Heliophila carnosa*

J F M A M J J A S O N D

Tussock-forming shrublets to 60 cm with annual stems from a woody base and thread-like leaves subtended by minute stipules; bears large, white, pink or violet flowers; the oblong fruits are 25–80 mm long. Dry hillsides from Namibia along the southern seaboard to Gauteng.

**5** *Heliophila scoparia*

J F M A M J J A S O N D

Leafy shrublet to 1 m with rod-like, longitudinally ridged stems and narrowly lance-shaped leaves subtended by minute stipules; bears a few smallish, white, pink or purple flowers on short-shoots; the narrow fruits are held erect and are 30–120 mm long. Sandstone slopes in the southwestern Cape.

**6** *Heliophila juncea*

J F M A M J J A S O N D

(=*Brachycarpaea juncea*) **Wild stock, blouriet**  Wand-like shrublet to 1 m with narrow to oblong leaves; bears racemes of white to pink or purple flowers with narrowly paddle-shaped petals 8–20 mm long; fruits are discus-shaped and warty. Rocky sandstone slopes in Namaqualand and the southwestern and southern Cape, flowering best after fire; very variable in growth form and flower size.

**①** *Heliophila cornuta*

J F M A M J **J A S O** N D

Slender shrublet to 1.5 m with willowy or straggling stems and fleshy, narrow or thread-like leaves lacking stipules; bears white, mauve or blue flowers with the petals flexed back and hairless or minutely haired sepals; the lightly beaded fruits are 30–100 mm long. Rocky slopes in arid fynbos from southern Namibia to the Eastern Cape.

▸ **ANNUALS**

**②** *Heliophila africana*

J F M A M J J **A S O** N D

More or less rough-haired, annual herb to 40 cm, often somewhat sprawling, with lance-shaped leaves often lobed or toothed above; bears blue or mauve flowers with hairless or hairy sepals; the narrow fruits are not beaded and are 13–100 mm long. Sandy flats in Namaqualand and the southwestern Cape.

**③** *Heliophila arenaria*

J F M A M J **J A S** O N D

Almost hairless or hairy annual herb with stiffly erect stems to 50 cm and thread-like leaves, sometimes lobed; bears blue flowers with hairy sepals; the beaded fruits are 15–55 mm long. Sandstone slopes in Namaqualand and the southwestern Cape.

**④** *Heliophila coronopifolia*

J F M A M J J **A S O** N D

Annual herb with stiffly erect stems to 60 cm that are roughly hairy towards the base and thread-like or variously lobed leaves; bears blue flowers with a white or greenish centre and hairless, purplish sepals; the beaded fruits are 30–90 mm long. Widespread on sandy flats and slopes, often forming massed displays in Namaqualand and the southwestern Cape.

# ZYGOPHYLLACEAE — Twinleaf family

## *Roepera*  TWINLEAF, SPEKBOS

Shrubs or subshrubs with jointed stems, sometimes spiny. *Leaves opposite, fleshy, divided into 2 leaflets.* Flowers 1 or 2 together, mostly yellow or white with reddish marks at the base of the petals, sometimes irregular, the stamen *filaments with appendages at the base. Fruits with 4 or 5 ridges or wings.* Mainly drier parts of southern Africa, especially the winter-rainfall regions: ±50 spp; ±20 fynbos spp. The southern African species were previously included in the North African genus *Zygophyllum*. The vernacular name *spekbos* alludes to the value of the plants as fodder.

**⑤** *Roepera morgsana*  **Slymbos**

J F **M A M** J J **A S** O N D

(=*Zygophyllum morgsana*) Shrub or shrublet to 1.5 m with petiolate leaves divided into 2 asymmetrical, oval leaflets; bears pale yellow flowers with reddish markings, with only 4 petals marked with red; the large fruits have 4 conspicuous wings, each 15 mm wide. Sandy and stony slopes and flats, mostly coastal, from southern Namibia to the Eastern Cape.

**⑥** *Roepera flexuosa*  **Maerbos**

J F M A M **J J A S** O N D

(=*Zygophyllum flexuosum*) Sprawling shrublet to 70 cm with sessile leaves divided into 2 succulent oval leaflets; bears golden-yellow flowers with reddish markings, with 5 petals flexed back; the fruits are ±globular and wider than long with 5 sutures. Coastal sands and limestone in the southwestern and southern Cape.

**❶ *Roepera spinosa***  `J F M A M J J A S O N D`

(=*Zygophyllum spinosum*) Erect or sprawling shrublet to 1 m with sessile leaves divided into 2 succulent, cylindrical leaflets that are grooved beneath; bears yellow flowers with or without red markings, with 5 petals flexed back; the fruits are globular with 5 sutures when fresh, but 5-angled and slightly ribbed when dry. Coastal sands and rocky ridges in Namaqualand and the West Coast.

**❷ *Roepera fulva***  `J F M A M J J A S O N D`

(=*Zygophyllum fulvum*) Erect or straggling shrublet to 1 m with sessile leaves divided into 2 oval leaflets with smooth, bony margins; bears cream to yellow flowers with red markings, with 5 petals; the fruits are egg-shaped with 5 sutures when fresh, but 5-angled when dry. Sandy flats and rocky slopes along the West Coast and in the southwestern and southern Cape.

**❸ *Roepera sessilifolia*  Witspekbos**  `J F M A M J J A S O N D`

(=*Zygophyllum sessilifolium*) Sprawling or prostrate shrublet to 10 cm with sessile leaves divided into 2 oval leaflets with rough, bony margins; bears cupped, whitish flowers with red veins and markings, with 5 petals; the fruits are globular to oblong with 5 sutures when fresh, but 5-lobed and ribbed when dry. Shale and sandy slopes, often under bushes, in the southwestern Cape.

**❹ *Roepera rogersii*  Pink twinleaf**  `J F M A M J J A S O N D`

(=*Zygophyllum rogersii*) Soft shrublet to 20 cm with sessile, grey leaves divided into 2 cylindrical leaflets that are grooved beneath; bears strawberry-pink flowers with 5 petals; the fruits are round with 5 sutures when fresh, but 5-angled and slightly ribbed when dry. Rocky sandstone slopes in arid fynbos on the drier interior mountains of the southwestern Cape.

# GERANIACEAE  Geranium family

## *Geranium*  GERANIUM, CRANE'SBILL

Annual or perennial herbs, often with jointed stems. Leaves with stipules, palmately lobed or divided, with the segments also toothed or lobed. Flowers 1 or 2 on slender axillary peduncles, white, pink or mauve to purple with notched petals, *radially symmetrical; stamens 10, usually all fertile*. Fruit segments each topped with a coiled, usually hairless bristle or awn. Temperate and montane tropics; widely cultivated: 300 spp; 4 fynbos spp. The leaves of *Geranium incanum* were used as a tea and medicinally, and the vernacular name for the species derives from the bitter (Latin *amara*) taste.

**❺ *Geranium incanum*  Amarabossie**  `J F M A M J J A S O N D`

Diffuse, trailing perennial with leaves on long petioles, the blades divided to the base into 3–7, deeply lobed segments that are hairless or sparsely hairy above, with dense white hairs beneath; bears 1 or 2 pink to mauve (rarely white with pink veins) flowers 15–30 mm in diameter on slender axillary peduncles. Sandy and stony soils along the coast from the Cape Peninsula to the Eastern Cape; selected forms are very popular garden plants.

## *Monsonia*  MONSONIA, BOESMANSKERS

Annual or perennial herbs with glandular stems, or succulent shrublets with waxy, translucent bark and sometimes with persistent, spine-like petioles. Leaves often unequal, some either smaller or on longer petioles that become spiny, variously palmately toothed or lobed. Flowers 1 or more on axillary peduncles, white, yellow or pink, usually with *the petals irregularly toothed at the ends, radially symmetrical; stamens 15*, usually all fertile, sometimes in clusters. Fruit segments each with a coiled, crested or fringed bristle or awn. Widespread through Africa and southwest Asia: ±50 spp; 5 fynbos spp. The highly succulent species from the arid parts of southern Africa were previously treated as the separate genus *Sarcocaulon*.

**1** *Monsonia speciosa*  Sambreeltjie  `J F M A M J J A S O N D`

Sprawling perennial producing annual stems from a short rhizome, with toothed to finely divided, almost hairless leaves; bears large white to pink flowers 25–65 mm in diameter that are deep pink on the reverse. Clay and granite slopes and flats, mostly in renosterveld, in the southwestern Cape.

## *Pelargonium*  PELARGONIUM, MALVA

Perennial herbs or shrubs, sometimes climbing, tuberous perennials, or rarely annuals, mostly herbaceous but sometimes woody or succulent. Leaves unlobed to finely dissected, variously hairy and mostly glandular, often aromatic, sometimes with persistent, spine-like petioles. Flowers 1 or more in umbel-like clusters, variously coloured, often pink, *zygomorphic, sometimes with fewer than 5 petals, the upper sepal forming a hollow spur that is joined to the top of the pedicel*; stamens 10, *usually only 2–7 fertile*. Fruit segments each with a coiled, crested or fringed bristle or awn. Widespread through the western hemisphere, mainly in the winter-rainfall region of southern Africa: ±270 spp; ±150 fynbos spp. Hybrids of various South African species are widely grown as the florists' 'geranium'; the scented oils from certain species are important in the fragrance industry; the powdered root of tuberous species, such as *Pelargonium triste*, was used as a purgative, while a decoction of the leaves of *P. cucullatum* was also used medicinally.

▶ **TUBEROUS PERENNIALS WITH LEAVES IN A BASAL TUFT, SOMETIMES DRY AT FLOWERING**

**2** *Pelargonium lobatum*  Kaneelbol  `J F M A M J J A S O N D`

Tuberous perennial to 50 cm with leaves in a basal cluster, soft-haired, oval and more or less lobed, to 30 cm in diameter; bears long peduncles of up to 20 pale yellow flowers marked with black in the centre, 15–18 mm in diameter, clove- or anise-scented at night; the floral tube is 25–35 mm long. Gravelly soils, often on granite outcrops, in the southwestern and southern Cape.

**3** *Pelargonium triste*  Kaneeltjie  `J F M A M J J A S O N D`

Tuberous perennial to 50 cm with leaves in a basal cluster, soft-haired, finely twice- or thrice-divided into narrow segments, to 30 cm in diameter; bears long peduncles of up to 20 pale yellow flowers, variously marked with dark maroon to black in centre, 15–18 mm in diameter, clove-scented at night; floral tube is 25–35 mm long. Sandy flats and lower slopes, often coastal, from Namaqualand to the southern Cape.

**4** *Pelargonium dipetalum*  `J F M A M J J A S O N D`

Tuberous perennial to 35 cm with hairy leaves that are dry at flowering and once- or twice-divided into narrow segments, to 15×25 mm; bears up to 12 white or pink flowers feathered with red, ±15 mm in diameter, with only 2 spoon-shaped petals; the floral tube is 7–18(50) mm long. Lowlands along the southern Cape coast.

### **1** *Pelargonium carneum*

J F M A M J J A S O N D

Tuberous perennial to 40 cm with leaves that are dry at flowering and hairy beneath, usually once- or twice-divided into narrow segments, up to 500×30 mm; bears up to 13 large white, yellow or pink flowers ±45 mm in diameter, the upper 2 petals with dark red feathering; the floral tube is 30–75 mm long. Stony slopes in the southwestern and southern Cape.

### **2** *Pelargonium longiflorum*

J F M A M J J A S O N D

Tuberous perennial to 30 cm with hairless to densely hairy, lance-shaped leaves that are usually green at flowering, to 160×25 mm; bears up to 15 pale yellow or pink flowers ±30 mm in diameter with narrowly ribbon-shaped petals, the upper 2 with dark red feathering; the floral tube is (10)15–44 mm long. Sandy or stony places in Namaqualand and the southwestern Cape.

### **3** *Pelargonium longifolium*

J F M A M J J A S O N D

Tuberous perennial to 25 cm with hairless or sparsely hairy leaves, dry at flowering, lance-shaped to variously divided, to 120×18 mm; bears up to 9 white, pale yellow or pink flowers 20–25 mm in diameter with narrow petals, the upper 2 usually with conspicuous maroon blotches near the middle; the floral tube is 8–22 mm long. Sandy and stony places in the southwestern Cape.

### **4** *Pelargonium pinnatum*

J F M A M J J A S O N D

Tuberous perennial to 30 cm with hairy leaves that are often green at flowering, once-divided into oval segments, to 70 mm long; bears up to 8 white, pale yellow, pink or purple flowers ±18 mm in diameter with rather broad, spoon-shaped petals, the upper 2 with red feathering; the floral tube is 11–35(45) mm long. Clay or sandstone slopes and flats in the southwestern Cape.

### **5** *Pelargonium rapaceum* **Bergpatat**

J F M A M J J A S O N D

Tuberous perennial to 40 cm with soft-haired leaves that are often drying at flowering, finely twice-divided and carrot-like with narrow segments, to 250 mm long; bears up to 50 white, pale yellow or pink flowers ±25 mm in diameter on branching peduncles, pea-like with the 3 lower petals forming a keel; the floral tube is 12–55 mm long. Stony slopes and flats from Namaqualand to the Eastern Cape.

## ▶ SUCCULENT-STEMMED SHRUBLETS

### **6** *Pelargonium magenteum* **Persmalva**

J F M A M J J A S O N D

Twiggy, succulent-stemmed shrublet to 1 m with rounded, shallowly lobed, grey-velvety leaves to 15 mm in diameter; bears clusters of up to 9 magenta-purple flowers ±20 mm in diameter; the floral tube is ±30 mm long. Rocky sandstone outcrops in arid fynbos in the interior mountains of the southwestern Cape.

### **7** *Pelargonium fulgidum* **Rooimalva**

J F M A M J J A S O N D

Succulent-stemmed shrublet to 40 cm with once-divided, densely silvery-silky leaves 10–17 cm in diameter; bears clusters of 4–9 scarlet flowers 15–20 mm in diameter; the floral tube is 20–40 mm long. Rocky slopes, often coastal granite, in Namaqualand and the West Coast.

185

### 1 *Pelargonium gibbosum*

J F M A M J J A S O N D

**Gouty geranium** Sprawling shrublet with joined stems conspicuously swollen at the nodes and leaves that are dry at flowering, once-divided, leathery and greyish, 13–17.5 cm in diameter; bears clusters of 3–14 greenish-yellow flowers ±15 mm in diameter, scented at night; the floral tube is 20–25 mm long. Among shrubs on rock outcrops along the Namaqualand coast and the West Coast.

## ▶ WOODY-STEMMED SHRUBS, USUALLY WITH AROMATIC LEAVES

### 2 *Pelargonium scabrum* Hoenderbos

J F M A M J J A S O N D

Roughly hairy, aromatic shrub to 1.2 m with deeply lobed, roughly hairy, lemon-scented leaves ±5 cm in diameter; bears clusters of up to 6 white to pink flowers ±20 mm in diameter; the floral tube is 3–12 mm long. Rocky sandstone slopes from Namaqualand to the Eastern Cape.

### 3 *Pelargonium hispidum*

J F M A M J J A S O N D

Large shrub to 1.8 m with hairy, deeply 3–5-lobed, aromatic leaves that have a balm-like scent, 5–8 cm in diameter; bears up to 12 pale pink flowers on short axillary peduncles, ±18 mm in diameter; the floral tube is 3–4 mm long. Near watercourses on sandstone slopes in the southwestern Cape. *Pelargonium glutinosum* has sticky leaves.

### 4 *Pelargonium crispum*

J F M A M J J A S O N D

Shrublet to 70 cm with 2 ranks of small, rough, lemon-scented, fan-shaped leaves that have crinkly margins, to 1 cm in diameter; bears 1–3 pink flowers on short peduncles, ±25 mm in diameter; the floral tube is 5–8 mm long. Rocky lower slopes in the southwestern Cape.

### 5 *Pelargonium betulinum* Kanferblaar

J F M A M J J A S O N D

Shrub to 1.5 m with oval to elliptic, somewhat leathery, leaves ±20 mm long; bears axillary clusters of up to 6 white to pink flowers ±50 mm in diameter; the floral tube is 3–8 mm long. Coastal dunes in the southwestern and southern Cape.

### 6 *Pelargonium cucullatum* Wildemalva

J F M A M J J A S O N D

Roughly hairy shrub to 2 m with more or less round, toothed leaves ±7 cm in diameter; bears clusters of up to 13 pinkish-purple flowers ±40 mm in diameter with widely overlapping petals; the floral tube is 5–12 mm long. Sandstone and granite slopes along the coast in the southwestern Cape.

### 7 *Pelargonium capitatum* Kusmalva

J F M A M J J A S O N D

Sprawling, softly velvety shrublet to 50 cm with aromatic, rounded, lobed and crisped leaves ±5 cm in diameter; bears clusters of up to 20 pink to purple flowers 15–25 mm in diameter; the floral tube is 3–8 mm long. Coastal dunes and flats from the West Coast to KwaZulu-Natal.

## ▶ SOFT-STEMMED PERENNIALS OR ANNUALS

**1 *Pelargonium ovale***

J F M A M J J A S O N D

Tufted, rhizomatous perennial to 30 cm with densely hairy, elliptical, toothed leaves ±4×1–3 cm; bears up to 7 white to pink flowers on well-developed, branching peduncles, 25–40 mm in diameter, with the upper petals overlapping and much larger; the floral tube is 2–13 mm long. Open places on mountains in the southwestern and southern Cape.

**2 *Pelargonium senecioides***

J F M A M J J A S O N D

Annual herb to 40 cm, branching mainly from the base, with twice- or thrice-divided leaves 7–16 cm in diameter; bears short peduncles of 2–4 white flowers marked with purple on the upper petals and veined with purple on the undersides, 8–18 mm in diameter; the floral tube is 6–9 mm long. Deep sand, often coastal, in Namaqualand and the southwestern Cape.

**3 *Pelargonium incarnatum***

J F M A M J J A S O N D

Weak-stemmed perennial to 30 cm, branching from a persistent rootstock, with rounded, palmately lobed leaves; bears few, almost radially symmetrical, pale pink flowers with a reddish eye; the floral tube is reduced to a shallow depression much shorter than the pedicel. Rocky sandstone slopes in the extreme southwestern Cape.

**4 *Pelargonium elongatum***

J F M A M J J A S O N D

Soft shrublet to 25 cm with heart-shaped, hairy leaves 4–5 cm in diameter, often with a reddish zonal marking; bears clusters of up to 6 cream-coloured flowers ±15 mm in diameter; the floral tube is 10–15 mm long. Stony slopes in the southwestern and southern Cape.

**5 *Pelargonium elegans***

J F M A M J J A S O N D

Tufted perennial to 45 cm with hairless or hairy, somewhat leathery, elliptical leaves ±3×2.5 cm; bears clusters of up to 7 pink flowers ±50 mm in diameter; the floral tube is 10–15 mm long and shorter than the pedicels. Coastal fynbos along the Cape south coast and the Eastern Cape.

**6 *Pelargonium patulum***

J F M A M J J A S O N D

Straggling shrublet to 30 cm with greyish, leathery, heart-shaped to rounded leaves, variously toothed along the margins and usually with a reddish zonal marking, ±3 cm in diameter; bears clusters of 2 or 3 pink flowers ±25 mm in diameter; the floral tube is 15–20 mm long. Sandstone slopes in fynbos in the southwestern and southern Cape.

**7 *Pelargonium myrrhifolium***

J F M A M J J A S O N D

Sprawling shrublet to 50 cm with leaves ±5×3 cm and twice-divided into thread-like or linear to ribbon-shaped segments; bears clusters of up to 5 white, pink or purple flowers 20–25 mm in diameter with the upper 2 petals markedly wider; the floral tube is 4–10 mm long. Open places on stony sand from Namaqualand to the Eastern Cape.

**① *Pelargonium suburbanum*** | J | F | M | A | M | J | J | A | S | O | N | D |

Sprawling shrublet to 50 cm with once- or twice-divided leaves 3–7 cm in diameter, subtended by large stipules 10×8 mm; bears clusters of up to 6 cream to purple flowers near the branch tips, 30–40 mm in diameter, with the upper 2 petals much wider; the floral tube is 8–50 mm long. Coastal dunes from the Cape Peninsula to the Eastern Cape.

**② *Pelargonium longicaule*** | J | F | M | A | M | J | J | A | S | O | N | D |

Creeping or straggling shrublet with once-divided leaves ±4×3 cm, subtended by stipules ±6×5 mm; bears clusters of up to 6 white to pale pink or pale yellowish flowers on well-developed branches, 30–60 mm in diameter, with the upper 2 petals much wider; the floral tube is 30–55 mm long. Sandy, often coastal flats in the southwestern Cape.

# RUTACEAE                                           Citrus family

▸ STYLE MUCH SHORTER THAN THE PETALS

## *Acmadenia*  ACMADENIA, DUINEBUCHU

Ericoid shrublets, usually single-stemmed at the base. Leaves needle-like to round, erect or spreading and often overlapping. Flowers 1–3 at the branch tips, sometimes crowded at the end of the stems on short-shoots, white or pink, the petals usually erect below and forming a throat; stamens each tipped with a sessile or sunken gland, without alternating staminodes or the staminodes minute; *ovary completely enveloped by a fleshy disc; the style shorter than the petals.* Winter-rainfall parts of South Africa in fynbos, mainly southwestern Cape: 33 spp, all fynbos.

**③ *Acmadenia obtusata*** | J | F | M | A | M | J | J | A | S | O | N | D |

Single-stemmed, aromatic shrublet to 30 cm with erect, needle-like leaves 10–11×1.5 mm that have minutely fringed margins and are closely pressed against the stem; bears bright pink flowers that are often crowded on short branchlets near the branch tips. Limestone hills and calcareous sands along the southern and Eastern Cape coasts.

**④ *Acmadenia mundiana*** | J | F | M | A | M | J | J | A | S | O | N | D |

Single-stemmed, aromatic shrub to 1 m with slightly spreading, broadly elliptical leaves up to 11×5 mm that are minutely haired on the margins; bears several pink flowers crowded at the branch tips. Limestone hills on the Agulhas Plain.

## *Adenandra*  CHINA FLOWER, PORSELEINBLOM

Ericoid shrublets. Leaves elliptical or needle-like, often with 2 glands at the base of the petiole. Flowers 1 to few at the branch tips, in heads, flat-topped clusters or short racemes, *glistening* white or, rarely, pink above and pink to red on the reverse; *stamens each tipped with a stalked gland* alternating with hairy, thread-like staminodes; ovary surrounded by a cup-shaped, fleshy disc, *the style shorter than the petals.* Winter-rainfall parts of the Western Cape in fynbos: 18 spp, all fynbos.

## FLOWER CLUSTERS NOT GUMMY

**1** *Adenandra villosa*

J F M A M J J A S O N D

Aromatic shrub to 1 m with ascending or spreading, sometimes loosely overlapping, elliptical to oblong leaves 4–13×2–5 mm, leathery, with thickened margins; bears heads of 2–6 white flowers that are reddish on the reverse, with petals 7–14 mm long and reddish, usually broad sepals. Sandstone slopes in the southwestern Cape.

**2** *Adenandra uniflora*

J F M A M J J A S O N D

Aromatic shrublet to 50 cm with ascending to spreading, oblong to lance-shaped leaves 4–14×1.5–3.5 mm, relatively thin-textured, with the margins rolled under; bears solitary (rarely more) white to pink flowers that are reddish on the reverse, with petals 6–16 mm long and large, leaf-like sepals. Sandstone slopes in the extreme southwestern Cape; very similar to *Adenandra villosa* and thought to hybridise with it on the Cape Peninsula.

## FLOWERS IN GUMMY HEADS

**3** *Adenandra gummifera*

J F M A M J J A S O N D

Single-stemmed, aromatic shrublet to 1.5 m, gummy on the young parts, with erect to spreading, closely overlapping, oblong leaves 8–14×2–3 mm, thick and leathery, with the margins rolled under; bears gummy heads of 1–4 white to pink flowers, with petals 13–20 mm long. Sandstone slopes on Potberg.

**4** *Adenandra obtusata*

J F M A M J J A S O N D

Aromatic shrublet to 50 cm, gummy on the young parts, with erect to spreading, closely overlaping, oblong leaves 4–6×2–3 mm, thick and leathery, with the margins rolled under; bears gummy heads of 1–4 white flowers that are pink on the reverse, with petals 8–12 mm long. Limestone hills and flats on the Agulhas Plain.

**5** *Adenandra viscida*

J F M A M J J A S O N D

Aromatic shrublet to 50 cm, almost hairless, with ascending, sometimes loosely overlapping, lance-shaped to elliptical, pointed leaves 6–12×1.5–3.5 mm, leathery, with the margins rolled under; bears gummy heads of 2–10 white flowers that are reddish on the reverse with petals 7–10 mm long and reddish-purple sepals. Sandstone or limestone hills from Hermanus to Agulhas.

## *Coleonema*　CAPE MAY, CONFETTI BUSH

Ericoid, usually single-stemmed shrubs with wand-like branches. Leaves needle-like or narrowly lance-shaped. Flowers solitary in the axils, sometimes clustered at the branch tips, white or pink; stamens with a minute terminal gland, the *staminodes situated within a groove in the petals* and joined to them at the base; ovary situated within a cup-shaped nectar-disc; *the style shorter than the petals*. Winter-rainfall South Africa, mainly southwestern Cape in fynbos: 8 spp, all fynbos.

**6** *Coleonema album*

J F M A M J J A S O N D

Shrub to 2 m with sweet-smelling, needle-like to oblong leaves 12–14×1.3–1.5 mm; bears clusters of white flowers 6–7 mm in diameter. Coastal sandstone or granite outcrops in the southwestern Cape.

**1** *Coleonema juniperinum*  J F M A M J J A S O N D

Shrublet to 50 cm with erect, resin-scented, needle-like leaves 5–7×1 mm; bears solitary white flowers 3–4 mm in diameter with finely warty petals. Sandstone slopes in the southwestern Cape.

## *Diosma*  DIOSMA, BITTERBOEGOE

Ericoid shrublets, usually single-stemmed at base. Leaves needle-like to round, erect or spreading and often overlapping. Flowers 1 to few at branch tips, white or cream, sometimes slightly reddened; stamens each tipped with a sessile or immersed gland, *without alternating staminodes, ovary surrounded by a shallow, undulating nectar-disc, style shorter than the petals.* Mainly winter-rainfall parts of South Africa in fynbos, mostly southwestern Cape: 28 spp; all fynbos.

▶ **LEAVES MOSTLY OPPOSITE**

**2** *Diosma oppositifolia* **Bitterboegoe**  J F M A M J J A S O N D

Shrublet to 1 m, many-stemmed from a woody rootstock, with opposite, needle-like to lance-shaped leaves, recurved at the tips, 5–10×1–1.5 mm; bears small, flat-topped clusters of white flowers. Rocky slopes in the southwestern Cape.

**3** *Diosma subulata*  J F M A M J J A S O N D

Single-stemmed shrub to 1.8 m with mostly opposite, erect, needle-like or lance-shaped leaves 5–17×2–3 mm; bears small clusters of white flowers. Coastal dunes around Agulhas.

▶ **LEAVES ALTERNATE**

**4** *Diosma aspalathoides* **Haasboegoe**  J F M A M J J A S O N D

Shrub to 1 m, many-stemmed from a woody rootstock, with short, petiolate, needle-like to lance-shaped leaves with recurved tips, 3–10×±1 mm; bears small clusters of white flowers. Sandy, mostly coastal flats, along the West Coast.

**5** *Diosma hirsuta*  J F M A M J J A S O N D

**Rooiboegoe, kanferboegoe** Shrublet to 50 cm coppicing from a woody rootstock, with needle-like, sharply pointed leaves 10–22×±1 mm; bears short racemes of white flowers that are grouped at the branch tips, with the petals persisting below the fruits. Sandstone and clay slopes in the southwestern and southern Cape.

## *Euchaetis*  EUCHAETIS

Ericoid shrublets, usually single-stemmed at the base. Leaves needle-like to round, sometimes folded. Flowers 1 to few at the branch tips, sometimes in tight clusters, white or pink, with the *narrow bases of the petals erect and forming a cage around the ovary, conspicuously bearded in the throat;* stamens each tipped with a sessile or immersed gland, *without alternating staminodes,* ovary completely enveloped within the nectar-disc, *the style shorter than the petals.* Mainly winter-rainfall parts of South Africa in fynbos: 23 spp, all fynbos.

**6** *Euchaetis burchellii*  J F M A M J J A S O N D

Dense shrub to 1 m with ascending, recurved, oval leaves up to 4.5×1.5 mm; bears white or pink flowers in pairs at the branch tips. Coastal sands in the southern Cape.

**① *Euchaetis meridionalis***  J F M **A M J J A** S O N D

Dense shrublet to 1.5 m with ascending, folded leaves that are hairy on the margins, 2–3×1.5–2 mm; bears clusters of 4–6 white or pink flowers at the branch tips. Coastal limestone on the Agulhas Plain.

**② *Euchaetis longibracteata***  J F M A **M J J** A S O **N D**

Shrublet to 80 cm with ascending, oval to lance-shaped leaves ±10×2.5–3 mm, the upper leaves whitish and petal-like; bears tight clusters of pink flowers surrounded by a conspicuous collar formed by the upper leaves. Limestone hills on the Agulhas Plain.

▶ **STYLE LONGER THAN THE PETALS**

## *Agathosma*  BUCHU, BOEGOE

Ericoid shrubs or shrublets. Leaves needle-like to orbicular. Flowers 1 to few in the axils or more usually in clusters at the branch tips, white, pink or mauve; stamens usually with a terminal gland, *alternating with variously shaped staminodes, these often petal-like*; ovary surrounded by a deeply cup-shaped nectar-disc, *the style longer than the petals*. Southern Africa, mainly winter-rainfall parts of the southwestern Cape: ±150 spp; ±140 fynbos spp. *Agathosma betulina* and, to some extent, *A. crenulata* are used to make some of the most important traditional medicines in the Cape pharmacopoeia and have achieved international usage in the flavour and fragrance industry on account of their blackcurrant-like odour. The vernacular name derives from the original Koisan name for several species of shrubby members of the family, the dried leaves of which were used to treat stomach ailments, or powdered and mixed with sheep fat for anointing the body.

▶ **FLOWERS SOLITARY IN THE LEAF AXILS**

**③ *Agathosma betulina* Buchu**  J F M A M **J J A S** O N D

Coppicing, broad-leafed shrub to over 2 m with oval leaves, mostly 10–20 mm long, concave and minutely toothed; bears large, white to pink flowers in the axils with petals 8–10 mm long and lance-shaped staminodes; ovary and fruits are 5-segmented. Rocky sandstone slopes on the mountains inland of the West Coast. *Agathosma crenulata*, from south of Ceres, has elliptical leaves, mostly 15–35 mm long.

▶ **FLOWERS IN CLUSTERS; STAMINODES WIDEST ABOVE THE MIDDLE**

**④ *Agathosma bisulca* Steenbokboegoe**  J F M A **M J J A** S O N D

Rounded shrub to over 1 m, branching at ground level with needle-like to lance-shaped leaves, mostly 10–12 mm long and often 2-grooved beneath; bears loose clusters of white flowers, the petals 5–6 mm long, with long, slender stalks and thread- or paddle-shaped staminodes; ovary and fruits are 2- or 3-segmented. Lower and middle slopes and flats in deep sand along the West Coast, especially near Clanwilliam.

**⑤ *Agathosma thymifolia***  J F M A M J J **A S O** N D

Single-stemmed shrub to over 1 m, branching near ground level, with broadly rounded leaves 3.5–4 mm long, flat or convex above; bears loose clusters of pink or mauve flowers with petals 4 mm long and paddle-shaped staminodes; ovary and fruits are 3- or 4-segmented. Coastal sand and dunes on limestone near Langebaan.

### ❶ *Agathosma lanceolata*

J F M **A M J J A S O** N D

**Heuningboegoe** Single-stemmed, tangled and spreading shrublet to 50 cm with liquorice-scented, elliptical to rounded leaves 4–6 mm long, flat or convex above and sometimes hairy on the margins; bears loose clusters of pink to deep mauve flowers with petals 4–4.5 mm long and paddle-shaped staminodes; ovary and fruits are 3-segmented. South-facing sandstone slopes on the Cape Peninsula.

### ❷ *Agathosma imbricata*

**J** F M A M **J J A S O N D**

Coppicing shrub to 1 m with sweetly or herb-scented, lance-shaped to rounded leaves 2.5–5 mm long, concave above and hairy on the margins; bears dense clusters of white, pink or purple flowers with petals 4–7.5 mm long and spoon-shaped staminodes; ovary and fruits are 3-segmented. Granite, calcareous or sandy, well-drained or seasonally damp slopes and flats in the southwestern and southern Cape.

## ▶ FLOWERS IN CLUSTERS; STAMINODES WIDEST AT OR BELOW THE MIDDLE

### ❸ *Agathosma capensis*

**J F M A M J J A S O N D**

Coppicing shrub to 90 cm with sweetly spice-scented, needle-like to oval leaves 1.5–7 mm long, almost concave above and hairless or hairy; bears loose clusters of white, pink or purple flowers with petals 3–5 mm long and peg-like or lance-shaped staminodes; ovary and fruits are 3-segmented. Slopes and flats on shale, granite or coastal sands, less often on acid sand, from Namaqualand to the southern and Eastern Cape; a very variable and widespread species.

### ❹ *Agathosma serpyllacea*

J F M A **M J J A S O** N D

Single-stemmed shrublet to 80 cm with needle-like to lance-shaped leaves, mostly 5–10 mm long, concave and hairless or variously hairy; bears clusters of white, pink or purple flowers with petals 3.5–5.5 mm long and peg-like or lance-shaped staminodes; ovary and fruits are 3-segmented. Coastal or inland sand or limestone flats and slopes in the southwestern and southern Cape.

### ❺ *Agathosma cerefolium*

J F M A M J J **A S O N D**

**Anysboegoe, strandboegoe** Single-stemmed shrublet to 1.4 m with strongly aniseed-scented, needle-like to rounded leaves, mostly 3–5 mm long, varying from slightly concave to convex above and hairy on the margins; bears loose clusters of white, pink or mauve flowers with petals 3–5 mm long and lance-shaped staminodes; ovary and fruits are 3-segmented. Mostly coastal, calcareous sands and limestone hills in the southern Cape.

### ❻ *Agathosma ciliaris*

J F M A **M J J A S O N D**

Dense, rounded shrublet to 45 cm with aniseed-scented, lance-shaped leaves 4–8 mm long, concave above and often hairy on the margins; bears clusters of white or mauve flowers with petals 4.5–5.5 mm long and lance-shaped staminodes; ovary and fruits are 3-segmented. Coastal flats to lower sandstone slopes and shale bands in the extreme southwestern Cape.

### ❼ *Agathosma collina*

J F M A M J J A S **O N D**

Dense, rounded, single-stemmed, yellowish-green-leafed shrub to over 1 m with mildly aromatic, oval to lance-shaped leaves 3.5–5 mm long, concave above; bears dense clusters of white flowers with petals 4.5 mm long and thread-like staminodes joined to the base of the petals; ovary and fruits are 3-segmented. Stabilised dunes on the Agulhas Plain.

199

**❶ *Agathosma riversdalensis*** `J F M A M J J A S O N D`

Single-stemmed, slender shrublet to 60 cm with herb-scented, oval leaves 2.5–3.5 mm long, flat or concave above; bears clusters of white to purple flowers with petals 4 mm long and narrowly lance-shaped staminodes; ovary and fruits are 3-segmented. Limestone flats on the Agulhas Plain.

## *Macrostylis*  MACROSTYLIS

Ericoid shrublets, single-stemmed at the base or coppicing. Leaves needle-like to round. Flowers 1 to few at the branch tips, sometimes in tight clusters, white or cream *with a beard-like tuft of hairs near the middle of the petals*; stamens each tipped with a sessile or immersed gland, *elongating and carrying the spent anthers beyond the petals*, alternating with minute staminodes, the ovary completely enveloped within the nectar-disc, and *the style longer than the petals; the ovary and fruits 3-segmented*. Winter-rainfall parts of South Africa in fynbos: 10 spp, all fynbos.

**❷ *Macrostylis villosa*** `J F M A M J J A S O N D`

Rounded shrublet to 30 cm with ±sessile, ascending, overlapping, lance-shaped leaves 4–14 mm long; flowers 11–14 at the branch tips, white. Sandy coastal flats on the Cape Peninsula and nearby West Coast.

## *Phyllosma*  PHYLLOSMA

Ericoid shrublets. Leaves oblong and leathery with the margins rolled under. Flowers 1 to few at the branch tips, sometimes in tight clusters, *pink, the petals with a narrow, hairy stalk*; stamens each tipped with a sessile or immersed gland, *elongating and carrying the spent anthers beyond the petals, without alternating staminodes*; ovary situated in a saucer-like nectar-disc, *the style longer than the petals*. Southwestern Cape in fynbos: 2 spp, both fynbos.

**❸ *Phyllosma capensis*** `J F M A M J J A S O N D`

Shrublet to 40 cm with foetid, narrowly oblong, leathery leaves, the margins rolled under, 6–15×1.5–2 mm; bears clusters of pale pink flowers at the branch tips. Sandstone crevices in the Cedarberg and Ceres mountains. *Phyllosma barosmoides*, from the Hex River Mountains, has rounded leaves 6–8x3–4 mm.

## *Empleurum*  EMPLEURUM, VLEIBOEGOE

Ericoid or willowy shrublets. Leaves narrowly elliptical to oblong with smooth or finely serrated margins that are slightly rolled under. Flowers 1–3 in the leaf axils, insignificant, *unisexual* or bisexual, *without petals*; male flowers with 4 large stamens, each tipped with a sessile or sunken gland; *ovary comprising a single carpel segment with a blade-like style arising to one side*. Southwestern and southern Cape in fynbos: 2 spp, both fynbos.

**❹ *Empleurum unicapsulare*** `J F M A M J J A S O N D`

Willowy shrub or small tree to 4 m with narrowly lance-shaped, gland-dotted and resin-scented leaves 20–60 mm long, with finely serrated margins; bears 1 or 2 unisexual or bisexual greenish flowers in the leaf axils; fruits ±10 mm long with a blade-like style of similar length. Streambanks or seeps in the mountains of the southwestern and southern Cape. *Empleurum fragrans* from the Langeberg Mountains is a smaller ericoid shrub with oblong leaves 6–8 mm long.

# LINACEAE

## Flax family

### Linum  FLAX

Perennials. Leaves opposite, alternate or whorled, with or without stipular glands at the base. Flowers in an open or more dense panicle, *yellow, usually reddish on the reverse*, the *petals rolled like an umbrella in bud, soon falling*; stamens 5, joined at the base, sometimes with minute staminodes between them, styles 5, separate or partially joined. Worldwide in tropical and temperate regions, with 14 species in southern Africa (mainly the winter-rainfall parts in fynbos): ±230 spp; 14 fynbos spp.

**❶ *Linum africanum***     J F M A M J J A S O N D

Perennial to 50 cm with slender stems from a persistent woody base and opposite, narrowly lance-shaped leaves with small glands at the base; bears loose panicles of yellow flowers flushed red on the reverse, with the styles joined for up to half their length. Sandstone and limestone slopes and flats in the southwestern and southern Cape.

# MALVACEAE

## Hibiscus family

### Anisodontea  AFRICAN MALLOW, BERGROOS

Shrubs or perennials. Leaves unlobed or 3–7-lobed. Flowers 1 to several in the axils, *white, pink or magenta, surrounded by an epicalyx of 3–5 bracts*; stamens many, *joined into a staminal column that is split at the top into numerous filaments*, stigmas apical and globular. *Fruits splitting into numerous segments.* South Africa and Lesotho, mainly in the drier parts, especially the winter-rainfall Karoo: 21 spp; 12 fynbos spp.

**❷ *Anisodontea scabrosa*  Sandroos**     J F M A M J J A S O N D

Shrub to 2 m, thinly to densely covered in gland-tipped hairs, with obscurely 3-lobed or elliptical toothed leaves; bears 1 to few pink flowers in the axils, surrounded by an epicalyx of narrow lobes and with a hairy staminal column more than 5 mm long. Coastal sands and granite outcrops from the West Coast to KwaZulu-Natal.

### Hibiscus  HIBISCUS, WILDESTOKROOS

Shrubs, subshrubs, or annual or perennial herbs. Leaves unlobed or lobed. Flowers usually solitary in the axils, *often large*, usually *yellow or pink with a dark eye, surrounded by an epicalyx of 5–20 bracts*; stamens many, *joined into a staminal column that bears anthers throughout its length or only in the upper half*, stigmas usually *disc-like*. Fruits a capsule, not splitting into segments. Each flower lasts just a single day. Worldwide in the tropics and subtropics, poorly represented in fynbos: ±300 spp; 6 fynbos spp.

**❸ *Hibiscus aethiopicus***     J F M A M J J A S O N D

Sprawling subshrub to 30 cm from a woody rootstock with oval to elliptical leaves, sometimes coarsely toothed at the ends, 3–5-veined from the base and hairy beneath but almost hairless above; bears cream to yellow flowers in the axils, often with a dark centre, surrounded by an epicalyx of 10–12 narrow lobes and with a staminal column ±10 mm long. Stony sandstone or clay slopes from the southwestern Cape to KwaZulu-Natal.

## *Hermannia*  DOLL'S ROSE, POPROSIE

Shrublets or perennials, often covered with star-shaped hairs and thus appearing granular or mealy. Leaves unlobed, toothed or variously divided, usually *subtended by leaf-like stipules*. Flowers axillary, *often in raceme- or panicle-like inflorescences*, yellow to red or pink, the sepals forming a *globular to bell-shaped calyx* and the *petals spirally twisted*; stamens 5, opposite the petals, joined at the base, the *filaments with membranous wings or lobes* and the *anthers tapering to a pointed or hairy tip*. Mainly southern Africa, especially the drier winter-rainfall regions: ±180 spp; 60 fynbos spp. Some species were used medicinally to treat syphilis ('pokkies').

▸ **STAMEN FILAMENTS ABRUPTLY WIDENED NEAR THE MIDDLE OR CROSS-SHAPED, AND BEARDED**

**1 *Hermannia saccifera***    J F M A M J J **A S O** N D

Hairless, sticky, sprawling shrublet to 40 cm with regularly toothed, elliptical to oblong leaves; bears axillary pairs of bell-shaped yellow flowers with the bracts joined into a small cup below the calyx. Stony clay slopes from the southwestern to the Eastern Cape.

**2 *Hermannia pinnata***    J F M A M J J **A S O** N D

Almost hairless, creeping shrublet to 15 cm, often forming mats, with narrow leaves, sometimes deeply lobed above and often spuriously whorled because the stipules are divided into 2 or 3 narrow lobes; bears scented yellow to pale orange flowers with furled petals on axillary peduncles, with narrow bracts below the calyx. Sandy coastal flats and dunes along the West Coast.

**3 *Hermannia heterophylla***    J F M A M J J A **S O** N D

Sprawling to creeping, slightly sticky shrublet to 50 cm with paddle-shaped leaves, toothed above and subtended by leafy stipules; bears 1 or 2 mauve flowers with tightly furled petals on slender axillary and terminal peduncles, the bracts partly united in a cup below the calyx. Sandy flats, often coastal, along the West Coast.

**4 *Hermannia grossularifolia***    J F M A M J J A **S O** N D

Sprawling to creeping, roughly hairy subshrub to 15 cm with wedge-shaped leaves, toothed or lobed above; bears terminal clusters of few yellow flowers with tightly furled petals that are covered with star-shaped hairs; the fruits are globular and swollen and covered with coarse hairs. Sandy flats and slopes in the southwestern Cape, flowering mostly after fire.

▸ **STAMEN FILAMENTS PADDLE-SHAPED; FLOWERS BELL-SHAPED WITH GRADUALLY FLARING PETALS**

**5 *Hermannia alnifolia***    J F M A M J **J A** S O N D

Rounded, grey-green shrub to 1 m, the young branchlets hairy, with wedge-shaped to oval leaves, toothed above and covered with granular hairs beneath; bears numerous small yellow flowers in elongate terminal clusters. Shale or rocky slopes in the southwestern and southern Cape.

**1** *Hermannia althaeifolia* **Pokkiesblom** J F M A M J J A S O N D
Soft-haired, grey-green shrublet to 50 cm, sometimes erect and single-stemmed, with conspicuously petiolated, oval to elliptical leaves, toothed and crisped on the margins and subtended by broad, leafy stipules; bears yellow flowers in terminal and axillary clusters, the calyx swollen and reddish, fading to cream. Clay, granite and limestone slopes in Namaqualand and the southwestern and southern Cape.

**2** *Hermannia trifurca* J F M A M J J A S O N D
Roughly hairy shrublet to 1.5 m with oblong leaves, 3-toothed above; bears bell-shaped, mauve flowers with dark venation, in horizontal, 1-sided racemes. Stony and sandy soils in Namaqualand and the southwestern Cape.

▸ **STAMEN FILAMENTS PADDLE-SHAPED; FLOWERS WITH A PIN-HOLE THROAT AND ABRUPTLY SPREADING PETALS**

**3** *Hermannia trifoliata* J F M A M J J A S O N D
Grey-green shrublet with stiffly erect branches to 40 cm and ascending, closely overlapping, sessile, wedge-shaped leaves; bears terminal clusters of orange to red flowers ±10 mm long, with a pin-hole throat and ± swollen, papery calyx. Coastal limestone soils in the southern Cape.

**4** *Hermannia ternifolia* J F M A M J J A S O N D
Grey-green shrublet with sprawling branches to 20 cm and wedge-shaped leaves, usually subtended by large, leafy stipules; bears terminal clusters of orange to red flowers ±13 mm long, with a pin-hole throat and swollen, papery calyx. Coastal sands and limestones along the West Coast to Agulhas.

**5** *Hermannia concinnifolia* J F M A M J J A S O N D
Erect shrublet to 90 cm with wedge-shaped leaves recurved at the tips and subtended by large stipules; bears terminal clusters of yellow flowers with a pin-hole throat and large, roughly hairy and usually reddish calyx. Coastal limestones on the Agulhas Plain.

**6** *Hermannia hyssopifolia* **Pokkiesblom** J F M A M J J A S O N D
Greyish, twiggy shrub to 2 m with wedge-shaped leaves, toothed above; bears dense terminal clusters of cream to pale yellow flowers with a pin-hole throat and a much swollen, urn-shaped, papery calyx. Stony granite and clay slopes from the Cape Peninsula to the Eastern Cape.

# APOCYNACEAE                                        Milkweed family

▸ **SAP WHITE AND MILKY**

## *Asclepias* **MILKWEED, WILDE KAPOK**

Spreading perennials or annuals *with milky sap*. Leaves opposite, usually sessile, variously shaped. Flowers in *erect, stalked, flat-topped clusters arising next to the axils and at the branch tips*, variously coloured, the petals spreading and the *corona lobes hollowed and boat-shaped*. Fruits usually solitary by abortion, smooth or with fleshy projections. Africa and America: ±150 spp; 3 fynbos spp. Although toxic, the dried leaves were used medicinally.

### ❶ *Asclepias crispa*  Bitterwortel

Sprawling perennial to 30 cm with narrow, roughly hairy leaves that are wavy or crinkly on the margins; bears stalked clusters of greenish or purple flowers with greenish corona lobes. Sandy flats and slopes from the West Coast to the Eastern Cape.

## *Gomphocarpus*  WILD COTTON, KATOENBOS

*Erect* perennials or shrublets *with milky sap.* Leaves opposite, variously shaped. Flowers in *nodding, stalked, flat-topped clusters arising next to the axils and at the branch tips,* variously coloured, the petals spreading and the *corona lobes hollowed and boat-shaped.* Fruits usually *inflated and balloon-like* with fleshy projections; the silky tufts of hairs on the seeds aid in wind-dispersal. Africa and Asia: ±30 spp; 2 fynbos spp.

### ❷ *Gomphocarpus cancellatus*

J F M A M J J A S O N D

**Gansiebos**  Rigid, hairy shrub to 1.5 m with milky sap and opposite, leathery, oblong to elliptical leaves that are rounded at the base; bears nodding clusters of cream-coloured flowers; the fruits are swollen and egg-shaped with tapering tips. Stony slopes from southern Namibia to the Eastern Cape.

### ❸ *Gomphocarpus fruticosus*

J F M A M J J A S O N D

**Vleiklapper**  Soft shrub 1–3 m tall, branching mainly from the base, with milky sap and opposite, narrow leaves that taper gradually towards the base; bears nodding clusters of cream-coloured flowers; the fruits are swollen and egg-shaped with tapering tips. Disturbed areas throughout southern Africa and elsewhere.

## *Cynanchum*  CYNANCHUM, BOKHORINKIES

*Climbers* or twiggy shrublets *with milky sap.* Leaves opposite, oval to elliptical. Flowers in *small clusters outside the axils, cup-shaped,* greenish to brown with a *cup-shaped or tubular corona* that is often deeply lobed or toothed. Cosmopolitan, often coastal: ±100 spp; 6 fynbos spp.

### ❹ *Cynanchum africanum*

J F M A M J J A S O N D

Climber to 60 cm with horizontal runners, sometimes hairy, with milky sap, and opposite, slightly fleshy, oval leaves; bears axillary clusters of fragrant flowers, brown or sometimes green with twisted petals and a white crown or corona that is twice as deep as wide; the style-column is clearly stalked and as long as the corona. Sandy soils, mainly coastal, from Namaqualand to the Eastern Cape.

### ❺ *Cynanchum obtusifolium*

J F M A M J J A S O N D

Climber to 3 m with a woody base and milky sap, and opposite, oval to elliptical leaves, often lightly crisped on the margins; bears axillary clusters of dull green flowers with a white crown or corona that is shallow and deeply lobed; the style-column is not stalked. Coastal bush from the Cape Peninsula to Mozambique. *Cynanchum ellipticum,* from east of George, has a shallowly toothed corona.

## *Microloma* WAX CREEPER, MELKTOU

*Climbers* or twiggy shrublets with clear sap. Leaves opposite, *narrow*, erect to pendent. Flowers in small clusters outside the axils, tubular to urn-shaped and ribbed, greenish yellow, *orange, red or pink*, the *petals usually closing the mouth of the tube. Fruits pendent.* Southern Africa, mainly arid areas: 10 spp; 2 fynbos spp. The small pink flowers are visited by sunbirds, the pollen-sacs attaching to the birds' tongues in a uniquely specialised form of bird pollination.

**1** *Microloma sagittatum* **Bokhorinkies** | J | F | M | A | M | J | J | A | S | O | N | D |

Slender climber with oblong leaves 7–35 mm long; bears tapering, fine-haired pink to red flowers 5–11 mm long with pointed petals. Widespread from Namaqualand to the Eastern Cape in a variety of drier habitats, from rock outcrops to sandy coastal flats.

**2** *Microloma tenuifolium* **Kannetjies** | J | F | M | A | M | J | J | A | S | O | N | D |

Slender, deciduous climber with narrow or thread-like leaves 20–70 mm long; bears urn-shaped, shiny and hairless, orange to red flowers 6–8 mm long with rounded petals. Moister mountain slopes and stony hills from the southwestern to the Eastern Cape.

## *Sarcostemma* SARCOSTEMMA, SPANTOU

*Leafless climbers or trailing shrublets with milky sap. Flowers in small axillary clusters, cup-shaped,* yellowish with a *ring- or cup-shaped corona.* Old World in arid areas: 10 spp; 1 fynbos sp.

**3** *Sarcostemma viminale* | J | F | M | A | M | J | J | A | S | O | N | D |

Leafless, succulent scrambler or climber to 3 m with smooth, grey-green stems and milky sap; bears dense umbels of fragrant, yellowish flowers with a white corona or central crown. Widespread throughout the more arid parts of Africa in bush on stony slopes.

▸ **SAP CLEAR AND WATERY**

## *Orbea* TOAD PLANT, AASBLOM

Clumped or mat-forming, leafless succulents with *hairless stems bearing 4 rows of tubercles and clear sap.* Flowers usually >30 mm in diameter with smooth or wrinkled petals, often with a *thickened, circular ring* in the centre, yellowish to brownish and foetid. Southern Africa, mainly drier parts: 20 spp; 1 fynbos sp. The stench of the flowers attracts carrion flies, which act as pollinators.

**4** *Orbea variegata* | J | F | M | A | M | J | J | A | S | O | N | D |

Mat-forming, leafless succulent with clear sap, the stems 15–25 mm in diameter, with conical tubercles loosely arranged in 4 rows; bears large speckled flowers 70–110 mm in diameter with a raised, shallowly bowl-shaped centre. Mainly coastal on granite or shale outcrops in the southwestern and southern Cape.

### *Stapelia* CARRION FLOWER, AASBLOM

Clumped or mat-forming, leafless succulents with *velvety stems bearing 4–6 rows of tubercles and with clear sap*. Flowers star- to funnel-shaped, usually with *wrinkled and often variously hairy petals*, yellowish to brownish and foetid. Africa, mainly drier parts of southern Africa: 43 spp; 8 fynbos spp. The stench of the flowers attracts carrion flies, which act as pollinators.

**①** *Stapelia hirsuta* **Haasoor**

| J | F | M | A | M | J | J | A | S | O | N | D |

Leafless, usually fine-haired succulent with clear sap, the 4-angled stems 10–20 mm in diameter, forming dense clumps; bears reddish to purple flowers 70–110 mm in diameter, hairless or soft-haired around the centre and along the petal margins, smelling of rotting fish. Stony, often sandstone, slopes from Namaqualand to the southern and Eastern Cape.

# OXALIDACEAE                                   Oxalis family

### *Oxalis* SORREL, SURING

Perennial or, rarely, annual herbs, *often stemless, with sour, acidic sap*. Leaves in a basal tuft or alternate, usually *divided into 3 (or more) leaflets* that are often *bilobed or notched at the tips*, sometimes with small orange or brownish warts or calluses at the tips, sometimes *drooping and closing at night*. Flowers solitary or in umbels, funnel-shaped and *furled at night*, mostly pink, yellow or white; the *stamens in 2 series at different heights with the stigmas at a third level*. Cosmopolitan with centres of diversity in South America and winter-rainfall South Africa: ±500 spp; ±120 fynbos spp. Plants are rich in oxalic acid and have been used culinarily and as a vermifuge.

▸ **PEDUNCLES WITH MORE THAN 1 FLOWER EACH**

**②** *Oxalis livida* **Steentjiesuring**

| J | F | M | A | M | J | J | A | S | O | N | D |

Perennial with stem to 20 cm, often branched, with the leaves often not fully expanded at flowering, divided into 3 deeply bilobed leaflets that are usually hairless and purple beneath; bears clusters of 2–6 rose pink or lilac flowers with a yellowish tube. Rocky slopes in shaded or sheltered situations in the southwestern Cape.

**③** *Oxalis pes-caprae* **Geelsuring**

| J | F | M | A | M | J | J | A | S | O | N | D |

Stemless perennial with the leaves mostly in a basal tuft, divided into 3 wedge-shaped, notched leaflets that are usually hairless above and hairy beneath; bears clusters of 3–20 canary yellow flowers. Widespread and common from Namaqualand to the Eastern Cape, often along verges and in fields.

▸ **PEDUNCLES WITH ONLY 1 FLOWER EACH; LEAVES WITH MORE OR LESS THAN 3 LEAFLETS**

**④** *Oxalis flava* **Bobbejaanuintjie**

| J | F | M | A | M | J | J | A | S | O | N | D |

Stemless perennial with the leaves often not fully expanded at flowering, hairless, leathery and greyish, with large brown stipules, divided into 2–12 narrow to elliptical, folded leaflets; bears yellow, white or pale lilac flowers. Flats and lower slopes, often on sand, from Namaqualand to the southern Cape.

**⑤** *Oxalis monophylla*

| J | F | M | A | M | J | J | A | S | O | N | D |

Stemless perennial with the leaves comprising a single leaflet covered in gland-tipped hairs; bears white or pale lilac flowers with a yellow tube. Rocky sandstone slopes along the Cape Peninsula and West Coast.

213

**① *Oxalis burtoniae***

J F M A M **J** J A S O N D

Perennial with wiry stem to 10 cm and leaves divided into 5–7 thread-like leaflets; bears bright yellow flowers. Granite and limestone outcrops around Saldanha Bay.

**② *Oxalis tomentosa* Vingersuring**

J F M **A M** J J A S O N D

Stemless perennial with silky-haired leaves divided into 10–20 oblong or narrowly wedge-shaped, minutely notched leaflets, often not fully expanded at flowering; bears white flowers with a yellow tube. Stony flats and lower slopes, often on clay, on the Cape Peninsula and along the West Coast.

▸ **PEDUNCLES WITH ONLY 1 FLOWER EACH; LEAVES WITH 3 WEDGE-SHAPED TO ROUNDED LEAFLETS; PEDUNCULAR BRACTS OPPOSITE AND AT A JOINT**

**③ *Oxalis bifida***

J F **M A M J J** A S O N D

Perennial with branched stem to 30 cm and leaves divided into 3 wedge-shaped leaflets that are bilobed to the middle; bears rose pink flowers with a greenish tube on jointed peduncles. Damp stony slopes in the southwestern Cape.

**④ *Oxalis lanata***

J F M A **M J J A S O** N D

Perennial with stem to 10 cm and leaves divided into 3 densely hairy, heart-shaped leaflets; bears white or pink flowers with a yellow tube on jointed peduncles. Stony slopes and screes in the extreme southwestern Cape.

**⑤ *Oxalis luteola* Sandsuring**

J F M A **M** J J A S O N D

Stemless perennial with the leaves divided into 3 broadly wedge-shaped leaflets that are hairless or hairy, conspicuously veined and often purple beneath; bears bright yellow flowers on an articulated peduncle. Sandy flats and lower slopes, often coastal, in the southwestern Cape.

**⑥ *Oxalis obtusa* Geeloogsuring**

J F M A M **J J A S O** N D

Stemless perennial with the leaves divided into 3 broadly wedge- or heart-shaped leaflets that are hairless or hairy; bears pink, brick red, yellow or white flowers with darker veins and a yellow tube on jointed peduncles that are covered with down-facing hairs. Mostly damp clay and granite slopes from Namaqualand to the Eastern Cape; widespread and common.

▸ **PEDUNCLES WITH ONLY 1 FLOWER EACH; LEAVES WITH 3 WIDE, BROADLY WEDGE-SHAPED TO ROUNDED LEAFLETS; PEDUNCULAR BRACTS NOT OPPOSITE AT A JOINT**

**⑦ *Oxalis natans***

J F M A M J J A **S O N** D

**Waterklawer, watersuring** Aquatic perennial with slender, flexible, branching stems and leaves floating in terminal clusters, divided into 3 broadly heart-shaped leaflets; bears shallowly cup-shaped, white flowers with a yellow cup. Seasonal pools and streams on the West Coast coastal plain and on the Cape Peninsula; rare.

### ❶ *Oxalis eckloniana*

J F M **A M J J** A S O N D

Stemless perennial with leaves divided into 3 broadly elliptical to heart-shaped leaflets that have fine hairs along the margins and are often purple beneath; bears yellow, white or pink to orange flowers with a rather long yellow tube and anthers that are distinctly arrow-shaped and spread widely when the petals are removed. Usually damp slopes in the southwestern Cape.

### ❷ *Oxalis purpurea*

J F M A **M J J A S** O N D

**Grand duchess sorrel**  Stemless perennial with leaves divided into 3 broadly heart-shaped leaflets that have fine hairs on the margins and are purple beneath, developing black streaks when dry; bears large purple, pink, yellow or white flowers with a yellow tube. Widespread and common on damp flats and slopes from Namaqualand to the Eastern Cape.

### ❸ *Oxalis suavis*

J F M A **M J** J A S O N D

Usually stemless perennial to 8 cm with leaves divided into 3 wedge- or heart-shaped leaflets that are hairy and glandular on the margins and with minute reddish-brown spots. Bears yellow or white flowers with a yellow tube. Lower slopes and flats near Hopefield.

### ❹ *Oxalis tenella*

J F M A **M J J** A S O N D

Perennial with slender stems to 10 cm and leaves terminal and divided into 3 wedge-shaped leaflets that have short hairs along the margins and beneath; bears white or pale lilac, rarely yellow, flowers with a yellow tube. Clay flats inland of the West Coast, especially around Clanwilliam.

▸ **PEDUNCLES WITH ONLY 1 FLOWER EACH; LEAVES WITH 3 NARROW, FOLDED, THREAD-LIKE TO OBLONG LEAFLETS**

### ❺ *Oxalis versicolor*  Candycane sorrel

J F M A **M J J A S O N D**

Perennial with partly leafy stem to 20 cm, sometimes branching, the leaves mostly terminal and divided into 3 thread-like, folded leaflets; bears white flowers with a yellow tube and reddish-purple petal margins. Flats and slopes in the southwestern Cape.

### ❻ *Oxalis argyrophylla*

J F M A **M J J** A S O N D

Perennial with stems to 20 cm and leaves that are terminal and divided into 3 silky, narrowly wedge-shaped, folded leaflets; bears white or lilac flowers with a yellow cup and often reddish petal margins. Flats and lower slopes, mainly on the Cape Peninsula.

### ❼ *Oxalis polyphylla*

J F **M A M J** J A S O N D

Perennial with a slender stem to 20 cm, the leaves terminal and divided into 3(7) thread-like, folded leaflets that sometimes have sparse hairs beneath; bears rose, lilac or white flowers with yellow tube and often slightly darker margins. Flats and rock outcrops in light or heavy soils in the southwestern and southern Cape.

### ❶ *Oxalis glabra* Tapytsuring

J F M **A M J J A S O N** D

Perennial with a partly leafy stem 5–20 cm and a small bulb less than 10 mm in diameter, spreading by runners and forming dense carpets, the leaves mostly terminal and divided into narrowly wedge-shaped, folded leaflets; bears red, pink or white flowers with a yellow tube and long, narrow sepals. Sandy flats and slopes in the southwestern Cape.

### ❷ *Oxalis pusilla*

J F M A **M J J** A S O N D

Perennial with a partly leafy stem 5–20 cm and a small bulb less than 10 mm in diameter, the leaves terminal and divided into thread-like to narrowly wedge-shaped, folded leaflets; bears white or pale rose flowers with a yellowish tube, sometimes with a purple mouth. Flats and dampish places on the Peninsula and along the West Coast.

### ❸ *Oxalis hirta*

J F M **A M J** J A S O N D

Perennial with a leafy stem 5–30 cm, often branching, and ±sessile, grey-green leaves divided into 3 narrowly elliptical, folded leaflets that are hairy beneath; bears mauve, magenta or white flowers with a yellow, sometimes elongate, tube. Flats and lower slopes along the West Coast.

# CONVOLVULACEAE
# Convolvulus family

## *Convolvulus* BINDWEED, KLIMOP

Sprawling or *twining perennials*. Leaves often *heart- or arrow-shaped*, sometimes lobed. Flowers 1 to few in axillary clusters, subtended by small bracts, funnel- to cup-shaped, white to pink or magenta; the *style dividing into 2 slender stigmas*. The flowers each last just a single day. Worldwide, mainly in temperate and subtropical regions: ±250 spp; 5 fynbos spp.

### ❹ *Convolvulus capensis*

J F M A M J J A **S O** N D

**Cape bindweed** Sparsely hairy, perennial climber to 2 m with arrow-shaped to deeply lobed leaves, often toothed; bears white to pale pink flowers 15–35 mm long, the sepals blunt, 6–10 mm long, and usually silky. Widespread on drier stony slopes from Namaqualand to the Eastern Cape.

## *Falkia* FALKIA, OORTJIES

*Creeping, mat-forming perennials*. Leaves *oval to kidney-shaped*. Flowers solitary in the axils, white to pink; the *ovary deeply 4-lobed with 2 styles arising between the lobes*. Africa, mainly southern Africa: 2 or 3 spp; 1 fynbos sp.

### ❺ *Falkia repens*

J F M A M J J A S **O N D**

Sparsely hairy, mat-forming perennial with short, erect branches to 5 cm and heart- to kidney-shaped leaves; bears small white, pink or mauve flowers. Damp coastal flats and seeps from the Cape Peninsula to the Eastern Cape.

# PLUMBAGINACEAE    Plumbago family

## *Limonium*   SEA-PINK, PAPIERBLOM

Perennial herbs or shrubs, the *stems often rough and scurfy* and the older parts covered with persistent leaf bases. Leaves often in basal rosettes or tufted, narrow and spoon- or paddle-shaped. Flowers in flat-topped or rounded panicles made up of *1-sided spikes*; the calyx is funnel-shaped or tubular and ribbed, often *expanded at the top and umbrella-like, persistent and papery in fruits*; the petals are separate or shortly joined at the base; the ovary has *5 separate styles*. Old World maritime and arid regions, mainly Mediterranean: ±350 spp; 13 fynbos spp. The larger-flowered species are segregated by some authorities as the genus *Afrolimon*; the long-lived, papery calyces act as parachutes in seed dispersal and several species are valuable ornamentals.

▶ **CALYX ±5 MM IN DIAMETER AT MATURITY**

**❶ *Limonium scabrum***    | J | F | M | A | M | J | J | A | S | O | N | D |

**Sea lavender, brakbossie** Roughly scurfy, tufted dwarf perennial to 25 cm with paddle-shaped leaves to 80×10 mm; bears densely branched, erect or spreading inflorescences of mauve flowers with the lower branchlets often sterile and the stems sometimes developing tufts of leaves in the lower axils, the calyx to 5 mm in diameter. Coastal dunes and estuaries from the Cape Peninsula to the Eastern Cape. *Limonium equisetinum* from the West Coast has leaves 10–30×5–10 mm and 2-ranked flowers.

**❷ *Limonium anthericoides***    | J | F | M | A | M | J | J | A | S | O | N | D |

**Brakblommetjie** Roughly scurfy, tufted perennial to 30 cm with paddle-shaped leaves in a basal rosette, 15–35×7–15 mm; bears erect, widely branching inflorescences of white to mauve flowers, the calyx to 5 mm in diameter with whisker-like lobes. Seasonally moist coastal flats and pans on the Agulhas Plain.

▶ **CALYX 10–20 MM IN DIAMETER AT MATURITY**

**❸ *Limonium capense***    | J | F | M | A | M | J | J | A | S | O | N | D |

**Rounded,** densely leafy shrublet to 60 cm with scurfy and minutely pitted, paddle-shaped leaves 18–25×3–4 mm; bears spikes of pink flowers, the calyx 17 mm in diameter. Coastal limestone flats around Saldanha Bay.

**❹ *Limonium longifolium***    | J | F | M | A | M | J | J | A | S | O | N | D |

Scurfy, tufted perennial to 60 cm with narrowly paddle-shaped leaves 60–200× 5–10 mm, mostly near the base; bears long-stemmed inflorescences of pink to peach and white flowers, the calyx 15–17 mm in diameter. Sandy flats, mainly along the West Coast, and near Riversdale.

**❺ *Limonium perigrinum***    | J | F | M | A | M | J | J | A | S | O | N | D |

**Strandroos, papierblom** Shrub to 1 m with the branches leafy at the tips and rough, sometimes pitted, paddle-shaped leaves 40–80×10–20 mm; bears flat-topped clusters of pink and magenta flowers, the calyx 15–17 mm in diameter. Coastal dunes in Namaqualand and on the West Coast.

**①** *Limonium purpuratum*

`J F M A M J J A O N D`

Tufted shrublet to 60 cm with smooth, paddle-shaped leaves to 80×20 mm; bears long-stemmed clusters of mauve flowers, the calyx 15–17 mm in diameter. Sandy coastal flats along the West Coast.

# GENTIANACEAE Gentian family

## *Sebaea*  SEBAEA

Annual, biennial or perennial herbs, erect or sprawling. Leaves basal or scattered along the stem, well-developed or reduced, narrow to round. Flowers *few to many in flat-topped clusters, yellow or white*; the stamens are inserted within the tube or in the mouth and the *ovary is 2-chambered*. Old World tropics and subtropics, mainly Africa, in damp situations: ±60 spp; ±20 fynbos spp.

**②** *Sebaea albens*

`J F M A M J J A S O N D`

Annual herb to 30 cm with oval leaves; bears 4-petalled, yellow or white flowers with sepals that are rounded on the back and a corolla tube that is shorter than the petals and 2–6 mm long. Damp, sandy coastal flats in the southwestern Cape.

**③** *Sebaea aurea*

`J F M A M J J A S O N D`

Annual herb to 30 cm with oval leaves; bears 4-petalled, yellow or white flowers with sepals that are keeled on the back and a corolla tube that is shorter than the petals and 2–6 mm long. Moist, sandy flats and slopes in the southwestern and southern Cape.

**④** *Sebaea exacoides*

`J F M A M J J A S O N D`

Annual herb to 30 cm with oval leaves; bears 5-petalled, yellow or cream flowers with orange streaks in the throat, sepals that are strongly winged on the back and a corolla tube 6–19 mm long, almost as long as the lobes; stamens arise within the tube below the level of the petals. Moist, sandy flats and slopes in the southwestern Cape.

## *Chironia*  WILD CENTAURY, BITTERWORTEL

Annual or perennial herbs. Leaves scattered along the stem and in a basal rosette (but sometimes deciduous), narrow to oval, sometimes reduced. Flowers *few to many in a flat-topped cyme, pink to magenta*, rarely white, and the *sepals are keeled*; the stamens are inserted in the mouth of the tube, the style is flexed downwards. Africa and Madagascar, in moist or saline situations: ±30 spp; 10 fynbos spp. *Chironia baccifera* was used medicinally but is potentially toxic. The name *aambeibossie* derives from its use in the treatment of haemorrhoids, primarily on account of a fancied resemblance to its fleshy fruits following the medieval 'doctrine of signatures'.

▸ **COROLLA TUBE 3–5 MM LONG; FRUITS ROUNDED**

**⑤** *Chironia baccifera*

`J F M A M J J A S O N D`

**Christmas berry, aambeibossie** Tangled shrublet to 1 m with narrow, spreading leaves; bears small pink flowers with a tube 3–5 mm long that is constricted above the ovary; the fruits are fleshy, bright red berries. Sandy flats and slopes from Namaqualand to KwaZulu-Natal.

**1** *Chironia linoides*

Shrublet to 90 cm with narrow, erect or spreading leaves; bears pink flowers with a cylindrical tube 3–5 mm long; the fruits are rounded. Sandy or marshy flats and slopes in Namaqualand and the southwestern Cape.

▶ **COROLLA TUBE 6–14 MM LONG; FRUITS POINTED**

**2** *Chironia jasminoides*

Shrublet to 90 cm with erect, narrow to oval leaves; bears pink flowers with a tube 9–14 mm long, and a calyx that is lobed nearly to the base; the fruits are pointed. Marshy slopes in the southwestern and southern Cape.

**3** *Chironia tetragona*

Sticky, willowy annual or biennial to 60 cm with narrow to oval leaves; bears sticky, pink flowers with a tube 6–10 mm long that is thickened in the throat, and a calyx that is lobed to halfway; the fruits are pointed. Coastal sands and limestones from the Cape Peninsula to the Eastern Cape.

## *Orphium*  SEA ROSE

*Shrublet with finely velvety stems and leaves*. Leaves rather crowded and leathery. Flowers *solitary in the upper axils or in clusters, glossy pink*; the sepals are *rounded on the back*; the stamens are inserted within the tube and the anthers are twisted; the style is flexed downwards. Western Cape in coastal areas: 1 sp. The twisted anthers release their pollen from pores at their tips, like a salt-cellar, when vibrated or buzzed by specialised solitary bees.

**4** *Orphium frutescens*

Velvety shrublet to 80 cm with paddle-shaped leaves that have the margins rolled under; bears 1 or 2 glossy, pink flowers in the upper axils with the anthers twisted and opening through apical pores. Coastal sands and pans in the southwestern and southern Cape.

# ERICACEAE                                   Erica family

## *Erica*  HEATH, HEIDE

Shrublets or, rarely, small trees. Leaves *mostly in whorls of 3 or 4*, small and leathery, often *needle-like with the margins rolled under* ('ericoid'). Flowers in various types of axillary racemes, variously coloured, cup-shaped to tubular, usually with a 4-lobed calyx and *4-lobed corolla that is firm-textured and long-lived*; the stamens are usually 8 with the filaments hairy at the base, the *anthers shed their pollen through small or long pores* at one end, and are sometimes *ornamented with crests or spurs*. Africa, Madagascar and Europe, with 80 per cent of the species confined to southern Africa: ±860 spp; 660 fynbos spp. Easily the largest genus in the fynbos, accounting for over 7 per cent of all fynbos species; several are cultivated.

## ▶ STAMENS 4

**❶ *Erica equisetifolia***  J F M A M J J A S O N D

Erect, compact shrublet to 20 cm; bears small tubular to narrowly cup-shaped, pink flowers with 4 protruding anthers. Mountain slopes in the extreme south-western Cape.

**❷ *Erica glabella***  J F M A M J J A S O N D

Erect to sprawling shrublet to 50 cm; bears small, tubular, egg-shaped, pink flowers with 4 protruding anthers, lightly honey-scented. Sandy flats and lower slopes in the southwestern Cape.

**❸ *Erica labialis***  J F M A M J J A S O N D

Erect, compact shrublet to 50 cm; bears heads of small to medium-sized, 2-lipped, tubular to funnel-shaped, pink flowers with 4 protruding anthers. Rocky, sandy slopes and flats in the extreme southwestern Cape.

## ▶ STAMENS 8; FLOWERS SMALL TO MEDIUM-SIZED, UP TO 15 MM LONG

**❹ *Erica caffra*  Water heath, waterheide**  J F M A M J J A S O N D

Erect shrub or small tree to 4 m; bears medium-sized, fine-haired, conical, white flowers. Beside streams on flats and mountain slopes from the southwestern Cape to southern KwaZulu-Natal.

**❺ *Erica denticulata*  Lekkerruikheide**  J F M A M J J A S O N D

Erect shrublet to 50 cm; bears medium-sized, urn-shaped, waxy, white to cream or pinkish flowers that are distinctly fragrant. Flats to upper slopes in the southwestern Cape.

**❻ *Erica glomiflora***  J F M A M J J A S O N D

Erect shrublet to 1 m; bears slightly sticky, small to medium-sized, urn-shaped to conical, white to deep pink flowers. Coastal flats to middle slopes in the southern Cape.

**❼ *Erica hirtiflora***  J F M A M J J A S O N D

Erect shrublet to 1 m; bears numerous small, hairy, ovoid, mauve to pink flowers. Moist flats and slopes in seepages in the extreme southwestern Cape, forming dense stands on the Cape Peninsula.

**❽ *Erica hispidula***  J F M A M J J A S O N D

Erect shrublet to 1(1.8) m with hairy leaves and sepals; bears small urn-shaped to bell-shaped white, pink or red flowers with a broad, piston-like stigma. Widespread and common throughout the southwestern and southern Cape.

J F M A M J J A S O N D

**❾ *Erica multumbellifera***

Erect shrublet to 40 cm; bears umbels of small, broadly urn-shaped, purple to red, musty-scented flowers. Sandy flats and mountains in the southwestern Cape.

### ❶ *Erica pulchella*

`J F M A M J J A S O N D`

Erect shrublet to 60 cm; bears dense, cylindrical spikes of small, urn- to cup-shaped, pink to dark red flowers. Sandy flats and lower slopes in the southwestern and southern Cape.

### ❷ *Erica nudiflora*

`J F M A M J J A S O N D`

Erect, compact to sprawling shrublet to 30 cm; bears small, tubular to narrowly bell-shaped, pink to red flowers with protruding anthers. Coastal flats to inland mountains in the southwestern Cape.

### ❸ *Erica transparens*

`J F M A M J J A S O N D`

Small, multi-stemmed, resprouting shrublet to 40 cm; bears small, narrowly tubular, pink or white flowers with spreading, star-like petal-tips. Moist south slopes and ledges in the southwestern and southern Cape.

### ❹ *Erica lutea*  Geelrysheide

`J F M A M J J A S O N D`

Erect shrublet to 90 cm; bears small to medium-sized, narrowly urn-shaped, yellow to white flowers with spreading petal tips and prominent sepals. Middle to upper slopes in the extreme southwestern Cape.

### ❺ *Erica baccans*  Berry heath

`J F M A M J J A S O N D`

Sturdy, somewhat willowy shrub to 3 m; bears small, globular, rose pink flowers with prominent, keeled, rather dry sepals. Mountainsides on the Cape Peninsula, in dense stands, colouring the slopes pink.

### ❻ *Erica canaliculata*

`J F M A M J J A S O N D`

Erect shrub to 2 m; bears small, cup-shaped, pink flowers with prominent sepals and conspicuously protruding style. Moist flats and lower slopes in the southern Cape.

### ❼ *Erica seriphiifolia*

`J F M A M J J A S O N D`

Erect, usually compact shrublet to 30 cm; bears small, open, cup-shaped, pink flowers with prominent sepals, clustered at the branch tips. Moist areas on lower to middle slopes in the southern Cape.

### ❽ *Erica placentiflora*  Klokkiesheide

`J F M A M J J A S O N D`

Erect shrublet to 60 cm; bears small, broadly urn-shaped, pink flowers with prominent sepals and protruding anthers. Flats and slopes in the southwestern Cape.

### ❾ *Erica coriifolia*

`J F M A M J J A S O N D`

Erect shrublet to 1 m; bears small to medium, urn-shaped, pink flowers with a narrow mouth, soon turning brown at the tips, with prominent sepals. Common on sandy flats and middle to upper slopes in the extreme southwestern Cape.

### ❿ *Erica bruniades*  Kapokkie

`J F M A M J J A S O N D`

Erect shrublet to 50 cm; bears small, urn-shaped, woolly flowers with protruding anthers, corolla white-haired, calyx covered in silvery, white, pink to purple hairs. Sandy flats, lower slopes and plateaus in the southwestern Cape.

## ▶ STAMENS 8; FLOWERS LARGE, MORE THAN 15 MM LONG

**❶ *Erica coccinea***    `J F M A M J J A S O N D`

Erect, stiff shrub to 1.2 m with the leaves often conspicuously tufted; bears large, tubular, yellow, orange or red flowers with conspicuously protruding anthers; bracts and bracteoles pressed against the calyx. Common on rocky flats and mountains in the southwestern and southern Cape.

**❷ *Erica plukenetii*  Hangertjie**    `J F M A M J J A S O N D`

Erect shrub to 2 m; bears medium to large, swollen-tubular, white, pink, red, green or yellow flowers with protruding anthers; bracts and bracteoles at the base of the pedicel. Widespread in Namaqualand and the southwestern Cape.

**❸ *Erica daphniflora***    `J F M A M J J A S O N D`

Erect shrublet to 1 m; bears small clusters of medium to large, urn-shaped to narrowly urn-shaped, white, yellow, pink or red flowers in cylindrical spikes. Sandy flats and slopes, often beside water, in the southwestern Cape.

**❹ *Erica urna-viridis***    `J F M A M J J A S O N D`

**Sticky green heath, groentaaiheide**  Erect, lanky shrub to 1.5 m; bears sticky, urn-shaped, pale green flowers. Mountain plateaus in damp places and along streams on the Cape Peninsula.

**❺ *Erica cerinthoides***    `J F M A M J J A S O N D`

**Fire heath, rooihaartjie**  Resprouting shrub, mostly compact and to 30 cm, sometimes sparse and to 1.2 m; bears tight clusters of large, swollen-tubular, densely hairy, orange-red flowers. Sandy flats and slopes, flowering especially after fire, from the southwestern Cape to Mpumalanga.

**❻ *Erica mammosa***    `J F M A M J J A S O N D`

**Ninepin heath, rooiklossieheide**  Erect shrub to 1.5 m; bears large, swollen-tubular flowers with a closed mouth and dimples at the base, cream, pale green, pink, orange or red. Sandy flats and lower mountain slopes in the southwestern Cape.

**❼ *Erica curviflora***    `J F M A M J J A S O N D`

**Water heath, waterbos**  Erect, soft to stout shrub to 1.6 m with leaves in whorls of 3; bears large, tubular, hairy or hairless, orange, red or yellow flowers, on hairy pedicels. Widespread in damp or wet areas on flats to high altitude from the southwestern to the Eastern Cape.

**❽ *Erica densifolia***    `J F M A M J J A S O N D`

Erect shrub to 1.5 m with leaves in whorls of 3; bears large, tubular, curved, hairy, red flowers with greenish-yellow lobes, on hairless pedicels. Flats to middle slopes on the mountains of the southern Cape.

**❾ *Erica discolor***    `J F M A M J J A S O N D`

Dense, resprouting shrublet to 1 m with leaves in whorls of 3; bears large, tubular, pink to dark red flowers with pale tips, on hairy pedicels. Flats and lower mountain slopes in the southwestern and southern Cape.

**1 *Erica versicolor*** J F M A M J J A S O N D
Erect or sprawling shrub to over 2 m with leaves in whorls of 4; bears large, tubular, pink or red flowers with paler or greenish tips, on hairy pedicels. Sandstone slopes in the mountains of the southwestern and southern Cape.

**2 *Erica perspicua*** J F M A M J J A S O N D
**Prince-of-Wales heath, veerheide** Erect shrub to 2 m; bears medium to large, tubular, hairy, white or pink flowers with white tips. Marshy slopes and flats between Betty's Bay and Hermanus.

**3 *Erica pinea*** J F M A M J J A S O N D
Erect shrublet to 1.5 m; bears large, tubular, usually hairy, white or yellow flowers with white tips, rarely purplish pink, with the anthers just protruding from the mouth. Rocky slopes and plateaus in the extreme southwestern Cape.

**4 *Erica longifolia*** J F M A M J J A S O N D
Erect shrublet to 1 m; bears large, tubular, sometimes hairy, white, yellow, orange, red, purple or greenish, sometimes bicoloured, flowers. Sandy or stony slopes in the extreme southwestern Cape.

**5 *Erica sessiliflora* Green heath** J F M A M J J A S O N D
Erect shrub to 2 m; bears dense spikes of large, tubular, light green flowers with distinctive, fleshy, fruiting inflorescences on the older branches. Moist flats and seepages on lower slopes in the southwestern and southern Cape.

**6 *Erica abietina* Red heath, rooiheide** J F M A M J J A S O N D
Erect shrublet to 1.5 m; bears large, slightly sticky, tubular, yellow, orange, red or magenta flowers, sometimes with protruding anthers. Dry lower to middle slopes in the southwestern Cape.

# PENAEACEAE                    Penaea family

## *Brachysiphon* **BRACHYSIPHON, SISSIES**

Shrublets. Leaves leathery, overlapping in 4 ranks. Flowers in small, axillary clusters at the branch tips, *pink to purple*, the floral tube cylindrical or cup-shaped and *up to 15 mm long*; the *anthers just protruding from the tube on short filaments; bracts narrow*. Winter-rainfall Western Cape in fynbos: 5 spp, all fynbos. The vernacular name is derived from the Afrikaans *sussie* (little sister), an allusion to the clustering of the pink flowers.

**7 *Brachysiphon acutus*** J F M A M J J A S O N D
Compact, rounded shrublet with closely overlapping, leathery, oval to elliptical leaves; bears clusters of pale pink flowers with a reddish tube in the upper axils; the floral tube is 7–14 mm long and 3–4 times longer than wide. Rocky sandstone slopes in the extreme southwestern Cape.

233

### 1 *Brachysiphon fucatus*

Compact, rounded shrublet to 1 m with closely overlapping, leathery, oval to elliptical leaves; bears clusters of pink to reddish flowers with a darker tube in the upper axils; the floral tube is 5–6 mm long and up to twice as long as wide. Cool, rocky sandstone slopes on the Cape Peninsula.

## *Sonderothamnus* SONDEROTHAMNUS

Shrublets. Leaves leathery, overlapping in 4 ranks. Flowers in clusters at the branch tips, *pink*, the floral tube cylindrical or cup-shaped and *up to 15 mm long*; the *anthers ±sessile in the throat of the tube*; the *bracts broader than the leaves, with minutely fringed margins*. Winter-rainfall Western Cape in fynbos: 2 spp, both fynbos.

### 2 *Sonderothamnus petraeus*

J F M A M J J A S O N D

Sparsely branched shrublet to 35 cm, coppicing from a woody rootstock, with overlapping, broadly oval leaves, the margins of especially the upper leaves minutely toothed to fringed; bears terminal heads of pink flowers with a darker tube 7–8 mm long and petals ±5 mm long. Crevices in sandstone rocks and cliffs around Kogelberg. *Sonderothamnus speciosus* is taller, to 60 cm, with petals ±8 mm long.

## *Endonema* ENDONEMA

Shrublets with 4-ridged branches. Leaves leathery, in 4 ranks. Flowers solitary in the upper leaf axils, *yellow to red*, subtended by *4 or 6 bracteoles*, the floral tube cylindrical and *20–30 mm long*; the *ovary with 4 ovules in each locule*. Winter-rainfall Western Cape on the Riviersonderend Mountains: 2 spp, both fynbos. The large, brightly coloured flowers are adapted to sunbird pollination.

### 3 *Endonema retzioides*

J F M A M J J A S O N D

Shrub to 1 m, coppicing from a woody rootstock, with narrowly elliptical leaves that have the margins rolled under; bears orange-red flowers with a yellow tube 20–30 mm long. Rocky southern sandstone slopes on the Riviersonderend Mountains. *Endonema lateriflora* from the western Riviersonderend Mountains has oval to heart-shaped leaves and yellow flowers.

## *Saltera* SALTERA, VLIEËBOSSIE

Sparsely branched shrublets with 4-ridged branches. Leaves leathery and overlapping in 4 ranks, oval. Flowers few at the branch tips, *glossy pink*, the floral tube cylindrical and *20–30 mm long*; the *bracts broader than the leaves and gummy, with minutely fringed margins*. Southwestern Cape in fynbos: 1 sp. The bright pink flowers are pollinated by Orange-breasted Sunbirds, a species endemic to fynbos.

### 4 *Saltera sarcocolla*

J F M A M J J A S O N D

Sparsely branched shrub with slender stems to 1.5 m, coppicing from a woody base, with leathery, closely overlapping, oval to almost diamond-shaped leaves; bears a few large, glossy, pink flowers in head-like spikes, subtended by sticky bracts with fringed margins. Rocky sandstone slopes in the extreme southwestern Cape.

235

## Penaea  PENAEA

Shrublets with 4-ridged branches. Leaves leathery, overlapping in 4 ranks. Flowers in the axils, yellow or cream, the floral tube cylindrical or cup-shaped and *up to 7 mm long*; the *style 4-winged* and the *anthers thick and fleshy with small pollen-sacs near the base*. Winter-rainfall Western Cape in fynbos: 4 spp, all fynbos.

**1 Penaea cneorum**

| J | F | M | A | M | J | J | A | S | O | N | D |

Shrubs to 4 m with smooth, hairless branches and narrowly elliptical to heart-shaped leaves; bears small yellowish flowers in short spikes subtended by broadly diamond-shaped bracts. Damp sandstone slopes and streambanks in the southern Cape east of False Bay and into the Eastern Cape.

**2 Penaea mucronata**

| J | F | M | A | M | J | J | A | S | O | N | D |

Shrub, sometimes to 1.3 m, with slightly hairy to papillate branches, coppicing from a woody base, and with heart- to lance-shaped leaves; bears small yellow to reddish flowers in short spikes subtended by broadly diamond-shaped bracts. Mostly rocky sandstone slopes in the southwestern and southern Cape. *Penaea acutifolia*, from the Outeniqua Mountains, has slender, tapering sepals.

# THYMELAEACEAE                    Daphne family

▶ FLOWERS WITH PETAL-LIKE SCALES AROUND THE MOUTH OF THE TUBE

## Gnidia  SAFFRON BUSH, SAFFRAAN

Shrublets or shrubs, often ericoid. Leaves opposite in 4 ranks or alternate, narrow to round. *Flowers usually in heads* surrounded by whorls of leaves, sometimes solitary or in short spikes, usually white or cream to yellow; the 4 (rarely 5) sepals are joined in a long, cylindrical or funnel-shaped tube with *0–8 petal-like scales at the mouth*, these either flat and membranous or fleshy; the *8 or 10 stamens are in two whorls at different heights within the tube*. Mainly Africa with a few species extending into Madagascar and India: ±130 spp; ±50 fynbos spp. The tubular flowers of most species are fragrant at night and adapted to moth pollination. The vernacular name refers to the early usage of the yellow flowers of *Gnidia deserticola* as a source of dye for leather.

▶ FLOWERS WITH A FUNNEL-SHAPED, BRIGHT YELLOW TUBE WITH 4 MEMBRANOUS PETAL-LIKE SCALES AT THE MOUTH

**3 Gnidia simplex**

| J | F | M | A | M | J | J | A | S | O | N | D |

Shrublet to 30 cm with narrowly lance-shaped to awl-like leaves, and similar involucral leaves; bears 2–4 yellow flowers at the branch tips, unscented, with a hairless, funnel-shaped tube and 4 membranous petal-like scales at the mouth. Mountain slopes in the southwestern and southern Cape.

**4 Gnidia juniperifolia**

| J | F | M | A | M | J | J | A | S | O | N | D |

Erect or spreading shrublet to 50 cm with scattered, narrow to awl-like leaves and slightly broader involucral leaves; bears pairs of yellow flowers at the branch tips, unscented, with a hairless, funnel-shaped tube and 4 membranous petal-like scales at the mouth. Mountain slopes in the southwestern and southern Cape.

## ► FLOWERS WITH A CYLINDRICAL, WHITE TO PALE YELLOW TUBE, WITH 4 FLESHY PETAL-LIKE SCALES AT THE MOUTH

**① *Gnidia oppositifolia* Basbos**  J F M A M J J A S O N D

Erect, willowy shrub to 3 m with opposite, lance-shaped, hairless leaves, and similar involucral leaves that are edged with crimson; bears clusters of 4–6 pale yellow flowers at the branch tips, scented at night, with a silky, ribbed tube and 4 fleshy, petal-like pale yellow scales at the mouth, turning brown when dry. Sandstone slopes from the southwestern to the Eastern Cape.

**② *Gnidia pinifolia***  J F M A M J J A S O N D

Shrub to 1 m with crowded, alternate, needle-like to narrowly oblong, sharply pointed, hairless leaves, and wider involucral leaves; bears clusters of ±10 white flowers at the branch tips, scented at night, with a silky tube and 4 fleshy, densely silky, petal-like scales at the mouth. Sandy flats and lower slopes in the south-western Cape.

**③ *Gnidia tomentosa***  J F M A M J J A S O N D

Shrub to 1 m with alternate, oval to lance-shaped, hairless leaves that are warty beneath, and similar involucral leaves; bears clusters of ±6 white flowers at the branch tips, scented at night, with a silky tube and 4 fleshy, hairy, petal-like yellow scales at the mouth. Marshy sandstone slopes in the extreme southwestern Cape.

## ► FLOWERS WITH A CYLINDRICAL WHITISH OR BLUE TUBE, WITH EITHER 0 OR MORE THAN 4 PETAL-LIKE SCALES AT THE MOUTH

**④ *Gnidia penicillata***  J F M A M J J A S O N D

Shrublet to 40 cm with narrow leaves, at first with densely fringed margins, and similar involucral leaves; bears 2–6 bright blue or pink flowers at the branch tips, with a silky tube and 16 minute, hairy, petal-like scales at the mouth. Marshy flats and lower slopes in the extreme southwestern Cape.

**⑤ *Gnidia geminiflora***  J F M A M J J A S O N D

Erect shrub to 60 cm with opposite, narrowly lance-shaped leaves that are hairless or silky-haired above, and similar involucral leaves; bears pairs of creamy yellow flowers at the branch tips, scented at night, with a silky tube and 4 fleshy, 2-lobed, petal-like scales at the mouth. Sandy flats in Namaqualand and the West Coast.

**⑥ *Gnidia ornata***  J F M A M J J A S O N D

Shrublet to 30 cm or more with opposite or alternate, oblong to lance-shaped leaves that are sparsely hairy beneath, and involucral leaves that are similar but more densely hairy on the margins and beneath; bears 1 to few white flowers at the branch tips, with a silky tube without petal-like scales at the mouth. Marshy flats and lower slopes east of Hermanus.

**⑦ *Gnidia squarrosa***  J F M A M J J A S O N D

Slender, many-branched, willowy shrub to 2 m with alternate, narrowly lance-shaped leaves that are hairless, and slightly broader, whorled involucral leaves that are sometimes hairy on the margins; bears clusters of pale creamy green flowers tinged with pink, scented at night, with a hairy tube and 8 finger-like petal-scales at the mouth. Coastal limestone and sandy slopes from the Cape Peninsula to the Eastern Cape; especially common around Hermanus lagoon.

## *Struthiola*
## FEATHERHEAD, VEERTJIE, JUFFERTJIE-ROER-BY-DIE-NAG

Shrublets or shrubs, often ericoid. Leaves opposite in 4 ranks or alternate, narrow to round. *Flowers solitary in the upper axils, often forming long spikes,* usually white or cream; the 4 sepals are joined in a long, cylindrical tube with *4, 8 or 12 fleshy, petal-like scales at the mouth surrounded by stiff hairs;* the *4 stamens are in 1 whorl* within the tube. South Africa, mostly winter rainfall or near-coastal: ±40 spp; ±25 fynbos spp. The tubular flowers are fragrant at night and are adapted to moth pollination. The vernacular name *veertjie* refers either to the plumose flower spikes or, more probably, the usage of the flexible stems as dusters (*vee*, wipe).

### ▶ PETAL-LIKE SCALES 4 OR 12

**①** *Struthiola striata*  **Roemanaggie**

| J | F | M | A | M | J | J | A | S | O | N | D |

Shrub to 1 m, hairy on the young branches, with overlapping oval or lance-shaped, pointed leaves that are strongly ridged beneath and fringed along the margins at first; bears cream, yellow or pinkish flowers, scented at night, with a hairless tube 8–15 mm long and 4 petal-like scales at the mouth. Flats and lower slopes mainly in the southwestern and southern Cape.

**②** *Struthiola argentea*  **Aandgonna**

| J | F | M | A | M | J | J | A | S | O | N | D |

Shrub to 2 m with hairs pressed to the branches, and closely overlapping, elliptical to almost round leaves that are faintly ribbed below and densely fringed along the margins; bears yellow to reddish-orange flowers, scented at night, with a silky tube 15–20 mm long and 12 petal-like scales at the mouth. Coastal flats or slopes from the southwestern to the Eastern Cape.

**③** *Struthiola tomentosa*

| J | F | M | A | M | J | J | A | S | O | N | D |

Slender shrublet to 60 cm with silky woolly branches, and overlapping, elliptical to oval, pointed or rounded leaves that are white-silky when young; bears yellow to pale orange flowers, vanilla-scented at night, with a woolly tube 8–15 mm long and 12 narrow petal-like scales at the mouth. Mostly lower rocky sandstone slopes in the southwestern and southern Cape.

### ▶ PETAL-SCALES 8

**④** *Struthiola ciliata*  **Stroopbossie**

| J | F | M | A | M | J | J | A | S | O | N | D |

Erect shrub to 1.5 m with wand-like branches and tapering, pointed, narrowly lance-shaped to oval leaves that are usually erect and overlapping, faintly ribbed beneath and fringed on the margins; bears cream, pink or reddish flowers, scented at night, with a sparsely hairy or silky tube 15–20 mm long and 8 petal-like scales at the mouth. Sandy flats and lower slopes in Namaqualand and the southwestern Cape.

**⑤** *Struthiola leptantha*

| J | F | M | A | M | J | J | A | S | O | N | D |

Branching shrub to 2 m with rather blunt, narrowly elliptical leaves that are often rather spreading, at first hairy beneath but later hairless; bears cream or sometimes reddish flowers, scented at night, with a silky tube 15–20 mm long with 8 petal-like scales at the mouth. Stony flats and mountain slopes in Namaqualand and the southwestern Cape.

**1** *Struthiola myrsinites*

J F M A M J J A S O N D

Erect shrub to 2 m with pointed, narrowly elliptical leaves; bears white or pale pink flowers, scented at night, with a hairless tube 15–20 mm long and 8 petal-like scales at the mouth. Sandstone slopes from the southwestern to the Eastern Cape.

**2** *Struthiola dodecandra* Soetgonna

J F M A M J J A S O N D

Erect shrub to 80 cm with wand-like branches and pointed, lance-shaped leaves that are smooth or faintly ribbed beneath; bears white or pink flowers with a hairless tube 8–16 mm long and 8 petal-like scales at the mouth. Stony flats and lower slopes mainly in the southwestern and southern Cape.

▸ **FLOWERS WITHOUT PETAL-LIKE SCALES AROUND THE MOUTH OF THE TUBE**

*Lachnaea* **MOUNTAIN CARNATION, BERGANGELIER**

Shrublets or shrubs, often ericoid. Leaves opposite in 4 ranks or alternate, narrow to round. *Flowers solitary or in heads at the branch tips,* usually white or pink; the 4 sepals are joined in a cylindrical to funnel-shaped tube *without any petal-like scales at the mouth*; the *8 stamens are in 2 whorls, with the outer ones protruding from the tube and the inner ones hidden within it, with 8 minute scales between the 2 whorls.* Winter-rainfall South Africa in fynbos: 30 spp, all fynbos.

▸ **FLOWERS SOLITARY**

**3** *Lachnaea grandiflora*

J F M A M J J A S O N D

Erect, usually compact, resprouting shrub 20–60(100) cm, sometimes to 1 m, with the leaves ascending or pressed to the stem, narrowly oval to elliptical; bears solitary, large pink or white flowers that are silky outside with pointed hairs; the stigma is head-like. Sandy flats and lower slopes in the southwestern Cape. *Lachnaea uniflora,* which flowers from July to March, always has narrow leaves, flowers with blunt hairs towards the base of the tube, and a narrowly conical stigma.

▸ **FLOWERS IN HEADS OR CLUSTERS**

**4** *Lachnaea capitata*

J F M A M J J A S O N D

Slender, single-stemmed, willowy shrub to 1.8 m with ascending, awl-like to narrowly elliptical leaves; bears small cream-coloured flowers in heads 5–16 mm in diameter, with the floral scales hidden within the tube. Sandy flats and lower slopes along the West Coast and the Cape Peninsula.

**5** *Lachnaea densiflora*

J F M A M J J A S O N D

Slender shrublet to 50 cm with ascending, awl-like to narrowly elliptical leaves; bears small cream to dark pink flowers in heads 10–16 mm in diameter, with the floral scales protruding from the tube. Sandy flats and lower slopes in the extreme southwestern Cape.

**6** *Lachnaea filamentosa* Bergaster

J F M A M J J A S O N D

Erect, moderately branched shrub to 1.5 m with ascending, narrowly to broadly oval leaves; bears many cream, lilac blue or blue flowers in rounded heads 30–100 mm in diameter, with the outer sepal 2–3 times larger than the others. Sandy or stony slopes in seasonally damp areas in the interior mountains along the West Coast.

**1** *Lachnaea eriocephala* **Bergangelier** J F M A M J J A S O N D

Erect, sparsely to moderately branched shrublet to 60 cm with ascending, narrowly elliptical leaves; bears many cream to mauve flowers in heads 25–55 mm in diameter, with the outer sepals larger than the others, and with a brush-like stigma. Sandstone slopes, 100–500 m, in the southwestern Cape.

**2** *Lachnaea aurea* J F M A M J J A S O N D

Slender, erect shrub to 1 m with ascending to spreading, narrowly elliptical leaves; bears many yellow flowers in daisy-like heads 20–55 mm in diameter, with the inner sepal much smaller than the others. Coastal slopes from Hermanus to Agulhas.

## *Passerina* PASSERINA, GONNA

Ericoid shrublets. Leaves opposite in 4 ranks, usually pressed to the stem, small and concave with the upper surface lined with woolly hairs. *Flowers small, in heads or short spikes, subtended by larger bracts*; the 4 sepals are joined in a *flask-shaped tube without any scale-like petals in the mouth*; the *8 stamens are in 2 unequal whorls, both protruding well beyond the tube.* Eastern and southern Africa, mainly winter-rainfall South Africa: ±20 spp; 15 fynbos spp. The small flowers with their conspicuously protruding anthers are adapted to wind pollination. The vernacular name *gonna* is a Khoisan word applied to various members of the Daphne family whose stringy bark was used for binding thatch, firewood, etc.

**3** *Passerina ericoides* J F M A M J J A S O N D

**Christmas berry, dronkbessie** Willowy shrublet to 1 m with oblong leaves that are hairy beneath and 2–3 mm long; bears flowers subtended by leaf-like bracts that are widened below; the floral tube is initially 3 mm long but elongates rapidly in fruit and is without a neck; the fruits are fleshy red berries. Coastal sand dunes in the extreme southwestern Cape.

**4** *Passerina truncata* J F M A M J J A S O N D

Shrub or shrublet with blunt or hump-backed leaves that are hairy beneath and 2–4 mm long; bears dense spikes of flowers subtended by larger ribbed bracts; the floral tube is ±3.5 mm long with a very short neck; the fruits are dry. Sandy and stony flats in Namaqualand, the southwestern and southern Cape.

**5** *Passerina corymbosa* J F M A M J J A S O N D

(=*Passerina vulgaris*) Shrub or small tree to 2 m with awl-like leaves that have a hairy groove beneath and are 3.5–10 mm long; bears flowers subtended by tapering oval bracts that have folded wings; the floral tube is ±4 mm long with a slender neck ±2 mm long; the fruits are dry. Sandy, often disturbed flats and slopes, such as roadsides, from the southwestern to the Eastern Cape.

245

# PROTEACEAE                                 Protea family

## *Protea*  PROTEA, SUGARBUSH

Shrubs or small trees, erect or creeping, sometimes stemless. Leaves mostly elliptical but sometimes needle-like or round, leathery, hairless or hairy. *Flowers clustered into terminal heads at the branch tips, surrounded by enlarged, colourful bracts*; the individual flowers or florets are 2-lipped, with 3 of the petals joined into a sheath and the fourth separate, sometimes tipped with a beard of hairs. Southern and tropical Africa, mainly the southwestern Cape: 115 spp; ±70 fynbos spp. The colourful involucral bracts, which serve to attract various pollinating animals and insects, have made many species and their hybrids popular in gardens and as cut flowers. The vernacular name *suikerbos* (sugarbush) was applied originally to *Protea repens* on account of the copious sugary nectar contained in the flowerheads, which was collected and boiled down to make a syrup (*bossiestroop*). The *waboom*, *Protea nitida*, was widely exploited, with thousands of trees felled annually in the late 19th century. The wood was used for firewood and charcoal, wagon parts and furniture, the bark for tanning leather, and the leaves to make ink.

▶ STYLE 12–35(40) MM LONG

**❶ *Protea acaulos*  Ground protea**      J F M A M **J J A S O N** D

Mat-forming, resprouting shrublet with erect, hairless, narrowly lance-shaped to oval leaves 60–250 mm long; bears cup-shaped flowerheads 30–60 mm in diameter, with hairless, green involucral bracts that have red tips; the style is 25–35 mm long. Sandy flats and lower slopes in the southwestern Cape.

**❷ *Protea scabra***      J F **M A M J J A S O** N D

Mat-forming, resprouting shrublet with rough, erect, needle-like to narrow, channelled leaves 100–300 mm long; bears cup-shaped flowerheads 30–50 mm in diameter with cream-coloured, rusty-haired involucral bracts; the style is 30–35 mm long. Sandstone slopes in the extreme southwestern Cape, flowering mainly after fire.

**❸ *Protea amplexicaulis***      J F M A M **J J A S** O N D

Sprawling shrublet to 40 cm with spreading, grey-green, heart-shaped leaves 30–80 mm long, clasping the stem; bears cup-shaped flowerheads 60–80 mm in diameter, concealed near the base of the branches and yeast-scented, with ivory-coloured involucral bracts that are densely chocolate-velvety on the outer surface; the style is 25–30 mm long. Warmer, sunny sandstone slopes in the mountains of the southwestern Cape.

**❹ *Protea scolymocephala***      J F M A M J **J A S O N** D

Erect shrub to 1.5 m with hairless, narrowly spoon-shaped leaves 35–90 mm long; bears bowl-shaped flowerheads 35–45 mm in diameter with hairless, cream or pale green involucral bracts; the style is 12–25 mm long. Sandy flats and lower slopes in the southwestern Cape.

247

### **1** *Protea witzenbergiana*

J F **M A M J** J A S O N D

**Creeping mountain rose** Sprawling or mat-forming shrublet to 50 cm high and 3 m in diameter; leaves greyish, needle-like, 15–55 mm long with a sharp black tip, usually held erect along the upper side of the stems; bears nodding, cup-shaped flowerheads 40–70 mm in diameter with reddish-brown involucral bracts that are minutely fringed along the margins; the style is 25–30 mm long. Sandstone slopes in the interior mountains along the West Coast. The true Mountain rose, *Protea nana*, from the mountains south of Tulbagh, is an erect plant with hairless, fresh green leaves.

▶ **STYLE 40–130 MM LONG AND LONGER THAN THE INVOLUCRAL BRACTS OR MORE CONSPICUOUS THAN THE BRACTS**

### **2** *Protea glabra* **Chestnut sugarbush**

J F M A M J **J A S O N** D

Multi-stemmed shrub or tree to 5 m with hairless, elliptical greyish leaves 40–75 mm long; bears bowl-shaped flowerheads 70–120 mm in diameter with short, hairless or velvety, dull brownish involucral bracts; the style is 40–50 mm long. Dry sandstone slopes and plateaus on the interior mountains of the West Coast.

### **3** *Protea nitida* **Waboom**

J F M A M J J A S O N D

Tree 5–10 m with hairless, elliptical, olive- to silvery grey leaves 80–180 mm long; bears cup-shaped flowerheads 80–160 mm in diameter, with short, sometimes silky, silver-grey involucral bracts; the style is 60–80 mm long. Sandstone slopes in the southwestern and southern Cape.

### **4** *Protea punctata*

J F M A M J **J** A S O N D

Shrub to 4 m with oval greyish leaves 35–80 mm long, hairless when mature; bears bowl-shaped flowerheads 20–25 mm in diameter with spreading, silky, pink or white involucral bracts that have fringed margins; the style is ±50 mm long. Rocky slopes in the interior mountains of the southwestern and southern Cape.

### **5** *Protea mundii*

J F M A M J J A S **O** N D

Shrub or tree to 8(12) m with elliptical to lance-shaped leaves 60–120 mm long, hairless when mature; bears narrowly cup-shaped flowerheads 65–80 × 40–65 mm with silky, white to pink involucral bracts that have fringed margins; the style is 55–65 mm long. Moist slopes and forest margins in the coastal mountains of the southwestern and southern Cape.

### **6** *Protea aurea*

J F M A M J J A S O N D

Shrub or tree to 5 m with hairless, oblong to oval leaves 40–90 mm long, with a lobed base; bears shuttlecock-like flowerheads 90–120 mm long with silky, pink to creamy green involucral bracts; the style is 85–105 mm long. South-facing mountain slopes in the southern Cape.

**❶ *Protea cynaroides*  King protea**

J F M A M J J A S O N D

Multi-stemmed, resprouting shrub to 3 m with hairless, long-petioled leaves that have an elliptical to rounded blade 120–300 mm long; bears large cup-shaped flowerheads 120–300 mm in diameter with pale or deep pink involucral bracts that are often silky outside; the style is 80–95 mm long. Moist sandstone slopes in the southwestern, southern and Eastern Cape.

**❷ *Protea repens***

J F M A M J J A S O N D

**Sugarbush, suikerbos**  Shrub or tree to 4.5 m with hairless, narrow to spoon-shaped leaves 50–150 mm long; bears narrowly cup-shaped flowerheads 100–160×70–90 mm with cream to red or bicoloured involucral bracts covered wth a sticky gum; the style is 70–90 mm long. Sandstone and clay flats and slopes from the West Coast to the southern and Eastern Cape.

**❸ *Protea obtusifolia***

J F M A M J J A S O N D

Large shrub to 4 m with elliptical to lance-shaped leaves 100–150 mm long, curved upwards and tapering at the base, hairless when mature; bears narrowly cup-shaped flowerheads 90–120×50–80 mm with downy, cream to red involucral bracts, the inner ones spoon-shaped; the style is ±65 mm long. Limestone flats and hills on the Agulhas Plain.

**❹ *Protea susannae***

J F M A M J J A S O N D

**Stinkblaarsuikerbos**  Shrub to 3 m with elliptical leaves 80–160 mm long, curved upwards and tapering at the base, and with a sulphurous odour; bears narrowly cup-shaped flowerheads 80–100×70–110 mm with pinkish-brown involucral bracts covered with a sticky brown varnish; the style is 60–70 mm long. Coastal limestone and sand on the Agulhas Plain.

**❺ *Protea compacta*  Bot River protea**

J F M A M J J A S O N D

Lanky shrub to 3.5 m with oblong to oval leaves 50–130 mm long, curved upwards and lobed at the base, hairless when mature; bears narrowly cup-shaped flowerheads 90–120×70–100 mm with downy pink or white involucral bracts, the inner ones spoon-shaped; the style is 60–70 mm long. Coastal slopes and flats in the extreme southwestern Cape.

**❻ *Protea eximia***

J F M A M J J A S O N D

Shrub to 5 m with hairless, oval to oblong leaves 60–100 mm long, spreading and lobed at the base; bears narrowly cup-shaped flowerheads 100–140×80–120 mm with downy pink involucral bracts, the inner ones spoon-shaped and the florets tipped with velvety black hairs; the style is 60–75 mm long. Sandstone slopes in the mountains of the southern Cape.

**1** *Protea longifolia*

J F M **A M J J A S** O N D

Sprawling shrub to 1.5 m with hairless, narrow to spoon-shaped leaves 90–20 mm long, curved upwards and tapering at the base; bears narrowly cup-shaped flowerheads 80–160×40–90 mm with hairless, greenish to pink involucral bracts, the innermost narrow and densely fringed, the florets forming a woolly black cone longer than the bracts; the style is 40–65 mm long. Gravel flats and lower slopes in the extreme southwestern Cape.

## ▶ ▶ INNER INVOLUCRAL BRACTS WITH A DISTINCT BEARD

**2** *Protea neriifolia*

J **F M A M J J A S O N** D

Shrub to 3 m with oblong, green leaves 100–180 mm long, hairless when mature; bears cylindrical flowerheads 100–130×60–80 mm with silky, cream to pink involucral bracts, the outer ones with horny brown margins and the inner ones with a dense, white or black beard, with fine, silvery hairs below the beard; the style is 55–70 mm long. Sandstone and clay slopes in the southwestern, southern and Eastern Cape.

**3** *Protea laurifolia*

J F M **A M J J A S O N** D

Small tree to 8 m with elliptical, greyish leaves 80–140 mm long, hairless when mature with a horny margin and midrib; bears cylindrical flowerheads 100–130×40–60 mm with silky, cream to pink involucral bracts, the outer ones with horny brown margins and the inner ones with a dense, blackish beard; the style is 65–70 mm long. Sandstone slopes in the southwestern Cape.

**4** *Protea lepidocarpodendron*

J F M **A M J J A S** O N D

**Black-bearded protea**  Like *Protea neriifolia* but with black hairs below the beard on the inner involucral bracts. Mainly sandstone slopes in the extreme southwestern Cape.

**5** *Protea coronata*

J F M **A M J J A S** O N D

Erect shrub or small tree to 5 m with hairless or silky, elliptical, green leaves 70–120 mm long; bears cylindrical flowerheads ±100×60 mm in diameter with bright green involucral bracts, the tips curved inwards and fringed with a white beard; the style is ±60 mm long. Clay slopes in the southwestern, southern and Eastern Cape.

**6** *Protea lorifolia*

J F M **A M J** J A S O N D

Rounded shrub or small tree to 3(5) m with narrowly elliptical, bluish-grey leaves 120×250 mm long with thickened, reddish or yellow margins and midrib, hairless when mature and partially concealing the flowerheads; bears ovoid flowerheads 70–130×25–50 mm, with silky, dull pink or cream involucral bracts with a white or brown beard; the style is 55–65 mm long. Dry sandstone slopes thoughout the southern Cape.

**7** *Protea speciosa*

J F M A M **J J A S O N D**

Multi-stemmed, resprouting shrub to 1.2 m with oval leaves 90–160 mm long, hairless when mature with horny margins; bears cylindrical flowerheads 90–140×±70 mm with silky, greenish to pink involucral bracts with a dense, rusty brown or whitish beard 10–15 mm long; the style is 65–75 mm long. Sandstone flats and slopes in the southwestern Cape.

**1** *Protea stokoei*

Shrub to 2 m with oval leaves 70–120 mm long, hairless when mature; bears cylindrical flowerheads 90–130×±60 mm with silky, pink involucral bracts with a short, heavy, brown beard 5–7 mm long; the style is 65–70 mm long. Sandstone seeps in the mountains of the extreme southwestern Cape.

**2** *Protea magnifica* **Queen protea**

J **F** M A M **J J A S O** N D

Sprawling shrub to 2.5 m with oblong, grey leaves 100–210 mm long that have undulating, horny, red or yellow margins; bears cup-shaped flowerheads 140×150 mm with silky, pink or cream bracts curved back at the tips with a dense, white or black beard; the style is 60–70 mm long. Sandstone slopes in the southwestern Cape.

## *Aulax* FEATHER BUSH

Hairless shrubs *with the sexes on separate plants*. Leaves narrow or needle-like, leathery. *Flowers in racemes at the branch tips; the male florets in loose racemes and the female florets in short heads surrounded by leafy involucral bracts, yellowish*. Southwestern Cape: 3 spp, all fynbos.

**3** *Aulax cancellata*

J **F** M A M J J A S O N D

Single-stemmed shrub to 2.5 m with needle-like or very narrow, channelled leaves; bears unisexual yellow flowers in racemes. Sandstone slopes in the southwestern and southern Cape. *Aulax pallasia* is a multi-stemmed, resprouting shrub with a large, woody rootstock and the leaves are not channelled.

**4** *Aulax umbellata*

J **F** M A M J J A S O N D

Single-stemmed shrub to 2.5 m with flat, narrowly lance-shaped leaves; bears unisexual yellow flowers in racemes. Sandstone slopes and flats in the extreme southwestern and southern Cape.

## *Leucadendron* CONE BUSH, TOLBOS

Shrubs or trees, erect or creeping, *with the sexes on separate plants*. Leaves mostly elliptical but sometimes needle-like, hairless or hairy. *Flowers in dense spikes at the branch tips, the male florets in small, rounded or conical heads and the female florets in cones formed by overlapping, woody bracts, often scented*. Fruiting cones either remain intact until burned or the individual scales open when mature to expose the fruits. South Africa, mainly southwestern Cape: 83 spp, all fynbos. The vernacular name *tolbos* alludes to the tendency of the woody, fruiting cones of many species to spin like a top when droppped or kicked, and probably not to any resemblance to the toy itself. The silver tree, *Leucadendron argenteum*, was extensively exploited for firewood on the Cape Peninsula in the 17th and 18th centuries.

▸ **CONE SCALES RECURVING AND OPENING WITHIN THE SAME SEASON TO SHED THE FRUITS**
▸ ▸ **INVOLUCRAL LEAVES SIMILAR TO THE FOLIAGE LEAVES**

**5** *Leucadendron brunioides*

J F M A M J J A S **O N** D

Resprouting shrub with many slender stems to 2 m and narrow to oblong, hairless leaves ±23 mm long with the involucral leaves similar; the male flowerheads are ±17 mm in diameter and the female heads are ±11 mm in diameter and foetid-smelling. Sandy flats in the southwestern Cape.

**1 Leucadendron pubescens**   J F M A M J **J A S O** N D

Single-stemmed shrub to 2.5 m with paddle-shaped, hairless or rarely silver-haired leaves 16–28 mm long (male) or 25–57 mm long (female), the involucral leaves similar; the male flowerheads are 9–18 mm in diameter and the female heads are 10–20 mm in diameter and sweetly or yeast-scented with silky bracts. Sandstone slopes in the southwestern Cape.

**2 Leucadendron loranthifolium**   J F M A M J **J A S** O N D

Single-stemmed shrub to 2 m with elliptical to lance-shaped, hairless, blue-green leaves 38–70 mm long with cartilaginous margins, the involucral leaves similar; the male flowerheads are 20–40 mm in diameter and the female heads are ±15 mm in diameter and foetid-smelling. Sandstone slopes along the interior West Coast mountains and in the Hex River Mountains.

**3 Leucadendron glaberrimum**   J F M A M J J **A S O** N D

Spreading, well-branched, single-stemmed shrub to 1.3 m with lance-shaped, hairless or hairy leaves 20–30 mm long, sometimes purplish, the involucral leaves similar; the male flowerheads are 12–17 mm in diameter and the female heads are ±10 mm in diameter and sweetly scented or foetid-smelling. High sandstone slopes in the interior mountains of the West Coast.

## ▶ ▶ INVOLUCRAL LEAVES MORE BRIGHTLY COLOURED THAN THE FOLIAGE LEAVES

**4 Leucadendron arcuatum**   J F M A M J J **A S O** N D

Sprawling or erect, resprouting shrub with many stems to 1.3 m, arising from a woody rootstock, with broadly paddle-shaped, hairless leaves 55–80 mm long with thickened, red margins, the involucral leaves similar but yellow; the male flowerheads are 22–35 mm in diameter and the female heads are 14–33 mm in diameter and sweetly scented. High sandstone slopes in the interior mountains of the West Coast.

**5 Leucadendron nitidum**   J F M A **M J J A S O** N D

Erect to spreading shrub to 2 m, branching at the base from a single stem, with narrowly paddle-shaped, silver-haired leaves 9–15 mm long (male) or 11–20 mm long (female), the involucral leaves twice as long and yellow; the male flowerheads are 15–20 mm in diameter and the female heads are 12–18 mm in diameter and sweetly scented. Sandstone plateaus in the interior mountains of the West Coast.

**6 Leucadendron daphnoides**   J F M A M J **J A S** O N D

Single-stemmed shrub to 1.5 m with elliptical to lance-shaped, hairless leaves to 60 mm long with the involucral leaves broader and yellow, turning ivory-white and then red; the male flowerheads are ±42 mm in diameter and the female heads are ±23 mm in diameter, with a citrus scent. Granite slopes in the extreme southwestern Cape.

**7 Leucadendron sessile**   J F M A M J **J A** S O N D

Single-stemmed shrub to 1.5 m with narrowly elliptical, hairless leaves to 64 mm long (male) or 80 mm long (female), the involucral leaves similar but yellow or red; the male flowerheads are ±35 mm in diameter with erect, brown bracts and the female heads are 14–18 mm in diameter and lemon-scented. Granitic slopes and flats in the southwestern Cape; especially visible on Sir Lowry's Pass.

257

**① *Leucadendron tinctum*** 〔J F M A M J **J A** S O N D〕

Bushy, single-stemmed shrub to 1.3 m with oblong to elliptical, hairless leaves to 90 mm long (male) or 115 mm long (female), the involucral leaves larger and yellow, turning red; the male flowerheads are ±35 mm in diameter with recurved, oily yellow bracts and the female heads are ±27 mm in diameter and spice-scented. Sandstone slopes in the southwestern and southern Cape.

▶ **CONE SCALES REMAINING TIGHTLY CLOSED AND RETAINING THE FRUITS FOR SEVERAL SEASONS UNTIL BURNED**

▶ ▶ **MATURE LEAVES SILVERY SILKY, AT LEAST WHEN YOUNG**

**② *Leucadendron album*** 〔J F M A M J J A S O **N D**〕

Single-stemmed shrub to 2 m with silvery, silky, narrowly paddle-shaped leaves 28–42 mm long (male) or 45–59 mm long (female), the involucral leaves larger; the male flowerheads are ±15 mm in diameter and the female heads are ±26 mm in diameter and slightly scented. Sandstone slopes in the southern Cape.

**③ *Leucadendron argenteum*** 〔J F M A M J J A **S O** N D〕

**Silver tree, witteboom** Tree to 10 m with silvery, silky, lance-shaped leaves to 150 mm long with fringed margins, the involucral leaves similar; the male flowerheads are ±50 mm in diameter and the female heads are ±40 mm in diameter. Granite and clay slopes from the Cape Peninsula to Somerset West.

**④ *Leucadendron uliginosum*** 〔J F M A M J J A S **O N D**〕

Single-stemmed, bushy shrub to 4 m with oblong, silvery-silky leaves (hairless when mature in subsp. *glabratum*), 20–35 mm long, the involucral leaves slightly larger and ivory to pale yellow; the male flowerheads are ±15 mm in diameter and the female heads are ±12 mm in diameter and slightly scented. Sandstone slopes in the southern Cape.

▶ ▶ **MATURE FOLIAGE LEAVES HAIRLESS AND SIMILAR TO THE INVOLUCRAL LEAVES**

**⑤ *Leucadendron rubrum*** 〔J F M A M J J **A** S O N D〕

Single-stemmed shrub to 2.5 m with paddle-shaped leaves to 34 mm long (male) or to 70 mm long (female), hairless when mature, the involucral leaves similar; the male flowerheads are clustered and ±5 mm in diameter and the female heads are ±20 mm in diameter and top-shaped with brown-edged bracts. Sandstone slopes in the southwestern and southern Cape.

**⑥ *Leucadendron conicum*** 〔J F M A M J J A S **O N** D〕

Single-stemmed shrub or tree to 6 m with narrowly paddle-shaped, soft, sharply pointed, dark green leaves 40–50 mm long, silky when young, the involucral leaves similar and few but the involucral bracts conspicuously spreading and yellowish or purple; the male flowerheads are ±15 mm in diameter and the female heads are ±12 mm in diameter and slightly fruit-scented. Sandstone slopes near streams in the southern Cape.

### ❶ *Leucadendron salicifolium*

J F M A M J **J A S** O N D

Single-stemmed shrub to 3 m with narrowly sickle-shaped, hairless leaves to 60 mm long and twisted below, the involucral leaves few, similar and creamy yellow but the involucral bracts conspicuously spreading and yellow; the flowerheads are 9–10 mm in diameter and slightly fruit-scented. Streams and seeps on flats and slopes in the southwestern Cape.

▶ ▶ INVOLUCRAL LEAVES BRIGHTLY COLOURED AND MORE CONSPICUOUS THAN THE FOLIAGE LEAVES

### ❷ *Leucadendron comosum*

J F M A M J J A **S O N D**

Single-stemmed shrub to 1.7 m with needle-like leaves, the upper narrowly paddle-shaped, 35 mm long (male) or to 45 mm long (female), with the involucral leaves similar but pale green to yellow; the male flowerheads are 10–13 mm in diameter and the female heads are ±16 mm in diameter and sweetly scented with disc-like scales that are scarcely overlapping. Sandstone slopes in the southern Cape.

### ❸ *Leucadendron spissifolium*

J F M A M J J **A S** O N D

Resprouting shrub with many stems to 1.3 m from a woody rootstock and narrowly paddle-shaped, hairless leaves 25–63 mm long (male) or 27–80 mm long (female) and twisted at the base, the involucral leaves larger and ivory or pale green; the male flowerheads are ±18 mm in diameter and the female heads are 13–15 mm in diameter and lemon-scented. Sandstone slopes in the southwestern Cape and southern KwaZulu-Natal.

### ❹ *Leucadendron salignum*

J F M **A M J J A S O N** D

Sprawling or erect, resprouting shrub with many stems to 1(2) m and narrowly paddle-shaped, hairless leaves 20–47 mm long (male) or 48–58 mm long (female) and twisted below, the male involucral leaves slightly longer and yellow or sometimes red and the female larger and ivory or red; the male flowerheads are 10–14 mm in diameter and the female heads are 9–12 mm in diameter and sweetly or yeast-scented. Sandy and clay slopes and flats throughout the southwestern and southern Cape.

### ❺ *Leucadendron procerum*

J F M A M J J **A S** O N D

Single-stemmed shrub to 3 m with hairless, paddle-shaped leaves 26–37 mm long (male) or 37–47 mm long (female), the involucral leaves larger and pale green to ivory; the male flowerheads are ±20 mm in diameter with red flowers and the female heads are ±12 mm in diameter. Sandstone slopes in the interior mountains of the West Coast.

### ❻ *Leucadendron strobilinum*

J F M A M J J A **S** O N D

Single-stemmed shrub to 2.6 m, branching near the base, with elliptical leaves to 67 mm long (male) or to 80 mm long (female) and fringed along the margins, the involucral leaves larger and ivory-coloured; the male flowerheads are 24–36 mm in diameter and the female heads are 18–25 mm in diameter and yeast-scented. Damp, south-facing sandstone slopes on the Cape Peninsula.

### 1 *Leucadendron microcephalum*

`J F M A M J J A S O N D`

Single-stemmed shrub to 2 m with oblong, hairless leaves to 90 mm long, the involucral leaves similar but yellow; the male flowerheads are ±18 mm in diameter and the female heads are ±11 mm in diameter with conspicuous, oily, brown bracts. Sandstone slopes in the extreme southwestern Cape.

### 2 *Leucadendron coniferum*

`J F M A M J J A S O N D`

Shrub or small tree to 4 m with narrowly paddle-shaped leaves to 77 mm long (male) or 83 mm long (female), hairless when mature and twisted, the involucral leaves broad below and yellow; the male flowerheads are ±18 mm in diameter and the female heads are ±14 mm in diameter. Coastal sands in the extreme southwestern Cape.

### 3 *Leucadendron eucalyptifolium*

`J F M A M J J A S O N D`

Single-stemmed shrub or tree to 5 m with narrowly lance-shaped leaves to 105 mm long, hairless when mature, the involucral leaves longer and yellow; the male flowerheads are ±16 mm in diameter and the female heads are ±12 mm in diameter and fruit-scented. Forest margins and open sandstone slopes in the southern Cape.

### 4 *Leucadendron meridianum*

`J F M A M J J A S O N D`

Densely branched, single-stemmed shrub to 2 m with narrowly paddle-shaped, silky or hairless leaves ±40 mm long, the involucral leaves longer and yellow; the flowerheads are ±12 mm in diameter and slightly scented. Limestone flats on the Agulhas Plain.

### 5 *Leucadendron xanthoconus*

`J F M A M J J A S O N D`

Single-stemmed shrub to 2 m with narrowly oblong or sickle-shaped leaves to 65 mm long, twisted at the base and silky when young but hairless when mature, the involucral leaves larger and yellow; the flowerheads are 10–11 mm in diameter. Sandstone slopes in the extreme southwestern Cape.

### 6 *Leucadendron laureolum*

`J F M A M J J A S O N D`

Single-stemmed shrub to 2 m with oblong leaves to 75 mm long (male) or to 95 mm long (female), hairless when mature, the involucral leaves larger, yellow and concealing the young heads; the male flowerheads are ±20 mm in diameter and the female heads are ±14 mm in diameter and slightly fruit-scented. The cones have a spiral of 8 shallow grooves. Sandstone slopes in the extreme southwestern Cape.

### 7 *Leucadendron gandogeri*

`J F M A M J J A S O N D`

Rounded, single-stemmed shrub to 1.6 m with elliptical, hairless leaves 42–85 mm long (male) or 60–105 mm long (female), with cartilaginous margins, the involucral leaves larger and yellow-tinged with red; the male flowerheads are ±24 mm in diameter and the female heads are ±18 mm in diameter and fruit-scented. Rocky sandstone slopes in the extreme southwestern Cape.

## Mimetes PAGODA BUSH, STOMPIE

Shrubs or trees. Leaves overlapping, elliptical to oblong, *leathery with 1 or more horny teeth at the tips, usually silky. Flowers in headlets arranged in dense spikes at the branch tips*, either surrounded individually by *coloured involucral bracts* or in the *axils of enlarged, often coloured, inflorescence leaves*. Southwestern Cape: 13 spp, all fynbos. The vernacular name *stompie*, also applied to *Brunia*, refers to the stumps that invariably remain after the woody shrubs have burned in periodic veldfires.

### 1 *Mimetes hirtus*

J F M A **M J J A S O N** D

Single-stemmed shrub to 2 m with almost hairless, oval to lance-shaped leaves 25–45 mm long and similar inflorescence leaves; the flower spikes comprise headlets of 9–14 white flowers surrounded by bright yellow involucral bracts 15–40 mm long with red tips; the style is red and 50–55 mm long. Peaty marshes in the extreme southwestern Cape.

### 2 *Mimetes pauciflorus*

J F M A M J J **A S O N** D

Single-stemmed shrub, 2–4 m, with oval leaves 25–40 mm long, hairy when young, pressed against the stems, and similar inflorescence leaves; the flower spikes comprise headlets of 3–4 cream-coloured flowers surrounded by orange-yellow bracts 10–25 mm long; the style is orange with a red tip and 45–50 mm long. Moist, south-facing mountain slopes in the southern Cape.

### 3 *Mimetes cucullatus* Rooistompie

J F M A M - J J A S O N D

Multi-stemmed shrub to 1.4 m, resprouting from a woody base, with hairless, oblong to elliptical leaves 25–55 mm long and spoon-shaped red inflorescence leaves; the flower spikes comprise headlets of 4–7 white flowers surrounded by small bracts; the style is red and 45–50 mm long. Sandstone slopes and flats mainly in the southwestern and southern Cape.

### 4 *Mimetes fimbriifolius*

J F M A M J J A S O N D

Tree to 4 m with oblong to elliptical leaves 40–70 mm long, densely fringed with hairs and dull, spoon-shaped, reddish-yellow inflorescence leaves; the flower spikes comprise headlets of 4–7 white flowers surrounded by small bracts; the style is yellow with a red tip and 55–60 mm long. Rocky slopes on the Cape Peninsula.

### 5 *Mimetes argenteus*

J F **M A M J** J A S O N D

Single-stemmed shrub to 3.5 m with spreading, silvery, silky, elliptical leaves 40–65 mm long and spoon-shaped, carmine to pale mauve inflorescence leaves; the flower spikes comprise headlets of 6–9 pink flowers surrounded by small bracts; the style is yellow and 40–45 mm long with a kink at the tip. Moist, south-facing slopes in the extreme southwestern Cape. *Mimetes arboreus* is a single-stemmed tree to 6 m with lance-shaped leaves 50–82 mm long and headlets of 8–13 flowers.

## Sorocephalus CLUSTERHEAD

Shrublets. *Leaves closely overlapping* and often pressed against the stem, needle- or awl-like. *Flowers in headlets*, clustered together into *dense, compound heads* at the branch tips; the individual florets are straight in bud. Southwestern Cape: 11 spp, all fynbos.

**1** *Sorocephalus lanatus*

Erect or sprawling shrublet to 80 cm with hairless or hairy, needle-like leaves 5–18 mm long, pressed to the stems; bears pink to purple flowers with darker tips in dense heads 10–30 mm in diameter. Sandstone slopes at high altitude along the interior mountains of the West Coast.

## *Spatalla*  FUZZYBUDS

Shrublets. *Leaves closely overlapping* and needle- or awl-like, hairless or hairy. Flowers in headlets arranged in *short spikes at the branch tips*; the individual florets are curved in bud. Southwestern Cape: 20 spp, all fynbos.

**2** *Spatalla curvifolia*

J F M A M J J A S O N D

Rounded shrublet to 80 cm with channelled, needle-like leaves 25–50 mm long; bears single-flowered headlets of cream-coloured flowers with unequal-sized petals in racemes 30–100 mm long on peduncles 20–30 mm long; the style is straight and ±7 mm long. Sandstone slopes in the extreme southwestern Cape.

**3** *Spatalla mollis*

J F M A M J J A S O N D

Rounded shrublet to 80 cm with needle-like leaves 15–20 mm long; bears single-flowered headlets of white or mauve flowers with unequal-sized petals in sessile racemes 30–40 mm long; the style is straight, hairy below and ±5 mm long. Streamsides on sandstone slopes in the extreme southwestern Cape.

**4** *Spatalla parilis*

J F M A M J J A S O N D

Shrub to 1.5 m; leaves needle-like, 15–20 mm long; bears single-flowered headlets of silvery pink flowers with unequal-sized petals in sessile racemes 30–60 mm long; the style is straight and ±6 mm long. Moist, sandstone slopes in the southwestern and southern Cape.

## *Paranomus*  DOLL'S BUSH, POPPIESBOS

Shrubs. *Leaves either all divided into narrow or needle-like segments or only the lower ones divided and the upper ones paddle-shaped to oval. Flowers in whorls of 4, arranged in spikes at the branch tips.* Southwestern Cape: 18 spp, all fynbos. The vernacular name refers to the fancied resemblance of the flower spikes to miniature dolls.

**5** *Paranomus bracteolaris*

J F M A M J J A S O N D

Shrub to 2.5 m with all the leaves finely divided, 30–60 mm long and shaggy-haired when young; bears flowerheads of purple flowers ±14 mm long in loose spikes 40–90 mm long, faintly scented. Rocky, sandstone slopes and plateaus in the interior mountains of the West Coast.

**6** *Paranomus dispersus*

J F M A M J J A S O N D

Shrub to 1.5 m with all the leaves sparsely divided into flattened segments, 40–80 mm long; bears flowerheads of pink flowers 14–18 mm long in loose spikes 25–90 mm long. Sandstone slopes in the southwestern and southern Cape.

## *Serruria*  SPIDERHEAD, SPINNEKOPBOS

Shrubs or shrublets, erect or creeping. *Leaves needle-like or divided into narrow or needle-like segments. Flowers clustered in 1 or more small heads at the branch tips,* usually pink or silvery. Southwestern Cape: ±50 spp, all fynbos. The vernacular name derives from the finely divided, silky leaves that give the impression of being covered with spiders' webs.

▸ **FLOWERHEADS CLUSTERED**

**❶ *Serruria decipiens***

| J | F | M | A | M | J | J | A | S | O | N | D |

Rounded shrublet to 1 m with almost hairless, finely divided leaves 30–45 mm long; a very short, thick peduncle bears clusters of 5–10 flowerheads of 6–10 fragrant, creamy white flowers without involucral bracts; the style is 8–9 mm long. Sandy flats and slopes, mainly coastal, along the West Coast.

**❷ *Serruria fasciflora***

| J | F | M | A | M | J | J | A | S | O | N | D |

Sprawling to erect shrublet to 1 m with sparsely hairy, finely divided leaves 30–70 mm long; a short, hairy peduncle bears clusters of many flowerheads of 5–7 sweetly scented, silvery pink flowers with lance-shaped involucral bracts; the style is 5–7 mm long. Sandy flats and lower slopes in the southwestern Cape.

**❸ *Serruria elongata***

| J | F | M | A | M | J | J | A | S | O | N | D |

Erect shrub to 1.5 m with fleshy, finely divided leaves 50–150 mm long, the upper ones arranged in whorls; an elongate peduncle 15–30 cm long bears loose clusters of flowerheads of 5–25 fragrant, silvery pink flowers without involucral bracts; the style is 7–11 mm long. Sandy flats and slopes in the extreme southwestern Cape.

▸ **FLOWERHEADS SOLITARY**

**❹ *Serruria aitonii***

| J | F | M | A | M | J | J | A | S | O | N | D |

Rounded shrublet to 1 m with crinkly-haired, finely divided leaves 20–45 mm long; a soft-haired peduncle 5–65 mm long bears a solitary (rarely up to 8) flowerhead of 15–20 fragrant, silvery grey flowers with oval involucral bracts; the style is 7–10 mm long. Sandstone slopes in the interior mountains of the West Coast.

**❺ *Serruria villosa***

| J | F | M | A | M | J | J | A | S | O | N | D |

Compact, rounded shrublet to 80 cm with silky, finely divided leaves 20–40 mm long; bears a solitary, sessile flowerhead of 18–22 fragrant yellow flowers nested among the leaves with lance-shaped involucral bracts; the style is ±10 mm long. Sandstone slopes and flats on the southern Cape Peninsula.

**❻ *Serruria acrocarpa***

| J | F | M | A | M | J | J | A | S | O | N | D |

Rounded, resprouting shrublet to 50 cm with almost hairless, finely divided leaves 20–50 mm long; a densely hairy peduncle 10–32 mm long bears a solitary flowerhead of 10–25 sweetly scented, silvery pink to greenish flowers with oval involucral bracts; the style is ±7 mm long. Sandy flats and slopes in the southwestern Cape.

## *Diastella*  SILKY PUFF

Shrublets, erect or creeping. *Leaves overlapping, oval to needle-like. Flowers clustered in a small head at the branch tips, usually pink.* Southwestern Cape: ±7 spp, all fynbos.

**❶ *Diastella divaricata***

J F M A M J J A S O N D

Sprawling, single-stemmed shrublet to 0.5×3 m with elliptical leaves 2–18× 2–7 mm; bears pink flowerheads 10–15 mm in diameter. Sandstone flats and slopes in the extreme southwestern Cape. *Diastella proteoides* has narrow, oblong leaves 5–15 × 1–2 mm that are hairy when young.

## *Leucospermum*  PINCUSHION, SPELDEKUSSING

Shrubs or trees, erect or creeping. *Leaves oval to narrow, leathery with 1 or more horny teeth at the tips, hairless or silky. Flowers clustered in medium-sized to large heads containing more than 15 florets at the branch tips, often yellow to red.* South Africa to Zimbabwe, mainly southwestern Cape: 48 spp; 45 fynbos spp. Several species and their hybrids are popular for the garden and as cut-flowers. The vernacular name *luisiesbos* refers to the resemblance of the nutlets of several species to lice.

▶ STYLE 10–35 MM LONG

**❷ *Leucospermum oleifolium***

J F M A M J J A S O N D

Rounded shrub to 1 m with hairless or hairy, oval to lance-shaped leaves 40–60 mm long with 1–5 apical teeth; bears flat-topped flowerheads 25–40 mm in diameter, yellow-green, fading to red; the style is straight and 25–30 mm long. Sandstone slopes in the extreme southwestern Cape.

**❸ *Leucospermum calligerum***

J F M A M J J A S O N D

Shrub to 2 m with hairy, lance-shaped to elliptical grey leaves 12–36 mm long with 1(3) apical teeth; bears globular flowerheads 20–35 mm in diameter, cream-coloured, fading to dull red; the style is slightly curved inwards and 21–25 mm long. Dry sandy slopes in the southwestern Cape.

**❹ *Leucospermum bolusii***

J F M A M J J A S O N D

Rounded shrub to 1.5 m with almost hairless, oval to elliptical leaves 25–45 mm long with 1 apical tooth; bears rounded flowerheads ±20 mm in diameter, cream-coloured, fading to pale pink; the style is straight and 15–20 mm long. Rocky sandstone slopes above Gordon's Bay.

**❺ *Leucospermum truncatulum***

J F M A M J J A S O N D

Sparsely branched, slender shrub to 2 m with densely felted, elliptical grey leaves 10–25 mm long with 1 apical tooth; bears globular flowerheads 15–20 mm in diameter, yellow, fading to red; the style is straight or slightly curved and 14–16 mm long. Sandy slopes and flats in the extreme southwestern Cape.

**❻ *Leucospermum rodolentum***

J F M A M J J A S O N D

Erect or spreading shrub to 3 m with densely velvety, elliptical to wedge-shaped grey leaves 40–65 mm long with 3–6 apical teeth; bears globular flowerheads 30–35 mm in diameter, bright yellow; the style is usually straight and 15–25 mm long. Sandy flats and lower slopes in southern Namaqualand and the southwestern Cape. *Leucospermum tomentosum*, from the West Coast, is a resprouting shrub to 1 m with narrow, channelled leaves with 1–3 teeth at the tips.

**1** *Leucospermum hypophyllocarpodendron*

J F M A M J J A S O N D

Sprawling to creeping shrublet with trailing stems and hairless or felted, narrow and channelled to lance-shaped, grey leaves 40–130 mm long, all pointing upwards, with 2–4 apical teeth; bears rounded, slightly flattened flowerheads 30–40 mm in diameter, bright yellow; the style is straight or slightly curved inwards and 20–26 mm long. Sandy coastal flats in the southwestern Cape.

**2** *Leucospermum truncatum*

J F M A M J J A S O N D

Rounded shrub to 2 m with almost hairless, narrowly wedge-shaped leaves 45–90 mm long with 3 apical teeth; bears globular flowerheads 30–40 mm in diameter, yellow, fading to orange; the style is straight or slightly curved and 18–35 mm long. Coastal limestones on the Agulhas Plain. *Leucospermum muirii*, from around Still Bay, has leaves with 3–7 apical teeth and smaller flowerheads 20–30 mm in diameter.

▸ **STYLE 30–60 MM LONG**

**3** *Leucospermum cuneiforme*

J F M A M J J A S O N D

Multi-stemmed shrub to 2 m, resprouting from a woody rootstock with the stems warty below, with hairless, wedge-shaped leaves 45–110 mm long with 3–10 apical teeth; bears oval flowerheads 50–90 mm in diameter, yellow, fading to red; the style is slightly curved and 38–55 mm long. Sandstone slopes and flats in the southern and Eastern Cape.

**4** *Leucospermum praecox*

J F M A M J J A S O N D

Rounded shrub to 3 m with hairless, oval to wedge-shaped leaves 35–70 mm long with 5–11 apical teeth; bears globular flowerheads ±60 mm in diameter, yellow, fading to orange; the style is curved inwards and 38–48 mm long. Sandy coastal flats on the eastern Agulhas Plain.

**5** *Leucospermum conocarpodendron*

J F M A M J J A S O N D

**Kreupelhout** Rounded shrub or tree to 5 m with densely hairy branches and almost hairless or felted, elliptical to wedge-shaped leaves 60–115 mm long, with 3–10 apical teeth; bears globular to oval flowerheads 70–90 mm in diameter, bright yellow; the style is slightly curved and 45–55 mm long. Dry rocky slopes in the extreme southwestern Cape.

**6** *Leucospermum tottum*

J F M A M J J A S O N D

Rounded shrub with spreading branches to 1.3 m and hairless, oblong to lance-shaped leaves 25–60 mm long with 1–3 apical teeth; bears rounded, slightly flattened flowerheads 90–150 mm in diameter, pinkish; the style is curved inwards at first but later straight and spreading and ±50 mm long. Rocky slopes in the south-western Cape.

**7** *Leucospermum lineare*

J F M A M J J A S O N D

Erect to sprawling shrub to 2 m with hairless, narrow and often channelled leaves 40–100 mm long with 1–3 apical teeth; bears rounded, slightly flattened flowerheads 60–90 mm in diameter, yellow to red, with hairless floral tubes; the style is curved inwards and 50–60 mm long. Clay slopes in the extreme south-western Cape.

273

**1** *Leucospermum cordifolium*

J F M A M J J A S O N D

Rounded shrub with drooping branches to 1.5 m and almost hairless, oval leaves 20–80 mm long that are lobed at the base and with 1–6 apical teeth; bears rounded, slightly flattened flowerheads 100–120 mm in diameter, orange to scarlet and borne at right angles to the stem; the style is spreading to incurved and 45–60 mm long. Rocky sandstone slopes in the extreme southwestern Cape. *Leucospermum patersonii*, from coastal limestones around Stanford, is a tree to 4 m with erect flowerheads and silky floral tubes.

**2** *Leucospermum vestitum*

J F M A M J J A S O N D

Rounded shrub to 2.5 mm with hairless, oval to elliptical leaves 50–70 mm long with 2–4 apical teeth; bears rounded flowerheads 70–90 mm in diameter, orange to scarlet, with silky floral tubes; the style is curved inwards and 50–60 mm long. Rocky, sandstone slopes in the interior mountains of the West Coast.

▶ **STYLE 70–90 MM LONG**

**3** *Leucospermum catherinae*

J F M A M J J A S O N D

Shrub to 3 m with hairless, elliptical leaves 90–135 mm long with 3 or 4 apical teeth; bears rounded, slightly flattened flowerheads ±150 mm in diameter, orange to coppery bronze; the style is flexed and twisted clockwise near the tip and 70–80 mm long. Sandstone slopes along streams in the interior mountains of the West Coast.

# SOLANACEAE                                        Potato family

## *Lycium*  HONEY THORN, KRAALDORING

Shrublets or small trees, *often with thorny branches*. Leaves *often in tufts*, usually elliptical. *Flowers solitary*, 4- or 5-lobed, white to purple, *cup-, bell- or urn-shaped to cylindrical*; the calyx is cup-shaped and 3–5-lobed; *the stamens are inserted in the lower half of the tube*. The fruits are berries. Widespread in warm and temperate regions of the world: ±200 spp; 5 fynbos spp.

**4** *Lycium afrum*

J F M A M J J A S O N D

**Kraal honey thorn, kraalkriekdoring** Stiffly branched, thorny shrub or small tree to 3 m with narrow, leathery leaves in tufts on short-shoots; bears tubular, purple flowers 12–20 mm long with the petals about a quarter as long as the tube; the stamens are inserted halfway up the tube and are enclosed within it. Mostly dry, stony slopes and flats in the southwestern and southern Cape.

**5** *Lycium tetrandrum*  **Boksdoring**

J F M A M J J A S O N D

Stiffly branched, thorny shrub to 2 m with succulent to leathery, oval leaves in tufts on short-shoots; bears white to pale mauve flowers to 12 mm long with the tube abruptly constricted below and with the petals half to one-third as long as the tube; the anthers and style are exposed. Sandy, coastal flats in Namaqualand and along the West Coast.

**① *Lycium ferocissimum* Slangbessie** J F M A M J J A S O N D

Stiffly branched, thorny shrub to 2 m with leathery, paddle-shaped leaves in tufts on short-shoots; bears bell-shaped, white to mauve flowers to 12 mm long, with the petals half to one-third as long as the tube; the anthers and style are exposed. Dry, stony flats from Namaqualand to Lesotho.

## *Solanum* NIGHTSHADE, BITTERAPPEL

Herbs or shrubs, sometimes climbing, unarmed or spiny. *Leaves sometimes lobed.* Flowers in *branched clusters*, 5-lobed, white or mauve to purple, *usually saucer-shaped*, sometimes with a cup-shaped tube; the calyx is 5–10-lobed or -toothed; the *stamens are inserted at the mouth of the tube* and the *anthers open by means of terminal pores or slits.* Cosmopolitan, mainly tropical, with many weedy species: ±1 400 spp; 15 fynbos spp. Certain species are toxic.

▸ **PLANTS WITHOUT PRICKLES**

**② *Solanum africanum* Dronkbessie** J F M A M J J A S O N D

Scrambling or creeping, semi-succulent shrub to 3 m long with the young stems square in section and lance-shaped to oval leaves to 6 cm long, the lower ones often lobed; bears terminal clusters of ±30 white, mauve or purple flowers 10 mm in diameter; the berries are purplish black and up to 15 mm in diameter. Coastal dunes in bush from the Cape Peninsula to KwaZulu-Natal.

**③ *Solanum guineense*** J F M A M J J A S O N D

Erect or sprawling shrub to 1.5 m with softly leathery, oval to elliptical leaves to 7 cm long; bears 1 to few mauve to light blue flowers to 18 mm in diameter in the axils; the berries are yellow, orange or red and up to 15 mm in diameter. Coastal dunes, slopes and river banks from Namaqualand to the Eastern Cape.

▸ **PLANTS ARMED WITH PRICKLES**

**④ *Solanum linnaeanum* Bitterappel** J F M A M J J A S O N D

Prickly shrub to 1 m, the prickles to 12 mm long, straight and yellow, with deeply lobed, usually spiny leaves to 15 cm long; bears 1 to few mauve to purple flowers 15 mm in diameter in the axils; the berries are yellow and 25 mm in diameter. Rocky slopes and flats and roadsides from the southwestern Cape to KwaZulu-Natal.

**⑤ *Solanum giftbergense*** J F M A M J J A S O N D

Prickly shrub to 1.5 m, the prickles to 12 mm long, slender, straight, yellow to reddish brown, with oval, bluntly lobed leaves to 4 cm long, spiny on the veins; bears clusters of 1–4 mauve to purple flowers to 10 mm in diameter; the berries are orange to red and 10 mm in diameter. Rocky sandstone slopes in Namaqualand and the West Coast.

**⑥ *Solanum tomentosum* Slangappel** J F M A M J J A S O N D

Yellowish-green, densely felted, prickly shrub to 1 m, the prickles to 12 mm long, straight or slightly curved, with oval, rarely spiny, leaves to 8 cm with wavy margins; bears clusters of a few mauve or purple flowers to 15 mm in diameter; the berries are orange and to 20 mm in diameter. Stony slopes and flats from Namaqualand to Lesotho.

# BORAGINACEAE Forget-me-not family

## *Anchusa* CAPE FORGET-ME-NOT, OSSETONG

Annual or perennial herbs. Leaves mostly basal, narrow, rough. Flowers in racemes or branched cymes, blue or white, with a cylindrical tube that is *occluded at the mouth by 5 hairy scales opposite the petals*; the stamens arise in the middle of the tube and are included within it. *Fruits of 4 wrinkled nutlets* that are rounded on the back with a *rim or wing around the margin*. North Africa and Eurasia, with 1 species in southern Africa: ±35 spp; 1 fynbos sp.

**1** *Anchusa capensis*    J F M A M J J A S O N D

Softly or roughly hairy annual to 1 m with narrowly lance-shaped leaves in a basal tuft; bears coiled cymes of blue flowers that lengthen in fruit. Sandy flats, often in disturbed places and along roadsides throughout the drier parts of southern Africa.

## *Echiostachys* ECHIOSTACHYS

*Perennial herbs with annual stems* from a somewhat woody rootstock. *Leaves mostly basal*, narrow, roughly hairy. *Flowers in a dense, spike-like inflorescence* comprised of numerous clusters of flowers, white or pink to pale blue, funnel-shaped; the *stamens protrude conspicuously from the tube* and have hairs at or near the base. Fruits of 4 almost smooth to wrinkled nutlets. Southwestern Cape: 3 spp, all fynbos.

**2** *Echiostachys incanus*    J F M A M J J A S O N D

Tufted perennial from a woody base to 40 cm with narrowly lance-shaped leaves tapering to a point, in a basal tuft, covered with white hairs; bears a dense spike of white or blue flowers more than 10 mm long that are hairy along the midline of each petal; the hairs at the base of the filaments are tufted. Moist clay flats, mostly in renosterveld, in the southwestern Cape. The remaining 2 species have blunt leaves and scattered hairs at the base of the filaments: *Echiostachys spicatus*, from sandy places on the West Coast, has white flowers; *E. ecklonianus*, from the Hottentots Holland Mountains, has smaller purple or red flowers.

## *Lobostemon* LOBOSTEMON, AGTDAEGENEESBOS

*Shrubs or shrublets*, usually hairy. *Leaves scattered on the stems*, often roughly hairy. Flowers cylindrical or funnel-shaped, usually blue to pink, rarely white or red; the stamens are either included within the tube or project beyond it and have hairy scales or ridges at their base. Fruits of 4 almost smooth to wrinkled nutlets. Winter-rainfall South Africa: 30 spp, all fynbos. A decoction of the plants was used as an antiseptic.

▸ **FLOWERS MOSTLY UP TO 15 MM LONG, USUALLY HAIRLESS OUTSIDE; STAMINAL SCALES WITH WELL-DEVELOPED LATERAL LOBES**

**3** *Lobostemon glaucophyllus*    J F M A M J J A S O N D

Shrublet, 30–80 cm, with the young branches hairless and narrowly lance-shaped leaves hairy only along the midrib and margins; bears blue to pink flowers 7–15 mm long that are hairless outside; the staminal scales are rounded with hairy lateral lobes and the style is hairy. Sandy flats and slopes in the south-western Cape.

### 1 *Lobostemon dorotheae*

J F M A M J J **A S O N** D

Shrublet, 30–80 cm, with the young branches hairless and narrowly lance-shaped leaves hairy only along the midrib and margins; bears blue to pink flowers 7–15 mm long that are hairless outside with the sepals unequal in width and with the stamens protruding and curved at the tips; the staminal scales are triangular with hairy lateral lobes and the style is hairy. Rocky sandstone slopes in the interior mountains along the West Coast.

### 2 *Lobostemon glaber*

J F M A M J J **A S O N** D

Shrublet, 30–60 cm, with hairy, narrowly lance-shaped leaves; bears white or pale pink to blue flowers 7–25 mm long that are hairless outside; the staminal scales are triangular with hairy lateral lobes and the style is almost hairless. Stony slopes in the southwestern Cape.

### 3 *Lobostemon trichotomus*

J F M A M J J **A S O N** D

Shrublet, 30–100 cm, with hairy, somewhat leathery, narrowly lance-shaped leaves; bears white or blue flowers 7–25 mm long that are hairless or hairy outside with the sepals dissimilar in width and velvety; the staminal scales are slightly triangular with lateral lobes and the style is hairless or hairy. Sandy slopes and flats in the southwestern Cape.

### 4 *Lobostemon echioides*

J F M A M J J **A S O N** D

Shrublet, 20–80 cm, with oblong to elliptical, soft, silvery-haired leaves; bears small, salver-shaped, blue flowers 7–15 mm long that are hairy outside with the stamens prominently protruding; the staminal scales are triangular with hairy lateral lobes. Stony slopes and flats from Namaqualand to the Eastern Cape.

▸ **FLOWERS MORE THAN 15 MM LONG, HAIRY OUTSIDE ON THE MIDRIB; STAMINAL SCALES REDUCED TO RIDGES WITHOUT LATERAL LOBES**

### 5 *Lobostemon fruticosus*

J F M A **M J J A S O N D**

**Douwurmbos, luibos**  Shrublet, 50–80 cm, with hairy, elliptical or oval leaves; bears blue to pink flowers 15–25 mm long that are hairy outside; the staminal scales are ridge-like without lateral lobes and the style is hairy. Sandy flats in Namaqualand and the southwestern Cape.

### 6 *Lobostemon lucidus*

J F M A M J J **A S O N** D

Shrublet, 20–30 cm, with hairy, narrowly lance-shaped leaves that have persistent woody bases; bears pink to mauve flowers 15–25 mm long that are hairy outside; the staminal scales are ridge-like without lateral lobes and the style is hairy. Sandy flats and lower slopes on the Agulhas Plain.

281

### ❶ *Lobostemon montanus*

J F M A M J **J A S** O N D

Shrub, 0.8–1.2 m, with oval to lance-shaped, silver-haired leaves; bears blue or turquoise flowers 15–25 mm long that are hairy outside; the staminal scales are ridge-like without lateral lobes and the style is hairy. Coastal sandstone in the extreme southwestern Cape.

### ❷ *Lobostemon curvifolius*

J F M A M J J **A S O** N D

Shrublet, 30–60 cm, with narrow, silver-haired leaves often recurved at the tips; bears pink to blue flowers >25 mm long that are hairy outside; the staminal scales are ridge-like without lateral lobes and the style is hairy. Sandy flats on the Agulhas Plain.

### ❸ *Lobostemon argenteus*

**J** F **M A M J J A S O N D**

Shrublet, 30–60 cm, with hairy, narrowly lance-shaped leaves that have the margins rolled under; bears a spike-like inflorescence of blue flowers 15–25 mm long with 1 flower per bract, hairy outside on the midveins and margins; the staminal scales are reduced to ridges and the style is hairy. Shale slopes from the southwestern to the Eastern Cape.

### ❹ *Lobostemon sanguineus*

J **F M A** M J J A S O N D

Shrub, 50–120 cm, with sparsely hairy, elliptical to oval leaves that have hairy margins; bears red flowers >25 mm long that are hairy outside; the staminal scales are reduced to ridges and the style is hairy. Sandstone slopes on the Agulhas Plain.

# VIOLACEAE Violet family

## *Viola*  VIOLET

Erect or trailing herbs or shrublets. Leaves entire or toothed, subtended by toothed or leafy stipules. Flowers usually solitary in the axils, 2-lipped with the sepals extended slightly at the base, the *lower petal smaller than the others and with a spur or pouch at the base*; the stamens are joined in a cone around the ovary, with the lower 2 drawn into nectar-secreting tails that protrude into the spur of the lower petal. Worldwide, mainly north temperate: ±300 spp; 1 fynbos sp. The pansy, *Viola odorata*, and heartsease, *V. tricolor*, are popular garden plants.

**①** ***Viola decumbens*  Wild violet**    J F M A M J **J A S O N D**

Slender shrublet to 25 cm with narrow or thread-like leaves; bears nodding, faintly scented, *Viola*-like, mauve to purple flowers in the axils. Damp sandstone slopes in the southwestern Cape.

# MELIANTHACEAE Melianthus family

## *Melianthus*  HONEY FLOWER, KRUIDTJIE-ROER-MY-NIE

Shrubs, *often with an unpleasant smell*. Leaves *subtended by leafy stipules, once-divided into unequally sided, toothed leaflets*. Flowers in racemes with 1–4 flowers at each node, reddish to greenish with an *unequally 5-lobed calyx* that may have a sac at the base and *with 5 unequal petals*; the ovary is surrounded by a nectar-secreting disc from within which the 4 stamens arise. Fruits globular or ellipsoidal, often covered with protuberances. Southern Africa: 6 spp; 3 fynbos spp. The curiously shaped flowers are visited by various birds for nectar; the fresh leaves and roots were used medicinally as an antiseptic.

**②** ***Melianthus elongatus***    J F M A M J **J A S** O N D

Shrub to 2 m with leathery leaves divided into toothed leaflets that are white-felted beneath and have the margins rolled under; bears axillary racemes with 2–4 flowers at each node, the petals red in bud and brown in flower and longer than the sepals; the ovary and fruits are velvety. Granite slopes and sandy flats in Namaqualand and the West Coast. *Melianthus comosus* has flat leaves and pendulous racemes with 1 flower at each node.

**③** ***Melianthus major*  Heuningblom**    J F M A M J J **A S** O N D

Foetid shrub to 2 m with large leaves that have a distinct greyish bloom, divided into toothed leaflets; bears large, long-stalked racemes with 2–4 flowers at each node and reddish petals shorter than the maroon to greenish sepals; the ovary and fruits are hairless. Mostly along streams in the southwestern and Eastern Cape.

285

# FUMARIACEAE

# Fumitory family

## Cysticapnos  AFRICAN FUMITORY

*Brittle, climbing or scrambling annuals with clear or yellow, watery sap. Leaves twice-divided* with the *apical leaflet often developed into a tendril.* Flowers in racemes, pink to purple, 2-lipped with 2 sepals that are often scale-like and deciduous, and 4 petals in 2 very unequal series, the upper sac-like or spurred at the base; the 6 stamens are in 2 groups. *Fruits dry and papery,* sometimes inflated, *many-seeded.* Southern Africa: 4 spp; 2 fynbos spp.

**❶ *Cysticapnos vesicaria*  Klappertjies**

J F M A M J J **A S O** N D

Straggling annual herb with a greyish bloom and leaves that are often tendrilled and are twice-divided into wedge-shaped, 3-lobed leaflets; bears racemes of strongly 2-lipped, pink flowers with broadly winged, flaring petals 10 mm long; the fruits are swollen and balloon-like, 20–30 mm long. Climbs among bushes on sandy flats and slopes in Namaqualand and the southwestern Cape. *Cysticapnos cracca* has smaller flowers 5–6 mm long and flattened, lance-shaped fruits 10–15 mm long.

# POLYGALACEAE

# Polygala family

## Polygala  BUTTERFLY BUSH, ERTJIEBOS

Shrubs or perennials. Leaves small or large. Flowers in terminal or axillary racemes or solitary, pink to purple, with *the inner 2 sepals greatly enlarged, petal-like and spreading like wings;* the lower petal is keeled with an apical crest and the *lateral 2 petals are usually reduced and sometimes 2-lobed;* there are usually *8 fertile stamens. Fruits dry and flattened.* Worldwide in temperate and warm countries: ±600 spp; ±30 fynbos spp.

▶ **WOODY SHRUBLETS TO 2 M TALL**

**❷ *Polygala fruticosa***

J F M A M J J **A S O N D**

Hairy or hairless shrub to 2 m with opposite, more or less heart-shaped leaves; bears pale greenish or purple flowers 8–15 mm long, with the tips of the inner sepals often green, in short racemes at the tips of the branchlets; the side petals are deeply and unequally bilobed with the lower lobe often longest. Rocky sandstone and clay slopes from the southwestern Cape to KwaZulu-Natal.

**❸ *Polygala myrtifolia*  Septemberbos**

J F M A M J **J A S O N D**

Sprawling or erect shrub to 2 m, often velvety on the young stems, the leaves either ascending and narrow with the margins slightly rolled under, or broadly elliptical and flat; bears large purple flowers 12 mm long, in short terminal racemes; the side petals are bilobed with the lower lobe much longer than the upper. Rocky slopes in the southwestern, southern and Eastern Cape.

**❹ *Polygala virgata***

J F M A M J **J A S O N D**

Willowy, single-stemmed shrub, branching above, sometimes to 2 m, leafy only at the top, mostly with elliptical leaves; bears many purple flowers 10–15 mm long, in slender, arching racemes on hairy pedicels; the side petals are unlobed. Sandstone, clay or limestone slopes, often on forest margins, from the southern Cape to tropical Africa.

## ▶ SOFTLY WOODY PERENNIALS TO 50 CM TALL

**❶ *Polygala garcinii***

`J F M A M J J A S O N D`

Soft shrublet to 40 cm with slender, trailing branches from a woody rootstock, and needle-like leaves; bears purple flowers 8–11 mm long, in long racemes; the side petals are blunt and sparsely hairy below. Sandy and clay slopes in the southwestern and southern Cape.

**❷ *Polygala umbellata***

`J F M A M J J A S O N D`

Slender shrublet to 40 cm with sprawling branches from a woody rootstock and needle-like to narrowly elliptical leaves; bears dense, umbel-like clusters of purple flowers 8–11 mm long; the side petals are blunt. Sandy and clay flats and lower slopes in the southwestern and southern Cape.

**❸ *Polygala refracta***

`J F M A M J J A S O N D`

Slender subshrub to 40 cm with erect, ridged stems from a woody rootstock and narrow leaves pressed to the stems; bears short axillary racemes of purple flowers 9–10 mm long; the side petals are shortly bilobed. Marshy sandstone slopes and flats in the southwestern and Eastern Cape. *Polygala nematacaulis* has smaller flowers to 7 mm long and scattered, scale-like leaves.

## *Muraltia*   PURPLE GORSE, KROESBOSSIE

Shrublets or shrubs, *often ericoid, sometimes thorny*. Leaves small and *often sharply pointed or spine-tipped, often in tufts*. Flowers solitary in the upper axils, purple, pink or white with all 5 sepals similar in size and rather dry in texure, or the inner 2 sepals petal-like and much longer than the outer 3; the lower petal is keeled with an apical crest and the lateral 2 petals are narrow and about as long as or longer than the lower; there are *7 stamens. Fruits dry, usually with 4 horns or warts, or rounded and fleshy*. Tropical and southern Africa, mainly winter-rainfall region: ±120 spp; ±110 fynbos spp. The species with fleshy fruits were until recently placed in the separate genus *Nylandtia*; a decoction of the branch tips of these species was used medicinally, and the fruits, although astringent, were eaten by early inhabitants at the Cape and favoured by ostriches and other animals, including tortoises, hence the common name skilpadbessie, or tortoiseberry. The vernacular name, kroesbossie, derives from the tufted, curly arrangement of the leaves of many of the species, suggestive of the tightly curled hair of some African peoples.

## ▶ INNER 2 SEPALS LARGE AND PETAL-LIKE; FRUITS ROUNDED AND FLESHY

**❹ *Muraltia scoparia*  Duinebessie**

`J F M A M J J A S O N D`

(=*Nylandtia scoparia*) Willowy shrub, sometimes tree-like, to 2.5 m with slender, wand-like branches and small oblong leaves; bears fragrant, pinkish flowers in the upper axils with the inner 2 sepals petal-like and much longer than the others; the fruits are red and thinly fleshy. Sandy flats and slopes on the West Coast.

**❺ *Muraltia spinosa***

`J F M A M J J A S O N D`

(=*Nylandtia spinosa*) **Nylandtia, skilpadbessie**  Stiffly-branched, thorny shrub with short, spike-like lateral branchlets, to 1 m with small oblong leaves; bears purplish or pink and white flowers in the upper axils with the inner 2 sepals petal-like and much longer than the others; the fruits are yellow to red and fleshy. Sandy flats and rocky slopes from Namaqualand to the Eastern Cape.

▸ **SEPALS ALL SIMILAR; FRUITS DRY AND HORNED**

▸ ▸ **CALYX SMALL, LESS THAN HALF THE LENGTH OF THE PETALS**

**❶ *Muraltia harveyana***

J F M A M J J A **S O N D**

Stiffly branched, closely leafy, almost hairless shrub to 60 cm with solitary, paddle-shaped leaves that are sharply pointed and have a prominent midrib beneath; bears pink flowers fading to white on short pedicels; the fruits are roughly hairy with long, slender horns. Limestone hills along the West Coast.

**❷ *Muraltia heisteria***

J F **M A M** J J A **S O N D**

Erect, usually sparsely branched shrub with wand-like stems to 1.5 m that are finely haired when young and tufts of hard, lance-shaped, channelled leaves that are spine-tipped and often fringed along the margins; bears purple flowers, sometimes with white side-petals, on short pedicels; the fruits have long, slender horns. Rocky, mainly sandstone, slopes in fynbos in the southwestern Cape. *Muraltia macropetala* is a similar stiffly branched shrublet from gravel flats and clay slopes in the southwest, but has fruit with short horns.

**❸ *Muraltia satureioides***

J F M A M J J A **S O N D**

Sprawling shrublet to 60 cm with tufts of narrow to oblong leaves that are spine-tipped and shortly fringed on the margins and keel; bears pink or white flowers on short pedicels; the fruits are stiff-haired and prominently horned. Coastal calcareous sands in the southwestern and southern Cape.

▸ ▸ **CALYX AT LEAST HALF THE LENGTH OF THE PETALS**

**❹ *Muraltia collina***

**J** F M A M J J A **S O N D**

Almost hairless shrublet to 35 cm with tufts of elliptical, channelled leaves that are fringed with hairs along the margins and tipped with spines; bears pink flowers on short pedicels; the fruits have long, slender horns. Lower sandstone slopes in the southwestern Cape.

**❺ *Muraltia filiformis***

J F M A M J J A **S O N D**

Slender, hairless shrublet to 30 cm, branching mainly at the base, with solitary or tufted, needle-like to narrowly lance-shaped leaves that are minutely pointed; bears sessile, pink flowers; the fruits have slender horns. Sandy flats, often in damp sites, in the extreme southwestern Cape.

# FABACEAE                                   Pea family

▸ **LEAVES PINNATELY COMPOUND, NOT GLAND-DOTTED; FLOWERS PINKISH OR RED**

## *Virgilia*   VIRGILIA, KEURBOOM

*Trees. Leaves pinnate* with oblong leaflets, stipules narrow. Flowers in axillary racemes, *pink to magenta; calyx pushed in at the base and 2-lipped* with the upper lip 2-lobed; *stamens all separate.* Pods narrow, woody. Southwestern and southern Cape: 2 spp, both fynbos. *Virgilia divaricata*, in particular, is a popular garden tree.

**1** *Virgilia divaricata*

Small tree to 16 m with pinnate leaves that have oblong, almost hairless leaflets; bears magenta flowers 15–25 mm long, in axillary racemes, subtended by small bracts, 2–5 mm long, that drop before the buds are 5 mm long. Forest margins and streamsides in the southern Cape east of George, and in the Swartberg.

**2** *Virgilia oroboides*

J F M A M J J A S O N D

Small tree to 20 m with pinnate leaves that have oblong leaflets finely haired beneath; bears pale pink and white flowers 15–25 mm long, in axillary racemes, subtended by large bracts, 7–15 mm long, that persist until the buds are 10 mm long. Forest margins and streamsides in the southwestern and southern Cape.

## *Lessertia* BALLOON PEA, BLAASERTJIE

Herbs or shrubs. Leaves *pinnately compound, leaflets many*, stipules present. Flowers in axillary racemes, pink to purple or red, calyx ± equally lobed; stamens joined with the upper one separate, equal. *Pods membranous*, flat or more or less swollen, opening at the tip; seeds rough. Southern and eastern tropical Africa: ±55 spp; ±15 fynbos spp. The leaves of *Lessertia frutescens* are widely used as a tonic under its old name *Sutherlandia*.

**3** *Lessertia rigida*

J F M A M J J A S O N D

Stiff, somewhat spinescent shrublet to 50 cm with leaves divided into oblong leaflets; bears loose racemes of pink to purple flowers 6–8 mm long, on stiff peduncles that are longer than the leaves, and that become somewhat spine-like with age; the pods are broadly oval and swollen in the middle. Stony and sandy flats and slopes in the southwestern Cape.

**4** *Lessertia frutescens*

J F M A M J J A S O N D

(=*Sutherlandia frutescens*) **Sutherlandia, kankerbos** Shrublet to 1 m with leaves divided into oblong, greyish-green leaflets that are hairless or sparsely hairy above; bears red flowers 25–35 mm long with very small wing petals hidden within the calyx; the pods are large, swollen, papery and hairless. Sandstone and shale flats and slopes throughout southern South Africa. *Lessertia canescens* from coastal sands in Namaqualand and the southwestern Cape has broader leaflets that are densely silver-haired on both surfaces.

▸ CLIMBERS WITH PINNATELY 3-FOLIOLATE LEAVES WITH ASYMMETRICAL LATERAL LEAFLETS

## *Dipogon* CAPE SWEET PEA, BOSKLIMOP

*Perennial climber*, sparsely hairy or almost hairless. Leaves pinnately 3-foliolate and petiolate, leaflets rhombic (diamond-shaped), *the lateral leaflets asymmetrical*, stipules present. Flowers in short racemes on long peduncles, magenta, calyx with *equal, very short, blunt lobes*; stamens joined in a tube with the upper one separate, *style thickly bearded on the upper side near the tip*. Pods oblong. Western and Eastern Cape: 1 sp.

**5** *Dipogon lignosus*

J F M A M J J A S O N D

Woody climber with pinnately 3-foliolate leaves and diamond-shaped leaflets that are greyish beneath; bears pedunculate racemes of magenta or pink flowers 10–15 mm long. Scrub or forest margins in the southwestern, southern and Eastern Cape.

## Bolusafra  TAR PEA, TEERERTJIE

*Glandular, hairy, aromatic scrambler.* Leaves pinnately 3-foliolate, hairy, leaflets oval, the *lateral leaflets asymmetrical,* stipules present. Flowers bright yellow in axillary racemes, *calyx with long lobes,* the upper 2 slightly joined; stamens joined in a tube with the upper one separate, anthers equal. Pods oblong, swollen, glandular and hairy. Southwestern Cape: 1 sp.

**① *Bolusafra bituminosa***

| J | F | M | A | M | J | J | A | S | O | N | D |
|---|---|---|---|---|---|---|---|---|---|---|---|

Scrambling, resinous, tar-scented shrublet with hairy, pinnately 3-foliolate leaves and oval leaflets; bears sparse racemes of bright yellow flowers 13–20 mm long. Mountain fynbos, often along streamsides, in the southwestern Cape.

▸ **LEAVES GLAND-DOTTED, DIGITATE OR 3-FOLIOLATE; FLOWERS BLUE OR PINK**

## Otholobium  OTHOLOBIUM, SKAAPBOSTEE

Shrubs or herbaceous perennials. Leaves 3-foliolate, *dotted with black or translucent glands,* stipules streaked with glands and hairy, sometimes joined to the base of the petiole. Flowers almost sessile, in pairs or trios subtended by a single bract and collected into spikes, white, pale blue or yellow, calyx with the upper lobes partially joined and the lower much larger; stamens joined in a tube with the upper one separate, uniform. Pods *1-seeded, covered with gland-tipped hairs* and swollen. Southern and eastern Africa; possibly also South America: ±60 spp; 43 fynbos spp. Some species have been used medicinally.

**② *Otholobium striatum***

| J | F | M | A | M | J | J | A | S | O | N | D |
|---|---|---|---|---|---|---|---|---|---|---|---|

Willowy shrub to 2.5 m with digitately 3-foliolate leaves and elliptical leaflets that are covered with pressed hairs when young, subtended by hairy stipules; bears spikes of white to cream flowers with purple-tipped keels 6–8 mm long; calyx white-haired, glandular, enlarging in fruit. Mountain fynbos in the southwestern Cape.

**③ *Otholobium bracteolatum***

| J | F | M | A | M | J | J | A | S | O | N | D |
|---|---|---|---|---|---|---|---|---|---|---|---|

Sprawling shrub to 2 m with petiolate, digitately 3-foliolate leaves and symmetrical, glandular, wedge-shaped leaflets, subtended by fringed, glandular stipules; bears dense spikes of blue, white and violet flowers 8–10 mm long; calyx soft-haired, glandular, with the lowest sepal larger. Coastal sandveld and limestone hills in the southwestern and southern Cape.

**④ *Otholobium fruticans***

| J | F | M | A | M | J | J | A | S | O | N | D |
|---|---|---|---|---|---|---|---|---|---|---|---|

Straggling subshrub to 40 cm with digitately 3-foliolate leaves and oval leaflets, subtended by fringed stipules; bears spikes of lilac and purple flowers 8–10 mm long; calyx sparsely silky and glandular, with the lowest sepal much larger than the others and leaf-like. Mountain fynbos on the Cape Peninsula.

## *Psoralea*   BLUE PEA, BLOUKEURTJIE

Shrubs or small trees. Leaves 3-foliolate or pinnate, sometimes reduced, *dotted with black or red glands, stipules clasping the stem and joined to the base of the petiole.* Flowers in groups of 1–5, each *subtended by a lobed cupule that is itself subtended by 2 bracts,* usually blue or lilac with a dark-tipped keel, calyx almost 2-lipped; stamens joined in a tube, mostly with the upper one separate. *Pods 1-seeded and glandular and included within the calyx at maturity.* Southern Africa: ±50 spp, all fynbos.

▶ **RUSH-LIKE PERENNIAL**

**1 *Psoralea restioides***

J F M A M J J A S O N D

Soft, rush-like perennial to 50 cm with needle-like leaves to 30 mm long, subtended by large stipules joined to the petioles; bears solitary blue and white flowers on pedicels to 10 mm long with a hairless calyx. Mountain and lowland fynbos in marshy areas in the extreme southwestern Cape.

▶ **STIFF, TREE-LIKE SHRUBS, EITHER WITH 3 BROAD LEAFLETS OR 5–9 NARROW LEAFLETS**

**2 *Psoralea aculeata***

J F M A M J J A S O N D

Tree-like shrub to 2 m with 3-foliolate leaves and leathery, wedge-shaped leaflets up to 8 mm long, with downcurved tips; bears small clusters of mauve and white flowers on pedicels to 13 mm long with a hairless calyx. Lowland fynbos in the extreme southwestern Cape.

**3 *Psoralea affinis***

J F M A M J J A S O N D

Slender, erect shrub to 3 m with 5–9-foliolate leaves and narrowly oblong to thread-like leaflets to 50 mm long, subtended by small stipules; bears small clusters of blue flowers on pedicels to 45 mm long with a densely black-haired calyx. Mountain, lowland and coastal fynbos, often in marshy areas in the southwestern and southern Cape.

**4 *Psoralea pinnata***

J F M A M J J A S O N D

Willowy tree to 4 m with 7–9-foliolate leaves and thread-like leaflets to 50 mm long, subtended by small stipules; bears small clusters of blue flowers on pedicels up to 25 mm long with a hairless or hairy calyx. Mountain fynbos, forest margins and riverbeds in the extreme southwestern Cape.

▶ **WILLOWY SHRUBS OR TREES WITH WEEPING BRANCHES BEARING 1–3 NARROW OR SCALE-LIKE LEAFLETS**

**5 *Psoralea oligophylla***

J F M A M J J A S O N D

Slender, willowy shrub to 2 m with weeping branches and 1–3-foliolate leaves with narrow leaflets up to 45 mm long; bears small clusters of dirty-white and purple flowers on pedicels to 30 mm long with a hairless calyx. Mountain fynbos along streamsides in the southwestern and southern Cape.

**6 *Psoralea aphylla*  Fonteinbos**

J F M A M J J A S O N D

Erect, broom-like shrub to 4 m with drooping branches and very small, scale-like leaves 5–17 mm long, present only on the young branches; bears small clusters of blue and white flowers with a hairless calyx. Mountain and lowland fynbos, often along stream banks in the southwestern Cape.

**1** *Psoralea fleta*

J F M A M J J A S O N D

Willowy tree to 6 m with drooping branches and 1–3-foliolate, scale-like leaves present only on the young branches; bears small clusters of blue and pale mauve flowers with a hairless calyx. Mountain fynbos along seeps and streams in the mountains above Wellington.

▶ **LEAVES USUALLY DIGITATELY 3-FOLIOLATE, SOMETIMES TUFTED, NEVER GLAND-DOTTED**

## *Aspalathus* **CAPE GORSE**

Prostrate to erect shrubs, *often spiny. Leaves usually in clusters, sessile,* simple or 3-foliolate, needle-like to almost round, fleshy or leathery and often spine-tipped, *stipules absent.* Flowers usually in heads or racemes, sometimes axillary, usually yellow, rarely lilac, pink or white, calyx usually more or less equally lobed; *stamens joined in a tube slit down the top,* alternate anthers larger. *Pods 1-seeded,* narrow to broad. South Africa, mainly winter-rainfall region: 278 spp, mostly fynbos. *Aspalathus linearis* is the source of rooibos tea, low in tannin and high in minerals and anti-oxidants, while *A. crenata* was used as a diuretic.

▶ **LEAVES UNDIVIDED, NEVER TUFTED**

**2** *Aspalathus linearis*

J F M A M J J A S O N D

**Rooibostee, bush tea** Erect or sprawling shrub to 2 m with needle-like leaves 15–60 mm long; bears scattered, pale to bright yellow or partly purple or violet flowers with a hairy keel and hairless calyx. Mountain fynbos in the southwestern Cape.

**3** *Aspalathus cordata*

J F M A M J J A S O N D

Stiff shrub to 1 m with hard, spine-tipped, oval to heart-shaped leaves 12–25 mm long, 11–21-veined from the base; bears bright yellow flowers fading to bright red, crowded at the branch tips, with a hairy keel and white-haired calyx. Mountain fynbos on lower slopes in the southwestern Cape.

**4** *Aspalathus crenata* **Stekeltee**

J F M A M J J A S O N D

Erect or sprawling shrub to 1 m with leathery, spine-tipped, oval to heart-shaped leaves 10–40 mm long with minutely toothed margins, 7–11-veined from the base; bears yellow flowers fading to red or brown, crowded at the branch tips, with a hairless keel and hairless calyx. Mountain fynbos in the southwestern Cape.

▶ **LEAFLETS STIFF, SHARP AND NEEDLE-LIKE**

**5** *Aspalathus astroites*

J F M A M J J A S O N D

Erect shrub to 1.3 m with whitish-haired branch tips and 3-foliolate leaves with sharp, tufted, needle-like leaflets 6–15 mm long; bears small heads of bright yellow flowers fading to orange with a hairless, beak-like keel and hairless or sparsely hairy calyx with spiny lobes. Lowland fynbos in the extreme southwestern Cape.

**6** *Aspalathus abietina*

J F M A M J J A S O N D

Erect or sprawling shrub to 60 cm with 3-foliolate leaves with sharp, tufted, needle-like leaflets 4–20 mm long; bears scattered, bright yellow flowers fading to orange, with a hairless, beak-like keel and hairless or sparsely hairy calyx with spiny lobes. Mountain fynbos on lower slopes in the southwestern Cape.

### ❶ *Aspalathus chenopoda*

J F M A M J J A S O N D

Stiff shrub to 2 m with densely hairy branches and 3-foliolate leaves with sharp, needle-like, hairless or sparsely whiskered leaflets 4–15 mm long; bears bright yellow flowers in terminal heads with a hairless keel and densely woolly calyx with needle-like lobes. Mountain fynbos on lower slopes in extreme southwestern Cape.

### ❷ *Aspalathus hirta*

J F M A M J J A S O N D

Shrub to 2 m with 3-foliolate leaves and sharp, needle-like or slightly angular leaflets 5–15 mm long; bears scattered, bright yellow flowers, the keel with short hairs below, and a short-haired calyx with needle-like lobes. Mountain fynbos in the southwestern and southern Cape.

## ▸ LEAFLETS CYLINDRICAL AND ± FLESHY, NOT SHARP AND NEEDLE-LIKE

### ❸ *Aspalathus ericifolia*

J F M A M J J A S O N D

Erect or sprawling shrublet to 60 cm with 3-foliolate leaves and almost cylindrical, hairy or hairless leaflets 1–6 mm long; bears scattered, pale or bright yellow flowers, usually with a hairy keel, and short-haired calyx with slender, thread-like lobes. Mountain and lowland fynbos in the southwestern Cape.

### ❹ *Aspalathus pinguis*

J F M A M J J A S O N D

Sparsely branched shrublet with erect, tail-like branches to 1 m and 3-foliolate leaves with cylindrical leaflets 1–26 mm long; bears scattered, bright yellow or partly red flowers with a hairless keel and calyx. Renosterbos-fynbos scrub in the southwestern and southern Cape.

### ❺ *Aspalathus incurvifolia*

J F M A M J J A S O N D

Shrublet with densely leafy, brush-like branches to 1 m and 3-foliolate leaves with cylindrical or thread-like leaflets 8–18 mm long; bears scattered, pale yellow flowers with a hairless keel and hairless or short-haired calyx with reduced lobes. Lowland fynbos on limestone on the Agulhas Plain.

### ❻ *Aspalathus capensis*

J F M A M J J A S O N D

Stiffly erect shrub to 3 m with 3-foliolate leaves and fleshy, cylindrical leaflets 5–10 mm long; bears 1–3 large bright yellow flowers at the branch tips, with hairless keel and fleshy, hairless calyx with oval lobes. Lowland fynbos on the southern Cape Peninsula.

### ❼ *Aspalathus capitata*

J F M A M J J A S O N D

Erect shrub or small tree to 2 m with 3-foliolate leaves and fleshy, sparsely hairy, cylindrical leaflets 7–15 mm long; bears bright yellow flowers with a hairless, pointed, beak-like keel in terminal heads, and fleshy, almost hairless calyx with oval lobes. Lowland and mountain fynbos on the northern Cape Peninusla.

### ❶ *Aspalathus carnosa*

J F M A M J J **A S O N D**

Erect shrub to 2 m with 3-foliolate leaves and fleshy, cylindrical leaflets 3–7 mm long; bears bright yellow flowers in terminal heads or sometimes scattered, with hairless keel and fleshy, almost hairless, calyx with more or less rounded lobes. Lowland fynbos in the extreme southwestern Cape.

### ❷ *Aspalathus pachyloba*

J F M A M J J A S **O N D**

Shrub or shrublet to 2 m with 3-foliolate leaves and cylindrical leaflets 5–10 mm long; bears scattered, bright yellow flowers fading to black when dry, with hairless keel and almost hairless calyx with narrow, pointed lobes. Mountain fynbos in the southwestern Cape.

### ❸ *Aspalathus costulata*

J F M A M J J **A S O N D**

Shrublet to 1.5 m with densely white-velvety young branches and 3-foliolate leaves with sausage-shaped leaflets 1–3 mm long; bears small clusters of fragrant, pinkish to mauve flowers near the branch tips, with hairless keel and ± hairless calyx with narrow, pointed lobes. Arid mountain fynbos on sandy plateaus in the southwestern Cape interior.

### ❹ *Aspalathus cephalotes*

J F M A M J J **A S O N D**

Shrub to 1 m with 3-foliolate leaves and thread-like or very narrow, sparsely hairy leaflets 4–10 mm long; bears pale violet or rose, rarely almost white, flowers in a spike or head, with silky keel and silky calyx with awl-like lobes. Mountain fynbos on lower slopes in the southwestern Cape. *Aspalathus nigra* with slate-blue to violet flowers has calyx lobes mostly shorter than 3 mm.

### ❺ *Aspalathus forbesii*

**J F M A M J J J A S O N D**

Shrub or shrublet to 2.5 m with 3-foliolate leaves and almost cylindrical leaflets 2–8 mm long; bears white or cream flowers, sometimes with pink on the wings, in terminal heads, with hairless keel and silky, short-haired calyx, the upper lobes deeply separated. Coastal fynbos, limestone and marine sands in the extreme southwestern Cape.

▶ **LEAFLETS ALMOST FLAT**

### ❻ *Aspalathus quinquefolia*

J F M A M J J **A S O N D**

Erect or sprawling shrub to 1.5 m with 3-foliolate leaves and silky grey-haired or almost hairless, oblong to elliptical leaflets 3–10 mm long; bears pale to bright yellow flowers in terminal spikes, with a silky keel and silky calyx. Coastal, lowland and mountain fynbos in the southwestern Cape.

### ❼ *Aspalathus aspalathoides*

J F M A M J J A S **O N D**

Shrublet to 40 cm with 3-foliolate leaves and hairless or sparsely hairy, narrowly lance-shaped leaflets 10–20 mm long; bears bright yellow flowers, often partly reddish on the standard, in terminal heads, with a hairy keel and silky calyx with tapering lobes. Lowland fynbos in the extreme southwestern Cape.

### ❽ *Aspalathus securifolia*

**J F M A M J J A S O N D**

Shrub to 1.2 m with 3-foliolate leaves and leathery, hairless, paddle-shaped leaflets 5–20 mm long; bears pale yellow flowers on long pedicels in terminal heads, with a silky keel and short-haired calyx. Mountain fynbos on lower slopes in the southwestern Cape.

**1 *Aspalathus tridentata***

J F M A M J J A S O N D

Shrub or shrublet to 1 m with 3-foliolate leaves and narrow, hairless or silky leaflets 3–25 mm long, with the leaf bases usually forming a spine; bears pale yellow flowers in terminal heads surrounded by a whorl of bracts, with a silky keel and silky calyx. Fynbos and renosterbos on lower slopes in the southwestern Cape.

## *Lebeckia*   LEBECKIA

Shrubs or herbs, sometimes spiny. Leaves usually 3-foliolate, rarely reduced to a single leaflet, leaflets thread-like to oval, *stipules absent*. Flowers in pedunculate racemes, yellow, *calyx equally lobed*; *stamens joined in a tube split down the top*, unequal. Pods narrow, many-seeded. Southern Africa: ±45 spp; ±20 fynbos spp.

### ▶ LEAVES UNDIVIDED AND THREAD-LIKE

**2 *Lebeckia plukenetiana***

J F M A M J J A S O N D

Sprawling or ascending subshrub to 40 cm with unjointed, thread-like leaves; bears racemes of yellow flowers with the keel shorter than the standard petal and the calyx lobes shorter than the tube. Sand-plain fynbos along the West Coast, 200–300 m, flowering especially after fire.

**3 *Lebeckia sepiaria***

J F M A M J J A S O N D

(=*Lebeckia simsiana*) **Wildeviolette**  Spreading shrublet to 50 cm with jointed, thread-like leaves; bears racemes of yellow flowers with the keel as long as or longer than the standard petal and the calyx lobes shorter than the tube; pods spongy, up to 40 mm long. Sandy flats, mostly above 300 m along the West Coast and in the southwestern Cape.

**4 *Lebeckia pauciflora***

J F M A M J J A S O N D

Slender, erect shrublet to 80 cm with long, jointed, thread-like leaves; bears racemes of yellow flowers with a spirally twisted keel as long as or longer than the standard petal, and slender calyx lobes longer than the tube; pods 60–120 mm long. Mountain fynbos in the southwestern Cape, flowering especially after fire.

### ▶ LEAVES 3-FOLIOLATE

**5 *Lebeckia sericea***

J F M A M J J A S O N D

Shrub to 1.5 m with 3-foliolate leaves and silky, elliptical leaflets; bears racemes of bright yellow or cream flowers with a silky calyx and pods. Karroid scrub and coastal thicket in Namaqualand and along the West Coast.

**6 *Lebeckia cytisoides***

J F M A M J J A S O N D

Shrub or small tree to 2 m with 3-foliolate leaves and silky, elliptical leaflets; bears racemes of bright yellow flowers with a hairless calyx and pods. Karroid scrub, renosterveld and fynbos along the West Coast and Breede River valley.

## *Lotononis*   LOTONONIS

Herbs or shrubs. Leaves usually digitately 3-foliolate, *stipules usually solitary at each node*. Flowers axillary or terminal, solitary or in heads, yellow or blue, *without bracteoles*; calyx usually with the upper 4 lobes joined and the lower lobe narrower; *stamens joined in a tube slit down the top*, unequal. Pods narrow or broad, seeds on long pedicels. Southern and eastern Africa, Eurasia and Pakistan: ±150 spp; ±40 fynbos spp.

305

**❶ *Lotononis prostrata***

J F M A M J J A S O N D

Prostrate or creeping shrublet with 3-foliolate leaves and sparsely hairy, wedge-shaped leaflets, subtended by solitary or unequal stipules; bears solitary, yellow flowers 10–15 mm long, on slender peduncles. Renosterveld and lowland fynbos in the extreme southwestern Cape.

**❷ *Lotononis umbellata***

J F M A M J J A S O N D

Prostrate shrublet with thick, woody branches to 10 cm and 3-foliolate leaves with sparsely hairy, wedge-shaped leaflets, subtended by solitary stipules; bears flat clusters of a few yellow flowers 8–10 mm long, on slender peduncles. Mountain and coastal fynbos in the southwestern and southern Cape.

## *Wiborgia*  PENNYPOD

Shrubs, often spinescent. Leaves digitately 3-foliolate, *stipules small or absent*. Flowers in terminal, *often 1-sided racemes*, creamy yellow to bright yellow, calyx mainly 2-lipped; *stamens joined in a tube that is slit down the top*, unequal. *Pods woody and indehiscent*, elliptical to orbicular *with a peripheral wing along the upper edge*. Winter-rainfall South Africa: 10 spp; 9 fynbos spp.

**❸ *Wiborgia fusca***

J F M A M J J A S O N D

Erect or spreading, somewhat thorny shrub to 1.5 m with hairless, greyish branches and 3-foliolate leaves with elliptical, pointed leaflets; bears racemes of pale greenish-yellow flowers 5–7 mm long; the pods have a wing along the upper edge and are 12–30×9–15 mm. Mountain and lowland fynbos in Namaqualand and along the West Coast.

**❹ *Wiborgia mucronata***

J F M A M J J A S O N D

Erect or spreading, thorny shrub to 1.5 m with hairless branches and 3-foliolate leaves with elliptical leaflets; bears terminal racemes of yellow flowers 6–8 mm long; the pods are irregularly ridged on the sides with a wing along the upper edge and are 12–30×9–15 mm. Mountain fynbos or renosterbos-fynbos scrub in Namaqualand and the southwestern Cape.

**❺ *Wiborgia obcordata***

J F M A M J J A S O N D

Slender, stiffly branched or willowy shrub to 3 m with velvety branches when young and 3-foliolate leaves with wedge-shaped leaflets that are sparsely hairy beneath; bears racemes of bright yellow flowers 6–8 mm long; the pods have a narrow crest along the upper edge and are 7–12×4–7 mm. Sandy flats and slopes, from southern Namaqualand to the southern Cape.

## *Cyclopia*  BUSH TEA, BOERTEE

Erect shrubs. Leaves digitately or palmately *3-foliolate*, leaflets narrow or broad, hairless or hairy, often with the margins rolled under. Flowers solitary in the axils, yellow; calyx pushed inwards at the base; *stamens separate or joined only at the base* with the *filaments widened at the base*. Pods oblong; seeds with a waxy appendage. Southwestern and southern Cape: 23 spp, all fynbos. *Cyclopia genistoides* is the original heuningtee (honeybush tea), but today other species, including *C. subternata*, are harvested commercially.

**❶ *Cyclopia subternata*  Vleitee**  J F M A M J J A **S O N** D

Erect, single-stemmed shrub to 3.5 m with 3-foliolate, hairless leaves and elliptical to lance-shaped leaflets, the margins slightly curved down, 8–30×3–10 mm; bears yellow flowers. Sandstone seeps up to 1 000 m in the mountains of the southern Cape.

**❷ *Cyclopia genistoides***  J F M A M J J A **S O N** D

**Honeybush tea, heuningtee**  Erect, resprouting shrub to 2 m with 3-foliolate, hairless leaves and narrow, needle-like leaflets, the margins rolled under, 8–30×1–2 mm; bears clusters of yellow flowers. Lowland fynbos on seasonally marshy flats and slopes in the southwestern Cape.

**❸ *Cyclopia galioides***  **J F M A M** J J A S O N D

Robust, soft-haired, resprouting shrub to 1 m with 3-foliolate, more or less silky leaves and needle-like leaflets, the margins rolled under, 8–27×1–2 mm; bears clusters of yellow flowers. Lowland fynbos on the Cape Peninsula.

## *Hypocalyptus*  HYPOCALYPTUS

Shrubs or small trees. Leaves digitately 3-foliolate, leaflets elliptical to oval, stipules present. Flowers in racemes, *pink to purple with a yellow nectar guide; calyx brown and membranous, pushed in at the base* with the upper 2 lobes joined; *stamens joined together in a closed sheath* with alternate anthers larger. Pods narrow, seeds 5 or 6 with a fleshy appendage. Southwestern Cape: 3 spp, all fynbos.

**❹ *Hypocalyptus coluteoides***  J F M A M J J A **S O N D**

Tree-like shrub to 3 m with 3-foliolate leaves and elliptical leaflets 10–45 mm long that are paler beneath; bears racemes of 6–15(25) pink to magenta flowers with a short-haired calyx; the pods are somewhat swollen. Moist sandstone slopes in the southwestern and southern Cape.

**❺ *Hypocalyptus sophoroides***  J F M A M J J A S **O N D**

Shrub or small tree to 6 m with erect, 3-foliolate leaves and wedge-shaped, pointed leaflets 10–35 mm long; bears dense racemes of 30 or more magenta flowers with a hairless calyx; the pods are narrow and almost segmented between the seeds. Moist sandstone slopes and streamsides in the southwestern Cape.

## *Indigofera*  INDIGO

Herbs or shrubs, mostly covered with forked hairs. Leaves (1)3(9)-foliolate, sometimes reduced to scales, stipules present. Flowers in axillary or terminal racemes, *shades of pink, petals often deciduous, the keel petals each with a sac or spur on the side and a fringed upper margin,* calyx more or less equally lobed; stamens joined in a tube with upper 1 separate, *anthers distinctly pointed.* Pods narrow or broad. Worldwide in tropics and subtropics: 720–730 spp; ±75 fynbos spp.

▸ WILLOWY SHRUB, ALMOST LEAFLESS EXCEPT WHEN YOUNG

**❻ *Indigofera filifolia***  J F M A M J J A **S O N D**

Erect, almost leafless shrub with willowy stems to 3 m and leaves mostly on younger plants or shoots, with 6–8-foliolate leaves with elliptical leaflets that are sparsely hairy beneath, and petioles 4–6 cm long; bears white to pink or purple flowers 9–11 mm long in racemes on peduncles shorter than the leaves, the back of the standard petal hairless. Mountain and lowland fynbos along streamsides in southwestern Cape.

## ▶ TRAILING OR SPRAWLING PERENNIALS WITH 3 LEAFLETS

**❶ *Indigofera heterophylla***

`J F M A M J J A S O N D`

Erect or sprawling to prostrate shrublet with pinnately or digitately 3-foliolate leaves and lance-shaped to oval, sparsely hairy leaflets; bears orange-pink to reddish-purple flowers in racemes on robust peduncles, with the back of the standard petal hairy and the calyx sparsely hairy with awl-like lobes up to 3 times as long as the tube. Renosterveld and fynbos, from Namaqualand to the Eastern Cape.

**❷ *Indigofera procumbens* Lewertjie**

`J F M A M J J A S O N D`

Spreading or trailing perennial to 10 cm with the stems often running underground and digitately 3-foliolate leaves with oval or rhomboidal leaves that are hairless or sparsely hairy above; bears orange, copper, rose or purple flowers in racemes on fleshy peduncles. Lowland renosterveld and coastal fynbos along the West Coast.

**❸ *Indigofera psoraloides***

`J F M A M J J A S O N D`

Erect or straggling shrublet to 80 cm with digitately 3-foliolate leaves and narrowly lance-shaped, short-haired leaflets; bears pink, red or purple flowers in racemes on robust peduncles. Lowland fynbos along the West Coast.

## ▶ SHRUBS WITH 5–7 LEAFLETS

**❹ *Indigofera flabellata***

`J F M A M J J A S O N D`

Erect, densely hairy, mass-flowering shrub to 1.5 m with ±sessile, almost digitately (3)5–7-foliolate leaves and narrowly lance-shaped, minute-haired leaflets, the margins rolled under; bears ±sessile, pink or purple flowers in racemes on peduncles shorter than the leaves, with persistent petals and the back of the standard petal hairy; the densely hairy calyx is 5-toothed. Mountain and lowland fynbos in the southern Cape.

**❺ *Indigofera brachystachya***

`J F M A M J J A S O N D`

Dense, mass-flowering shrub to 1.5 m with densely grey-haired stems and ±sessile, pinnately 5–7-foliolate leaves and narrowly wedge-shaped leaflets that are short-haired above and densely grey-haired beneath, the margins strongly rolled under; bears ±sessile, mauve to pink flowers in dense racemes on long or short peduncles, with persistent petals and the back of the standard petal with silky white hairs. Coastal fynbos and limestone in the southwestern Cape.

**❻ *Indigofera cytisoides***

`J F M A M J J A S O N D`

Erect, single-stemmed shrub to 3 m with ±sessile or shortly petiolate, pinnately (3)5-foliolate leaves and elliptical, minutely haired leaflets 20–50 mm long; bears purple to pink flowers to 11 mm long in racemes on robust peduncles about as long as the leaves, with the back of the standard petal densely hairy. Mountain and riverine fynbos in the extreme southwestern Cape.

311

▶ LEAVES SIMPLE, ALMOST SESSILE, STIPULES SMALL OR ABSENT

## *Rafnia*  INK PEA

Shrubs, *completely hairless and usually bluish, often turning black on drying. Leaves simple, hairless, stipules absent.* Flowers solitary or in racemes, yellow, calyx usually with the lowest lobe narrower; *stamens joined in a tube that is slit down the top,* unequal. Pods narrow. South Africa, mainly winter-rainfall region: 19 spp, all fynbos. The roots of *Rafnia amplexicaulis* were used as a liquorice substitute, and a decoction of *R. perfoliata* as a diuretic.

**❶ *Rafnia schlechteriana***

| J | F | M | A | M | J | J | A | S | O | N | D |

Erect shrublet to 60 cm with broadly elliptical to orbicular leaves that are opposite on the flowering branches; bears yellow flowers 11–15 mm long with a blunt keel, clustered in large, conical, compound inflorescences at the ends of the branches, the calyx lobes up to as long as the tube. Sandstone slopes in the mountains along the West Coast. *Rafnia ovata* has larger flowers with a sharp, beak-like keel.

**❷ *Rafnia angulata***

| J | F | M | A | M | J | J | A | S | O | N | D |

Erect or sprawling shrublet with wand-like stems to 2 m and needle-like to oval leaves; bears axillary racemes of 1–6 yellow flowers 8–20 mm long, with a sharp, beak-like keel, the calyx lobes as long as or longer than the tube. Stony slopes in the southwestern Cape.

**❸ *Rafnia perfoliata***

| J | F | M | A | M | J | J | A | S | O | N | D |

Prostrate or trailing shrublet to 30 cm, forming clumps to 1 m in diameter, with heart-shaped leaves often clasping the stem and opposite on flowering branches; bears solitary yellow flowers 9–14 mm long with a sharp, beak-like keel, the calyx lobes as long as or much longer than the tube. Stony slopes in the mountains of the southwestern Cape. *Rafnia amplexicaulis* is an erect shrub with the calyx lobes shorter than the tube.

## *Liparia*  MOUNTAIN PEA

Shrubs or shrublets. *Leaves simple,* narrow to round, *3- or more-veined from the base, often drying black,* stipules small. Flowers in terminal heads, yellow to orange *with large, leaf-like bracts, calyx pushed in at the base* with long lobes, the upper 4 often partly joined and the *lowermost much larger;* stamens joined in a tube with the upper 1 separate, unequal. Pods oval or oblong, sparsely hairy, seeds with a fleshy appendage. Winter-rainfall South Africa: 20 spp, all fynbos. The striking flowers of *Liparia splendens* are pollinated by sunbirds, especially the Orange-breasted Sunbird, while *L. parva* is adapted to pollination by rodents.

**❹ *Liparia vestita***

| J | F | M | A | M | J | J | A | S | O | N | D |

Multi-stemmed, resprouting shrub to 2.5 m with concave, broadly elliptical to almost circular leaves; bears racemes of yellow flowers 11–15 mm long, in alternating groups of 4 with the bracts clasping the base of the calyx. Mountain fynbos up to 1 000 m in the extreme southwestern Cape.

**❺ *Liparia splendens***

| J | F | M | A | M | J | J | A | S | O | N | D |

**Mountain dahlia, skaamblom** Erect or creeping, resprouting shrub to 1 m with elliptical leaves; bears nodding heads of 15–17 orange to red flowers 35–40 mm long, among conspicuous, dark reddish-brown bracts. Mountain and lowland fynbos in the southwestern Cape.

**① *Liparia parva***  J F M A M J J A S O N D

Prostrate, resprouting shrublet to 20 cm with elliptical leaves; bears heads of up to 7 pale yellowish-green flowers 15–20 mm long, among dark reddish bracts. Lowland and mountain fynbos below 300 m on the Cape Peninsula.

## *Xiphotheca*  SILVER PEA

Shrubs. *Leaves simple*, elliptical to round, *stipules small or absent. Flowers in pairs collected into short, axillary racemes*, yellow, calyx mostly 2-lipped with the lower lip largest; stamens joined into a tube with the upper 1 separate. Pods leathery, silky; seeds with a fleshy appendage. Winter-rainfall South Africa: 9 spp, all fynbos.

**② *Xiphotheca fruticosa***  J F M A M J J A S O N D

Single- or multi-stemmed shrub to 2 m with dense, silvery, silky hairs and elliptical leaves; bears yellow flowers 10–15 mm long, crowded in sessile, head-like terminal clusters nested among the leaves with the calyx lobes shorter than the tube. Sandstone slopes in fynbos in the southwestern Cape. *Xiphotheca lanceolata* from lowlands on the Cape Flats has the calyx lobes longer than the tube.

## *Amphithalea*  AMPHITHALEA

Shrubs or shrublets, usually hairy. *Leaves simple*, usually sessile, narrow to broad, flat or with the margins curved up or down, *stipules absent*. Flowers small, axillary and ±sessile, sometimes in spikes, *white, pink to purple* or rarely yellow, without bracteoles; calyx unequally lobed with the upper 2 lobes larger and often joined, *keel petals with a sac or spur on the side*; stamens joined in a tube with the upper one separate, with alternate anthers longer and basifixed, others versatile. Pods oval to oblong, silky; seeds 1–4 with a fleshy appendage. South Africa, mainly southwestern Cape, especially southern Cape: 42 spp, all fynbos.

**③ *Amphithalea imbricata***  J F M A M J J A S O N D

Erect shrub to 1.8 m with silky, flat, oval leaves that have distinct venation, 7–20×4–11 mm; bears heads of deep mauve flowers 5–10 mm long; ovules and seeds 2. Mountain and lowland fynbos below 750 m in the extreme southwestern Cape.

**④ *Amphithalea alba***  J F M A M J J A S O N D

Erect, single-stemmed shrub to 1.2 m with silky, oval leaves, the margins turned down, 4.5–10×1.5–3 mm; bears heads of white or cream flowers 7–8 mm long; ovule and seed 1. Lowland fynbos on limestone below 150 m on the Agulhas Plain.

**⑤ *Amphithalea ericifolia*  Persblom**  J F M A M J J A S O N D

Erect, resprouting shrublet to 1 m with silky, lance-shaped leaves, the margins strongly turned down, 5–15×1.5–4 mm; bears clusters of pink, rose and dark pink flowers 4–6 mm long; ovule and seed 1. Mountain and lowland fynbos below 1 500 m in the southwestern Cape.

## *Podalyria*  CAPE SWEETPEA, KEURTJIE

*Silvery-silky or hairy shrubs. Leaves simple,* narrow to almost round. *Flowers 1–4 on axillary peduncles, pink, purple or white; calyx shaggy and pushed in at the base,* sometimes split on one side; *stamens joined only at the base* with the filaments widened at the base. Pods shaggy, seeds with a fleshy collar. Mainly winter-rainfall South Africa: 19 spp; 18 fynbos spp.

### ❶ *Podalyria pearsonii*

| J | F | M | A | M | J | J | A | **S** | O | N | D |

Willowy, resprouting shrub to 1 m with elliptical to narrowly elliptical leaves 10–20×2–5 mm that are hairless and shining above and silky beneath; bears magenta to pink flowers 10–15 mm long, subtended by rounded bracts. Sandstone slopes in the northern mountains.

### ❷ *Podalyria leipoldtii*

| J | F | M | A | M | J | J | **A** | S | O | N | D |

Stiff, resprouting shrub to 2 m with small, paddle-shaped leaves 7–17×3–7 mm that are silvery silky on both surfaces; bears pink flowers 15–25 mm long, subtended by lance-shaped bracts. Sandstone slopes in the northern mountains.

### ❸ *Podalyria sericea*

| J | F | M | **A** | **M** | J | J | A | S | O | N | D |

Single-stemmed shrublet to 1 m with elliptical leaves 10–30×6–15 mm that are silky on both surfaces; bears small pink flowers 8–10 mm long, subtended by lance-shaped bracts. Sandstone and granite outcrops below 500 m along the West Coast.

### ❹ *Podalyria myrtillifolia*

| J | F | M | A | M | **J** | **J** | **A** | **S** | O | N | D |

Rounded, single-stemmed or sometimes resprouting shrub to 2 m with oval or paddle-shaped leaves 10–20×5–10 mm that are silky on both surfaces; bears pink flowers 10–16 mm long, subtended by lance-shaped bracts. Sandstone, limestone or shale flats and lower slopes in the southwestern and southern Cape.

### ❺ *Podalyria calyptrata*

| J | F | M | A | M | J | J | **A** | **S** | O | N | D |

Small tree to 5 m with elliptical to oval leaves 20–60×10–30 mm that are silky on both surfaces when young; bears bright pink flowers 20–30 mm long, subtended by very broad bracts that are joined into a cap or sheath covering the bud. Sandstone slopes in marshy places in the extreme southwestern Cape.

# AIZOACEAE Ice plant family

▸ SEPALS COLOURED AND PETAL-LIKE; FLOWERS WITHOUT PETALS OR STAMINODES

## *Tetragonia*  SEA CORAL, KLAPPERBRAK

Annual or perennial herbs or shrublets, often sprawling. Leaves alternate, semi-succulent, often rhombic and minutely warty. Flowers 1 to many, mainly axillary, green, cream to yellow or magenta, *with 5(7) petal-like sepals; ovary inferior or half-inferior,* stamens few to many, often in bundles. Fruits *1-seeded, usually 4-winged, indehiscent.* Africa, South America and Australia: ±60 spp; ±10 fynbos spp.

▸ **TUBEROUS HERBS**

**1 *Tetragonia chenopodioides***   J F M A M J **J A S** O N D

Tuberous perennial with sprawling branches to 40 cm with rhombic leaves that are often reddish beneath; bears ±sessile, yellow-green flowers in axillary and terminal clusters, with styles twice as long as the sepals; the fruits are 8-ridged. Coastal sands along the West Coast.

**2 *Tetragonia nigrescens***   J F M A M J **J A S O** N D

Tuberous perennial with sprawling stems to 50 cm, and paddle-shaped to ±orbicular leaves that are often red beneath; bears yellow or cream (rarely orange) flowers 3–4 mm in diameter, often purple on the reverse, on slender pedicels in axillary and terminal clusters; the fruits are winged. Sandy and clay slopes and flats, from Namaqualand to the southern Cape. *Tetragonia halimoides*, from the West Coast, has larger flowers 4–5 mm in diameter, and fruits 20–25 mm long.

**3 *Tetragonia herbacea***   J F M A M **J J A** S O N D

Tuberous perennial with sprawling stems to 50 cm and paddle-shaped leaves; bears bright yellow flowers 4–6 mm in diameter, on long pedicels in terminal flower clusters and solitary in the upper axils; the fruits are pear-shaped and smooth but ridged when dry. Mostly clay and granite slopes in the southwestern Cape.

▸ **SOFTLY WOODY SHRUBS OR SUBSHRUBS**

**4 *Tetragonia decumbens***   **J F M** A M J J **A S O N D**

Sprawling perennial with branches to 1 m with oblong or lance-shaped, glistening leaves that are warty or hairy; bears yellow flowers 3–4 mm in diameter, in branched, axillary clusters shorter than the leaves; the fruits have stiff wings. Coastal dunes from southern Namibia to the Eastern Cape.

**5 *Tetragonia fruticosa*  Kinkelbossie**   J F M A M J J **A S O N D**

Sprawling shrub with long branches, often trailing through scrub, with oblong leaves, the margins rolled under; bears yellowish flowers 3–4 mm in diameter, in terminal racemes, or 1 to few in the upper axils; the fruits are broadly winged with knobs between the wings. Granite and sandstone slopes, especially along the coast, from Namaqualand to the Eastern Cape. *Tetragonia spicata* is a stiffly erect shrub.

**1** *Tetragonia rosea*

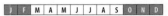

Subshrub with sprawling branches to 60 cm and rhombic to paddle-shaped leaves; bears 1 to few, ±sessile or pedicellate, magenta flowers in the upper axils and terminally, with the sepals joined at the base; the fruits are 4-winged with knobs between the wings, and 15–20 mm long. Sandstone slopes in the mountains along the West Coast.

## *Acrosanthes*  ACROSANTHES

Prostrate to sprawling, woody perennials with unequal branching. Leaves opposite, fleshy, *hairless*. Flowers apparently lateral, *solitary at the nodes, white, with 5 petal-like sepals*; stamens 8 to many, sometimes in bundles, ovary superior. *Fruit a 2-chambered capsule with 1 basal seed in each chamber*. Western Cape: 5 spp, all fynbos.

**2** *Acrosanthes teretifolia*

Sprawling, widely branching perennial to 80 cm from a woody base with cylindrical, pointed leaves 10–20 mm long; bears solitary white flowers at the nodes, with more than 25 stamens. Stony flats and slopes in the southwestern Cape.

## *Aizoon*  AIZOON, SKAAPVYGIE

Perennial or annual herbs or subshrubs, *all parts variously hairy*. Leaves mostly alternate, often crowded, flat to cylindrical. Flowers apparently solitary or in axillary groups, forming frond-like inflorescences, white inside and yellow or pink outside, *with 4 or 5 petal-like sepals*; stamens few to many, in bundles, ovary superior. *Fruit a 4- or 5-chambered capsule with many seeds per chamber*. Africa, Mediterranean and Australia: ±20 spp; 6 fynbos spp. The vernacular name, skaapvygie, refers to the value of the plants as browsing for stock.

**3** *Aizoon paniculatum*

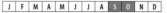

Prostrate or sprawling subshrub to 50 cm with the leaves mostly basal, lance-shaped and covered with pressed, silvery hairs; bears sessile magenta or sometimes cream-coloured flowers clustered in flattened, forked, terminal cymes. Dry sandstone and clay slopes and flats along the West Coast and adjacent interior.

**4** *Aizoon rigidum*

Prostrate subshrub to 15 cm with paddle-shaped leaves, covered with pressed, grey hairs; bears solitary, yellow flowers in the axils. Dry, stony slopes, often near the sea, in the southern and Eastern Cape.

## *Mesembryanthemum* ICE PLANT, BRAKSLAAI

Annual or perennial, often *sprawling, fleshy herbs*, often with *angled or winged stems*. Leaves opposite or alternate, *flat and petiolate to club-shaped, covered with rounded or flattened, glistening bladder cells*. Flowers solitary or clustered, 10–60 mm in diameter, open in sunlight, pink, yellow or white; staminodes present or absent. Fruits 5-segmented. Dry parts of southern Africa: 16 spp; ±6 fynbos spp.

**1** *Mesembryanthemum crystallinum*

| J | F | M | A | M | J | J | A | S | O | N | D |

Sprawling annual with oval or paddle-shaped leaves at the base, forming a small rosette, covered with large bladder cells; bears white or pinkish flowers 15–30 mm in diameter. Coastal sands in the Western and Eastern Cape.

**2** *Mesembryanthemum guerichianum*

| J | F | M | A | M | J | J | A | S | O | N | D |

Sprawling annual with oval or paddle-shaped leaves at the base, forming a small rosette, covered with small bladder cells; bears white or pinkish flowers 25–55 mm in diameter. Sandy flats and roadsides in the drier parts of southern Africa.

## *Dorotheanthus* DOROTHEANTHUS, BOKBAAIVYGIE

Annual herbs *covered with glistening bladder cells*, to 10 cm in flower. Leaves mostly alternate, lowermost in rosettes, *flat and petiolate*. Flowers solitary, to 40 mm in diameter, *on naked pedicels to 60 mm long*, white, yellow, orange, red or pink, usually with a paler halo in the middle and with *a dark centre*; opening in sunlight; *petals in 2 series; stamens sometimes brown or reddish, staminodes absent*. Fruits 5-segmented. Winter-rainfall South Africa: 7 spp; 4 fynbos spp. The vernacular name, Bokbaaivygie, alludes to the prevalence of the plants on the sands around Bokbaai on the West Coast.

**3** *Dorotheanthus bellidiformis*

| J | F | M | A | M | J | J | A | S | O | N | D |

**Livingstone daisy** Tufted annual with tongue-like to paddle-shaped leaves, covered with bladder cells; bears red, yellow, pink or white flowers 20–30 mm in diameter, on pedicels up to 25 mm long. Mostly on sandy flats in Namaqualand and the southwestern Cape. *Dorotheanthus apetalus*, from coastal flats in the southwestern Cape, has small white flowers with the petals shorter than the sepals.

**4** *Dorotheanthus clavatus*

| J | F | M | A | M | J | J | A | S | O | N | D |

Tufted annual with very narrow, strap-shaped leaves; bears pink, white or orange flowers 20–30 mm in diameter, on pedicels up to 25 mm long. Saline places between Darling and Hopefield.

## *Apatesia*  APATESIA, VETKOUSIE

*Sprawling annual herb.* Leaves opposite, *flattened with a petiole,* clasping the stem at the base, covered with waxy flakes. Flowers solitary on long pedicels, *yellow,* opening in sunlight, petals in 4 or 5 series, *the margins with minute hairs*; staminodes numerous. *Fruit 8–12-segmented.* Southwestern Cape: 3 spp, all fynbos.

### ❶ *Apatesia pillansii*

J F M A M J J A S O N D

Annual succulent to 15 cm, with flat, slightly succulent leaves; bears yellow flowers; the fruits are slightly domed above and the seeds are slightly warty. Coastal dunes along the West Coast. *Apatesia helanthoides* from further inland has fruits that are conical above and smooth seeds.

## *Carpanthea*  CARPANTHEA, VETKOUSIE

Annual herb with *glistening, hairy stems.* Leaves opposite, *flat, with scattered white hairs and fringed margins.* Flowers 1–3 at the stem tips, *golden yellow,* opening in sunlight and furling up tightly at night, petals in several series, narrow; staminodes numerous. *Fruit 12–18-segmented.* Southwestern Cape: 1 sp. The vernacular name, vetkousie, is part corruption and part translation of the original Khoisan name.

### ❷ *Carpanthea pomeridiana*

J F M A M J J A S O N D

Annual succulent to 20 cm with soft-haired stems and flat, slightly succulent leaves with hair-like papillae on the margins; bears yellow flowers with hair-like papillae on the calyx. Sandy flats along the West Coast and adjacent interior.

## *Conicosia*  CONICOSIA, GANSIES

Perennial or biennial herbs with trailing branches, often tuberous. Leaves opposite, in a basal tuft and scattered along the branches, 3-angled, smooth, elongated, *up to 40 cm long. Flowers solitary at the branch tips on long pedicels, yellow or whitish,* up to 130 mm in diameter, *opening in the afternoon, often unpleasantly scented*; petals in numerous series, narrow; staminodes numerous. *Fruits cone-shaped, 10–25-segmented.* Winter-rainfall South Africa: 2 spp; 1 fynbos sp.

### ❸ *Conicosia pugioniformis*  Varkslaai

J F M A M J J A S O N D

Tufted perennial to 40 cm with a thick tap root and trailing branches, and with long, 3-angled leaves; bears solitary, large yellow flowers that open in the afternoon. Sandy flats, mostly coastal, from Namaqualand to the Eastern Cape.

## *Carpobrotus*  SOUR FIG, SUURVY

*Robust, trailing perennials,* often forming large mats, with maroon to yellow stems that are sometimes narrowly winged. Leaves opposite, smooth and sharply 3-angled, *with a cartilaginous and often reddish, toothed keel and margins, up to 130 mm long.* Flowers solitary at the branch tips on a stout pedicel, *large, up to 150 mm in diameter,* white, yellow, pink or magenta; petals in several series; staminodes numerous; *ovary 2-ridged* and tapering into the pedicel. *Fruit fleshy, 4–20-segmented.* Southern Africa, Chile, California and Australia: 13 spp; 6 fynbos spp. The sap is used as an antiseptic and the fruits for jam.

**325**

### ① *Carpobrotus edulis*

J F M A M J J A S O N D

Succulent perennial with trailing stems to 2 m long, with straight or slightly curved leaves 8–18 mm in diameter; bears yellow flowers 50–80 mm in diameter, fading to pink with age, with the stigmas about as long as the stamens; the receptacle is top-shaped and tapers gradually into the pedicel. Coastal and inland slopes, from Namaqualand to the Eastern Cape. *Carpobrotus mellei* has pink or purple flowers, with the stamens shorter than the stigmas.

### ② *Carpobrotus acinaciformis*

J F M A M J J A S O N D

Succulent perennial with trailing stems to 2 m long, with robust, sabre-shaped leaves 15–25 mm in diameter; bears purple flowers 70–100 mm in diameter; the receptacle is oblong or ±globular, and curves abruptly into the pedicel. Coastal sands in the southwestern Cape. The following species with similar flowers have more or less straight leaves: *Carpobrotus deliciosus*, from the southern Cape, has leaves 12–18 mm in diameter; *C. muirii*, from the Agulhas Plain, has slender leaves 5–7 mm in diameter.

### ③ *Carpobrotus quadrifidus*

J F M A M J J A S O N D

(=*Carpobrotus sauerae*) Succulent perennial with trailing stems to 3 m long, and robust, scimitar-shaped leaves 18–25 mm in diameter; bears purple or pink flowers 120–150 mm in diameter; the receptacle is oblong or ±globular and curves abruptly into the pedicel. Coastal rocks from Namaqualand and the West Coast.

## *Jordaaniella*  JORDAANIELLA, STRANDVYGIE

*Prostrate perennials with long orange or yellow internodes. Leaves spindle-shaped (tapering at both ends).* Flowers solitary on short side branches, yellow to purple, rarely white, opening at midday; petals in several series; *staminodes absent. Fruits 10–25-segmented.* Winter-rainfall South Africa: 4 spp; 1 fynbos sp.

### ④ *Jordaaniella dubia*

J F M A M J J A S O N D

Prostrate succulent with stem internodes longer than 20 mm, and slender, spindle-shaped leaves without papillae; bears solitary, yellow, sometimes white or magenta, flowers 30–40 mm in diameter. Fruits ±globular, 10–15-segmented. Coastal sands in the southwestern Cape.

▶ ▶ TUFTED OR CUSHION-FORMING PERENNIALS OR WOODY SHRUBLETS, OR TRAILING, WITH FLOWERS RARELY YELLOW AND STYLES AND FRUIT SEGMENTS ONLY 4 OR 5

## *Phyllobolus*  PHYLLOBOLUS

Prostrate to erect *shrubs or perennials*, often with thickened or tuberous roots. Leaves opposite, almost cylindrical or flattened, *usually with conspicuous bladder cells.* Flowers solitary or in clusters, white, green, yellow, orange, red or pink, opening in sunlight; petals in several series; staminodes present or absent. Fruit 4- or 5-segmented. Southern Africa: 32 spp; ±7 fynbos spp.

### ⑤ *Phyllobolus canaliculatus*

J F M A M J J A S O N D

Geophyte with tuberous roots and long, creeping, softly woody branches that root at the nodes, the leaves opposite below but alternate in the inflorescence and with prominent bladder cells; bears pinkish flowers 20–30 mm in diameter, with the stamens exposed. Coastal dunes in the southwestern and southern Cape.

### ① *Phyllobolus caudatus*

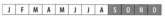

Geophyte with tuberous roots and creeping, softly woody stems, the leaves opposite below but alternate in the inflorescence and with prominent bladder cells; bears showy yellow flowers 40–60 mm in diameter, with the stamens exposed. Sandy flats and plateaus along the interior West Coast.

## *Prenia*   PRENIA

Erect or *creeping shrublets with soft, smooth, whitish bark.* Leaves mostly opposite, almost flat and 3-angled or almost cylindrical, *with a thick waxy layer that is easily wiped off.* Flowers in branched clusters, 20–40 mm in diameter, white, yellow or pink, opening in sunlight; petals joined to the stamens and staminodes at the base. Fruits 4-segmented. Mainly arid, winter-rainfall regions of southern Africa: 6 spp; 3 fynbos spp.

### ② *Prenia pallens*

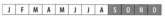

Prostrate perennial with whitish stems and narrowly oval, 3-angled leaves; bears whitish to yellow flowers. Mainly clay and granite slopes in Namaqualand and the southwestern Cape.

## *Delosperma*   DELOSPERMA, SKAAPVYGIE

Shrublets or perennials, *often with sprawling annual branches,* sometimes tuberous. Leaves opposite, sometimes hairy or prickly and with bladder cells, 3-angled to cylindrical, *usually soft, often bright green.* Flowers solitary or in 3s, white to pink or purple, rarely yellow or reddish; petals in 1–4 series; staminodes usually arranged in a cone, whitish; ovary usually 5-segmented. Mainly South Africa, especially eastern parts: ±158 spp; ±10 fynbos spp.

### ③ *Delosperma litorale*  Kalkklipvygie

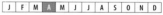

Sprawling shrublet with trailing stems to 35 cm long and erect branchlets to 15 cm; the spreading, sickle-shaped leaves have white margins; bears white or pink flowers in 3s on pedicels to 20 mm long. Coastal, limestone flats in the southwestern and southern Cape.

## *Disphyma*   DISPHYMA

*Creeping, mat-forming perennials* with internodes 20–30 mm long. Leaves opposite but *in small rosettes at the nodes,* 3-angled, *bright green, covered with translucent spots when seen against the light, up to ±30 mm long.* Flowers 1–3 at the branch tips, white or pink to magenta, ±40 mm in diameter, opening at midday; *petals in ±2 series;* staminodes absent. Fruits spongy, 5-segmented. Western Cape coast, Australia and New Zealand: 4 spp; 2 fynbos spp.

### ④ *Disphyma crassifolium*

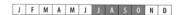

Mat-forming perennial, rooting at the nodes, with smooth, 3-angled, dark green leaves 25–35 mm long, covered with translucent dots; bears clusters of 1–3 white to rose red flowers 40 mm in diameter. Coastal rocks just above high-tide mark in the Western and Eastern Cape. *Disphyma dunsdonii,* from salt pans near Bredasdorp, has leaves 5–9 mm long and flowers 20–25 mm in diameter.

## *Drosanthemum*   DROSANTHEMUM, DOUVYGIE

Shrublets or loosely branched shrubs, often prostrate, the *stems with distinct internodes and often bristly.* Leaves opposite, *not joined at the base and easily shed, rounded at the tips* and up to ±50 mm long, *covered with glistening papillae or bladder cells.* Flowers solitary or in clusters, white, orange, red, pink or magenta, opening at midday; petals in 1 or 2 series; stamens either erect or widely spreading, staminodes present or absent. Fruit 5-segmented. Mainly winter-rainfall southern Africa: 110 spp; ±25 fynbos spp.

329

**① *Drosanthemum hispidum*** J F M A M J J A S O N D
Erect or spreading shrublet to 60 cm, with roughly hairy or bristly red branches and blunt, cylindrical leaves, mostly bending downwards and covered with glittering bladder cells; bears solitary, magenta flowers. Pioneer of disturbed areas and roadsides in the drier parts of southern Africa.

## *Erepsia*  EREPSIA, ALTYDVYGIE

Shrublets with smooth stems. Leaves 3-angled and *sharply pointed, often with translucent dots*. Flowers usually many, white, pink or magenta, *often remaining open day and night; petals in 1 or 2 series, slender, often spoon-shaped; stamens bending into the floral tube, almost completely covered by the staminodes*. Fruits 5-segmented (rarely more). Mainly southwestern Cape: 30 spp, all fynbos. The vernacular name refers to the characteristic flowers that always (*altyd*) remain open.

**② *Erepsia anceps*** J F M A M J J A S O N D
Slender, erect shrublet to 30 cm, sparsely branched from the base, with slender leaves less than 5 mm in diameter; bears pink or magenta flowers with spoon-shaped petals and papillate, bright yellow filamentous staminodes concealing the stamens; the fruits are 4–8 mm in diameter. Sandstone slopes to 1 000 m in the southwestern Cape, flowering mostly after fire.

**③ *Erepsia patula*** J F M A M J J A S O N D
Slender, erect, regularly branched shrublet to 30 cm, with slender leaves less than 5 mm in diameter; bears magenta flowers with a white centre and yellow filamentous staminodes, tipped with red, concealing the stamens; the fruits are 4–6 mm in diameter. Loamy soils, to 500 m, in slightly disturbed places on the Cape Peninsula.

**④ *Erepsia inclaudens*** J F M A M J J A S O N D
Densely branched shrublet to 40 cm, with red stems and red-tipped leaves 6–8 mm in diameter; bears small clusters of deep mauve flowers with spoon-shaped petals and minute filamentous staminodes concealing the stamens; the fruits are 8–10 mm in diameter. Rock crevices in the extreme southwestern Cape.

## *Lampranthus*  LAMPRANTHUS, VYGIE

Creeping or erect shrublets with smooth stems. Leaves opposite, *usually cylindrical*, blunt or tapering, *mostly smooth*, up to 50 mm long. Flowers solitary or in clusters, white, yellow, orange or pink to magenta, 7–70 mm in diameter, opening in sunlight; petals in several series; staminodes present or absent, spreading or collected in a cone. Fruits 5-segmented, *with funicular hairs*. Mainly winter-rainfall southern Africa: ±150 spp; ±120 fynbos spp. The vernacular name derives from the Dutch diminutive for fig, applied originally to the edible fruits of *Carpobrotus*.

▶ CREEPING PERENNIALS WITH LEAVES IN TUFTS

**⑤ *Lampranthus filicaulis*** J F M A M J J A S O N D
Mat-forming perennial to 10 cm with leaves crowded at the branch tips and curving inwards with the tips curved back, to 25×3 mm; bears solitary, rose to magenta flowers to 20 mm in diameter, with the filamentous staminodes and stamens collected in a central cone. Moist depressions on laterite clay in the southwestern Cape.

**1** *Lampranthus reptans*

J F M A M J J A S O N D

Mat-forming perennial with trailing branches and erect leaves in tufts, 15–25×5–6 mm; bears solitary white or yellow flowers on long pedicels. Sandy flats on the West Coast and Cape flats. *Lampranthus explanatus* is not mat-forming and has narrower leaves to 2 mm in diameter.

## ▶ SHRUBLETS WITH YELLOW OR ORANGE FLOWERS

**2** *Lampranthus aurantiacus*

J F M A M J J A S O N D

Sparsely branched shrublet to 45 cm with bluntly 3-angled, greyish leaves 20–30 mm long; bears solitary, orange flowers 40–50 mm in diameter. Sandy flats along the West Coast.

**3** *Lampranthus aureus*

J F M A M J J A S O N D

Erect perennial to 40 cm, with the leaves joined at the base and greyish, to 50 mm long; bears shiny, orange flowers to 60 mm in diameter. Granite outcrops around Saldanha Bay.

**4** *Lampranthus bicolor*

J F M A M J J A S O N D

Stiffly branched, erect shrublet to 30 cm with rough, almost 3-angled green leaves 12–25 mm long; bears groups of 1–3 yellow flowers with scarlet or copper undersides. Sandy flats or slopes in the extreme southwestern Cape.

## ▶ SHRUBLETS WITH WHITE, PINK OR MAGENTA FLOWERS

**5** *Lampranthus aduncus*

J F M A M J J A S O N D

Low shrublet with erect branches and leaves crowded at the branch tips, bearing short-shoots in the axils, joined at the base and spreading with hooked or recurved tips, 15–20×±2 mm; bears solitary, magenta-red flowers to 18 mm in diameter at the branch tips, with the stamens and staminodes collected in a central cone. Stony slopes along the interior West Coast and the Cape Peninsula.

**6** *Lampranthus aestivus*

J F M A M J J A S O N D

Erect, stiffly branched shrublet to 30 cm with erect, pitted, greyish leaves 10–15 mm long that are flattened from the side and widened like the prow of a boat above; bears numerous white or pink flowers ±25 mm in diameter, on pedicels to 20 mm long. Sandy coastal flats in the extreme southwestern Cape.

**7** *Lampranthus immelmaniae*

J F M A M J J A S O N D

Erect shrublet to 25 cm with ascending, tapering leaves covered with round papillae, 10–20×2 mm; bears white, pink or magenta flowers to 20 mm diameter. Deep sandy flats along the West Coast.

**8** *Lampranthus vernalis*

J F M A M J J A S O N D

Erect shrublet to 20 cm with erect to ascending green leaves that are sharply pointed and slightly recurved at the tips, ±30 mm long; bears pink flowers ±30 mm in diameter. Limestone outcrops along the West Coast.

333

**① *Lampranthus amoenus***

Shrublet to 40 cm with weakly spreading, cylindrical to 3-angled leaves that are shortly pointed and to 40 mm long; bears white to purple flowers in 3s, 35–40 mm in diameter. Sandy flats along the West Coast.

**② *Lampranthus watermeyeri***

Erect shrublet to 50 cm with ±cylindrical leaves 20–40×6 mm that are joined at the base; bears mostly solitary, white or magenta flowers to 70 mm in diameter on long pedicels, without staminodes. Sandstone outcrops from Namaqualand to the Olifants River Valley and Touws River.

## *Ruschia*   RUSCHIA, VYGIE

Shrubs or shrublets, usually erect but sometimes creeping. Leaves opposite, *sometimes joined together into a sheath at the base*, 3-angled, *bluish green and usually with darker dots*. Flowers usually in clusters, white or pink to purple, opening in sunlight; petals in 1 to several series, sometimes in bundles; *stamens arranged in a cone*, staminodes few to many. Fruit 5- (rarely 6-) segmented. Widespread through the dry parts of southern Africa: ±400 described species but probably fewer; ±60 fynbos spp.

▶ **CREEPING PERENNIALS WITH TRAILING STEMS**

**③ *Ruschia radicans***

Creeping shrublet, rooting at the nodes, with 3-angled, finely velvety leaves 10–15×6 mm at the base; bears solitary pink to magenta flowers 18 mm in diameter. Granite rocks along the West Coast.

**④ *Ruschia langebaanensis***

Robust, prostrate shrublet with stiff branches ±6 mm in diameter, and erect, sharply pointed, green to light blue leaves 35×4 mm; bears clusters of 3–5 magenta flowers ±20 mm in diameter. Rock crevices on granite outcrops around Saldanha Bay.

▶ **ERECT OR ±ERECT SHRUBLETS**

**⑤ *Ruschia indecora***

Erect shrublet to 50 cm with greyish leaves ±20×3 mm, recurved at the tips and with swollen sheaths; bears clusters of silvery white flowers 8–10 mm in diameter, with magenta-tipped staminodes. Deep sands along the West Coast at Koeberg.

**⑥ *Ruschia caroli***

Spreading shrub with sprawling, grey to reddish branches, and 3-angled leaves with green dots; bears clusters of magenta flowers. Rocky sandstone slopes in the Olifants River valley and Worcester Karoo.

335

**1** *Ruschia tumidula*

Erect shrublet to 40 cm with reddish branches, and almost cylindrical, slightly rough leaves; bears many-flowered clusters of white to pink flowers. Sandy coastal flats in the extreme southwestern Cape.

**2** *Ruschia macowanii*

Sprawling shrublet to 20 cm with almost cylindrical leaves 20–35×4 mm, with a swollen sheath ±5 mm long; bears clusters of pink flowers ±20 mm in diameter. Coastal rocks in the southwestern Cape.

**3** *Ruschia tecta*

Erect shrub to 1 m with erect, S-shaped leaves that are joined below into a long, slightly swollen sheath; bears clusters of purplish flowers ±20 mm in diameter, with a white centre; the fruits are 6-segmented. Sandy flats along the West Coast.

## *Oscularia*  OSCULARIA, SANDSTEENVYGIE

Dense shrublets with *reddish stems*. Leaves opposite, *triangular to 3-angled, short, up to ±20 mm long, mostly with a toothed keel and margins, waxy and greyish green to pale blue*. Flowers solitary or clustered, up to ±15 mm in diameter, *remaining open and almond-scented*, white to pink; *petals in ±1 series; stamens and staminodes collected in a cone*. Fruits 5-segmented. Winter-rainfall South Africa, mainly the mountains along the West Coast: ±25 spp; ±20 fynbos spp.

**4** *Oscularia deltoides*

Sprawling or rounded shrublet to 20 cm with shining reddish branches and triangular, greyish leaves with the keel and margins toothed; bears pink flowers in crowded cymes. Sandstone rocks in the mountains of the southwestern Cape.

**5** *Oscularia vredenburgensis*

Sprawling shrublet to 25 cm with crescent-shaped, bluish-grey leaves; bears pink flowers with a white centre in small cymes, the staminodes forming a red-tipped cone in the centre. Granite rocks along the West Coast.

## *Cheiridopsis*  CHEIRIDOPSIS

Compact, tufted, dwarf shrublets. Leaves opposite, *only 1 or 2 pairs per branch, joined at the base, with 1 pair withering to form a papery sleeve*, short or long, 3-angled, often with a few teeth along the keel or near the tip. *Flowers solitary at the branch tips, usually yellow*, rarely purple or red, 10–100 mm in diameter, opening at midday; staminodes absent. *Fruits 10–20-segmented*. Winter-rainfall southern Africa: 23 spp; 2 fynbos spp.

**6** *Cheiridopsis rostrata*

Compact, cushion-forming succulent with leaves triangular in section and covered with translucent spots on the underside; bears yellow flowers 30–40 mm in diameter, fading red. Granite outcrops on the West Coast. *Cheiridopsis namaquensis*, from inland, has serrated keels on the leaves, and fruits with more than 10 segments.

### *Conophytum* CONE PLANT, TOONTJIES

*Dwarf, stemless*, cushion-forming or single-bodied perennials. *Leaves only 2 per branch, united into a top-shaped or cylindrical body with a small, mouth-like opening at the top*, often spotted or lined. Flowers solitary, emerging from the central opening of the leaf-body, *with an elongate, floral tube*, variously coloured but often magenta, opening either during the day or at night; petals few to many in 1 or several series; staminodes vestigial. Fruits 3–8-segmented. Winter-rainfall southern Africa, rare in the southwestern Cape: 86 spp; ±10 fynbos spp. The species are popular with succulent collectors.

**1** *Conophytum minusculum*

| J | F | M | A | M | J | J | A | S | O | N | D |

Succulent perennial forming low mats, with leaf-bodies 5–15 mm long that are often flattened or slightly keeled, spotted and streaked; bears magenta or sometimes white flowers with a yellow tube and minute white to gold staminodes. Sandstone slopes and pavements in the interior mountains on the West Coast.

# MONTINIACEAE                    Montinia family

### *Montinia* MONTINIA, PEPERBOS

Shrubs or shrublets *with the sexes on separate plants*. Leaves deciduous, elliptical and leathery. Flowers cup-shaped, white, the males in clusters, the females 1 or 2, with *4 petals*. Fruits *dry and shuttle-shaped*, the husk splitting into 2 halves. Dry parts of southern Africa: 1 sp. The vernacular name, peperbos, alludes to the acrid taste of the foliage.

**2** *Montinia caryophyllacea*

| J | F | M | A | M | J | J | A | S | O | N | D |

Upright, greyish shrub to 1.5 m with leathery, elliptical, sometimes tufted leaves; bears white flowers, either in loose clusters in male plants, or 1 or 2 in female plants. Drier, rocky sandstone or granite slopes throughout southwestern Africa.

# ROSACEAE                          Rose family

### *Cliffortia* CLIFFORTIA

*Shrublets, shrubs* or small trees. Leaves alternate or in *tufts, sessile or shortly petiolate*, often *apparently simple*, sometimes small and hard, subtended by small *stipules joined to the petiole and sheathing the stem* (rarely lacking). *Flowers unisexual, without petals*: male flowers with 3 or 4 petal-like calyx lobes and 3–50 stamens, female flowers with the calyx tubular and ribbed, with 1–3 long, feathery styles. Tropical and southern Africa, mainly winter-rainfall South Africa in fynbos: ±120 spp; 115 fynbos spp.

**3** *Cliffortia obcordata*

| J | F | M | A | M | J | J | A | S | O | N | D |

Shrub to 1.3 m, the sexes on the same or different plants, with 3-lobed leaves, the midlobe heart-shaped and 3–7 mm long, and the side-lobes asymmetrically oval and 4–10×2–8 mm; the male flowers have 15 stamens, the female flowers have a shallowly 12-grooved calyx tube. Flats and lower slopes in the extreme southwestern Cape.

339

**①** *Cliffortia ruscifolia*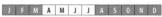
**Climber's friend, steekbos** Shrub to 1.5 m, the sexes on the same or different plants, with hard, narrowly lance-shaped, stiffly pointed leaves 10–12 mm long; the male flowers have pedicels 1–2 mm long and ±12 stamens, the female flowers have a furrowed, brownish calyx tube 3–4 mm long. Rocky sandstone soils from Namaqualand to the southern Cape.

**②** *Cliffortia graminea* **Vleirooigras**
Sprawling shrub to 2 m, the sexes on the same or different plants, with soft, grass-like leaves, sheathing the stem for 30–60 mm, with a narrowly lance-shaped blade 50–150×3–6 mm and subtended by narrowly triangular stipules 4–10 mm long; the male flowers have ±30 stamens, the female flowers have a furrowed, greenish calyx tube 4–5 mm long. Seeps and streamsides in the southwestern and southern Cape.

# NEURADACEAE Desert primrose family

## *Grielum* **DESERT PRIMROSE, DUIKERWORTEL**

Creeping, more or less white-woolly annuals with a *mucilaginous taproot and stems*. Leaves deeply lobed or divided. Flowers large, solitary in the axils, yellow, cup-shaped with the cup enlarging in fruit, and with the petals furled in bud; stamens 10. *Fruits flattened and pentagonal with a peripheral wing and central knobs*. Drier parts of southern Afrca: ±6 spp; 2 fynbos spp. The vernacular name, duikerwortel, refers to the predilection of that antelope for the succulent rootstock.

**③** *Grielum grandiflorum*
Creeping annual herb, often forming mats, with once- or twice-divided, white-woolly leaves with pointed lobes; bears glistening, pale yellow flowers with a green eye. Sandy and stony coastal flats from Namaqualand to Table Bay.

**④** *Grielum humifusum*
**Maritzwater, pietsnot** Creeping annual herb, often forming mats, with deeply lobed, sparsely white-woolly leaves that are almost hairless above and with rounded lobes; bears glistening, pale yellow flowers with a white eye or central ring. Sandy lower slopes and flats from southern Namibia to the southwestern Cape.

# CAMPANULACEAE Bellflower family

▶ FLOWERS RADIALLY SYMMETRICAL WITH THE ANTHERS MOSTLY WITHERED AT FLOWERING

## *Rhigiophyllum* **RHIGIOPHYLLUM**

Stiffly erect shrublets. Leaves closely *overlapping in 4 ranks, broad and leathery, hairless*. Flowers in heads at the branch tips intermixed with stiff bracts, deep blue, salver-shaped, with a *long, slender tube* and spreading petals; stamens *arising in the throat of the tube*, almost stalkless; stigma divided into *3 fleshy lobes*. Fruits opening by a lid at the top. Southwestern Cape in fynbos: 1 sp.

**1 *Rhigiophyllum squarrosum***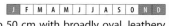

Densely leafy shrublet with erect branches to 50 cm with broadly oval, leathery leaves closely overlapping in 4 ranks; bears heads of tubular, deep blue flowers at the branch tips. South-facing sandstone slopes on the mountains around Bredasdorp, mainly seen after fire.

## *Merciera*  **MERCIERA**

Dwarf shrublets. Leaves stiff and needle-like, *often with coarse white bristles near the base*, usually with axillary tufts. Flowers solitary in the upper axils forming cylindrical spikes, white to blue or purple, *narrowly funnel- or salver-shaped with a slender tube*; stamens arising at the base of the tube, deciduous at flowering, stigma divided into *2 fleshy lobes*. Fruits opening by a lid at the top. Southwestern Cape in fynbos: 6 spp, all fynbos.

**2 *Merciera azurea***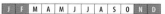

Subshrub to 30 cm with stiff, needle-like leaves that have short hairs and bristly margins rolled under; bears spikes of blue to purple flowers with a narrowly funnel-shaped tube 10–25 mm long. Lower sandstone slopes in the extreme southwestern Cape. *Merciera tenuifolia* has tufts of small leaves in the leaf axils and a cylindrical tube; *M. eckloniana* is a more slender species with scattered leaves.

**3 *Merciera leptoloba***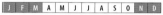

Subshrub to 30 cm with stiff, needle-like leaves that have short hairs and bristly margins rolled under, and with axillary tufts of hairless leaves; bears spikes of white flowers with a slender tube 3–6 mm long, and narrow petals. Sandy flats and lower slopes in the extreme southwestern Cape. *Merciera breviloba* has shorter leaves less than 8 mm long and oval petals; *M. tetraloba* has only 4 petals.

## *Prismatocarpus*  **PRISMATOCARPUS, STEELVRUG**

Slender-stemmed shrublets or perennial herbs. Leaves often narrow and leathery. Flowers *usually on wiry stems*, solitary or in clusters at the branch tips or in branching panicles, white to blue, *funnel-shaped to tubular*; stamens arising at the base of the tube, deciduous at flowering, stigma divided into *2 fleshy lobes*. *Fruits cylindrical*, often slender, at length *splitting longitudinally into 5 strips*. Africa, mainly southwestern Cape: 31 spp; 28 fynbos spp.

▶ **FLOWERS MOSTLY IN THE LEAF AXILS, WITH THE BRACTS LEAF-LIKE OR LARGER**

**4 *Prismatocarpus nitidus***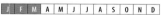

Prostrate, softly woody subshrub or perennial to 35 cm with alternate or ±opposite, oval to lance-shaped leaves, the margins slightly rolled under and toothed; bears 1–5 bell-shaped, white to pale blue flowers ±8 mm in diameter at the branch tips; the fruits are 15–25 mm long. Sheltered sandstone crevices on the Cape Peninsula. *Prismatocarpus debilis*, from the mountains east of the Peninsula, has more wiry stems.

**5 *Prismatocarpus spinosus***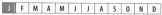

Stiffly erect, closely leafy, coarse-haired shrublet to 1 m with stiff, coarse-haired leaves, the margins prickly-toothed and rolled under; bears narrowly funnel-shaped or tubular, white flowers ±5 mm in diameter in the axils and at the branch tips; the ovary and calyx are coarse-haired; the fruits are ±8 mm long. Sandstone slopes on the Potberg.

## ▶ FLOWERS IN LEAFLESS TERMINAL INFLORESCENCES, WITH THE BRACTS SMALLER THAN THE LEAVES

### ① *Prismatocarpus fruticosus*

J F M A M J J A S O N D

Erect or sprawling, short-haired shrublet to 50 cm with needle-like leaves that have coarse hairs on the lower margins; bears deeply cup- or funnel-shaped, white flowers with brown or purple reverse in a leafless, branching inflorescence; the sepals are shorter than the floral tube; the fruits are 15–30 mm long. Sandy flats and lower slopes in the southwestern Cape. *Prismatocarpus pedunculatus* has shallowly dish- or bowl-shaped flowers.

### ② *Prismatocarpus brevilobus*

J F M A M J J A S O N D

Erect or sprawling, short-haired shrublet to 50 cm with needle-like leaves that have coarse hairs on the lower margins; bears cup- or funnel-shaped, white to blue flowers in a leafless, branching inflorescence; the sepals are shorter than the floral tube and broadly oval; the fruits are 15–30 mm long. Rocky sandstone slopes in the southwestern Cape.

### ③ *Prismatocarpus diffusus*

J F M A M J J A S O N D

Shrublet to 45 cm with short hairs on the young stems, and needle-like leaves with sparse hairs on the lower margins; bears salver-shaped, blue or white flowers with a slender, cylindrical tube ±10 mm long, in leafless, branching inflorescences; the anthers protrude shortly from the tube; the fruits are 10–20 mm long. Mainly sandstone slopes, in Namaqualand and the southwestern Cape, flowering well after fire. *Prismatocarpus pauciflorus*, from the northern Cedarberg Mountains, has the anthers included within the tube; *P. pilosus*, from the Koue Bokkeveld, has a fine-haired ovary and calyx.

## *Roella*  ROELLA

Shrublets. Leaves stiff and often recurved, usually *prickly along the margins and often with coarse white bristles near the base*, the upper leaves below the flowers often differing somewhat. Flowers sessile, solitary or in clusters at the branch tips, white to blue, rarely pink, *sometimes with dark blotches, bell-shaped*; stamens arising at the base of the tube, deciduous at flowering, stigma divided into *2 fleshy lobes*. Fruits opening by a lid at the top. South Africa, mainly Western Cape in fynbos: 20 spp; 19 fynbos spp.

### ▶ LEAVES OVAL TO ELLIPTICAL

### ④ *Roella muscosa*

J F M A M J J A S O N D

Creeping, mat-forming perennial to 5 cm with oval leaves that are softly prickly-toothed on the margins and whiskered towards the base; bears solitary white to pale blue flowers ±10 mm in diameter, with a hairless ovary; distinct floral bracts lacking. Sandstone rocks in the mountains of the extreme southwestern Cape.

### ⑤ *Roella squarrosa*

J F M A M J J A S O N D

Straggling shrublet to 50 cm with sharply pointed, oval, spreading-recurved leaves that are prickly-toothed on the margins and whiskered towards the base; bears 1–3 white or pale blue flowers ±10 mm in diameter, with a hairless ovary; the floral bracts are broadly oval to round. Sandstone slopes on the Cape Peninsula. Related species from the Peninsula include *Roella recurvata*, with leaf-like, hooked bracts, *R. aplexicaulis*, with almost round bracts, and *R. decurrens*, with scattered leaves.

## LEAVES NEEDLE- OR AWL-LIKE

### ① *Roella arenaria*

J F M A M J J A S O N D

Erect or sprawling shrublet to 50 cm with stiff, spreading, awl-like leaves that are whiskered on the margins and have a thickened midrib beneath, often with axillary tufts; bears solitary, white or pale blue flowers 10–15 mm in diameter, with a hairy ovary and hooked sepals; the floral bracts are like the leaves but more crowded. Sandy flats along the southwestern coast. *Roella prostrata* has ±erect leaves and straight sepals.

### ② *Roella ciliata*

J F M A M J J A S O N D

Erect or sprawling shrublet to 50 cm with stiff, awl-like leaves that are whiskered on the margins and have a thickened midrib beneath, often with axillary tufts; bears solitary, white or blue flowers 20–30 mm in diameter, with a dark ring or spots on the petals, and a hairless ovary; the floral bracts are larger than the leaves and conspicuously fringed with white whiskers. Stony sandstone slopes in the southwestern Cape.

### ③ *Roella incurva*

J F M A M J J A S O N D

Shrublet to 40 cm with stiff, awl-like leaves that are often prickly-toothed on the margins and whiskered, with a thickened midrib beneath, often with axillary tufts; bears 1–3 white or blue, sometimes pink or red (only Potberg), flowers 20–30 mm in diameter, mostly with dark spots on the petals, and a hairless ovary; the floral bracts are longer than the leaves. Sandy lower slopes in the southwestern Cape.

### ④ *Roella triflora*

J F M A M J J A S O N D

Erect shrublet with ascending branches to 20 cm with stiff, awl-like leaves that are prickly-toothed on the margins and whiskered towards the base, often with axillary tufts; bears 1–3 pale blue flowers 15–20 mm in diameter, with a dark eye, a hairy calyx and ovary; the floral bracts are larger and shortly hairy, with stiff, wire-like hairs on the margins. Sandy lower slopes on the Cape Peninsula. *Roella maculata*, from the southwest coast, has large dark spots in the gaps *between* the petals.

## *Wahlenbergia*  AFRICAN BLUEBELL, BLOUKLOKKIE, MUISTEPELKAROO

Annual or perennial herbs or shrublets. Leaves mostly alternate, narrow and stiff to broad and soft, sometimes toothed or lobed, often with coarse hairs. Flowers solitary or in panicles, white to blue, star-shaped to deeply cup-shaped; stamens attached to the base of the petals, withered at flowering; *ovary ± half-inferior, stigma with 2–5 lobes alternating with the petals. Fruits opening by 5 flaps at the tip.* Mainly southern temperate: ±125 spp; ±60 fynbos spp. The quaint vernacular name, muistepelkaroo, is used for the shrubby species in allusion to the resemblance of the unexpanded stigmas to the nipples of a mouse.

▸ **ANNUAL HERBS WITH A BASAL TUFT OF SOFT LEAVES; PETALS LESS THAN TWICE AS LONG AS BROAD**

### ⑤ *Wahlenbergia paniculata*

J F M A M J J A S O N D

Rough-haired annual herb to 15 cm, branching mainly from the base, with small, lance-shaped leaves that have thickened, minutely toothed margins; bears open, flat-topped panicles of bell-shaped, white or blue flowers 6–8 mm in diameter, with a white cup and dark ring in the throat, and an ovary that is sparsely hairy or velvety in bands; the fruits are ± hemispherical. Sandy flats, mainly coastal, in the southwestern Cape.

**1 *Wahlenbergia androsacea***　　J F M A M J J A **S O N** D

Tufted annual herb to 40 cm with rough-haired, paddle-shaped leaves mostly in a basal tuft, and with wavy or crisped margins; bears flat-topped panicles of cup-shaped, white to pale blue flowers 5–15 mm in diameter, with a hairless ovary, a 3-lobed stigma, and stamen filaments that are broadened at the base. Sandy flats, from southern Namibia to tropical Africa.

**2 *Wahlenbergia annularis***　　J F M A M J J **A S O N** D

Tufted annual herb to 40 cm with rough-haired, paddle-shaped leaves mostly in a basal tuft, and with wavy or crisped margins; bears flat-topped panicles of bowl-shaped, white to pale blue flowers 15–20 mm in diameter, with a hairless ovary, a style less than half as long as the corolla, and a 3-lobed stigma. Sandy flats and lower slopes in Namaqualand and the West Coast.

**3 *Wahlenbergia cernua***　　J F M A M J J A S **O** N **D**

Rough-haired annual herb to 60 cm with elliptical, toothed or jagged leaves scattered up the stem; bears mostly solitary or few, bowl-shaped, whitish to blue flowers 8–15 mm in diameter, with a hairless ovary and 3 large, rounded stigma lobes. Damp sandstone slopes in the mountains of the southwestern Cape.

**4 *Wahlenbergia capensis***　　J F M A M J J A **S O N D**

Hairy annual herb to 50 cm with paddle-shaped to elliptical, wavy or toothed leaves that are mostly scattered up the stem; bears solitary, bowl-shaped, pale blue flowers with a darker centre, on long stems, with a densely hairy ovary, and 5 broad stigma lobes. Sandstone slopes and flats in the southwestern and southern Cape.

▶ **SHRUBLETS WITH STIFF LEAVES; PETALS OFTEN MORE THAN TWICE AS LONG AS BROAD**

**5 *Wahlenbergia ecklonii***　　**J F** M A M J J A **S O N** D

Erect or sprawling perennial to 30 cm with narrow, stiff leaves that are slightly hairy, the margins slightly thickened and toothed; bears lax panicles of narrowly bell-shaped blue flowers 8–10 mm in diameter, with elongate sepals and a rough-haired ovary with a 5-lobed stigma; the fruits are hemispherical. Rocky slopes from Namaqualand to the Eastern Cape.

**6 *Wahlenbergia longifolia***　　**J** F M **A** M J J A S O N **D**

Erect shrublet to 40 cm with narrow, flat leaves that are sometimes recurved and slightly toothed towards the base, often in tufts; bears narrow, raceme-like panicles of star-shaped, white or cream flowers 5–8 mm in diameter, with a tube ±1 mm long and a hairy ovary. Coastal sands and limestone in the southwestern Cape.

**7 *Wahlenbergia calcarea***　　**J** F M **A** M J J A S **O N D**

Sprawling, often densely leafy shrublet to 30 cm with narrow leaves that have the margins strongly rolled under, often in tufts; bears tight, terminal clusters of star-shaped white flowers ±8 mm in diameter, with darker reverse, with a tube 2–3 mm long and a smooth or short-haired ovary. Coastal limestone on the Agulhas Plain.

349

**1** *Wahlenbergia tenerrima*

Sprawling shrublet to 50 cm with recurved, oval to lance-shaped leaves that are concave above and with thickened margins; bears star-shaped, blue or white flowers 5–7 mm in diameter, at the branch tips, with a tube ±1 mm long, and a half-inferior, short-haired ovary. Sandstone slopes in the southwestern, southern and Eastern Cape.

**2** *Wahlenbergia subulata*

J F M A M J J A S O N D

Erect or sprawling shrublet to 30 cm with spreading, often tufted, narrow or needle-like leaves; bears star-shaped, white to blue flowers ±6 mm in diameter that fade to yellow, with a tube up to 1 mm long, sepals that are bulbous below, and a half-inferior ovary that is usually hairy. Stony or gravelly lower slopes in the southwestern Cape.

## *Microcodon*  **MICROCODON**

Small, often somewhat wiry, annual herbs. Leaves alternate, narrow and toothed, coarsely hairy. Flowers in heads at the branch tips, blue, deeply cup-shaped; stamens attached to the base of the petals, *withered at flowering; ovary half-inferior, stigma with 5 slender lobes opposite the petals. Fruits opening by 5 flaps at the tip.* Winter-rainfall South Africa: ±3 spp, all fynbos.

**3** *Microcodon glomeratum*

J F M A M J J A S O N D

Annual herb to 15 cm, branching from the base, with narrow leaves that have thickened margins and stiff hairs towards the base; bears tight, leafy clusters of narrowly bell-shaped, pale blue flowers with a purple centre, 5–8 mm diameter, with long calyx lobes almost as long as the flowers. Clay or sandy flats in the southwestern Cape.

▸ FLOWERS ±2-LIPPED WITH THE ANTHERS PERSISTING AT FLOWERING

## *Cyphia*  **CYPHIA, BAROE**

*Erect or twining* perennial herbs, often with a *tuber.* Leaves basal or scattered along the stem, lance-shaped or deeply divided, usually toothed. Flowers in racemes or 1 to few in the upper leaf axils, white to mauve or purple, almost equally 5-lobed or 2-lipped, usually *split down the sides;* stamens not attached to the petals, with the anthers *separate from one another or only loosely attached* and usually bearded on the backs, rarely hairless. Africa, mainly the southwestern Cape: ±60 spp; ±20 fynbos spp. The tubers are edible. The vernacular name, baroe, derives from the original Khoi.

▸ STEM ERECT, NOT TWINING

**4** *Cyphia bulbosa*

J F M A M J J A S O N D

Erect, almost hairless perennial to 30 cm, with deeply divided leaves grading into the floral bracts and paler beneath, the margins lightly rolled under; bears a raceme of showy, white to mauve flowers 8–13 mm long that are 2-lipped, with the tube split down the sides; the stamens are ±6 mm long, with only 2 anthers bearded on the back. Sandy and stony flats and slopes along the interior West Coast and the Cape Peninsula, especially common after fire.

**5** *Cyphia incisa*

J F M A M J J A S O N D

Erect, sparsely hairy perennial to 30 cm with deeply toothed or divided leaves in a basal rosette; bears a naked raceme of whitish to mauve flowers 10–14 mm long that are 2-lipped, with the tube split down the sides; the stamens are ±6 mm long, with all the anthers bearded on the back. Sandy and stony flats and slopes along the interior West Coast and the Cape Peninsula.

351

### **1** *Cyphia phyteuma*

| J | F | M | A | M | J | J | A | S | O | N | D |

Erect, almost hairless perennial to 40 cm with slightly toothed leaves in a basal rosette; bears a minutely bracteate, spiralling, spike-like raceme of ±sessile, whitish to brown or mauve flowers16–20 mm long that are 2-lipped, with the tube split down the sides; the stamens are ±6 mm long, with all the anthers bearded on the back. Sandy and stony flats and slopes in the southwestern Cape.

## ▶ STEM TWINING; FLOWERS ± EQUALLY 5-LOBED, WITH THE TUBE NOT COMPLETELY SPLIT DOWN THE SIDES

### **2** *Cyphia subtubulata*

| J | F | M | A | M | J | J | A | S | O | N | D |

Twining perennial with narrowly lance-shaped, toothed leaves; bears showy, white to mauve flowers 15–15 mm long in the upper axils, weakly 2-lipped and partially split down the sides; the stamens are ±6 mm long, with all the anthers bearded on the back. Stony, often clay flats in Namaqualand and along the interior West Coast.

### **3** *Cyphia zeyheriana*

| J | F | M | A | M | J | J | A | S | O | N | D |

Twining perennial with narrowly lance-shaped or divided, slightly toothed leaves; bears showy, cream to mauve flowers 10–18 mm long in the upper axils, curved and equally 5-lobed, not split down the sides; the stamens are 3–5 mm long, with the anthers not bearded on the back. Sandstone slopes along the Olifants River valley.

## ▶ STEM TWINING; FLOWERS 2-LIPPED, WITH THE TUBE COMPLETELY SPLIT DOWN THE SIDES

### **4** *Cyphia crenata*

| J | F | M | A | M | J | J | A | S | O | N | D |

Twining perennial with oval to lance-shaped, toothed leaves that are often shortly lobed at the base and usually erect; bears clusters of 1–3 white to mauve flowers 9–11 mm long in the upper leaf axils, 2-lipped and split down the sides; the calyx is almost flat at the base and divided almost to the bottom; the stamens are 5–6 mm long, with all the anthers bearded on the back. Sandy flats and slopes, often coastal, in southern Namaqualand and along the West Coast.

### **5** *Cyphia digitata*

| J | F | M | A | M | J | J | A | S | O | N | D |

Twining perennial with leaves that are usually deeply 3–7 lobed and obscurely toothed, but sometimes lance-shaped; bears white to mauve flowers 7–14 mm long in the upper leaf axils, are 2-lipped and split down the sides; the stamens are 5–9 mm long and reach the mouth of the tube, with all or only 2 anthers bearded on the back. Sandstone and clay slopes throughout the southwestern and southern Cape.

### **6** *Cyphia volubilis*

| J | F | M | A | M | J | J | A | S | O | N | D |

Twining perennial with lance-shaped to deeply lobed and toothed leaves; bears showy, white to purple flowers 10–26 mm long in the upper leaf axils, 2-lipped and split down the sides; the stamens are 3–5 mm, less than half as long as the floral tube, with all the anthers bearded on the back. Sandy flats and slopes throughout the southwestern and southern Cape.

## *Monopsis*  MONOPSIS, WILD VIOLET

Small annual or perennial herbs. Leaves opposite or alternate, toothed. Flowers in racemes or solitary in the axils, often yellow or purple, almost *2-lipped*, with the pedicels twisted so that the upper lip is *3-lobed* and the lower lip 2-lobed *and split down the middle to the base*; stamens sometimes attached to the base of the petals, with the anthers *joined to one another* and with a *brush-like tuft of straight white hairs at the tips*; stigma with 2 slender lobes. Africa: ±20 spp; 8 fynbos spp.

**① *Monopsis lutea*  Yellow lobelia**  J F M A M J J A S O N D

Perennial herb with sprawling or trailing stems to 60 cm with narrowly elliptical, toothed leaves, often oriented along the upper side of the stem; bears stalkless, 2-lipped, bright yellow flowers clustered in spikes at the branch tips. Damp flats and lower slopes, often along seeps or streams, in the southwestern and southern Cape. *Monopsis flava*, from Namaqualand to Ceres, has stalked flowers; *M. variifolia*, from the Breede River valley, has fewer flowers nested among the leaves.

**② *Monopsis debilis***  J F M A M J J A S O N D

Loosely sprawling or tufted annual herb with slender stems to 25 cm and narrowly elliptical, toothed leaves; bears solitary, almost regular, purple flowers with broad, rounded petals and a darker centre on slender pedicels in the leaf axils, without a bracteole at the base opposite the subtending leaf. Damp sandy slopes and flats, often along seepages in Namaqualand and the southwestern Cape. *Monopsis simplex*, from sheltered places along the south coast, has 2-lipped flowers with narrower petals and a bracteole at the base of the pedicels opposite the subtending leaf.

## *Lobelia*  LOBELIA

Perennials or subshrubs, rarely annual herbs. Leaves alternate, opposite or whorled, variable, often toothed. Flowers in racemes or 1 to few in the upper leaf axils, often blue or purple, *2-lipped*, with the upper lip *2-lobed and split down the middle to the base* and the lower lip 3-lobed; stamens attached to the base of the petals, with the anthers *joined to one another* and with a *brush-like tuft of straight white hairs at the tips*. Worldwide: ±300 spp; ±35 fynbos spp. The resinous root of *Lobelia pinifolia* was used medicinally.

▸ **ALL ANTHERS WITH A TUFT OF WHITE HAIRS AT THE TIPS**

**③ *Lobelia setacea***  J F M A M J J A S O N D

Tufted, erect or sprawling perennial with slender, wiry stems to 60 cm and sparse, thread-like leaves less than 1 mm wide; bears branched racemes of hairless, blue or violet and white flowers 10 mm long. Sandstone slopes and sandy flats in the southwestern and southern Cape.

**④ *Lobelia linearis***  J F M A M J J A S O N D

Broom-like shrublet with erect, rod-like stems to 70 cm and narrow leaves, sometimes divided into thread-like segments, mainly towards the base of the stems, or almost leafless at flowering; bears branched or unbranched racemes of hairless, blue flowers 10–15 mm long. Dry, stony and sandy lower slopes in the southwestern and southern Cape.

**⑤ *Lobelia pinifolia***  J F M A M J J A S O N D

Shrublet with erect, densely leafy stems to 50 cm with overlapping, narrow or needle-like leaves 1–2 mm wide; bears 1 to few, hairy, blue flowers 10–15 mm long, on short or long naked stalks. Rocky, sandstone slopes and flats in the southwestern Cape.

**1** *Lobelia tomentosa*  J F M A M J **J A S O** N D

Tufted shrublet to 40 cm with somewhat sprawling, short-haired stems branching from the base, and narrow to thread-like, toothed leaves 2–5 mm wide, with the margins rolled under; bears 1–4 *shortly hairy*, blue, violet or pink flowers 10–15 mm long on wiry, leafless stalks 10–25 cm long. Stony lower slopes from the Cape Peninsula to southern Mozambique.

**2** *Lobelia coronopifolia*  J F **M A M** J J A S **O** N D

Tufted shrublet to 30 cm with somewhat sprawling, short-haired stems branching from the base, and narrow to lance-shaped, deeply toothed or lobed leaves 5–10 mm wide, with the margins slightly rolled under; bears 1 to few large, *hairless*, dark blue, pink or white flowers 15–30 mm long, on wiry, leafless stalks 10–28 cm long. Sandy and stony flats and lower slopes in the southwestern Cape. *Lobelia chamaepitys* has mostly solitary, smaller flowers, 10–16 mm long, on stems 7–12 cm long.

▶ **ONLY THE LOWER 2 ANTHERS WITH A TUFT OF WHITE HAIRS AT THE TIPS**

**3** *Lobelia comosa*  J **F M A M J J A S O** N D

Soft shrublet with rod-like stems to 50 cm, branching from the base, and hairless or sparsely hairy, lance-shaped, toothed leaves 5–10 mm wide; bears loose or dense racemes of hairless, bright blue flowers 10 mm long, on elongate stems. Sandy, coastal slopes in the southwestern Cape.

**4** *Lobelia valida*  Galjoenblom  J F **M A M** J J A S **O** N D

Soft, leafy shrublet with rod-like stems to 60 cm, and overlapping, broad, paddle-shaped, leathery leaves 10–15 mm wide; bears dense racemes of hairless, deep blue flowers 10–15 mm long. Coastal hills on the Agulhas Plain.

**5** *Lobelia pubescens*  J F **M A M** J J A S **O** N D

Spreading annual or perennial with fine-haired stems to 50 cm, and fine-haired, petiolate, lance-shaped to broadly oval, toothed leaves 8–20 mm wide; bears leafy racemes of sparsely hairy, white to pale blue flowers 10–15 mm long. Sheltered rocky slopes and damp rocks near the coast in the southwestern and southern Cape.

**6** *Lobelia anceps*  J F **M A M** J **J A S O** N D

Erect or sprawling perennial with flattened, narrowly winged stems to 50 cm, and lance- or paddle-shaped, obscurely toothed leaves 4–10 mm wide; bears racemes of hairless blue, mauve or white flowers 10 mm long. Damp places, usually near the coast, from the Cape Peninsula to KwaZulu-Natal.

**7** *Lobelia jasionoides*  J F **M A M** J **J A S O** N D

Erect or sprawling perennial to 50 cm with narrow or paddle-shaped, sharply toothed leaves 3–15 mm wide; bears dense spikes of small, 1-lipped, hairless, lilac and white flowers 5–8 mm long. Moist upper mountains in the southwestern Cape.

## Identifying members of the Carrot family

All members of the Carrot family have similar, very small flowers arranged in flat-topped clusters known as umbels, in which all the flower stalks arise from the same point, like the ribs of an umbrella. These clusters may be simple, comprising a single whorl of flowers, or they may be compound, comprising a whorl of individual, smaller clusters. An important distinction is made between **annual** species, with slender, fibrous roots; **perennials**, with fleshy or carrot-like roots, and leaves clustered at the base of the stem; and **shrubs**, with persistent, leafy, woody stems. Another useful distinction is between leaves that are **undivided**, or simple, and those that are **deeply divided**, or compound.

Many of the critical features for identifying the genera, however, are to be found in the mature **fruits**. Each fruit comprises two separate halves, or half fruits, that fall apart when ripe. In most genera each half fruit is more or less rounded in cross-section or slightly flattened from the sides so that it touches the other member of the pair along 1 edge. *Capnophyllum*, *Hermas* and *Peucedanum* species, however, have half fruits that are flattened from front to back, and thus lie face to face.

The surface sculpturing of the fruits is also important. In all *Anginon* species and many *Centella* species each half fruit is smooth or irregularly wrinkled, whereas most other genera develop 5 longitudinal ribs or ridges on the outer surface of each half fruit. Exceptions are *Annesorhiza* species, which have 3 enlarged ribs on 1 half fruit of each pair and 4 enlarged ribs on the other. The distinctive fruits of *Torilis*, like those of carrots, are burr-like and covered in barbed bristles.

The characteristic aroma and taste of the fruits, as enjoyed in culinary herbs such as fennel and coriander, come from oils contained in narrow ducts, usually visible as dark streaks. In most genera these oil ducts are located between the ribs on the half fruits but in *Lichtensteinia* they lie beneath each rib, and are completely lacking in the fruits of *Centella* species.

---

## FRUITS

*Complete fruit in side view (left) and top view (right); oil ducts shaded*

▶ **Stemless or tufted perennial herbs with the foliage leaves in a basal rosette**

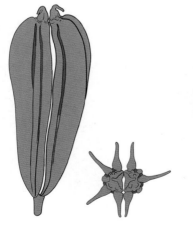

*Annesorhiza macrocarpa*

*Lichtensteinia lacera*

*Itasina filifolia*

5 mm

▶ **Shrublets or softly woody perennials with some leaves borne on the stem**

*Centella virgata*

*Anginon difforme*

*Peucedanum galbanum*

*Hermas villosa*

*Dasispermum suffruticosum*

▶ **Annual herbs**

*Sonderina caruifolia*

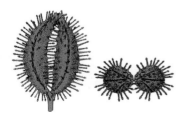

*Torilis arvensis*

*Capnophyllum africanum*

*Sonderina hispida*

## *Centella*  CENTELLA

Perennial herbs or shrublets. Leaves *simple*, needle-like to heart-shaped, often toothed above. Flowers either in *small, unisexual umbels or with a central bisexual flower surrounded by 4 male flowers*, each flower cluster surrounded by 2–4 bracts. Fruits flattened with the 2 halves edge to edge, each half *smooth or irregularly ribbed, without distinct oil ducts*. Mainly southern Africa, especially winter-rainfall region: ±50 spp, nearly all fynbos.

**❶ *Centella capensis***

J F M A M **J J A S O N** D

Loosely tufted perennial to 10 cm, spreading from underground stems, with petiolate, narrowly triangular to paddle-shaped leaves that are bluntly lobed at the tips and densely white- or rusty-haired; the flower clusters comprise either a sterile central flower surrounded by 4 male flowers, or a large fertile central flower surrounded by 4 sterile flowers, with the male flowers longer than the bracts and whitish with prominent purple style bases; the fruits are relatively large but shorter than the bracts, oval, ribbed, wrinkled and sparsely hairy. Flats and granite outcrops, often coastal, in the southwestern and southern Cape.

**❷ *Centella virgata***

J F M A M **J J A S O N** D

Erect or somewhat sprawling, willowy perennial to 60 cm with narrow or needle-like, hairless or densely woolly leaves; the flower clusters comprise either 1–5 male flowers, or a solitary female flower; the fruits are carried above the leaves and are variable in size, mostly relatively small but longer than the bracts, oval and slightly ribbed. Sandy flats and lower slopes from the southwestern to the Eastern Cape.

## *Anginon*  ANGINON, WILDEVINKEL

*Woody shrubs or shrublets.* Leaves *sometimes reduced to petioles* and thus apparently simple, especially the upper ones, *often pine-needle-like.* Flowers in compound umbels. Fruits elliptical, smooth or wrinkled but *not regularly ribbed or winged*, with a persistent style base. Mainly winter-rainfall region: 12 spp; 8 fynbos spp.

**❸ *Anginon difforme***

J F M A **M** J J A S O N **D**

Rigid, upright shrub with rod-like stems to 3 m and axillary tufts of stiff, quill-like green leaves, bearing compound flower clusters of yellowish flowers on stout peduncles; the fruits are egg-shaped, ridged and warty, with a collar at the base. Rocky sandstone slopes from Namaqualand to the Eastern Cape.

## *Hermas*  TINDERLEAF, TONTELBLAAR

Tufted perennials or shrublets. Leaves *simple, leathery* and *felted or woolly, at least on the underside*. Flowers in densely packed, compound umbels, resembling a simple umbel, *each umbel usually with a single female or bisexual flower surrounded by several male flowers* (thus only the central flower setting seed), white to cream. Fruits oblong or flattened with the *2 halves face to face* and usually separated by a deep furrow, *with many oil ducts*. Winter-rainfall South Africa: 7 spp, all fynbos. The woolly hairs were scraped from the leaves and, when dried, were used for dressing wounds, and also in tinder boxes, whence the vernacular name.

### ❶ *Hermas capitata*

J F M A M J J A S O N D

Tufted perennial to 25 cm with long petioles and oval to elliptical leaves that are lightly scalloped and white- or brown-felted beneath; bears white flowers in small compound flower clusters; the fruits are broadly oval. Damp sites on rocky sandstone slopes from the Cape Penninsula to the southern Cape.

### ❷ *Hermas quinquedentata*

J F M A M J J A S O N D

Tufted perennial to 45 cm with shortly petiolate, paddle-shaped leaves that are coarsely toothed and white-felted beneath; bears white flowers crowded in small, compound flower clusters; the fruits are broadly oval. Damp sites on rocky sandstone slopes in the extreme southwestern Cape.

### ❸ *Hermas villosa*

J F M A M J J A S O N D

Robust, single- or few-stemmed shrub to 1 m with sessile to shortly petiolate, oblong to elliptical leaves that are finely toothed and white-felted beneath; bears cream-coloured flowers in crowded flower clusters; the fruits are ±orbicular and winged. Rocky sandstone slopes in the extreme southwestern Cape. *Hermas gigantea* is a tufted perennial with large, petiolate leaves densely felted on both surfaces.

## *Dasispermum*  DASISPERMUM, DUINESELDERY

*Softly woody perennial.* Leaves finely divided, *somewhat fleshy.* Flowers in compound, *apparently axillary umbels*; involucral bracts none or few. Fruits *elliptical to oval; each half with 5 thick ribs or wings.* South Africa, widespread along the coastline: 1 sp, fynbos.

### ❹ *Dasispermum suffruticosum*

J F M A M J J A S O N D

Sprawling perennial with a woody base to 50 cm, with leathery or fleshy leaves, twice-divided into narrow, toothed leaflets that often curl inwards; bears compound flower clusters of small cream-coloured flowers; the fruits are broadly oval-shaped with thick ribs. Coastal sands from southern Namaqualand to KwaZulu-Natal.

## *Peucedanum*  HOG'S FENNEL, BERGSELDERY

Shrubs or perennials, often tufted, with a taproot. Leaves usually thrice-divided. Flowers usually in many-rayed, compound umbels; involucral bracts few to many. Fruits *flattened with the halves face to face*, each half with flattened margins, concave or flattened on the face and 3-ribbed on the back. Eurasia and Africa: ±120 spp; ±14 fynbos spp. The leaves of *P. galbanum* induce photosensitivity, leading to severe blistering in sunlight, and were used medicinally.

### ❺ *Peucedanum galbanum*

J F M A M J J A S O N D

**Blister bush** Robust, sparsely branched shrub to 3 m with leathery, greyish leaves twice-divided into diamond- to oval-shaped or sometimes 3-lobed, toothed, leaflets; bears small, yellow flowers in large, rounded, compound flower clusters on short axillary peduncles; the fruits are elliptical, ±6 mm long. Rocky, sandstone slopes in bush and on forest margins in the southwestern and southern Cape.

### ① *Peucedanum ferulaceum*

J F M A M J J A S O N D

Slender perennial with erect stems to 1.5 m, with finely divided leaves; bears small yellowish flowers in compound flower clusters on branched stems; the fruits are elliptical, ± 6 mm long. Rocky slopes and sandy flats in Namaqualand and the southwestern and southern Cape.

### ② *Peucedanum typicum* Hondewortel

J F M A M J J A S O N D

Tufted perennial to 1 m, with large, soft, trailing leaves, finely divided and carrot-like; bears small yellow flowers in compound flower clusters on branched stems, the uppermost cluster fertile and the lateral ones male; the fruits are round and broadly winged, 10-15 mm long. Coastal scrub along the western and southern coasts.

▸ STEMLESS OR TUFTED PERENNIAL HERBS WITH THE FOLIAGE LEAVES IN A BASAL ROSETTE

## *Itasina* GRASS-PARSLEY

Delicate perennial herb with a slender, carrot-like taproot. Leaves *simple, grass-like and blunt*. Flowers in compound umbels; involucral bracts few. Fruits oblong and ridged with persistent petals and style base, each half 5-ribbed. Winter-rainfall South Africa: 1 sp, fynbos.

### ③ *Itasina filifolia*

J F M A M J J A S O N D

Tufted perennial to 45 cm with slender, thread-like or narrowly spoon-shaped leaves in a basal tuft, usually dry at flowering; bears small white flowers in a compound flower cluster on branched peduncles; the fruits are narrowly oblong and ridged, often with persistent, slender, horn-like sepals. Sandstone and limestone flats in the southwestern and southern Cape.

## *Arctopus* ARCTOPUS, PLATDORING

*Stemless perennials* with a thick taproot; *sexes on separate plants*. Leaves prostrate, *simple, oval, lobed with bristly or spiny margins*. Male flowers in compound, stalked umbels, white or pinkish to cream; *female flowers in sessile umbels*, each umbel surrounded by 4, usually spiny, bracts. Fruits oblong and tapering at the end, ribbed. Winter-rainfall South Africa: 3 spp, all fynbos. The thick taproot was used medicinally.

### ④ *Arctopus echinatus* Sieketroos

J F M A M J J A S O N D

Stemless perennial with spongy petioles and lobed, glossy, oval to orbicular leaves with bristly margins and stiff spines arising directly from the base of the gaps between the lobes; male flowers cream to pink; female involucral bracts joined at the base and spine-tipped with 1 or 2 inflexed lateral spines, becoming hard and very spiny in fruit. Damp sand and granite flats and slopes from Namaqualand to the Eastern Cape.

### ⑤ *Arctopus monacanthus*

J F M A M J J A S O N D

Like *Arctopus echinatus* but with solid petioles and leaf spines arising on small flaps at the base of the gaps between the lobes; female involucral bracts separate, ±orbicular, sometimes with small lateral spines, enlarging greatly and becoming papery in fruit. Seasonally damp sandstone and clay slopes and flats along the West Coast and on the Cape Peninsula. *Arctopus dregei*, a rare species from the Hopefield district, has blunt involucral bracts that are tipped with 3–5 fine spines or bristles and which enlarge slightly and become leathery, with the margins rolled over, in fruit.

## *Annesorhiza*  ANNESORHIZA, ANYSWORTEL

Tufted, biennial or perennial herbs with almost *leafless scapes, and several swollen roots*. Leaves *basal, dry at flowering*, variously divided with *scale-like stem-leaves*. Flowers in compound umbels, yellow. Fruits oblong, more than 5 mm long, the halves similar or dissimilar, flat on the inner face and *with 3 or 4 ridges or wings on the outer face*. Southern Africa: 12 spp; ±8 fynbos spp.

**① *Annesorhiza macrocarpa***

J F M A M J J A S O N D

**Wildeanyswortel**  Perennial to 1.6 m, with numerous fleshy, often fluted roots and long, trailing leaves that are dry at flowering and finely dissected into minute segments, the long thin petioles usually covered with sand; the pale yellow flowers are unisexual, with the terminal flower cluster always female and the lateral ones usually male; the fruits are large with the 2 halves unequally winged. Coastal dunes and sandy slopes on the western and southern Cape coasts.

## *Lichtensteinia*  LICHTENSTEINIA, KALMOES

Tufted, biennial or perennial herbs with almost *leafless scapes*. Leaves *basal, green or beginning to dry at flowering*, variously toothed or divided, and with *scale-like leaves along the stem*. Flowers in compound umbels. Fruits ovoid or oblong to flattened, with the halves face to face, with a prominent style base, each half 5-ribbed on the outer face with *oil ducts in the ribs, not between them*. South Africa and St Helena: ±7 spp; 6 fynbos spp. The vernacular name, kalmoes, originally referred to *Calamus acorus* but was transferred to several members of the carrot family having aromatic roots that were used to treat stomach ailments.

**② *Lichtensteinia lacera***

J F M A M J J A S O N D

Tufted perennial to 1.4 m with leaves in a basal tuft, sometimes withered at flowering, large and oval or sometimes deeply cut, or divided into 3 segments, roughly toothed, each tooth tipped with a whisker; bears compound flower clusters of yellow flowers on long, branched, hollow peduncles; the fruits are narrowly oblong. Clay flats and lower slopes in the extreme southwestern Cape.

▶ ANNUAL HERBS

## *Sonderina*  SONDERINA

*Annual herbs*. Leaves finely divided. Flowers in compound, *apparently leaf-opposed umbels*; involucral bracts few, narrow. Fruits oval or oblong, sometimes with minute hairs, each half 5-ribbed. South Africa, mainly winter rainfall: 4 spp; 3 fynbos spp.

**③ *Sonderina hispida***

J F M A M J J A S O N D

Annual herb to 45 cm, branching from below, with leaves finely dissected into narrow leaflets; bears small white flowers on short-haired pedicels in compound, leaf-opposed flower clusters; fruits are oval and tapering, lightly ridged and with minute hairs. Sandy or limestone flats, usually coastal, in southwestern and southern Cape. *Sonderina caruifolia* has smooth pedicels and fruits.

## *Capnophyllum*  CAPNOPHYLLUM

*Annual herbs, with unisexual flowers in separate flower clusters on the same plant*. Leaves finely divided. Flowers in compound, *apparently leaf-opposed, flower clusters*; involucral bracts few. Fruits *flattened with the halves face to face*, each half with flattened or winged margins and 3 smooth or warty ribs on the back. Coastal in winter-rainfall South Africa: 2 spp, both fynbos.

**1 Capnophyllum africanum**

Sprawling, annual herb to 30 cm, branching from the base, with soft, finely divided leaves; bears unisexual, white flowers in compound flower clusters with warty ovaries; fruits elliptical with winged margins and warty ridges. Sand dunes on the West Coast south of Saldanha. *Capnophyllum leiocarpon*, from coastal sands north of Saldanha, has smooth, scarcely ribbed seeds without warts.

## *Torilis*  HEDGE-PARSLEY

*Annual herbs.* Leaves finely divided and carrot-like. Flowers in *leaf-opposed umbels*. Fruits oblong and grooved at the sides, *burr-like, covered with barbed bristles*. Mediterranean to Asia: ±15 spp; 1 sp. introduced to the Cape.

**2 Torilis arvensis**

J F M A M J J A S O N D

Sprawling, soft, annual herb to 40 cm with the leaves finely divided into toothed segments; bears a few white flowers in simple flower clusters; the fruits are burr-like and covered with barbed bristles. Flats and rocky slopes in sheltered sites in the southwestern and Eastern Cape; introduced from Europe.

# GRUBBIACEAE                            Grubbia family

## *Grubbia*  GRUBBIA

Evergreen shrubs with furrowed, short-haired branches. *Leaves opposite*, narrow and leathery, with the margins rolled under. *Flowers 2 to many in axillary clusters, very small*, with a pinkish, 4-lobed calyx but without petals; there are *8 stamens in 2 whorls* and the ovary is inferior. Winter-rainfall South Africa in montane fynbos: 3 spp, all fynbos.

**3 Grubbia rosmarinifolia**

J F M A M J J A S O N D

Ericoid shrublet to 1.5 m, with narrow, spreading, rosemary-like leaves 5–30×1–1.5 mm; bears 2 or 3 very woolly flowers in the axils. Damp sandstone slopes in the southwestern and southern Cape.

**4 Grubbia tomentosa**  Koolhout

J F M A M J J A S O N D

Shrublet to 1.5 m, multi-stemmed from a woody base, with ascending, narrowly elliptical, lavender-like leaves 25–65×5–7 mm; bears cone-like, axillary clusters of numerous short-haired, pinkish flowers. Damp, sandstone slopes in the southwestern and southern Cape. *Grubbia rourkei*, a local endemic on the Kogelberg, has similar cone-like clusters of flowers, but is single-stemmed, with narrow, roughly hairy leaves.

# RHAMNACEAE                            Phylica family

## *Phylica*  PHYLICA, HARDEBLAAR

Shrublets or shrubs, rarely small trees, often ericoid. Leaves leathery, needle-like to oval with the margins rolled under, *without stipules*. Flowers axillary or in spikes or heads, minute, with a cup-shaped, variously hairy calyx and minute petals or these absent; the ovary is inferior and the base of the style is surrounded by a *hairless, nectar-secreting disc*. Africa, Madagascar and S Atlantic islands, mainly winter rainfall in fynbos: ±180 spp; ±130 fynbos spp.

## ▶ FLOWERHEADS SURROUNDED WITH CONSPICUOUS, SILKY BRACTS

**1 Phylica pubescens**

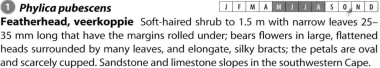

**Featherhead, veerkoppie** Soft-haired shrub to 1.5 m with narrow leaves 25–35 mm long that have the margins rolled under; bears flowers in large, flattened heads surrounded by many leaves, and elongate, silky bracts; the petals are oval and scarcely cupped. Sandstone and limestone slopes in the southwestern Cape.

**2 Phylica plumosa** **Veerkoppie** J F M A M J J A S O N D

Sparsely branched shrublet to 40 cm with narrow, rough-textured leaves 10–15 mm long that have the margins rolled under; bears flowers in dense spikes, subtended by feathery bracts longer than the leaves; the petals are cup-shaped. Mainly clay and granite soils in the southwestern Cape.

## ▶ FLOWERHEADS WITHOUT CONSPICUOUS BRACTS

**3 Phylica oleaefolia** **Blinkhardeblaar** J F M A M J J A S O N D

Shrub to 2 m with oval to broadly elliptical leaves 15–25 mm long that are grey-felted beneath and have the margins lightly rolled under; bears short racemes of stalked flowers sometimes arranged in panicles; the petals are cupped; the fruits are 8–10 mm long, hairless and glossy with a circumferential scar. Rocky slopes from Namaqualand and the southwestern Cape.

**4 Phylica buxifolia** **Bukshardeblaar** J F M A M J J A S O N D

Rounded shrub or small tree, sometimes to 4 m, with oval to elliptical leaves 15–25 mm long that are grey-felted beneath and have the margins lightly rolled under; bears small heads of sessile flowers; the petals are cupped; the fruits are 8–10 mm long and velvety. Lower mountain slopes in the extreme southwestern Cape.

**5 Phylica cephalantha** J F M A M J J A S O N D

Densely branched shrub, 40–90 cm, with narrow or needle-like leaves 5–8 mm long that have the margins rolled under; bears yellowish flowers in heads that are solitary or in groups; the petals are cupped. Sandy flats and lower slopes along the West Coast.

**6 Phylica ericoides** J F M A M J J A S O N D

Compact shrublet, sometimes to 1 m, with needle-like leaves mostly 5–8 mm long, and often rough, with the margins rolled under; bears white flowers in small, rounded heads that are either solitary or clustered; the petals are deeply hooded or helmet-like. Coastal slopes and deep sands in the southwestern and southern Cape.

---

## *Trichocephalus* **TRICHOCEPHALUS, HONDEGESIGGIE**

Ericoid shrublet. Leaves leathery, needle-like, with the margins rolled under, *subtended by minute, dry stipules*. Flowers in heads, minute, with a woolly, cup-shaped calyx and minute, cupped petals; the ovary is inferior and *the base of the style is surrounded by a hairy, nectar-secreting disc*. This species was included within *Phylica* for a long time. Winter-rainfall Western Cape: 1 sp, fynbos. The vernacular name is a fanciful allusion to the resemblance of the fruits to the face of a dog.

**1 *Trichocephalus stipularis***  J F M A M J J A S O N D

Rounded shrublet, sometimes to 90 cm, resprouting from a persistent rootstock, with narrow, leathery leaves 7–15 mm long that have the margins rolled under and are subtended by dry, awl-like stipules 2–3 mm long; bears solitary, rounded heads of small, honey-scented, pink flowers that are densely white-woolly on the outside. Sandy flats and lower slopes in the southwestern and southern Cape.

# SANTALACEAE                    Sandalwood family

## *Osyris*  CAPE SUMACH, PRUIMBOS

Small trees or shrubs, partially parasitic on the roots of other plants. Leaves leathery, mostly alternate, *elliptical and bluish or greyish green*. Flowers in axillary clusters, small, yellowish green, cup-shaped and *3- or 4-lobed*, the stamens with a tuft of hairs at the back. *Fruits are fleshy, 1-seeded, red or black berries.* Africa to India: 6 or 7 spp; 2 fynbos spp. The vernacular name derives from the plum-like colours developed by the ripening fruits.

**2 *Osyris compressa***  J F M A M J J A S O N D

(=*Colpoon compressum*) Greyish shrub or small tree to 5 m with oval to elliptical leaves that have thickened margins; bears delicate, terminal clusters of greenish flowers with the buds 2–2.5 mm in diameter; the fleshy fruits are 17–12 mm long. Rocky slopes, from the southwestern Cape to tropical Africa.

**3 *Osyris speciosa***  J F M A M J J A S O N D

(=*Colpoon speciosum*) Multi-stemmed, resprouting shrublet to 2 m with oval to elliptical leaves that have thickened margins; bears stout, terminal clusters of greenish flowers with the buds ±3 mm in diameter; the fleshy fruits are 21–25 mm long. Coastal sandstone and limestone flats and slopes in the extreme southwestern Cape, flowering after fire.

## *Thesium*  THESIUM, SWARTSTORM

Shrubs or herbs, usually hairless but sometimes shortly bristly, partially parasitic on the roots of other plants. *Leaves usually scale-like, rarely rounded.* Flowers in loose or compact clusters, spikes or heads, small, white, cup-shaped or shortly tubular and *5-lobed, the lobes sometimes fringed or bearded*, the stamens usually with a tuft of hairs at the back. *Fruits are greenish nuts,* crowned with the persistent floral remains, *usually 10-ribbed*. Widespread in the Old World, mainly temperate and subtropical: ±330 spp; ±80 fynbos spp. The roots of some species are used medicinally and the vernacular name alludes to their dark bark.

**4 *Thesium euphorbioides***  J F M A M J J A S O N D

Willowy, single-stemmed shrub to 2 m with angular branchlets and oval to ±orbicular, greyish leaves; bears head-like clusters of cream-coloured flowers among broad, yellowish bracts, without bearded lobes. Sandstone slopes in the southwestern and southern Cape.

**5 *Thesium capitatum***  J F M A M J J A S O N D

Densely leafy shrublet to 30 cm with narrow, strongly keeled leaves that have a hard point and translucent, minutely toothed margins; bears dense, bracteate heads of whitish flowers, with bearded lobes. Sandstone slopes in the southwestern and southern Cape.

# BRUNIACEAE                                    Brunia family

## *Audouinia*   FALSE HEATH, VALSHEIDE

Ericoid shrublet. Leaves small, overlapping and pressed to the stem. Flowers each surrounded by several bracts and *arranged in spikes, reddish; the stamens are shorter than the petals*, and the ovary is 3-chambered with 2 styles. Southwestern Cape in fynbos: 1 sp, fynbos.

**1** *Audouinia capitata*   J F M A M J J A S O N D

Loosely branched shrub to 1.5 m, coppicing from a woody rootstock, with small overlapping leaves pressed to the stems, with minutely haired margins; bears reddish flowers crowded in cylindrical spikes. Rocky flats and lower slopes in the extreme southwestern Cape.

## *Berzelia*   BERZELIA, KOLKOL

Ericoid shrubs. Leaves small, usually closely overlapping, mostly narrow. Flowers small, *many (>30) in ±globular heads*, whitish; the *stamens are longer than the petals*, the ovary is 1-locular with *1 style*. South Africa, mainly winter-rainfall region in fynbos: 12 spp, all fynbos. Leafing and flowering shoots are marketed in the cut-flower trade as 'Cape greens', and the vernacular name alludes to the appearance of the plants, visible from a distance as distinct patches (*kolle*) of bright green and white against the hillsides.

**2** *Berzelia lanuginosa*   J F M A M J J A S O N D

**Kolkol, vleiknoppiesbos**   Fine-leafed shrub, 1.5–2.0 m, with thread-like, spreading to ascending leaves less than 0.5 mm wide; bears small cream-coloured flowers in axillary heads 5–8 mm in diameter, arranged in short racemes and clustered terminally in loose corymbs. Damp sandstone slopes, seeps and stream banks in the southwestern Cape.

**3** *Berzelia abrotanoides*   J F M A M J J A S O N D

**Redlegs, rooibeentjies**   Shrub to 1.5 m, coppicing from a woody caudex, with keeled, elliptical, ascending leaves ±1 mm wide; bears small white flowers in rounded axillary heads 6–10 mm in diameter, aggregated in corymbs, on red peduncles that are often swollen and fleshy. Damp sandstone slopes and flats in the southwestern Cape.

## *Brunia*   BRUNIA, VOLSTRUISIES

Ericoid shrubs. Leaves usually closely overlapping, narrow to oblong. Flowers small, *many (>30) in ±globular heads*, whitish; the *stamens are longer than the petals and unequal in length*, the ovary is 2-chambered with 2 styles. South African winter-rainfall region in fynbos: 6 spp, all fynbos. The vernacular name, volstruisies, originally applied particularly to *Brunia noduliflora*, and alludes to the resemblance of the flowerheads to a brood of ostrich chicks; stompie, also applied to *Mimetes*, refers to the stumps that invariably remain after the woody shrubs have burned down in periodic veldfires.

**4** *Brunia laevis* **Vaalstompie, vaaltol**   J F M A M J J A S O N D

Rounded shrub to 1.5 m, coppicing from a woody rootstock, with oblong, ascending leaves 3–5 mm long that are incurved at the ends and with minute hairs on the upper surface; bears small cream-coloured flowers in globular heads 15–20 mm in diameter, arranged in loose clusters. Rocky sandstone and limestone slopes in the extreme southwestern Cape.

**1** *Brunia noduliflora* **Fonteinbos**

J F M A M J J A S O N D

Rounded shrub to 1.5 m, coppicing from a woody rootstock, with minutely hairy branches and overlapping triangular or lance-shaped leaves 2–3 mm long that are pressed to the stem; bears small white flowers in globular heads ±10 mm in diameter, arranged in loose clusters. Rocky sandstone slopes in the southwestern and southern Cape.

# *Nebelia* **NEBELIA**

Ericoid shrubs. Leaves usually closely overlapping, narrow and usually incurved. Flowers small, *many (>30) in ±globular heads*, whitish; the *stamens are longer than the petals and are all equal in length*, the ovary is 2-chambered with *2 styles*. South African winter-rainfall region in fynbos: 6 spp, all fynbos.

**2** *Nebelia paleacea*

J F M A M J J A S O N D

Shrub to 1.5 m, coppicing from a woody caudex, with sparsely hairy branches and overlapping, narrowly triangular leaves that are ascending and incurved; bears small cream-coloured flowers in heads 5–7 mm in diameter that are surrounded by a conspicuous whorl of slender, white bracts longer than the flowers. Sandstone slopes in the southwestern Cape.

# *Staavia* **STAAVIA**

Ericoid shrublets. Leaves needle-like or oblong, *more or less spreading*, with the *upper leaves forming a conspicuous, whitish whorl around the flowerhead*. Flowers small, in small heads, sometimes sticky; the *stamens are shorter than the petals*, the ovary is 2-chambered with 2 styles that are joined for most of their length and thus apparently single. South African winter-rainfall region in fynbos: 10 spp, all fynbos.

**3** *Staavia radiata* **Altydbos**

J F M A M J J A S O N D

Rounded, twiggy shrublet to 60 cm, coppicing from a woody rootstock, with narrowly lance-shaped leaves 4–10 mm long; bears small pink flowers in heads ±5 mm in diameter, surrounded by a whorl of small white bracts. Sandy flats near the coast in the southwestern Cape.

**4** *Staavia glutinosa*

J F M A M J J A S O N D

**Flycatcher bush, vlieëbos** Willowy shrub to 1.5 m, with narrow, sparsely hairy or hairless leaves mostly 10–15 mm long; bears sticky, pink flowers in heads ±10 mm in diameter, surrounded by a whorl of thread-like, white bracts. Cool, rocky slopes on Table Mountain.

**5** *Staavia dodii* **Diamondeyes**

J F M A M J J A S O N D

Willowy shrub to 1 m, with overlapping, elliptical leaves 10–12 mm long; bears sticky, pink flowers in heads ±10 mm in diameter, surrounded by a whorl of elliptical white bracts. Rocky, sandstone flats on the Cape Peninsula.

# ASTERACEAE

**Daisy family**

## Identifying members of the Daisy family

The genera of daisies are grouped into several tribes distinguished primarily by microscopic characters of the stigmas and anthers that are of little practical use in a field guide. Most of the genera, however, may be identified by a combination of more obvious characters, notably:

▶ **Bracts:** Each daisy flowerhead is surrounded by overlapping involucral bracts. The number of rows, or series, of these bracts is important, as well as the shape and texture of the individual bracts, which may be entirely green, or with conspicuous translucent membranous margins or tips, or entirely dry and papery.

▶ **Florets:** Each flowerhead contains a number of individual, small flowers, or florets, which may differ in form and sex within the head. Button-like or **discoid** flowerheads contain only funnel-shaped florets, each with 5 (rarely only 4) triangular petals, and a fertile ovary and anthers. The more familiar **radiate** flowerheads, in contrast, comprise 2 different types of florets: funnel-shaped, male or bisexual disc florets in the centre, plus a peripheral ring of strap-shaped ray florets that usually lack stamens and are thus female. Most genera have narrow rays but some have distinctive, broad, wedge-shaped rays, and others have rays that are reduced to small, inconspicuous lobes. In a few genera with radiate flowerheads, 2 of the petals of the ray florets remain separate as thread-like appendages opposite the main ray, and are thus 2-lipped. An intermediate type of flowerhead, known as **disciform**, has several peripheral rows of tubular, female florets surrounding the fertile disc florets. **HINT: Check the fruiting heads to determine which of the florets set seeds and are thus female/fertile. Those heads in which the disc florets are functionally male will set only a peripheral ring of seeds, developed from the outer florets.** The different types of floret are illustrated below.

▶ **Fruits:** One of the keys to the success of daisies lies in their highly specialised fruits, commonly misidentified as seeds. In many daisies each fruit is crowned with a ring of flat scales or thread-like bristles, known as the **pappus**, which aids in the dispersal of the fruits by wind. **HINT: The pappus is most evident at the fruiting stage, when it enlarges.** Fruits with a pappus of scales resemble miniature shuttlecocks or even dried florets, while those with bristles recall dandelions or dainty brushes. Relatively few daisies lack any form of pappus, and have flattened or winged fruits instead. Representative fruit types from each of the genera included in this guide are illustrated on pages 379–383.

## FLORETS

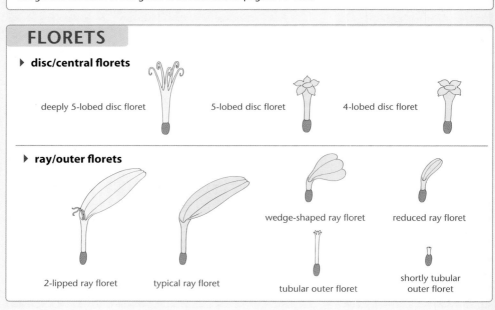

▶ **disc/central florets**

deeply 5-lobed disc floret     5-lobed disc floret     4-lobed disc floret

▶ **ray/outer florets**

wedge-shaped ray floret     reduced ray floret

2-lipped ray floret     typical ray floret     tubular outer floret     shortly tubular outer floret

▶ Involucral bracts dry and shining, often colourful and more conspicuous than the florets; heads discoid/disciform or with only 1 or 2 rays; pappus of bristles (everlastings, strawflowers, blombosse and the various renosterbosse)

*Stoebe aethiopica*

*Disparago ericoides*

*Elytropappus gnaphaloides*

5 mm

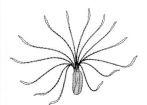

*Metalasia densa*

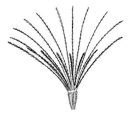

*Lachnospermum fasciculatum*

*Bryomorphe aretioides*

*Phaenocoma prolifera*
(outer fertile fruit)

*Edmondia sesamoides*

*Petalacte coronata*

*Phaenocoma prolifera*
(central sterile fruit)

*Helichrysum patulum*

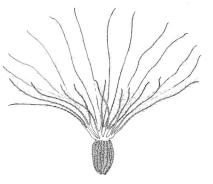

*Syncarpha speciosissima*

**379**

# FRUITS

▶ Plants resembling a monocotyledon, with strap-like leaves with parallel venation; flowerheads in clusters, individually 1-flowered, white or purple

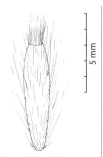

*Corymbium glabrum*

▶ Tufted perennials or gnarled shrubs with firm, leathery leaves that are densely felted beneath; ray florets 2-lipped and disc florets deeply cleft with curled petals; heads radiate, usually white or pinkish, including the disc, never bright yellow; pappus of long bristles

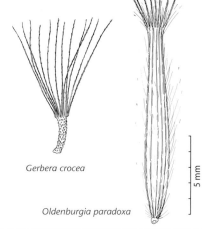

*Gerbera crocea*

*Oldenburgia paradoxa*

▶ Plants often thistle-like; flowerheads radiate with yellow, orange or red rays, sometimes with dark markings at the base; involucral bracts in 2 or more rows, spine-tipped and joined at the base into a cup; ray florets sterile, 4-toothed; pappus of scales, sometimes narrow, tapering and bristle-like, rarely absent

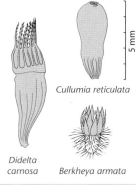

*Cullumia reticulata*

*Didelta carnosa*

*Berkheya armata*

▶ Flowerheads radiate with white, pink or yellow to reddish rays, sometimes with dark marks at the base; at least the inner involucral bracts with large, rounded, membranous tips; pappus of scales

*Haplocarpha lanata*

*Ursinia anthemoides*

*Ursinia cakilefolia*

*Arctotis bellidifolia*

*Arctotheca calendula*

*Arctotheca populifolia*

▶ Involucral bracts in 1(2) series, cohering along the margins and sometimes joined below, entirely green (sometimes with additional series of small bracteoles below); ray florets curling back at night; pappus of barbed bristles (sometimes soon dropping)

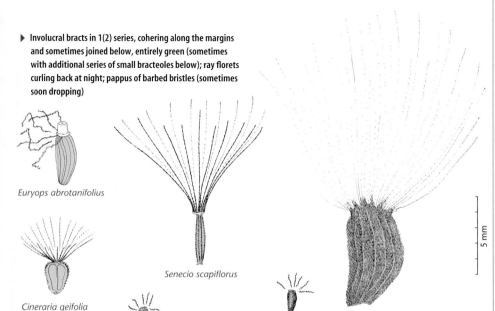

*Euryops abrotanifolius*

*Cineraria geifolia*

*Euryops tenuissimus*

*Senecio scapiflorus*

*Gymnodiscus capillaris*

*Othonna coronopifolia*

5 mm

▶ Flowerheads radiate with the disc florets mostly male and the rays yellow, orange or white; involucral bracts in 1–4 series, narrow and mostly green throughout; fruit large (mostly >5 mm long), without a pappus

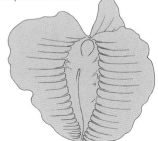

*Osteospermum ciliatum*

*Osteospermum grandiflorum*

*Dimorphotheca sinuata*
(disc fruit)

*Dimorphotheca sinuata*
(ray fruit)

*Osteospermum clandestinum*

*Osteospermum ilicifolium*

*Osteospermum incanum*

5 mm

# FRUITS

▶ Annuals, often with finely divided leaves; flowerheads discoid or with small or a few white or yellow rays; disc florets 4-lobed; receptacle often conical; pappus of scales or lacking

*Cotula turbinata*

*Foveolina tenella*

*Oncosiphon suffruticosum*
(floret still attached)

*Oncosiphon grandiflorum*

*Cotula coronopifolia*

5 mm

▶ Flowerheads radiate with yellow rays but otherwise not as any of the above

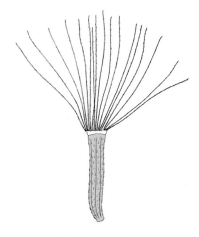

*Capelio caledonica*

*Oedera genistifolia*

*Relhania fruticosa*

5 mm

*Leysera gnaphalodes*

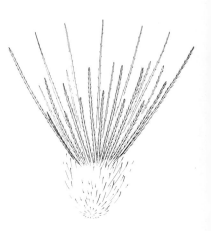

*Heterolepis aliena*

▶ Flowerheads discoid or radiate with white, pink or blue to purple rays that curl back at night, but otherwise not as any of the above

*Polyarrhena stricta*

*Osmitopsis asteriscoides*

*Hymenolepis crithmoides*

*Athanasia crithmifolia*

*Zyrphelis lasiocarpa* (ray fruit)

*Amellus asteroides*

*Eriocephalus racemosus*

*Mairia hirsuta* (ray fruit)

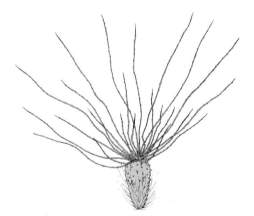

*Pteronia incana*

5 mm

*Mairia hirsuta* (sterile disc fruit)

*Chrysocoma ciliata*

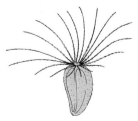

*Felicia amelloides*

## *Petalacte* **PETALACTE, WILDESEWEJAARTJIE**

Grey-felted shrublet. Leaves alternate, elliptical to paddle-shaped, flat, densely felted on both surfaces. Flowerheads in small clusters, disciform, with 4 rows of woolly bracts, the inner with *spreading, dry, papery white tips; receptacle with narrow scales.* Outer florets female, narrowly tubular; *fruits clasped by the subtending bract*, narrowly elliptical, smooth or papillate; pappus of twisted, barbed bristles. *Central florets male*, 5-lobed, *purple*. Southwestern Cape in fynbos: 1 sp.

**❶ *Petalacte coronata***

J F M A M J J A S O N D

Densely leafy shrublet to 50 cm, mostly grey-felted but golden-haired on the young parts, with paddle-shaped leaves; bears several clusters of small, disciform flowerheads, ±6 mm in diameter, at the branch tips, the bracts all with spreading, papery white tips. Coastal dunes and sandstone slopes in the southwestern Cape.

## *Helichrysum* **STRAWFLOWER, STROOIBLOM**

Annual or perennial herbs or shrubs, usually woolly or cobwebby. Leaves alternate, variously shaped but never toothed, flat or with the margins rolled under, mostly variously felted or woolly. Flowerheads solitary or often in flat-topped clusters at the branch tips, discoid or disciform, *with several rows of dry, chaffy or papery bracts coloured white, yellow, straw, brown, pink, purple or red*, at least *the inner with a translucent strip near the base*; receptacle without scales but sometimes fringed. Outer florets female, often narrowly tubular, yellow. Central florets fertile, 5-lobed with hairy petals, yellow. Fruits smooth or variously hairy; *pappus of barbed or somewhat feathery bristles*. Old World, mainly Africa: ±500 spp; ±70 fynbos spp. The leaves and twigs are an important traditional medicine, especially for chest complaints. *Helichrysum petiolare* is an important horticultural plant.

▶ FLOWERHEADS SMALL, 3–4 MM LONG, CYLINDRICAL TO BELL-SHAPED, MANY CROWDED IN FLAT-TOPPED CLUSTERS

**❷ *Helichrysum moeserianum***

J F M A M J J A S O N D

Grey-woolly to cobwebby, annual herb to 30 cm, branching from the base, with narrowly paddle-shaped, woolly leaves; bears many bell-shaped, discoid or disciform flowerheads 3–4×2–3 mm, with bright yellow bracts spreading at the tips. Sandy flats and slopes in the southwestern Cape. *Helichrysum versicolor*, from coastal sands east of Knysna, has oblong leaves.

**❸ *Helichrysum cymosum***

J F M A M J J A S O N D

Straggling, sparsely woolly shrub to 1 m with narrow to elliptical leaves that are sparsely silky above and white-felted beneath, and with the margins slightly rolled under; bears flat-topped clusters of many cylindrical, disciform or discoid flowerheads 3×1 mm, with bright yellow bracts. Sandy slopes in damp places from the southwestern Cape to Mpumalanga.

**1** *Helichrysum dasyanthum*

J F M A M J J A S O N D

Straggling, grey-woolly shrub to 1.5 m with narrow to elliptical grey-woolly leaves, the margins slightly rolled under; bears flat-topped clusters of bell-shaped, disciform flowerheads 4×3 mm, with silky, straw-coloured bracts. Sandy flats and slopes in Namaqualand and the southwestern and southern Cape.

▶ **FLOWERHEADS MEDIUM-SIZED, 5–10 MM LONG, BELL-SHAPED TO ±GLOBULAR**

**2** *Helichrysum revolutum*

J F M A M J J A S O N D

Sprawling, sparsely grey-woolly shrub to 2 m with narrowly lance-shaped leaves slightly eared at the base and often in axillary tufts, becoming hairless above and white-woolly beneath with the margins rolled under; bears compact clusters of bell-shaped, discoid flowerheads 5×4 mm, with straw-coloured bracts. Rocky or sandy flats and slopes from southern Namibia to the southwestern Cape.

**3** *Helichrysum pandurifolium*

J F M A M J J A S O N D

Straggling, grey-woolly shrublet or shrub with oval, grey-woolly leaves with crinkly margins that are narrowed and eared at the base and clasping the stem; bears clusters of bell-shaped, discoid flowerheads 5–8×6–10 mm, with hairless, pointed, cream-coloured bracts. Sandy flats and slopes in the southwestern and southern Cape.

**4** *Helichrysum patulum*

J F M A M J J A S O N D

Like *Helichrysum pandurifolium* but with blunt involucral bracts. Sandy flats and slopes along the coast in the southwestern Cape. *H. petiolare* from sheltered slopes and forest margins has paddle-shaped leaves that are abruptly and conspicuously petioled and not crinkly.

**5** *Helichrysum teretifolium*

J F M A M J J A S O N D

Straggling, thinly felted shrublet to 30 cm with stiffly spreading, needle-like leaves, hooked at the tips, more or less hairless above but white-woolly beneath, with the margins rolled under; bears dense clusters of bell-shaped, disciform or discoid flowerheads 5×5 mm, with creamy white bracts that are spreading at the tips. Sandy slopes and dunes from the southwestern Cape to KwaZulu-Natal.

**6** *Helichrysum stellatum*

J F M A M J J A S O N D

Rounded, grey-woolly shrublet to 45 cm, with spoon-shaped, grey-woolly leaves; bears clusters of widely bell-shaped, disciform flowerheads 7×7 mm, with golden-brown and white or sometimes pink involucral bracts that are spreading at the tips. Sandy flats and slopes in the southwestern Cape.

**7** *Helichrysum cochleariforme*

J F M A M J J A S O N D

**Gold-and-silver** Rounded, grey-woolly shrublet to 20 cm, with spoon-shaped, grey-woolly leaves; bears few, ±globular, disciform flowerheads 5–7×5–8 mm, with cupped, golden-brown involucral bracts, the inner ones tipped with white and minutely spreading. Coastal sands along the western and southern Cape coasts.

### 1 *Helichrysum grandiflorum*

Grey-woolly, somewhat tufted subshrub to 50 cm, with lance-shaped, densely woolly leaves; bears dense clusters of bell-shaped, discoid flowerheads 7×7 mm, on peduncle-like stems, with white involucral bracts, the inner ones spreading at the tips. Cool sandstone slopes on the Cape Peninsula.

▸ **FLOWERHEADS LARGE, 15–40 MM IN DIAMETER, SOLITARY OR FEW**

### 2 *Helichrysum foetidum*

J F M A M J J A S O N D

Robust, foetid, biennial to 1 m, covered with gland-tipped hairs, with oblong to lance-shaped leaves that are eared at the base and clasping the stem, roughly hairy above and grey-woolly beneath; bears leafy clusters of flattened-globular, disciform flowerheads 15–25 mm in diameter, with cream to yellowish bracts. Damp rocky slopes from the southwestern to Eastern Cape.

### 3 *Helichrysum retortum*

J F M A M J J A S O N D

Straggling, closely leafy, silvery shrublet to 50 cm with overlapping, oblong, channelled leaves that are spreading or curved backwards, hooked at the tips and covered with silvery-silky, tissue paper-like hairs; bears solitary, top-shaped, disciform flowerheads 25–40×±40 mm nested in the leaves, with glossy, hairless white bracts often flushed pink and brown. Coastal sands and cliffs in the southwestern Cape.

## *Syncarpha* EVERLASTING, SEWEJAARTJIE

Felted perennial herbs. Leaves alternate, narrow to lance-shaped, never toothed, *flat or slightly concave, densely grey- or silver-felted on both surfaces.* Flowerheads solitary or in clusters, usually *large and conspicuous, discoid,* with several rows of glossy, dry, papery bracts coloured white, yellow, pink or brown; receptacle without scales but fringed. Florets all fertile, yellow, 5-lobed. Fruits oblong, papillate; *pappus of feathery bristles joined at the base.* Southern Africa: 28 spp, all fynbos.

▸ **FLOWERHEADS LESS THAN 20 MM IN DIAMETER**

### 4 *Syncarpha gnaphaloides* Vlaktetee

J F M A M J J A S O N D

White-felted shrublet to 30 cm with slender, almost cylindrical leaves that have the margins rolled upwards; bears solitary, cylindrical, fragrant, discoid flowerheads ±10 mm in diameter, on long peduncles, with reddish-brown bracts that are dry and sharply bent downwards at the tips. Sandstone slopes in the southwestern and southern Cape.

### 5 *Syncarpha paniculata*

J F M A M J J A S O N D

Densely leafy, silvery-felted shrublet to 60 cm with narrow, sharply pointed leaves; bears few to several hemispherical, discoid flowerheads ±10 mm in diameter, in clusters, with conspicuous pointed, papery bracts that are yellow or pink in bud but age to white or cream. Coastal and lower slopes in the southwestern and southern Cape.

### 6 *Syncarpha argyropsis*

J F M A M J J A S O N D

**Witsewejaartjie** Densely leafy, silvery-felted shrublet to 70 cm with paddle-shaped leaves; bears few to several, hemispherical, discoid flowerheads 15–20 mm in diameter, in clusters, with conspicuous pointed, papery, white bracts. Coastal slopes, sometimes on limestone, in the southwestern and southern Cape.

389

**① *Syncarpha chlorochrysum***   J F M A M J J A S O N D

**Gold everlasting** Densely leafy, silvery-felted shrub to 1.5 m with oval, pointed, spreading to recurving leaves that are 5-veined from the base; bears several hemispherical, discoid flowerheads 10–12 mm in diameter, in loose clusters, with conspicuous pointed, papery, pale yellow bracts. Limestone hills in fynbos on the Agulhas Plain.

▶ **FLOWERHEADS MORE THAN 20 MM IN DIAMETER**

**② *Syncarpha canescens***   J F M A M J J A S O N D

**Pienksewejaartjie** Sparsely branched, grey-felted shrublet to 50 cm with small, elliptical leaves; bears mostly solitary, top-shaped, discoid flowerheads 25–35 mm in diameter, with conspicuous pointed, papery pink to red bracts. Drier rocky sandstone slopes and flats throughout the southwestern and southern Cape.

**③ *Syncarpha eximia***   J F M A M J J A S O N D

**Strawberry everlasting** Robust, mostly single-stemmed, silvery-felted shrub to 40 cm with oval leaves; bears crowded hemispherical, discoid flowerheads 20–25 mm in diameter, nested in the upper leaves, with rounded, papery, bright red bracts. Cool, moist, south-facing sandstone slopes in the southern Cape.

**④ *Syncarpha vestita* Cape snow**   J F M A M J J A S O N D

Softly woody, grey-woolly shrublet to 1 m, with paddle-shaped leaves; bears few to several, top-shaped, discoid flowerheads 35–40 mm in diameter, in loose clusters, often nested in the upper leaves, with pointed, papery white bracts. Rocky slopes and flats in the southwestern and southern Cape.

**⑤ *Syncarpha speciosissima***   J F M A M J J A S O N D

**Cape everlasting** Sprawling, white-woolly shrublet, 20–60 cm, with erect annual stems, and oblong to linear leaves clasping the stem at the base; bears solitary, hemispherical, discoid flowerheads 30–40 mm in diameter, on elongate peduncles, with pointed, papery, white to cream bracts. Sandstone slopes in the southwestern Cape.

## *Edmondia*   EDMONDIA, SEWEJAARTJIE

Slender shrublets. Leaves alternate, erect, overlapping, *hairless beneath and densely white-woolly above*, more or less differentiated into *longer, needle-like leaves with the margins rolled upwards on the vegetative branches* and *scale-like, concave leaves on the flowering stems. Flowerheads solitary on slender stems, large and showy*, discoid or disciform, with several rows of large, glossy, dry, papery bracts coloured white, yellow or pink; receptacle without scales but fringed. Outer florets sometimes female and then narrower. Inner florets fertile, 5-lobed, the petals covered with gland-tipped hairs. Fruits either ellipsoid and papillate, or flattened and smooth; pappus of somewhat feathery bristles joined at the base. Southwestern Cape: 3 spp, all fynbos.

**⑥ *Edmondia sesamoides***   J F M A M J J A S O N D

Sparsely white-woolly shrublet to 30 cm with the lower foliage leaves needle-like, their margins rolled upwards, and the upper leaves scale-like and pressed against the peduncles; bears solitary, discoid flowerheads 25–30 mm in diameter, with conspicuous glossy, papery, white to pink or creamy-yellow bracts; the fruits are elliptical. Rocky flats and slopes in the southwestern and southern Cape.

### ❶ *Edmondia pinifolia*

J F M A M J J A S O N D

Sparsely white-woolly shrublet to 60 cm with the lower foliage leaves needle-like, their margins rolled under, and the upper leaves smaller and pressed to the peduncle, grading into the involucral bracts through a series of papery, brown scales; bears solitary, discoid flowerheads 25–30 mm in diameter, with conspicuous, glossy, papery, white or pink bracts; the fruits are flattened and winged. Rocky, sandstone slopes in the southwestern Cape.

### ❷ *Edmondia fasciculata*

J F M A M J J A S O N D

Sparsely white-woolly shrublet to 30 cm with the lower foliage leaves needle-like, their margins rolled upwards, and the upper leaves scale-like and pressed against the peduncles, the uppermost grading into the involucral bracts through a series of brown scales; bears solitary, discoid flowerheads 25–30 mm in diameter, with conspicuous, glossy, papery, bright yellow bracts; the fruits are elliptical. Rocky, sandstone slopes in the southwestern Cape.

## *Phaenocoma*   FALSE EVERLASTING, ROOISEWEJAARTJIE

Stiffly branched shrublet with white-woolly stems bearing *numerous short-shoots at right angles to the branches*, each subtended by a brown bract. *Leaves small and granular or knob-like*, closely spaced, white-woolly on the upper surface, which is pressed to the stem. *Flowerheads solitary at the branch tips*, large, disciform, with several rows of large, dry, papery *bracts divided into a lower, woolly shaft, a central dark brown hinge, and an upper blade coloured glossy pink to red.* Outer florets female, slender; fruits flask-shaped and densely silky; pappus of many somewhat feathery bristles. Central florets male, 5-lobed *with hairy petals*; sterile fruits smooth and glossy; pappus of several somewhat feathery bristles. Southwestern Cape in fynbos: 1 sp.

### ❸ *Phaenocoma prolifera*

J F M A M J J A S O N D

Stiffly branched, white-stemmed shrublet to 60 cm with closely overlapping, granular leaves clustered on short-shoots; bears solitary, large, disciform flowerheads 30–40 mm in diameter, with conspicuous, glossy, papery, pink to red bracts. Sandstone slopes in fynbos in the southwestern and southern Cape.

## *Lachnospermum*   LACHNOSPERMUM, ROOIBLOMBOS

Shrublets with greyish-woolly branches. Leaves alternate, sometimes in tufts, stiff and leathery, small and *scale-like and/or needle-like and often twisted, with the margins rolled upwards and densely woolly in the groove,* but more or less hairless beneath. *Flowerheads mostly solitary* at the branch tips, discoid, with *several series of woolly bracts, the inner with dry, papery, often reddish tips*; receptacle sometimes with a few small scales. Florets often yellow, 5-lobed *with hairy petals*. Fruits spindle-shaped with hairy ribs; pappus of barbed bristles. Southwestern Cape in fynbos: 3 or 4 spp, all fynbos.

### ❹ *Lachnospermum fasciculatum*

J F M A M J J A S O N D

Tangled shrublet with felted stems to 60 cm with tufts of small, needle-like leaves 1–5 mm long; bears 1 to few discoid, narrowly cylindrical, yellow flowerheads ±5 mm in diameter, at the branch tips, with white-woolly bracts, the inner ones with erect or slightly spreading, papery tips. Sandy, lower slopes in the southwestern Cape. *Lachnospermum umbellatum* has distinctly clustered flowerheads with most of the bracts with papery, pinkish tips that are bent sharply backwards.

### 1 *Lachnospermum imbricatum*

J F M A M J J A S O N D

Shrublet with stiffly erect, felted stems to 50 cm with overlapping, oval leaves 5–10 mm long, pressed against the stems; bears a few discoid, cylindrical, pink to purple flowerheads ±8 mm in diameter, with partially woolly bracts, the inner ones with conspicuous, spreading, papery white tips. Coastal sands and limestone outcrops in the extreme southwestern Cape.

## *Metalasia* METALASIA, BLOMBOS

Shrublets with greyish-woolly branches. Leaves alternate, typically *of 2 sizes with a tuft of smaller leaves in the axils of the primary leaves*, stiff and leathery, small and usually *needle-like, often twisted, with the margins rolled upwards and densely woolly in the groove* but more or less hairless beneath. Flowerheads mostly crowded at the branch tips, small, discoid, *3–8-flowered*, with 4–6 series of woolly bracts, *the inner with dry, papery tips often coloured white, pink or yellow*; receptacle without scales. Florets often reddish, 5-lobed. Fruits elliptical, smooth or warty; pappus of many *barbed bristles swollen at the tips*. South Africa, mainly southwestern Cape: 52 spp, all fynbos. The long-lasting flowering stems, often garishly dyed, are used locally as graveside tributes.

### 2 *Metalasia densa*

Shrub to 2.5(4.0) m with lance-shaped to oval leaves 2–15 mm long that are twisted and often flexed downwards, and with axillary tufts; bears clusters of 3–5-flowered, discoid flowerheads, with erect or rarely spreading bracts, the inner ones petal-like and white or sometimes brownish, the outer ones papery and sharply pointed. Sandy or stony flats and slopes from Namaqualand to Limpopo.

### 3 *Metalasia muricata*

J F M A M J J A S O N D

Like *Metalasia densa* but the leaves typically hooked at the tips and the bracts brownish with the outer ones rather thick-textured, blunt and faintly keeled. Coastal sands from the southwestern Cape to southern KwaZulu-Natal.

### 4 *Metalasia pungens*

J F M A M J J A S O N D

Shrub to 2.5 m with erect lance-shaped leaves 2–25 mm long that are not twisted, and with axillary tufts; bears clusters of 3–5-flowered, discoid flowerheads, with erect bracts, the outer ones sharply pointed and the inner ones petal-like and whitish. Sandstone and limestone slopes from Agulhas to Grahamstown.

### 5 *Metalasia fastigiata*

J F M A M J J A S O N D

Shrublet to 1.5 m cm, with needle-like leaves 4–20 mm long that are flexed downwards and twisted, and with axillary tufts; bears clusters of 5-flowered, discoid flowerheads, with erect bracts, the inner ones petal-like and pink. Sandy flats and slopes in the southwestern Cape.

## *Elytropappus* RENOSTERBOS

Glandular shrubs. *Leaves usually small and scale-like*, upper surface often covered with matted hairs. *Flowerheads crowded in heads, spikes or more open clusters*, discoid, small, 2–6-flowered, with a few rows of dry bracts; receptacle without scales. Florets 5-lobed. Fruits ellipsoid, ribbed, smooth or short-haired, often with a well-developed apical collar; *pappus of feathery bristles* joined at the base. Southern Africa, mainly Western Cape: 10 spp, all fynbos. Comprises the dominant element of the renosterveld vegetation of clay soils in the southwestern Cape. Alcoholic infusions of the young branches were a traditional remedy for stomach ailments.

**1** *Elytropappus rhinocerotis*

J **F M A** M J J A S O N D

**Renosterbos** Resinous, sparsely grey-woolly shrub to 2 m with short, whip-like branches covered with closely pressed, scale-like leaves; bears few, small, mostly 3-flowered, discoid flowerheads at the tips of lateral branchlets. Dry shale and sandstone slopes and flats, typically the dominant shrub, from southern Namibia to the Eastern Cape.

**2** *Elytropappus glandulosus*

J F **M A M J J** A S O N D

Shrublet to 50 cm with needle-like leaves covered with gland-tipped hairs pressed to the branches or spreading and twisted; bears clusters of small, mostly 2-flowered, discoid flowerheads arranged in slender spikes. Sandstone slopes in the mountains of the southwestern Cape. *Elytropappus gnaphaloides* has the flowerheads in open panicles.

## *Stoebe*  STOEBE, SLANGBOS

Often tangled shrublets. Leaves small, *scale-like or needle-like and often twisted*, with the *margins rolled upwards and densely felted in the groove* but less hairy beneath. *Flowerheads crowded in tight heads or spikes*, these sometimes in open clusters, *small, 1-flowered*, with a few rows of dry, membranous bracts; receptacle without scales. Florets 5-lobed, white, pink or red. Fruit smooth or hairy, sometimes with an apical collar; *pappus of feathery bristles* or rarely lacking. Southern and south tropical Africa and Madagascar, mainly Western Cape: 34 spp; 22 fynbos spp. A tincture of the bruised roots was traditionally used as a diuretic. The vernacular name, slangbos, has probably been transferred from species of similar-looking *Elytropappus*, which were used as attempted antidotes for snakebite.

▶ FLORETS PURPLE, BROWN OR YELLOW WITH SMALL, ERECT PETALS

**3** *Stoebe plumosa* **Slangbos**

J F M **A M J J** A S O N D

Sprawling, white-woolly, softly woody shrub to 1 m with numerous widely branching short-shoots, and small, granular, tufted leaves; bears globular axillary heads of discoid flowerheads arranged in spike-like inflorescences, with brownish florets and pointed, golden-brown bracts. Rocky flats and slopes throughout southern and southeastern South Africa, often forming dense stands.

**4** *Stoebe cinerea* **Vaal haartebeeskaroo**

J F M **A M J J** A S O N D

Grey-woolly, much-branched shrub to 1.5 m with short-shoots and spreading, twisted, needle-like leaves that have a bulbous base; bears globular axillary heads of discoid flowerheads arranged in elongated, spike-like inflorescences, with purplish florets and pointed, golden-brown bracts. Rocky slopes, often on shale, in the extreme southwestern Cape.

**5** *Stoebe spiralis*

J F **M A M** J J A S O N D

Grey-woolly, ericoid shrublet to 60 cm, with twisted, recurved, needle-like leaves; bears globular heads of discoid flowerheads with yellow florets and short yellow bracts. Damp sandstone slopes in the mountains of the southwestern Cape. *Stoebe incana*, from the coastal mountains, has longer, golden-brown bracts and flowers.

▶ **FLORETS WHITE, PINK OR MAUVE, USUALLY WITH CONSPICUOUS, SPREADING PETALS**

**①** *Stoebe alopecuroides*

| J | F | M | A | M | J | J | A | S | O | N | D |

**Katstertslangbos** Robust, sparsely hairy shrub to 1 m with spreading, twisted stiffly needle-like leaves; bears numerous discoid flowerheads massed in elongated spikes, with conspicuous white florets and brown bracts. Forest margins and fynbos in the southern Cape.

**②** *Stoebe capitata*

| J | F | M | A | M | J | J | A | S | O | N | D |

Erect or spreading, sparsely cobwebby shrublet to 50 cm with spreading, twisted, needle-like leaves; bears dense, globular heads of flowerheads, with mauve to pink or white florets and brown bracts. Sandstone slopes and coastal sands in the southwestern and Eastern Cape.

**③** *Stoebe rosea*

| J | F | M | A | M | J | J | A | S | O | N | D |

Stiffly branched, densely leafy shrub to 50 cm with recurved and twisted, needle-like leaves; bears dense, globular heads of flowerheads, with pink florets concealing the bracts among the conspicuous, feathery pappus bristles. Sandstone slopes on the Cape Peninsula.

## *Disparago*  **DISPARAGO**

Often tangled shrublets. Leaves small, *scale-like or needle-like and often twisted*, with the *margins rolled upwards and densely felted in the groove* but less hairy beneath. *Flowerheads crowded in heads or cylindrical spikes*, small, 2–10-flowered, *all or some with 1 or 2 ray florets*, with 1–4 rows of dry, membranous bracts; receptacle without scales. Ray florets 0 or 1 per head, fertile, *white or pink*. Disc florets male or fertile, white or pink. Fruits smooth or hairy; pappus of barbed or feathery bristles, rarely lacking. South Africa, mainly Western Cape: 9 spp, all fynbos.

**④** *Disparago ericoides*

| J | F | M | A | M | J | J | A | S | O | N | D |

Sparsely cobwebby shrublet to 30 cm with spreading or recurved, twisted, needle-like leaves; bears globular, short-stalked heads of closely packed flowerheads, each with a single, sterile, pink ray floret; the ovary of the disc florets is densely woolly. Sandstone slopes in the southwestern Cape. *Disparago tortilis*, from the southern and Eastern Cape, has female ray florets, and flowers in winter and spring.

## *Bryomorphe*  **BRYOMORPHE**

*Dwarf, cushion-forming, moss-like shrublet.* Leaves closely overlapping, *needle- or scale-like and silvery grey with the upper surface woolly. Flowerheads 1–3 nested among the leaves at the branch tips, radiate, sometimes inconspicuously*, with several rows of bracts, the inner with dry, papery, purplish tips; receptacle honeycombed, without scales. *Ray florets 6 or 7 per head*, fertile, *white or pinkish*. Disc florets fertile, purplish. Fruits tending to adhere together, spindle-shaped, smooth; pappus of barbed bristles feathery at the tips. Southwestern Cape at high altitudes: 1 sp.

**⑤** *Bryomorphe aretioides*

| J | F | M | A | M | J | J | A | S | O | N | D |

Dwarf, silvery-woolly, densely leafy, moss-like, cushion-forming shrublet to 5 cm with silvery grey, needle- or scale-like leaves; bears radiate flowerheads nested among the leaves, with white or pinkish rays and a purplish disc. Sandstone rocks and crevices above 1 000 m in the southwestern Cape.

▶ PLANTS RESEMBLING A MONOCOTYLEDON, WITH STRAP-LIKE LEAVES WITH PARALLEL VENATION; FLOWERHEADS IN CLUSTERS, INDIVIDUALLY 1-FLOWERED, WHITE OR PURPLE

## *Corymbium*  CORYMBIUM, HEUNINGBOS

Tufted perennial herbs. Leaves in a basal tuft, *narrow with parallel venation, smooth or hairy*, often silky at the base. Flowerheads crowded in flat-topped or open clusters, discoid, *1-flowered, spindle-shaped*, with 2 rows of bracts; receptacle without scales. *Florets deeply 5-lobed with the petals longer than the tube, white, pink or purple*. Fruit spindle-shaped, silky; pappus short and crown-like or of fine bristles. Southwestern and southern Cape: 9 spp, all fynbos. The vernacular name, heuningbos, derives from the honey-like fragrance of the flowers.

▶ STEMS AND INVOLUCRAL BRACTS SMOOTH

**1** *Corymbium glabrum*

| J | F | M | A | M | J | J | A | S | O | N | D |

Tufted perennial to 60 cm with smooth stems and leathery, sword-shaped leaves with prominent veins; bears loose clusters of discoid, pink or white flowerheads with smooth bracts. Rocky sandstone slopes in the southwestern and Eastern Cape.

▶ STEMS AND INVOLUCRAL BRACTS ROUGH AND STICKY

**2** *Corymbium africanum*  Plampers

| J | F | M | A | M | J | J | A | S | O | N | D |

Tufted perennial to 30 cm with roughly hairy stems and thread- to strap-like leaves; bears dense clusters of discoid, purple, pink or white flowerheads with roughly hairy, sticky bracts. Sandy flats and slopes in the southwestern and Eastern Cape.

**3** *Corymbium villosum*

| J | F | M | A | M | J | J | A | S | O | N | D |

Tufted perennial to 30 cm with roughly hairy stems and sword-shaped leaves covered with gland-tipped hairs; bears dense clusters of discoid, mauve to white flowerheads with roughly hairy, sticky bracts. Lower sandstone slopes and flats in the southwestern Cape.

▶ TUFTED PERENNIALS OR GNARLED SHRUBS WITH FIRM, LEATHERY LEAVES THAT ARE DENSELY FELTED BENEATH; RAY FLORETS 2-LIPPED AND DISC FLORETS DEEPLY CLEFT WITH CURLED PETALS; HEADS RADIATE, USUALLY WHITE OR PINKISH, INCLUDING THE DISC, NEVER BRIGHT YELLOW; PAPPUS OF LONG BRISTLES

## *Oldenburgia*  OLDENBURGIA, KREUPELBOS

Gnarled, small trees or dwarf shrubs, sometimes cushion-forming. Leaves alternate but crowded at the branch tips, *elliptical, leathery, with the margins lightly rolled under, densely white-woolly beneath and silky at the base*. Flowerheads large, sessile or pedunculate, radiate, with several rows of firm, woolly bracts; receptacle without scales. Ray florets female, *2-lipped, the outer lip large and strap-shaped and the inner lip of 2 small, thread-like lobes, white*. Disc florets fertile, deeply 5-lobed with curled petals, *white or cream*. Fruits spindle-shaped and ribbed, smooth or silky; pappus of few to many barbed or feathery bristles. Southwestern and Eastern Cape: 4 spp; 3 fynbos spp.

**4** *Oldenburgia paradoxa*

| J | F | M | A | M | J | J | A | S | O | N | D |

Cushion-forming shrublet to 30 cm with leathery, elliptical leaves that are woolly beneath, the margins rolled under; bears solitary, sessile, white, radiate flowerheads nested in the leaves. Sandstone rocks at high altitude in the southwestern and southern Cape. *Oldenburgia intermedia* has the flowerheads borne on white-woolly peduncles; *O. papionum* is a larger shrublet to 1 m with flowerheads borne on more or less hairless peduncles.

## *Gerbera* GERBERA

Tufted perennial herbs, often with a woolly crown. Leaves basal, elliptical and toothed or lobed, *tough and leathery, often densely felted beneath*. Flowerheads solitary on long scapes, radiate, with several rows of bracts; receptacle without scales. Ray florets usually female, *2-lipped, the outer lip large and strap-shaped and the inner lip of 2 small, thread-like lobes, white, yellow, pink or red*. Disc florets fertile, *5-lobed and irregularly 2-lipped with curled petals, usually blackish*. Fruits narrowly flask-shaped and ribbed, with sparse short hairs; pappus of many barbed bristles. Africa, Asia and South America: 30 spp; ±6 fynbos spp.

▶ **FLOWER STALKS WITHOUT ANY BRACTS**

**①** *Gerbera piloselloides*  **Swarttee**  
`J F M A M J J A S O N D`

Tufted perennial to 30 cm with a rosette of elliptical leaves tapering towards the base and softly hairy or cobwebby on both surfaces; bears inconspicuously radiate, white, pink, red or yellow flowerheads on naked scapes that are swollen at the tip; the involucral bracts are hairy. Sandstone and limestone slopes from the southwestern Cape to tropical Africa.

▶ **FLOWER STALKS WITH SMALL SCALE-LIKE BRACTS**

**②** *Gerbera crocea*  **Dialstee**  
`J F M A M J J A S O N D`

Tufted perennial to 40 cm with a rosette of petiolate, lance-shaped to elliptical leaves that are hairless to sparsely cobwebby beneath, their margins lightly toothed and rolled under; bears radiate, white or pink flowerheads, maroon on the reverse, on scaly scapes; the involucral bracts are hairless to sparsely cobwebby. Sandstone slopes in the southwestern Cape, flowering after fire.

**③** *Gerbera serrata*  
`J F M A M J J A S O N D`

Tufted perennial to 30 cm with a rosette of petiolate, narrowly elliptical or oblong leaves that are yellow-felted beneath, their margins saw-toothed and rolled under; bears radiate, white flowerheads, maroon on the reverse, on scaly scapes; the involucral bracts are softly felted and are in ± distinct series. Sandstone slopes in the southwestern and southern Cape, flowering after fire. *Gerbera tomentosa* has broader leaves and ± evenly overlapping involucral bracts; *G. wrightii*, from the Cape Peninsula, has broad, rounded leaves that are white- or greyish-felted beneath.

**④** *Gerbera linnaei*  **Varingblom**  
`J F M A M J J A S O N D`

Tufted perennial to 40 cm with a rosette of narrow leaves that are yellow-felted beneath and cut into round, twisted lobes, their margins rolled under; bears radiate, cream, sometimes yellow, flowerheads, maroon on the reverse, on scaly scapes; the involucral bracts are hairless. Sandstone slopes in the exteme southwestern Cape, flowering after fire.

▶ PLANTS OFTEN THISTLE-LIKE; FLOWERHEADS RADIATE WITH YELLOW, ORANGE OR RED RAYS, SOMETIMES WITH DARK MARKINGS AT THE BASE; INVOLUCRAL BRACTS IN 2 OR MORE ROWS, SPINE-TIPPED AND JOINED AT THE BASE INTO A CUP; RAY FLORETS STERILE, 4-TOOTHED; PAPPUS OF SCALES, SOMETIMES NARROW, TAPERING AND BRISTLE-LIKE, RARELY ABSENT

## *Cullumia*  SNAKE THISTLE, STEEKHAARBOS

*Spiny shrublets, often sprawling, sometimes cobwebby. Leaves alternate, overlapping, small, with spiny or bristly margins* and *often spine-tipped.* Flowerheads solitary and sessile, radiate, with *4 rows of stiff, hairless, often recurved involucral bracts with spiny margins, joined at the base*; receptacle honeycombed, without scales. Ray florets sterile, 4-toothed, yellow. Disc florets fertile, deeply 5-lobed; fruits oblong or ellipsoid, smooth, *without a pappus.* Winter-rainfall South Africa: 15 spp, all fynbos.

▶ **LEAF MARGINS ROLLED UNDER AND MOSTLY COVERING THE UNDERSIDE**

**1** *Cullumia bisulca*

J F M A M J J A S O N D

Sprawling, densely leafy shrublet to over 1 m, cobwebby on the young parts, with strongly arched, needle-like leaves, the margins bristly and rolled under; bears radiate, yellow flowerheads, with the outer involucral bracts yellowish and dissimilar to the leaves. Dry sandstone slopes in the southwestern and southern Cape.

**2** *Cullumia squarrosa*

J F M A M J J A S O N D

Sprawling, densely leafy shrublet to 50 cm, cobwebby on the young parts, with spreading or arched, needle-like leaves (10)15–25 mm long, the margins bristly and rolled under; bears radiate, yellow flowerheads, with the inner involucral bracts unlike the outer and without prickles. Coastal bush in the extreme southwestern Cape.

▶ **LEAF MARGINS THICKENED AND TRANSLUCENT BUT NOT ROLLED UNDER**

**3** *Cullumia setosa*

J F M A M J J A S O N D

Sprawling, densely leafy shrublet to 60 cm, sometimes cobwebby, with arched, oval leaves with the tips flexed down and with thickened margins bearing mostly 1 row of bristles; bears radiate, yellow flowerheads. Lower mountain slopes in the southwestern Cape.

**4** *Cullumia reticulata*

J F M A M J J A S O N D

(=*Cullumia ciliata*)  Straggling, densely leafy shrublet to 60 cm with ascending, oval leaves with the tips flexed down and with thickened margins bearing 2 rows of opposed bristles; bears radiate, yellow flowerheads. Lower sandstone slopes in the southwestern Cape.

## *Didelta*  SALAD THISTLE, SLAAIBOS

Perennial herbs or shrubs, more or less succulent. Leaves alternate or opposite, with or without a few spiny teeth, fleshy, hairless or felted. Flowerheads solitary and sessile or on peduncles, radiate, *with 2 rows of bracts: an outer row of 3–5 large, triangular, leaf-like bracts and an inner row of several lance-shaped bracts*, sometimes with spiny margins; receptacle deeply honeycombed with the outer cells thick-walled, breaking into 3–5 woody outer parts, 1 attached to each of the outer bracts, with the fruits embedded in spine-fringed cells, and a central, thin-textured part. Ray florets sterile, yellow. Disc florets fertile or inner ones male, deeply 5-lobed; fruits flask-shaped, ribbed, smooth or hairy; pappus of narrow, fringed scales joined at the base. Winter-rainfall South Africa: 2 spp, both fynbos. The large, wing-like bracts attached to the outer, woody involucral segments aid in dispersal. The spiny pit margins deter seed predators, and the seeds germinate directly within the woody pits, 1 to a segment, thus extending their protective role to the seedling as well.

### ❶ *Didelta spinosa*

J F M A M J **J A S** O N D

Shrub to 2 m, cobwebby on the young parts, with somewhat fleshy, opposite, oval to elliptical leaves that are rounded at the base, their margins slightly rolled under and sometimes prickly; bears solitary, large, radiate, yellow flowerheads at the branch tips. Dry granite and sandstone slopes from southern Namibia to the West Coast. *Didelta carnosa*, from coastal dunes, is a smaller, often densely cobwebby shrublet with narrow leaves.

## *Berkheya*  WILD THISTLE, WILDEDISSEL

Thistle-like, perennial herbs or shrubs, often cobwebby or woolly. Leaves alternate or basal, rarely opposite, *more or less lobed and spiny-toothed*, sometimes continuing down the stem as leafy wings. Flowerheads usually several at the branch tips, radiate or discoid, with several rows of lance-shaped *involucral bracts joined only at the base*, usually with prickly or bristly margins and tips; *receptacle honeycombed with fringed margins to the pits*. Ray florets sterile, usually yellow, rarely white or lilac. Disc florets fertile or inner ones male, deeply 5-lobed; fruits flask-shaped, ribbed, smooth or hairy; pappus of short or long scales or barbed bristles. Southern and tropical Africa: ±75 spp; ±12 fynbos spp.

### ❷ *Berkheya armata*

J F **M A M J J A** S O N D

Tufted perennial to 40 cm, sprouting from a woody rootstock, with a basal rosette of lance-shaped leaves that are hairless above and white-felted beneath, the margins prickly-toothed and slightly rolled under; bears 1 to few radiate, yellow flowerheads on leafy peduncles; all of the involucral bracts are finely prickly along the margins. Clay and granite slopes and flats in the southwestern Cape.

### ❸ *Berkheya herbacea*

J **F M A M J J A S** O N D

Tufted perennial to 40 cm, sprouting from a woody rootstock, with a basal rosette of lance-shaped leaves that are hairless above and white-felted beneath, the margins often scarcely prickly-toothed; bears several radiate, yellow flowerheads on leafy peduncles; the inner involucral bracts have broad, smooth, horny margins. Sandstone slopes in the southwestern Cape.

### ❹ *Berkheya barbata*

J F M A M J **J J** A S O N D

White-felted shrublet to 60 cm, sprouting from a woody rootstock, with opposite, elliptical leaves that are slightly prickly-toothed and hairless above but white-felted beneath, the margins rolled under; bears solitary, large, radiate, yellow flowerheads. Rocky sandstone slopes in the southwestern Cape.

### ❶ *Berkheya rigida*

J F M A M J J A S O N D

Sparsely or more densely white-woolly perennial to 1 m with the leaves deeply dissected into narrow, prickly lobes, and the margins rolled under; bears clusters of discoid, yellow flowerheads on lateral branches. Clay and granite slopes and flats in the southwestern Cape, often in disturbed places.

## *Gazania*  GAZANIA, GOUSBLOM

Perennial or sometimes annual herbs, usually tufted, *with milky latex.* Leaves mostly basal or in a rosette, *narrow or deeply lobed* into narrow segments, usually *with the margins rolled under and white-felted beneath. Flowerheads solitary on hollow peduncles,* radiate, often brightly marked, with several rows of stiff bracts *joined into a smooth, hairless or roughly hairy cup;* receptacle without scales. Ray florets sterile, yellow, orange or red, *mostly with dark marks at the base.* Disc florets fertile or inner 1 sterile, deeply 5-lobed; fruits flask-shaped with rows of swollen cells, silky; pappus of many delicate, hair-like scales. Southern and tropical Africa: ±16 spp; ±8 fynbos spp. The vernacular name derives from the Dutch *goud* (gold), alluding to the rich, or golden, colours of the flowerheads.

▸ **SPRAWLING OR CREEPING PERENNIALS ROOTING ALONG THE STEMS**

### ❷ *Gazania maritima*

J F M A M J J A S O N D

Creeping perennial to 10 cm, rooting along the rhizome, with leathery leaves mostly divided into 3–7 elliptical lobes, their margins rolled under and white-felted beneath, often with bristly petioles; bears radiate flowerheads with yellow to orange rays with dark marks at the base; the involucre is more or less hairless. Coastal rocks and sands in the southwestern Cape.

### ❸ *Gazania rigens*  Strandgazania

J F M A M J J A S O N D

Sprawling, mat-forming perennial to 20 cm with most leaves simply lance-shaped, rarely lobed, their margins rolled under and white-felted beneath with smooth petioles; bears radiate flowerheads with yellow rays, with or without dark marks at the base; the involucre is partially white-woolly. Coastal dunes and rocky outcrops along beaches from the southern Cape to southern Mozambique.

▸ **TUFTED, STEMLESS PERENNIALS OR ANNUALS**

### ❹ *Gazania pectinata*

J F M A M J J A S O N D

Tufted annual to 20 cm with the leaves mostly divided into narrow to elliptical lobes, their margins rolled under and white-felted beneath; bears radiate flowerheads with yellow or orange rays with dark marks at the base; the involucre is hairless, with the inner bracts very long and slender. Coastal flats and lower slopes in the southwestern Cape.

### ❺ *Gazania krebsiana*

J F M A M J J A S O N D

Tufted perennial to 20 cm with the leaves either undivided or divided into narrow segments, their margins rolled under and white-felted beneath; bears radiate flowerheads with yellow to orange or reddish rays with dark marks at the base; the involucre is hairless or sparsely hairy. Roadsides, flats and lower slopes throughout southern Africa to Tanzania.

**1** *Gazania rigida*  J F M A M J J A S O N D

Tufted perennial to 25 cm with the leaves usually divided into elliptical lobes, sometimes undivided, their margins rolled under and white-woolly beneath; bears radiate flowerheads with yellow or orange rays, usually with dark marks at the base; the involucre is roughly hairy. Flats and lower slopes in the southwestern and southern Cape.

▶ FLOWERHEADS RADIATE WITH WHITE, PINK OR YELLOW TO REDDISH RAYS, SOMETIMES WITH DARK MARKS AT THE BASE; AT LEAST THE INNER INVOLUCRAL BRACTS WITH LARGE, ROUNDED, MEMBRANOUS TIPS; PAPPUS OF SCALES

## *Arctotis* ARCTOTIS, GOUSBLOM

Annual or perennial herbs, sometimes tufted, or shrubs, *often felted and glandular*. Leaves alternate or basal, more or less lobed, more or less felted or woolly. Flowerheads solitary on short or long, *hollow peduncles*, radiate, often large, with 5 or 6 rows of bracts, the *outer often tailed and the inner bracts broad with large, membranous tips*; receptacle honeycombed, without scales. *Ray florets female*, white, yellow, orange, pink or purple, often with darker marks at the base. Disc florets fertile, 5-lobed. *Fruits ovoid, with 3–5 ribs on one side enclosing 2 furrows*, hairless or silky and often with a *tuft of long hairs at the base; pappus of 1 or 2 rows of scales*. Southern and south tropical Africa, mainly winter-rainfall parts: ±50 spp; ±30 fynbos spp.

▶ **ANNUAL HERBS**

**2** *Arctotis hirsuta* **Gousblom**  J F M A M J J A S O N D

Slightly fleshy, often robust annual to 45 cm with sparsely hairy, lyre-shaped, divided leaves, often with ear-like lobes at the base; bears radiate flowerheads with yellow, cream or orange rays and a dark disc, with shortly tailed outer bracts; the fruits have 2 rounded cavities, a short pappus, and a rudimentary basal tuft of hairs. Sandy slopes and flats, usually coastal, in the southwestern Cape.

**3** *Arctotis breviscapa*  J F M A M J J A S O N D

**Sandveldgousblom** Tufted annual herb to 20 cm with a basal rosette of divided leaves that are green and almost hairless above, but woolly beneath; bears radiate flowerheads on hairy scapes, with orange or yellow rays, red on the reverse, and a dark disc, the outer bracts with slender, woolly tips; the fruits have 2 elongated cavities, no pappus, and an obsolete basal tuft of hairs. Rocky sandstone slopes along the West Coast.

▶ **ROUGHLY HAIRY PERENNIALS**

**4** *Arctotis acaulis* **Renostergousblom**  J F M A M J J A S O N D

Tufted perennial to 20 cm with a basal rosette of lance- to lyre-shaped, toothed leaves that are roughly hairy above and grey-felted beneath; bears radiate flowerheads on hairy scapes, with orange, yellow or cream rays and a black disc, the outer bracts with slender, woolly tips; the fruits have 2 rounded cavities and a well-developed pappus and basal tuft of hairs. Clay, granitic, and limestone flats in the southwestern and southern Cape.

**① *Arctotis incisa*  Botterblom**

J F M A M J J A S O N D

Sprawling perennial to 30 cm with deeply lobed and toothed leaves that are roughly hairy above and white-felted below, the margins lightly rolled under; bears solitary, radiate flowerheads on hairy scapes, with white or orange rays and a dark disc, the outer bracts with long woolly tails; the fruits have 2 elongate, undulate cavities and a well-developed pappus and basal tuft of hairs. Sandy slopes and flats in the southwestern and southern Cape.

**② *Arctotis revoluta***

J F M A M J J A S O N D

Softly woody, aromatic shrub to 2 m with the leaves usually twice-divided into narrow segments, the margins rolled under, almost hairless above but grey-felted beneath; bears radiate flowerheads on hairy peduncles, with yellow to orange rays and a dark disc, the outer bracts tailed; the fruits have 2 wedge-shaped cavities and a well-developed pappus and basal hair tuft. Rocky slopes, often coastal, in Namaqualand and the southwestern Cape.

**③ *Arctotis aspera*  Taaigousblom**

J F M A M J J A S O N D

Sprawling perennial to 2 m, the stems and leaves covered with rough, gland-tipped hairs, the leaves once- or twice-divided into narrow lobes, with the margins rolled under, sometimes grey beneath; bears radiate flowerheads on hairy peduncles, with purple or white rays, dark on the reverse, and a dark disc, the outer bracts more or less tailed; the fruits have 2 elongate, undulate cavities and a well-developed pappus and basal hair tuft. Rocky slopes along the West Coast and onto the Cape Peninsula.

▶ **GREY- OR SILVERY-WOOLLY PERENNIALS**

**④ *Arctotis angustifolia***

J F M A M J J A S O N D

Creeping, sparsely white-woolly perennial with stems to 40 cm from a diffuse underground root system, with lance-shaped to oval, toothed to lobed leaves that are usually darker above, the margins lightly rolled under; bears radiate flowerheads on woolly peduncles, with white or yellow rays, reddish reverse and a dark disc, the outer bracts only obscurely tailed; the fruits have 2 rounded cavities and a well-developed pappus and basal hair tuft. Sandy slopes and flats in the southwestern Cape.

**⑤ *Arctotis stoechadifolia*  Kusgousblom**

J F M A M J J A S O N D

Sprawling, silvery-woolly perennial with erect shoots to 35 cm and white-felted, lance-shaped to lobed leaves; bears radiate flowerheads on woolly peduncles with cream-coloured rays, reddish reverse and a dark disc, the outer bracts with woolly tails; the fruits have 2 elongate cavities and a well-developed pappus and basal hair tuft. Dunes and sandy flats, mostly coastal, around the Cape Peninsula and Table Bay.

## *Haplocarpha*  HAPLOCARPHA, GOUSBLOM

Tufted or mat-forming perennial herbs. Leaves toothed or lobed, *strongly discolorous with the upper surface green and the lower densely white-felted*. Flowerheads solitary on *hollow peduncles*, with several rows of *bracts, with broad membranous margins and tips*. Ray florets fertile, yellow, often with reddish reverse. Disc florets fertile, deeply 5-lobed. *Fruits ovoid, weakly ribbed on one side, hairless or hairy; pappus of 2 or more rows of scales or lacking*. Tropical and southern Africa: 8 spp; 3 fynbos spp.

413

**① *Haplocarpha lanata* Brandblom**  J F M A M J J A S O N D

Tufted perennial herb to 15 cm with a rosette of coarsely toothed, elliptical to lance-shaped leaves that are rough above and densely white-felted beneath; bears solitary, radiate flowerheads on scapes covered with gland-tipped hairs, with yellow rays that are red on the reverse and a yellow disc; the fruits are silky, with a basal tuft of hairs longer than the fruit, and a pappus longer than the body of the fruit. Sandstone slopes in the southwestern Cape, flowering mainly after fire.

## *Arctotheca*  ARCTOTHECA

Felted annual or perennial herbs, tufted or creeping. Leaves alternate, more or less lobed, more or less felted or woolly. Flowerheads solitary on *hollow peduncles*, radiate, with several rows of *bracts with broad membranous margins and tips*; receptacle honeycombed, without scales. *Ray florets sterile*, yellow, sometimes with a dark base. Disc florets fertile, 5-lobed; *fruits ovoid*, thinly ribbed, *usually woolly or silky; pappus of small scales or a crown of scales or lacking*. Southern Africa: 5 spp, all fynbos.

**② *Arctotheca calendula* Cape weed**  J F M A M J J A S O N D

Tufted or sprawling annual herb to 20 cm with mostly basal leaves, scalloped to deeply divided and roughly hairy above, but white-woolly beneath; bears solitary, radiate flowerheads on roughly hairy scapes, with pale to deep yellow rays, often paler or darker at the base, and a black disc; the fruits are woolly with a small, chaffy pappus. Coastal areas or disturbed soil from Namaqualand to the Eastern Cape. *Arctotheca prostrata* is a sprawling perennial that roots along the stem, with white-tipped involucral bracts.

**③ *Arctotheca populifolia* Sea pumpkin**  J F M A M J J A S O N D

Mat-forming perennial with petiolate, white-felted, paddle-shaped leaves sparsely toothed on the margins; bears solitary, radiate, yellow flowerheads on woolly, shortly leafy scapes; the fruits are woolly with a small, crown-like pappus. Coastal dunes along the seashore from the West Coast to Mozambique.

## *Ursinia*  PARACHUTE DAISY, BERGMAGRIET

Annual or perennial herbs or shrubs. Leaves alternate, usually toothed or lobed, often with thread-like segments. Flowerheads solitary or in loose clusters on *long, slender peduncles*, radiate, with several rows of bracts, the *outer usually with dark margins and the inner broad with large, rounded, membranous tips; receptacle with scales enfolding the florets*. Ray florets usually sterile, yellow or rarely orange, reddish or white. Disc florets fertile, 5-lobed; fruits flask-shaped, straight or curved, sometimes with a basal tuft of web-like hairs; *pappus of large, papery, white scales*, sometimes with an inner row of smaller scales. Mainly winter-rainfall southern Africa with 1 species extending to North Africa: 38 spp; 32 fynbos spp.

▶ **ANNUAL OR WEAKLY PERENNIAL HERBS**

**④ *Ursinia anthemoides* Magriet**  J F M A M J J A S O N D

Annual herb to 50 cm with once- or twice-divided leaves 20–50 mm long; bears solitary, radiate flowerheads, 15–60 mm in diameter, on slender peduncles, with yellow or orange rays, sometimes darker at the base and on the reverse, and a dark disc; the pappus comprises 5 scales only. Sandy and gravel slopes and flats from southern Namibia to the Eastern Cape.

### ① *Ursinia cakilefolia*

J F M A M J **J A S O** N D

Sprawling annual herb to 45 cm with finely twice-divided leaves 20–50 mm long; bears solitary, radiate flowerheads ±25–50 mm in diameter, on long peduncles, with yellow or orange rays and a dark disc that is glossy in the centre; the pappus comprises 5 scales and 5 bristles. Sandy flats and slopes from Namaqualand to the southwestern Cape. *Ursinia speciosa* has the tips of all the involucral bracts rounded and papery.

### ② *Ursinia chrysanthemoides*

J F M A M J J **A S O** N D

Sprawling or creeping annual or weak perennial, rooting along the stem, with finely twice-divided leaves 20–50 mm long; bears solitary, radiate flowerheads ±25–50 mm in diameter, on long peduncles, with yellow, orange, white or red rays, darker reverse, and a glossy disc; the pappus comprises 5 scales and 5 bristles. Sandy and gravel slopes and flats from Namaqualand to the Eastern Cape.

## ▸ WOODY PERENNIALS OR SHRUBLETS

### ③ *Ursinia nudicaulis*

J F **M A M J J A** S O N D

Tufted dwarf shrublet to 50 cm with the leaves crowded at the base, finely divided, 15–70 mm long; bears solitary, radiate flowerheads 15–30 mm in diameter, on elongate peduncles, with yellow rays and disc, the outer bracts often papery above; the pappus comprises 5 scales only. Sandstone slopes, sometimes in wet places, in the mountains of the southwestern and southern Cape.

### ④ *Ursinia dentata*

J F **M A M J J A** S O N D

Shrublet to 50 cm with erect, shortly divided leaves 5–35 mm long, with finely pointed lobes; bears solitary, radiate flowerheads 40 mm in diameter, on elongate, wiry peduncles, with yellow rays, darker on the reverse, and a yellow disc; the pappus comprises 5 scales only. Sandstone or limestone slopes and flats in the southwestern Cape.

### ⑤ *Ursinia punctata*

J F M **A M J J A** S O N D

Sparsely hairy, erect or sprawling shrublet to 50 cm with finely divided leaves 10–20 mm long, with oblong lobes; bears solitary, radiate flowerheads 7–15 mm in diameter, on long, wiry peduncles, with yellow rays and disc; the pappus comprises 5 scales only. Damp sandstone slopes in mountains of the southwestern Cape.

### ⑥ *Ursinia paleacea* Geelmagriet

J F M A M J J **A S O** N D

Shrub to 90 cm with finely divided leaves 20–60 mm long; bears solitary, radiate flowerheads 20–50 mm in diameter, on elongate peduncles, with yellow or brownish rays, sometimes greenish at the base and dark on the reverse, and a yellow disc; the pappus comprises 5 scales only. Sandstone slopes in the southwestern and southern Cape, especially after fire.

▶ INVOLUCRAL BRACTS IN 1(2) SERIES, COHERING ALONG THE MARGINS AND SOMETIMES JOINED BELOW, ENTIRELY GREEN (SOMETIMES WITH ADDITIONAL SERIES OF SMALL BRACTEOLES BELOW); RAY FLORETS CURLING BACK AT NIGHT; PAPPUS OF BARBED BRISTLES (SOMETIMES SOON DROPPING)

## *Senecio*   GROUNDSEL, HONGERBLOM

Annual or perennial herbs, shrubs or climbers, sometimes succulent, hairless or hairy, sometimes glandular. Leaves alternate or basal, often variously toothed or lobed. Flowerheads 1 to many on short or long peduncles, radiate or discoid, *with 1 row of narrow, green involucral bracts cohering along the margins, with additional minute bracteoles at the base*; receptacle without scales. Ray florets when present female, usually yellow, sometimes purple or pink to white. Disc florets fertile, 5-lobed. *Fruits cylindrical* and ribbed, smooth or hairy; *pappus of many long, barbed bristles*. Cosmopolitan: ±1 250 spp; ±80 fynbos spp. Many species contain toxic alkaloids responsible for stock losses but the leaves of some are used externally to promote healing, and the vernacular name, hongerblom, derives from the purported use of certain species as a tea to promote the appetite.

▶ ANNUAL HERBS

### ① *Senecio littoreus* Geelhongerblom

| J | F | M | A | M | J | J | A | S | O | N | D |

Almost hairless or short-haired annual herb to 40 cm with toothed to shallowly lobed, oblong to lance-shaped leaves; bears loose clusters of radiate flowerheads with yellow rays and disc. Mainly coastal sands in southern Namaqualand and the southwestern Cape.

### ② *Senecio abruptus*

| J | F | M | A | M | J | J | A | S | O | N | D |

**Bastergeelhongerblom** Like *Senecio littoreus* but the leaves more deeply divided. Stony slopes in Namaqualand and the southwestern Cape.

### ③ *Senecio maritimus*

| J | F | M | A | M | J | J | A | S | O | N | D |

**Strandhongerblom** Sprawling to creeping, hairless, annual herb to 30 cm with fleshy, slightly toothed, oblong, rather blunt leaves; bears loose custers of radiate flowerheads with yellow rays and disc. Coastal dunes and slopes from southern Namaqualand and the southwestern Cape.

### ④ *Senecio sophioides*

| J | F | M | A | M | J | J | A | S | O | N | D |

Delicate, annual herb to 20 cm, covered with minute, gland-tipped hairs, with petiolate leaves divided into narrow lobes, each with a minute white callus at the tip; bears 1 to few radiate flowerheads with purple or yellow rays and a yellow disc. Stony slopes in the southwestern Cape.

### ⑤ *Senecio arenarius* Hongerblom

| J | F | M | A | M | J | J | A | S | O | N | D |

Annual herb, 15–40 cm, covered with gland-tipped hairs, with toothed or lobed leaves, the margins sometimes rolled under; bears branched clusters of radiate flowerheads, with mauve or white rays and a yellow disc; the involucre is cylindrical and covered with fine, gland-tipped hairs, with inconspicuous bracteoles at the base. Sandy flats from southern Namibia to the southwestern Cape.

### ① *Senecio elegans*  Veld cineraria

`J F M A M J J A S O N D`

Annual herb to 1 m, densely covered with gland-tipped hairs, with fleshy, deeply lobed or divided leaves, the margins rolled under; bears branched clusters of numerous radiate flowerheads, in dense corymbs, with purple rays and a yellow disc; the involucre is cup-shaped with conspicuous bracteoles at the base. Coastal sands from the southwestern to the Eastern Cape.

## ▶ TUFTED PERENNIALS WITH THE LEAVES MOSTLY IN A BASAL ROSETTE

### ② *Senecio lanifer*

`J F M A M J J A S O N D`

Tufted perennial to 60 cm, covered with gland-tipped hairs and with a basal rosette of lance-shaped, roughly lobed or toothed leaves; bears loose clusters of discoid, magenta or whitish flowerheads. Sandstone slopes in fynbos or grassland from the southwestern Cape to southern tropical Africa.

### ③ *Senecio scapiflorus*  Perskoppie

`J F M A M J J A S O N D`

Tufted, sparsely white-woolly perennial to 30 cm with a basal rosette of petiolate, lance- or heart-shaped, toothed to lobed or divided leaves; bears solitary, discoid, white or purple flowerheads on elongate, scaly peduncles. Rocky slopes and flats in Namaqualand and the southwestern Cape.

### ④ *Senecio hastifolius*

`J F M A M J J A S O N D`

Tufted perennial to 40 cm with a basal rosette of petiolate leaves, the blades often purple beneath and variously arrow-, heart- or lyre-shaped and lobed or toothed, with the terminal lobe largest; bears 1 to few radiate flowerheads on scaly scapes, with purple or white rays and a purple or yellow disc; the involucral bracts are broad. Damp sandstone slopes and marshes in the southwestern Cape, often flowering after fire.

### ⑤ *Senecio erosus*

`J F M A M J J A S O N D`

Tufted, hairless to roughly hairy perennial to 60 cm with a woolly crown and a mostly basal rosette of petiolate, lance-shaped and irregularly toothed to roughly lobed leaves; bears solitary or a few, radiate flowerheads on sparsely leafy scapes, with yellow rays and disc. Rocky slopes in Namaqualand and the southwestern Cape.

## ▶ SHRUBLETS WITH THE LEAVES SCATTERED ALONG THE STEMS

### ⑥ *Senecio pinifolius*

`J F M A M J J A S O N D`

Sparsely branched, densely leafy shrublet to 40 cm with needle-like leaves; bears mostly solitary, radiate flowerheads nested among the leaves at the branch tips, with yellow rays and disc. Sandstone slopes in fynbos in the southwestern, southern and Eastern Cape.

### ⑦ *Senecio pubigerus*  Takluisbossie

`J F M A M J J A S O N D`

Loosely branched, roughly hairy shrub with wand-like branches to 1 m, and oblong, coarsely toothed leaves, with the margins rolled under; bears small clusters of sparsely radiate flowerheads in white-woolly clusters scattered on slender, scaly branches, with yellow rays and disc. Dry, stony, clay or granite slopes, often in disturbed places, in the southwestern Cape.

### **1** *Senecio burchellii*

J F M A M J J A S O N D

**Geelgifbossie, Molteno disease plant** Softly woody shrublet to 40 cm, mostly hairless but sometimes roughly hairy below, with narrow leaves that have the margins rolled under and are sometimes sparsely toothed, usually with axillary tufts of smaller leaves; bears loose clusters of radiate flowerheads with yellow rays and disc; the involucre is conical. Sandy and stony slopes from Namibia to the Eastern Cape.

### **2** *Senecio rosmarinifolius*

J F M A M J J A S O N D

**Gryshongerblom** Softly woody, sparsely white-woolly shrublet to 80 cm with narrow leaves, the margins rolled under, and sometimes sparsely toothed, usually with axillary tufts of smaller leaves; bears dense clusters of radiate flowerheads with yellow rays and disc. Sandy and stony slopes from Namaqualand to the Eastern Cape.

### **3** *Senecio halimifolius* **Tabakbos**

J F M A M J J A S O N D

Sparsely white-cobwebby, greyish shrub to 1.5 m with lance-shaped leaves that are broader and coarsely toothed above; bears dense clusters of radiate flowerheads with yellow rays and disc. Coastal sands in damp places along seeps or lagoons in the southwestern Cape.

### **4** *Senecio rigidus* **Rough ragwort**

J F M A M J J A S O N D

Roughly hairy, densely leafy shrub with coarsely hairy stems to 1.5 m with oblong, irregularly toothed leaves, the margins rolled under, often woolly beneath with raised veins; bears branched clusters of small, radiate flowerheads with yellow rays and disc. Sandstone slopes and gullies in the southwestern and southern Cape.

### **5** *Senecio umbellatus*

J F M A M J J A S O N D

Hairless, wand-like perennial to 80 cm, sometimes sparsely hairy below, either with narrow, thread-like leaves, or these divided into thread-like lobes, with the margins rolled under and minutely toothed; bears loosely branched clusters of radiate flowerheads with magenta to pink or sometimes white rays and a yellow disc. Moist sandstone flats and slopes in the southwestern and southern Cape. *Senecio paniculatus* has discoid flowerheads.

### **6** *Senecio speciosissimus*

J F M A M J J A S O N D

Robust, densely leafy, sparsely white-woolly perennial to 2 m with lance-shaped leaves, the margins rolled under and slightly toothed; bears loosely branching clusters of radiate flowerheads with mauve or white rays and a yellow disc. Sandstone slopes above 800 m, near water, in the mountains of the extreme southwestern Cape. *Senecio coleophyllus*, from the Riviersonderend Mountains, is a smaller plant with deeply toothed leaves and fewer flowerheads on long stalks.

## *Cineraria* **CINERARIA**

Perennial herbs or subshrubs, sometimes grey-felted. Leaves alternate or sometimes basal, often *rounded and variously lobed and incised, mostly distinctly petiolate, often eared at the base.* Flowerheads in loose clusters, radiate (rarely discoid), *with 1 row of narrow green involucral bracts cohering along the margins, with additional minute bracteoles at the base;* receptacle without scales. Ray florets female, yellow. Disc florets all or mostly fertile, 5-lobed. *Fruits elliptical and flattened with a thickened margin,* smooth or hairy; *pappus of several long, barbed bristles.* Africa and Madagascar: ±50 spp; ±7 fynbos spp.

**1** *Cineraria lobata*

J F M A M J J A S O N D

Sparsely cobwebby to almost hairless, sprawling perennial to 40 cm with deeply lobed and irregularly, sharply toothed leaves that have ear-like lobes at the base of the petioles; bears loose clusters of radiate, yellow flowerheads with 5–7 rays. Damp slopes and gullies from the southwestern to the Eastern Cape and also Limpopo.

**2** *Cineraria geifolia*

J F M A M J J A S O N D

Roughly hairy, sprawling perennial to 40 cm with rounded, scalloped leaves that have ear-like lobes at the base of the petioles; bears loose clusters of radiate, yellow flowerheads with 7–11 rays. Mainly coastal bush in the southwestern Cape.

## *Othonna*  OTHONNA, BOBBEJAANKOOL

Perennial herbs, shrubs or climbers, *more or less succulent and usually hairless* although often woolly in the axils. Leaves alternate or basal, sometimes toothed or lobed, or cylindrical. Flowerheads solitary or several on short or long peduncles, radiate or disciform, with *1 row of smooth bracts joined at the base, without additional small bracteoles*; receptacle without scales. Ray florets when present usually yellow, rarely pink or white, fertile; *fruits ellipsoid, ribbed, smooth or hairy; pappus of many long, fine, barbed bristles, often elongating markedly and banded with brown. Disc florets male*, 5-lobed. Southern Africa: ±120 spp; ±30 fynbos spp. The vernacular name, bobbejaankool, derives from the cabbage-like appearance of the leaves of some species.

### ▶ TUBEROUS PERENNIALS WITH ANNUAL STEMS

**3** *Othonna filicaulis*  **Bobbejaanklimop**

J F M A M J J A S O N D

Straggling, succulent perennial to 70 cm with annual stems from a woolly crown, and leathery, lance-shaped to rounded leaves that are lobed at the base and clasping the stem; bears solitary, disciform, white or yellow flowerheads. Sandy flats and slopes, often coastal, from southern Namibia to the Eastern Cape.

**4** *Othonna bulbosa*

J F M A M J J A S O N D

Tuberous perennial to 30 cm with annual stems from a tuberous root, and leathery leaves, mostly in a basal tuft and woolly in the axils, the lower leaves petiolate and elliptical to lance-shaped and sometimes lobed; bears solitary, radiate, yellow flowerheads on sparsely leafy stems. Sandy slopes and flats in the southwestern Cape, especially conspicuous after fire. *Othonna heterophylla* has leaves that are usually toothed and more or less woolly beneath.

### ▶ SHRUBS OR SHRUBLETS

**5** *Othonna cylindrica*

J F M A M J J A S O N D

Brittle-stemmed, succulent shrub to 1 m with fleshy, spindle-shaped to cylindrical leaves clustered at the branch tips; bears loose clusters of radiate, yellow flowerheads on long peduncles. Sandy and stony flats and rocks from southern Namibia to the West Coast.

**6** *Othonna parviflora*  **Bobbejaankool**

J F M A M J J A S O N D

Robust shrub to 2 m with leathery, lance-shaped leaves that have smooth or finely toothed margins; bears dense, branched clusters of numerous small, radiate, yellow flowerheads. Sandstone slopes in the mountains of the southwestern and southern Cape.

**1** *Othonna quinquedentata*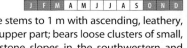

Erect shrub with several slender, wand-like stems to 1 m with ascending, leathery, lance-shaped leaves, often toothed in the upper part; bears loose clusters of small, radiate, yellow flowerheads. Rocky, sandstone slopes in the southwestern and southern Cape, often in damp places.

**2** *Othonna arborescens*

**Bobbejaankool** Brittle-stemmed, succulent shrublet to 60 cm with leathery, lance-shaped, usually lobed or toothed leaves crowded at the branch tips and woolly in the axils; bears mostly solitary, radiate, yellow flowerheads on elongate peduncles. Coastal dunes or rocks along the West Coast.

**3** *Othonna coronopifolia*

Semi-succulent shrub to 1.5 m with lance-shaped, often irregularly toothed leaves, usually in tufts on short branchlets; bears solitary, radiate, yellow flowerheads on long peduncles. Rocky sandstone and granite slopes along the West Coast and adjacent interior.

## *Euryops*  EURYOPS, HARPUISBOS

Shrubs or shrublets. Leaves alternate, sometimes in tufts, *usually lobed or forked, sometimes needle-like*. Flowerheads *apparently axillary, on wiry peduncles*, radiate or discoid, with *1 row of smooth, oval bracts joined at the base, without additional small bracteoles*; receptacle without scales. Ray florets female, yellow. Disc florets fertile, 5-lobed. *Fruits ellipsoid*, smooth to hairy, sometimes ribbed; *pappus of few, short, sinuous, barbed bristles that soon drop*. Southern Africa with 1 species extending to Arabia: 97 spp; ±30 fynbos spp. The resin was used by early farmers as a substitute for mastic or gum.

▸ **FLOWERHEADS MORE THAN 40 MM IN DIAMETER; DISC FLORETS CONICAL, WIDENING GRADUALLY FROM THE BASE**

**4** *Euryops pectinatus* **Wolharpuisbos**

Densely grey-felted shrub to over 1.5 m with leaves 40–100 mm long, toothed or divided into narrow lobes; bears large, solitary, radiate, yellow flowerheads on stout peduncles in the upper leaf axils; the involucre is cup-shaped and the disc florets are conical. Rocky, sandstone slopes in the southwestern Cape.

**5** *Euryops speciosissimus*

**Pronkharpuisbos** Slender shrub to over 2 m with leaves 60–200 mm long, divided into flexible, thread-like lobes; bears solitary, large, radiate, yellow flowerheads ±70 mm in diameter, on stout peduncles; the involucre is cup-shaped and the disc florets are conical. Rocky, sandstone slopes in the interior mountains along the West Coast. *Euryops wagneri*, from the northern Cedarberg mountains, has grey leaves, and deep yellow to orange flowerheads with broader rays, borne on longer peduncles more than twice the length of the leaves.

**6** *Euryops brevilobus*

Like *Euryops speciosissimus* but rarely over 1 m and with stiff leaves that have short lobes. Sandstone slopes in the Cedarberg and Koue Bokkeveld mountains. *E. serra*, from the mountains above Tulbagh, has very shortly lobed, almost toothed, leaves.

▶ **FLOWERHEADS USUALLY LESS THAN 40 MM IN DIAMETER; DISC FLORETS FUNNEL-SHAPED, WIDENING ABRUPTLY FROM A SLENDER BASE**

**①** *Euryops abrotanifolius*

| J | F | M | A | M | J | J | A | S | O | N | D |

**Bergharpuisbos** Densely leafy shrub to 1 m with leaves 60–90 mm long, divided into thread-like or needle-like lobes; bears solitary, radiate, yellow flowerheads that are woolly at the base; the fruits are hairless and closely ribbed, with a fleshy appendage. Sandstone slopes in the southwestern and southern Cape.

**②** *Euryops multifidus*

| J | F | M | A | M | J | J | A | S | O | N | D |

Shrub with stiffly erect branches to 1.5 m with leathery leaves 6–35 mm long, crowded on short-shoots and mostly 3-forked into cylindrical lobes, the lateral ones further toothed or lobed; bears solitary, radiate, yellow flowerheads on short peduncles in the leaf axils; the fruits are conspicuously woolly. Rocky slopes, often on rock outcrops, from Namaqualand to the southwestern Cape.

**③** *Euryops virgineus*  **Rivierharpuisbos**

| J | F | M | A | M | J | J | A | S | O | N | D |

Densely leafy shrub with stiffly erect stems to 3 m and small, narrowly lobed or toothed oval leaves 5–12 mm long; bears small, solitary, radiate, yellow flowerheads on short, wiry peduncles in the upper leaf axils. Damp sandstone slopes in the southern and Eastern Cape.

**④** *Euryops tenuissimus*

| J | F | M | A | M | J | J | A | S | O | N | D |

**Resin bush, grootharpuisbos**  Shrub to 2.5 m, often mealy on the young parts, with needle-like, or sometimes 3-lobed, leaves 15–150 mm long; bears solitary, radiate, yellow or orange flowerheads on short, wiry peduncles clustered among the leaves; the fruits are hairy, becoming mucilaginous when wet. Stony, karroid slopes from Namaqualand to the southern Cape. *Euryops linifolius*, from the West Coast, has hairless fruits.

**⑤** *Euryops rehmannii*

| J | F | M | A | M | J | J | A | S | O | N | D |

Shrub to 1.5 m, often resinous, with needle-like, or rarely 3-lobed, leaves (5)10–50 mm long; bears solitary, radiate, yellow flowerheads on wiry peduncles, usually well above the leaves, with the involucral bracts joined well above the middle into a deeply cup-shaped involucre; the fruits are short-haired, becoming mucilaginous when wet . Karroid scrub or arid fynbos in the interior mountains of the southwestern and southern Cape.

**⑥** *Euryops thunbergii*

| J | F | M | A | M | J | J | A | S | O | N | D |

Shrub to 1.2 m, densely cobwebby on the young parts, with spreading, needle-like leaves 10–50 mm long that have a thin line of wool along the midline below; bears solitary, radiate, yellow flowerheads on wiry peduncles, together forming loose clusters; the fruits are hairy, becoming mucilaginous when wet. Sandy flats and lower slopes in the southwestern Cape.

## *Gymnodiscus*   YELLOWWEED, GEELKRUID

*Hairless annual herb. Leaves in a basal rosette, leathery or succulent*, elliptical or wedge-shaped and usually lobed or spindle-shaped. *Flowerheads small, in loose clusters on long, slender, almost leafless stems*, radiate, with *1 row of smooth, oval bracts joined at the base, without additional small bracteoles*; receptacle without scales. Ray florets female, yellow; *fruits ovoid, papillate or almost smooth; pappus of many, short, sinuous, barbed bristles that soon drop (rarely absent).* Disc florets *male*, 5-lobed; pappus absent. Winter-rainfall South Africa: 2 spp; 1 fynbos sp.

**1** *Gymnodiscus capillaris*

| J | F | M | A | M | J | J | A | S | O | N | D |

Tufted, succulent annual herb to 20 cm with a rosette of lance- to lyre-shaped leaves, usually lobed below; bears clusters of small, shortly radiate, yellow flowerheads on branched scapes. Sandy flats and lower slopes from Namaqualand to the southern Cape.

▶ FLOWERHEADS RADIATE WITH THE DISC FLORETS MOSTLY MALE AND THE RAYS YELLOW, ORANGE OR WHITE; INVOLUCRAL BRACTS IN 1–4 SERIES, NARROW AND MOSTLY GREEN THROUGHOUT; FRUITS LARGE (MOSTLY >5 MM LONG), WITHOUT A PAPPUS

## *Osteospermum*   BONESEED, BIETOU

Annual or perennial herbs or shrubs, sometimes thorny or glandular. Leaves usually alternate, mostly coarsely toothed or lobed. Flowerheads usually solitary on short peduncles, radiate, *with 2–4 rows of narrow or lance-shaped bracts*; receptacle without scales. Ray florets female, *bright yellow*, sometimes with a dark base; *fruits variously shaped, more or less club-shaped to 3-angled or -winged, smooth, ribbed or warty, rarely fleshy, without a pappus.* Disc florets male, 5-lobed. Mainly Africa but extending to the Middle East: ±80 spp; ±35 fynbos spp. Some species produce prussic or hydrocyanic acid and are implicated in stock poisonings; selections of *Osteospermum ecklonis* from the southern Cape are widely cultivated as the garden osteospermum. The vernacular name, bietou, is one of the very few Khoi names still in use, surviving also in another spelling as the Biedouw Mountains. DNA studies show that the species previously placed in the separate genera *Chrysanthemoides, Gibbaria* and *Tripteris* are all most closely related to various species of *Osteospermum* and are thus appropriately included within it.

▶ FRUITS FLESHY AND EGG-SHAPED, GLOSSY BLACK WHEN RIPE

**2** *Osteospermum incanum*

| J | F | M | A | M | J | J | A | S | O | N | D |

(=*Chrysanthemoides incana*) **Grysbietou**   Sprawling, white-woolly, sparsely thorny shrublet to 80 cm with oval to elliptical, coarsely toothed leaves; bears small clusters of radiate flowerheads, with yellow rays and disc; the involucral bracts are densely woolly; the fruits are fleshy and glossy black when ripe, 6–8 mm long. Coastal dunes or sandy, inland slopes from Namibia to the southwestern Cape.

**3** *Osteospermum moniliferum*

| J | F | M | A | M | J | J | A | S | O | N | D |

(=*Chrysanthemoides monilifera*) **Tickberry, bosluisbessie**   Rounded shrub to over 1.5 m, sparsely woolly on the young parts, with oval to elliptical, toothed leaves; bears small clusters of radiate flowerheads, with yellow rays and disc; the involucral bracts are hairless or sparsely woolly; the fruits are fleshy and glossy black when ripe, 6–8 mm long. Sandstone and limestone slopes and flats from Namaqualand to tropical Africa.

## ▶ FRUITS PAPERY, LARGE AND CONSPICUOUSLY 3-WINGED WITH AN APICAL AIR CHAMBER

**❶ *Osteospermum scariosum***  `J F M A M J J A S O N D`
(=*Tripteris aghillana*) **Skaapbos** Roughly hairy or bristly perennial to 30 cm, with a woody base, and mostly basal, lance-shaped, often sharply toothed leaves; bears radiate flowerheads on elongate peduncles, with yellow or cream rays, sometimes with a dark base, and a dark disc; the fruits are 3-winged, 9–12 mm long. Rocky slopes and hills from the southwestern Cape to Mpumalanga.

**❷ *Osteospermum dentatum***  `J F M A M J J A S O N D`
(=*Tripteris dentata*) Sprawling, roughly hairy perennial to 60 cm with the lowermost leaves opposite, lance-shaped and toothed to lobed; bears branched clusters of radiate flowerheads, with yellow rays and disc; the fruits are 3-winged, 9–12 mm long. Sandstone slopes and flats along the West Coast.

**❸ *Osteospermum clandestinum***  `J F M A M J J A S O N D`
(=*Tripteris clandestina*) **Trekkertjie** Aromatic, annual herb to 40 cm, covered with gland-tipped hairs, and with lance-shaped, toothed to lobed leaves; bears branched clusters of radiate flowerheads, with pale yellow rays, often brownish at the base, and a dark purplish disc; the fruits are 3-winged, 8–9 mm long. Sandy and rocky flats from southern Namibia to the southwestern Cape.

## ▶ FRUITS HARD, SMOOTH, ANGLED OR SHORTLY WINGED BUT WITHOUT AN APICAL AIR CHAMBER

**❹ *Osteospermum ciliatum***  `J F M A M J J A S O N D`
Sprawling or straggling, sparsely cobwebby shrublet to 50 cm with elliptical leaves, the margins scalloped and slightly rolled under; bears few, small, radiate flowerheads, with yellow rays and disc, at the branch tips; the fruits are smooth and cylindrical, ±6 mm long. Damp places on mountain slopes in the extreme southwestern Cape.

**❺ *Osteospermum spinosum***  `J F M A M J J A S O N D`
Aromatic, intricately branched, thorny shrublet to 1.2 m, covered with gland-tipped hairs, and with narrow, lobed leaves; bears solitary, radiate flowerheads at the branch tips, with pale yellow rays and disc; the fruits are smooth and sometimes angled, ±8 mm long. Gravelly slopes and flats in the southwestern Cape.

**❻ *Osteospermum polygaloides***  `J F M A M J J A S O N D`
Densely leafy, almost hairless shrub to 2 m, often with stiffly erect branches, and leathery, oblong to oval leaves curved back at the tips; bears solitary, radiate flowerheads on short, roughly hairy peduncles, with yellow rays and disc; the fruits are ribbed and pitted, 5–7 mm long. Rocky, mostly sandstone slopes from the southwestern Cape to KwaZulu-Natal.

**❼ *Osteospermum junceum***  `J F M A M J J A S O N D`
Softly woody, single-stemmed shrub with willowy branches to 3 m, white-woolly when young, and with lance-shaped, toothed leaves that decrease in size up the stem; bears loose clusters of radiate flowerheads on woolly peduncles, with yellow rays and disc, the fruits are smooth and slightly lobed, 5–7 mm long. Sandstone slopes in the southwestern and Eastern Cape.

### 1 *Osteospermum grandiflorum*

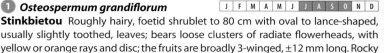

**Stinkbietou** Roughly hairy, foetid shrublet to 80 cm with oval to lance-shaped, usually slightly toothed, leaves; bears loose clusters of radiate flowerheads, with yellow or orange rays and disc; the fruits are broadly 3-winged, ±12 mm long. Rocky slopes in Namaqualand and on the West Coast.

### 2 *Osteospermum ilicifolium*

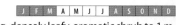

(=*Gibbaria ilicifolia*) Roughly hairy, sprawling, densely leafy, aromatic shrub to 1 m, sometimes sparsely woolly on the young parts, with oval to lance-shaped leaves, the margins rolled under and usually sharply toothed; bears solitary, radiate flowerheads at the branch tips, with yellow rays and disc; the fruits are kidney-shaped, warty and pitted with a small cavity on one side, 4–5 mm long. Sandstone or limestone slopes in the southwestern Cape.

## *Dimorphotheca*  MARGUERITE, MAGRIET

Annual or perennial herbs or shrubs. Leaves alternate, usually coarsely toothed. *Flowerheads large*, radiate, *with 1 or 2 rows of narrow bracts*, sometimes with membranous margins; receptacle without scales. Ray florets female or sterile, *2 or 3 times as long as the involucral bracts, lilac, white, cream or orange, with darker underside*, sometimes with dark base; *fruits 3-angled, often with various protuberances, without a pappus*. Disc florets sterile or fertile, 5-lobed; *fruits* (when present) *flattened, disc-like, with thickened margin, without a pappus*. Southern Africa: 13 spp; 10 fynbos spp.

### 3 *Dimorphotheca pluvialis*

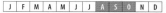

**Reënblommetjie** Erect to sprawling, annual herb to 30 cm, covered with gland-tipped hairs, with lance-shaped, lobed to toothed leaves; bears solitary, radiate flowerheads at the branch tips, with white rays, purple at the base and darker on the reverse, and a purple disc; the involucre is shallowly cup-shaped; the ray fruits are slender and warty and the disc fruits are flattened. Sandy and clay flats and slopes from southern Namibia to the southern Cape. *Dimorphotheca sinuata*, from Namaqualand and the northern parts of the West Coast, has beige to orange rays and a deeply cup-shaped involucre.

### 4 *Dimorphotheca chrysanthemifolia*

**Magriet** Perennial to 1 m, sparsely covered with gland-tipped hairs, with lance-shaped, toothed to lobed leaves; bears 1 to few radiate flowerheads at the branch tips, with yellow or orange rays and disc; the ray fruits are 3-angled and the disc fruits are flattened. Rocky sandstone slopes in the interior southwestern Cape.

### 5 *Dimorphotheca nudicaulis*

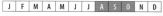

**Witmagriet** Perennial covered with gland-tipped hairs, with annual stems to 30 cm from a woody base, and basal tufts of narrowly lance-shaped, usually toothed, leaves with fringed margins; bears solitary, radiate flowerheads on sparsely leafy peduncles, with white rays, purple to copper on the reverse, and a purple disc; the ray fruits are vestigial and the disc fruits are flattened. Sandstone slopes in the southwestern and southern Cape. *Dimorphotheca tragus*, from Namaqualand and the northern West Coast, has orange or yellow rays.

**1** *Dimorphotheca fruticosa*

J F M A M **J J A S** O N D

(=*Osteospermum fruticosum*) **Rankbietou** Shortly hairy, sprawling to prostrate perennial, with fleshy, petiolate, oval, minutely toothed leaves; bears solitary, radiate flowerheads on naked peduncles, with white or mauve rays and a purple disc; the ray fruits are smooth and 3-angled, ±6 mm long. Coastal dunes and rocks from the West Coast to KwaZulu-Natal.

▶ ANNUALS, OFTEN WITH FINELY DIVIDED LEAVES; FLOWERHEADS DISCOID OR WITH SMALL OR A FEW WHITE OR YELLOW RAYS; DISC FLORETS 4-LOBED; RECEPTACLE OFTEN CONICAL; PAPPUS OF SCALES OR LACKING

## *Oncosiphon* STINKWEED, STINKKRUID

*Annual herbs, usually foetid or aromatic.* Leaves alternate, finely once- or twice-divided. Flowerheads solitary or in clusters on peduncles, radiate or discoid, with several rows of bracts with narrow membranous margins; receptacle without scales. Ray florets absent or female and then white. Disc florets fertile, *4-lobed, with a swollen and brittle tube,* yellow. Fruits flask-shaped and 4-ribbed with *glands between the ribs; pappus of small, irregular teeth.* Southern Africa, mainly winter-rainfall region: 6 spp; 5 fynbos spp. Traditionally used as an antispasmodic for stomach ailments.

**2** *Oncosiphon suffruticosum*

J F M A M J J A **S O N D**

**Stinkkruid, wurmbossie** Aromatic annual herb to 50 cm, much-branched above, with finely twice- to thrice-divided leaves; bears numerous discoid, yellow flowerheads 5–8 mm in diameter, in flat-topped clusters. Sandy flats and slopes, often coastal in waste ground, from southern Namibia to the West Coast.

**3** *Oncosiphon grandiflorum*

J F M A M J J **A S O N** D

**Grootstinkkruid** Aromatic annual herb to 45 cm with finely twice-divided leaves; bears solitary or few discoid, yellow flowerheads 8–10 mm in diameter, with sparsely woolly bracts. Sandy and stony flats and lower slopes from southern Namibia to the West Coast. *Oncosiphon intermedium*, from the northern Cedarberg, has long, pointed petals, giving the flowerheads a 'fluffy' look; *O. piluliferum*, from the drier southwest interior, has smaller flowerheads with hairless involucral bracts.

**4** *Oncosiphon africanum*

J F M A M J J A **S O** N D

**Wild chamomile** Erect to spreading annual herb to 30 cm with once- or twice-divided leaves; bears solitary, radiate flowerheads 10–15 mm in diameter, on stout peduncles, the rays white and the disc yellow. Found on the margins of seasonally waterlogged, often saline pans along the West Coast.

437

## Foveolina   WILD CHAMOMILE, WILDEKAMILLE

Silky, *annual herbs*. Leaves alternate, twice-divided. Flowerheads *solitary on long peduncles*, discoid, disciform or radiate, with 3–5 rows of blunt bracts with membranous margins; receptacle flat to conical, without scales. Outer florets female, tubular or rayed and then white. Disc florets fertile, 4- or 5-lobed, yellow. *Fruits small, 3-ribbed on one side and glandular; pappus crown- or ear-like*. Western South Africa in arid areas: 5 spp; 2 fynbos spp.

 **❶ *Foveolina tenella*  Lazy daisy**   J F M A M J J A S O N D

Sprawling, sparsely hairy, aromatic, annual herb to 25 cm with finely twice-divided leaves; bears solitary, radiate flowerheads 15–20 mm in diameter, on slender, naked peduncles, the rays white and the disc yellow. Sandy slopes and flats, mostly coastal, from Namaqualand and the West Coast. *Foveolina albidiformis*, from the drier interior, has disciform flowerheads.

## Cotula   BUTTONS, KNOPPIES

*Annual or creeping perennial herbs*. Leaves usually alternate, sometimes basal, *slender to finely twice-divided*. Flowerheads *solitary on slender or wiry peduncles* that are *sometimes inflated beneath the head*, usually disciform, rarely with small or large rays, *with 2 rows of bracts, sometimes almost round, with narrow membranous margins*; receptacle flat to conical, without scales. Outer or ray florets female, *mostly shortly stalked*, white or yellow. Disc florets fertile, *4-lobed, sometimes flattened or winged*, yellow. *Fruits usually stalked, flattened and elliptical*, usually papillate; *pappus lacking*. Southern hemisphere, mainly southern Africa: ±50 spp; ±20 fynbos spp.

▶ **FLOWERHEADS RADIATE; PEDUNCLES LEAFLESS, SWELLING AT THE TOP IN FRUIT**

 **❷ *Cotula macroglossa***   J F M A M J J A S O N D

Softly hairy annual herb to 10 cm with finely twice-divided leaves; bears conspicuously radiate flowerheads on slender, sometimes naked peduncles, with pale bluish or white rays, purple beneath, and a yellow disc; the involucral bracts are silky. Stony slopes in the interior mountains of the southwestern Cape.

 **❸ *Cotula turbinata*  Ganskos**   J F M A M J J A S O N D

Softly hairy, annual herb, 5–30 cm, with finely twice- or thrice-divided leaves; bears inconspicuously radiate flowerheads 8–12 mm in diameter, on wiry, leafless peduncles that become swollen at the top in fruit, with white or yellow rays and a yellow disc; the involucral bracts are broad and 3-veined. Sandy or disturbed places in the southwestern Cape, often in waste ground.

 **❹ *Cotula duckittiae***   J F M A M J J A S O N D

Like *Cotula turbinata* but more robust, up to 40 cm, with larger, conspicuous, bright orange flowerheads 15–20 mm in diameter. Sandy coastal slopes south of Yzerfontein.

▶ **FLOWERHEADS DISCOID; PEDUNCLES LEAFY, NOT SWELLING IN FRUIT**

 **❺ *Cotula bipinnata***   J F M A M J J A S O N D

Annual herb to 30 cm with finely twice- or thrice-divided leaves that are sheathing at the base; bears discoid, yellow or white flowerheads 8–10 mm in diameter, on slender, leafy peduncles. Near seasonal pools in Namaqualand and the southwestern Cape.

**1** *Cotula coronopifolia*

**Gansgras, eendekos** Erect or sprawling, annual herb to 30 cm with irregularly toothed to twice-divided leaves, sheathing at the base; bears discoid, bright yellow flowerheads 8–10 mm in diameter, on slender, minutely leafy peduncles. Seasonal seeps or in ephemeral pools from Namaqualand to Mpumalanga. *Cotula filifolia* has simple, thread-like leaves.

▶ **FLOWERHEADS RADIATE WITH YELLOW RAYS BUT OTHERWISE NOT AS ANY OF THE ABOVE**

## *Capelio*  MOUNTAIN DAISY

Woolly or felted perennial herbs or shrublets. Leaves alternate, elliptical and sometimes toothed, densely felted beneath and more or less woolly above. *Flowerheads large, 1 to few on long peduncles, with 2 rows of leathery involucral bracts*; receptacle without scales. Ray florets female, yellow. Disc florets fertile, 5-lobed. *Fruits oblong and ribbed, hairy; pappus of many barbed bristles.* Southwestern Cape: 3 spp, all fynbos. Previously known as the genus *Alciope*; often flowering only after fire.

**2** *Capelio tabularis*

(=*Alciope tabularis*) Grey-felted shrublet to 50 cm from a woody base with oval, petiolate leaves that are densely felted beneath, their margins sparsely toothed and rolled under; bears 1 to few, radiate, yellow flowerheads 30–40 mm in diameter, in loose clusters; the inner involucral bracts are hairless. Sandstone slopes in the extreme southwestern Cape, flowering mainly after fire. *Capelio tomentosa* (=*Alciope lanata*), from the interior mountains along the West Coast, has densely woolly inner involucral bracts.

## *Heterolepis*  ROCK DAISY

Shrublets with cobwebby branchlets. *Leaves alternate, stiff and narrow or needle-like, with the margins rolled under*, sometimes sparsely toothed, *sharply pointed and densely woolly beneath.* Flowerheads solitary on long or short, glandular peduncles, *large, radiate*, with 1–3 rows of green bracts with membranous margins, the inner bracts almost entirely membranous; receptacle honeycombed, without scales. Ray florets female, *with a thread-like lobe opposite the ray*, yellow. Disc florets fertile, deeply 5-lobed. *Fruits flask-shaped, densely silky; pappus of 2 unequal rows of stout, tawny, barbed, bristle-like scales.* Southwestern and southern South Africa: 4 spp; 3 fynbos spp.

**3** *Heterolepis aliena*

Sprawling, closely leafy shrublet to 30 cm with a woody rootstock and cobwebby branches, with needle-like leaves (10)15–30 mm long, the margins rolled under and sparsely toothed, densely woolly beneath; bears solitary, radiate, yellow flowerheads 40–50 mm in diameter, on short, roughly hairy peduncles to 50 mm long at the branch tips. Rocky, sandstone slopes and outcrops in the mountains of the southwestern Cape. *Heterolepis peduncularis* has the flowerheads on elongate peduncles ±10 cm long.

## *Leysera*  LEYSERA, GEELTEE

Slender shrublets or woody annuals, usually greyish-woolly. Leaves alternate, *needle-like, glandular. Flowerheads solitary on wiry peduncles,* radiate, with 4–7 rows of oblong, firm-textured, glandular involucral bracts; receptacle without scales. Ray florets female, yellow; fruits slender; pappus of narrow scales. Disc florets fertile, 5-lobed; fruits slender; *pappus of feathery bristles surrounded by short scales.* Southern Africa and Mediterranean to Asia: 3 spp; 2 fynbos spp. An infusion of the dried leaves was used as an emollient to treat coughs.

 **1** *Leysera gnaphalodes*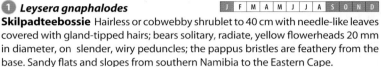

**Skilpadteebossie** Hairless or cobwebby shrublet to 40 cm with needle-like leaves covered with gland-tipped hairs; bears solitary, radiate, yellow flowerheads 20 mm in diameter, on slender, wiry peduncles; the pappus bristles are feathery from the base. Sandy flats and slopes from southern Namibia to the Eastern Cape.

 **2** *Leysera tenella*  **Vaalteebossie**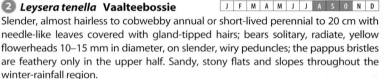

Slender, almost hairless to cobwebby annual or short-lived perennial to 20 cm with needle-like leaves covered with gland-tipped hairs; bears solitary, radiate, yellow flowerheads 10–15 mm in diameter, on slender, wiry peduncles; the pappus bristles are feathery only in the upper half. Sandy, stony flats and slopes throughout the winter-rainfall region.

## *Relhania*  RELHANIA, PERDEKAROO

Shrubs or shrublets, rarely annuals. Leaves alternate or rarely opposite, needle-like to rounded, *glandular, or sometimes woolly beneath. Flowerheads mostly solitary and sessile,* radiate, with ±5 rows of involucral bracts, sometimes with dry tips; *receptacle with narrow or broader scales.* Ray florets female, *yellow, often reddish or coppery beneath; fruits slender, hairless; pappus cup- or crown-like or of scales.* Disc florets fertile or sterile, 5-lobed. Southern Africa, mainly southwestern Cape: 13 spp; ±10 fynbos spp. Originally a Khoi name for the arid interior, the word *karoo* is also applied to many fodder plants, chiefly kinds of daisies, of that region.

 **3** *Relhania fruticosa*

Densely leafy shrublet to 50 cm with needle-like leaves that are densely white-woolly above, the margins rolled in and the tips curved back; bears solitary, radiate, yellow flowerheads 10 mm in diameter, at the branch tips. Clay or sandy flats in fynbos in the southwestern Cape.

## *Oedera*  OEDERA, PERDEKAROO

More or less stiffly erect, somewhat heath-like shrublets. *Leaves opposite or spirally overlapping,* narrow to broad, *hairless. Flowerheads sessile in clusters within a common cup of bracts, sometimes appearing simple,* radiate, with 3 or 4 rows of involucral bracts; *receptacle with scales, which are sometimes toothed.* Ray florets female, yellow. Disc florets fertile, 5-lobed. *Fruits slender, hairless; pappus crown-like or of short scales.* South Africa, mainly winter-rainfall region: 18 spp; ±12 fynbos spp.

 **4** *Oedera squarrosa*

Twiggy shrub to 1 m with the young leaves in 4 ranks, broadly oval and curved back with sharp tips and often gummy above; bears dense clusters of a few, radiate, yellow flowerheads 6–8 mm in diameter, at the branch tips. Stony sand or clay slopes and flats in the southwestern and southern Cape.

**① *Oedera uniflora***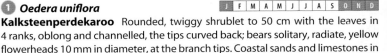
**Kalksteenperdekaroo** Rounded, twiggy shrublet to 50 cm with the leaves in 4 ranks, oblong and channelled, the tips curved back; bears solitary, radiate, yellow flowerheads 10 mm in diameter, at the branch tips. Coastal sands and limestones in the southwestern and southern Cape.

**② *Oedera capensis***
Densely leafy, sprawling shrublet to 30 cm with the leaves spreading or curved back, narrowly lance-shaped, the margins covered with rough, gland-tipped hairs, sometimes silky; bears several radiate, yellow or orange heads crowded together to form a single large, false head 20–25 mm in diameter (individual heads can be discerned within the 'disc'). Dry, stony flats and slopes in the southwestern Cape. *Oedera hirta* has the leaves covered with gland-tipped hairs beneath and often twisted; *O. imbricata* has broader, lance-shaped to oval leaves.

▶ FLOWERHEADS DISCOID OR RADIATE WITH WHITE, PINK OR BLUE TO PURPLE RAYS, WHICH CURL BACK AT NIGHT, BUT OTHERWISE NOT AS ANY OF THE ABOVE

## *Pteronia*  GUMBUSH, GOMBOS

Shrublets or shrubs, *often gummy*, rarely spiny. Leaves *mostly opposite*, sometimes alternate or in tufts, smooth, warty or woolly, *never toothed, but the margins sometimes fringed*. Flowerheads solitary or in clusters, *discoid*, with 4–10 rows of bracts; receptacle without scales, sometimes fringed. Florets usually yellow, rarely purple or greenish, 5-lobed. Fruits top-shaped or ovoid, smooth or hairy; *pappus of 2 rows of stout, tawny or purplish, barbed or feathery bristles*, often joined at the base; often flowering from late summer to winter. Mainly arid parts of southern Africa: ±80 spp; ±20 fynbos spp.

**③ *Pteronia uncinata* Strandgombos**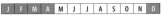
Erect shrublet to 90 cm with spreading, hairless, almost needle-like leaves that are keeled beneath and hooked at the tips; bears loose clusters of narrowly cylindrical, discoid, yellow flowerheads 10×3 mm; the involucral bracts are hairless. Coastal sands in the southwestern Cape.

**④ *Pteronia camphorata* Sandgombos**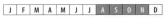
Slender, aromatic shrub to 1 m with more or less thread-like leaves, shortly fringed along the margins; bears 1 to few shortly cylindrical, discoid, yellow flowerheads 15×15 mm; the involucral bracts are shortly and densely fringed. Coastal to upper slopes from Namaqualand to the southern Cape.

**⑤ *Pteronia divaricata* Geelgombos**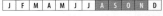
Rounded, leafy shrub to 2 m with broadly oval, rough-textured leaves; bears dense clusters of cylindrical, discoid, yellow to whitish flowerheads 15 mm long; the involucral bracts are oval or lance-shaped and hairless. Sandy and stony slopes and flats from southern Namibia to the southwestern Cape.

445

**1** *Pteronia incana*  **Asbossie**

| J | F | M | A | M | J | J | A | S | O | N | D |

Widely branched, grey-leafed shrublet to 1 m with small, oblong and channelled, white-woolly leaves; bears solitary, cylindrical, discoid, yellow flowerheads 15×10 mm at the branch tips; the involucral bracts are hairless. Stony slopes on sand or clay throughout the southwestern and Eastern Cape. *Pteronia ovalifolia* has larger flowerheads 20–30 mm long, with the involucral bracts partially grey-felted.

## *Athanasia*  ATHANASIA, KOUTERBOS

Shrubs, smooth or more *often with mealy hairs*. Leaves alternate, *leathery*, narrow or lance-shaped, often toothed or lobed. Flowerheads usually *in dense, flat-topped clusters, discoid*, with 3–5 rows of chaffy bracts; *receptacle usually with scales*. Florets 5-lobed, usually with stalked glands on the tube, yellow. Fruit *cylindrical or flask-shaped*, 5–12-ribbed, smooth or rarely glandular, sometimes *topped with a ring of stalked glands; pappus lacking*. Southern Africa: 40 spp; 36 fynbos spp. The vernacular name, kouterbos, derives from the propensity for plants of *Athanasia trifurcata* to pack up against the colter (*kouter*) of the plough.

**2** *Athanasia dentata*

| J | F | M | A | M | J | J | A | S | O | N | D |

Densely leafy shrublet to 1.5 m with hairless, broadly oval or almost round, toothed, bright green leaves that curve backwards; bears branched clusters of narrowly cylindrical, discoid, yellow flowerheads, each containing 7–15 florets. Sandy coastal slopes in the southwestern and southern Cape.

**3** *Athanasia trifurcata*  **Klaaslouwbos**

| J | F | M | A | M | J | J | A | S | O | N | D |

Shrublet to 1.5 m with more or less erect, hairless to scurfy, wedge-shaped grey leaves 3–5-toothed at the tips; bears unbranched clusters of broadly cylindrical, discoid, yellow flowerheads, each containing 50–100 florets. Flats and rocky slopes from Namaqualand to the Eastern Cape, in disturbed ground, along roadsides and especially in overused lands.

**4** *Athanasia crithmifolia*

| J | F | M | A | M | J | J | A | S | O | N | D |

Shrub to 2 m with the leaves deeply divided into thread-like lobes; bears branched or unbranched clusters of shortly cylindrical, discoid, yellow flowerheads, each containing 30–65 florets. Sandy flats and slopes, often along drainage lines, in the southwestern Cape.

## *Hymenolepis*  FALSE KAROO, BASTERKAROO

Shrubs, smooth or more *often with mealy hairs*. Leaves alternate, *leathery*, narrow or lance-shaped, sometimes lobed. Flowerheads *small and narrow, 6–10-flowered, in dense, flat-topped clusters, discoid*, with 3–5 rows of chaffy bracts; *receptacle usually with scales*. Florets 5-lobed, usually with stalked glands on the tube, yellow. Fruit *cylindrical or flask-shaped*, 5–10-ribbed, smooth; *pappus of fringed scales*. South Africa, mainly southwestern Cape: 7 spp; ±5 fynbos spp.

**5** *Hymenolepis crithmoides*

| J | F | M | A | M | J | J | A | S | O | N | D |

(=*Hymenolepis parviflora*) Shrub to 3 m, densely leafy at the branch tips, with large, leathery leaves that are finely divided into needle-like segments, the margins rolled under; bears small, discoid yellow flowerheads massed together in densely branched, flat-topped clusters, honey-scented. Rocky sandstone slopes in Namaqualand and the southwestern Cape, often along roadsides.

## *Eriocephalus*  WILD ROSEMARY, KAPOKBOSSIE

Aromatic, mostly grey-silky shrublets. Leaves mostly opposite, *often in tufts, narrow and often scale-like*, or deeply lobed, leathery. Flowerheads small, *in clusters on short, wiry peduncles, with 1 row of 4–6 rounded bracts*, often with membranous margins, disciform or sparsely radiate; receptacle with scales, the outer ones *hard and woolly and enclosing the outer florets and fruits, the entire head shed as a single, woolly unit. Outer florets 2 or 3*, female, either slender or developed into white, pink or purple rays; *fruit elliptical, woolly*; pappus lacking. Disc florets male, 5-lobed. Drier parts of southern Africa: ±34 spp; ±5 fynbos spp. Brandy-based infusions of wild rosemary were used traditionally as a diuretic, but today the plant is an important source of aromatic essential oils for perfumes.

**1** *Eriocephalus racemosus* **Kapokkie**  J F M A M J **J A S** O N D
Erect shrub to 1.5 m with narrow, sometimes tufted, silvery-silky leaves; bears disciform flowerheads in the leaf axils, forming long racemes. Coastal dunes and hills from southern Namaqualand to the southern Cape.

**2** *Eriocephalus africanus* **Kapokbossie**  J F M A M J J A S O N **D**
Twiggy shrub to 1 m with tufts of narrow, sometimes forked, silvery-silky leaves; bears small, flat-topped clusters of conspicuously radiate flowerheads at the branch tips, with blunt, white rays. Mostly clay or granite hillsides from southern Namaqualand to the Eastern Cape.

## *Osmitopsis*  MOUNTAIN DAISY, BELSKRUIE

Shrubs or shrublets, sometimes felted, *aromatic and camphor-scented*. Leaves usually alternate, narrow and sometimes toothed, sometimes felted. *Flowerheads solitary or few on short peduncles, radiate*, with 2–4 rows of green bracts; *receptacle with long, narrow scales*. Ray florets female or sterile, *white*. Disc florets fertile, 5-lobed, yellow. Fruit ovoid and somewhat 3- or 4-angled, smooth; *pappus crown- or collar-like or of short or slender scales*, often with the *stubby base of the style in the centre*. Southwestern Cape, often damp sandstone slopes: 9 spp, all fynbos. A brandy tincture (*belsbrandewyn*) of the leaves is a traditional remedy for chest and stomach complaints and was also used as a tonic and antiseptic.

**3** *Osmitopsis dentata* **Kaapsebelskruie**  J F **M A M J J A S** O **N D**
Perennial with erect stems to 50 cm from a woody rootstock, and lance-shaped, sharply toothed leaves 5–45 mm long, the lower ones larger and spreading and the upper ones ascending; bears solitary, radiate flowerheads with white rays and a yellow disc; pappus of ±equal scales. Damp rocky slopes on the Cape Peninsula.

**4** *Osmitopsis asteriscoides* **Belskruie**  J F **M A M J J A S** O N **D**
Sparsely branched, aromatic shrub with erect stems to 2 m that are densely leafy above, having ascending, smooth or felted, lance-shaped leaves 10–60(80) mm long; bears loose clusters of radiate flowerheads with white rays and a yellow disc; pappus lacking. Marshes and seeps on sandstone in the extreme southwestern Cape.

449

## *Chrysocoma* **BITTERBUSH, BITTERBOS**

Shrublets. Leaves alternate, usually *needle-like*. Flowerheads *solitary on slender peduncles*, usually *discoid*, with 4 rows of green bracts with narrow membranous margins; receptacle without scales. Florets 5-lobed, yellow. Fruit *flattened and elliptical with a thickened margin, with 2 small resin sacs at the top*, short-haired; *pappus of many barbed bristles* surrounded by an outer ring of minute scales. Southern Africa: ±20 spp; ±8 fynbos spp. Although palatable to stock animals, the bitter bushes can cause illness if consumed in large quantities. *Chrysocoma ciliata* has been used medicinally.

**1 *Chrysocoma ciliata***

J F M A M J J A S O N D

Slender-stemmed, closely leafy shrublet to 60 cm with ascending, hairless, needle-like leaves 2–14 mm long; bears solitary, discoid, yellow flowerheads. Rocky slopes and flats from Namaqualand to Mpumalanga.

**2 *Chrysocoma coma-aurea***

J F M A M J J A S O N D

Closely leafy shrublet to 50 cm with spreading to recurved, hairless, needle-like leaves 3–20 mm long, often with the tips curved upwards; bears solitary, discoid, yellow flowerheads. Coastal flats and lower slopes in the extreme southwestern Cape.

## *Felicia* **FELICIA, ASTERTJIE**

Annual or perennial herbs or shrublets. Leaves alternate, opposite or basal, narrow or broader, rarely toothed, usually hairy. Flowerheads solitary on peduncles, usually *radiate*, with 2–4 rows of green bracts with narrow membranous margins; receptacle without scales. *Ray florets usually fertile, blue, pink or white*. Disc florets fertile, 5-lobed, yellow or rarely blue. *Fruit flattened and elliptical with a thickened margin*, usually hairy; *pappus of barbed bristles*, sometimes soon dropping, rarely lacking in ray florets. Southern and tropical Africa to Arabia: 85 spp; ±50 fynbos spp.

▸ **PERENNIALS OR SHRUBLETS**

**3 *Felicia fruticosa***

J F M A M J J A S O N D

**Wildeaster, bosastertjie**   Much-branched shrublet to 1 m with tufts of small, fleshy, lance-shaped leaves; bears radiate flowerheads on wiry peduncles, with blue to mauve rays and a yellow disc; the involucral bracts are in 3 or 4 series. Rocky, lower slopes in the extreme southwestern Cape and in Limpopo.

**4 *Felicia filifolia* Draaibossie**

J F M A M J J A S O N D

Much-branched shrublet to 1 m with tufts of fleshy, needle-like leaves; bears radiate flowerheads on wiry peduncles, with blue to mauve rays and a yellow disc; the involucral bracts are in 3 or 4 series. Flats and rocky slopes, widespread through southern Africa.

**5 *Felicia hyssopifolia***

J F M A M J J A S O N D

Slender, sparsely hairy or hairless shrublet to 60 cm with narrow, pointed leaves; bears radiate flowerheads on wiry peduncles, with blue, mauve, pink or white rays and a yellow disc; the involucral bracts are in 3 or 4 series. Sandy flats or lower slopes from Namaqualand to the Eastern Cape and also in Lesotho.

**1** *Felicia echinata* **Bloublommetjie**   J F M A M J J A S O N D

Stiff, densely leafy shrublet to 1 m with white-woolly stems closely covered with overlapping, oval leaves curved back at the ends and with bristly margins; bears radiate flowerheads crowded at the branch tips among the leaves, with mauve or blue rays and a yellow disc; the involucral bracts are in 3 or 4 series. Coastal bush in the southern Cape.

**2** *Felicia amoena*   J F M A M J J A S O N D

Softly hairy biennial or perennial, 10–25 cm, with soft-textured, lance-shaped leaves; bears radiate flowerheads on elongate peduncles, with blue or white rays and a yellow disc; the involucral bracts are in 2 series. Stony slopes from the southwestern to the Eastern Cape.

**3** *Felicia aethiopica* **Bloublommetjie**   J F M A M J J A S O N D

Sparsely hairy, soft shrublet to 1 m with elliptical to oval leaves that are often flexed downwards; bears radiate flowerheads on elongate peduncles, with blue rays and a yellow disc; the involucral bracts are in 2 series, with 3 veins each. Rocky flats and slopes from the southwestern Cape to KwaZulu-Natal. *Felicia amelloides,* from coastal scrub in the southeastern Cape, has spreading, oval leaves that are 3-veined from the base, and the involucral bracts have just 1 vein each.

**4** *Felicia elongata*   J F M A M J J A S O N D

Coarsely hairy, shrubby perennial to 30 cm with lance-shaped leaves mostly clustered at the base, the margins rolled under; bears radiate flowerheads 30–40 mm in diameter, with white to mauve rays boldly marked with maroon at the base and a yellow disc; the involucral bracts are in 2 series. Coastal limestone sands around Saldanha Bay.

▶ **ANNUAL HERBS**

**5** *Felicia australis*   J F M A M J J A S O N D

Sparsely hairy, sprawling annual, 5–25 cm, with narrow, sometimes lightly toothed leaves that are sparsely hairy along the margins; bears radiate flowerheads with blue to mauve rays and a yellow disc; the involucral bracts are in 3 or 4 series. Sand or clay flats from Namaqualand and the interior southwestern Cape.

**6** *Felicia tenella*   J F M A M J J A S O N D

Sparsely hairy annual, 5–25 cm, with narrow leaves that are coarsely bristly on the margins; bears radiate flowerheads with blue, violet or white rays and a yellow disc; the involucral bracts are in 3 or 4 series. Near water or on coastal dunes in the southwestern Cape.

**7** *Felicia bergeriana*   J F M A M J J A S O N D

Slender, hairy annual to 20 cm with oval or lance-shaped leaves; bears radiate flowerheads on elongate peduncles, with blue (sometimes white) rays and a yellow disc, the ray florets sometimes without pappus bristles; the involucral bracts are in 2 series. Rocky lower slopes and flats in the southwestern Cape.

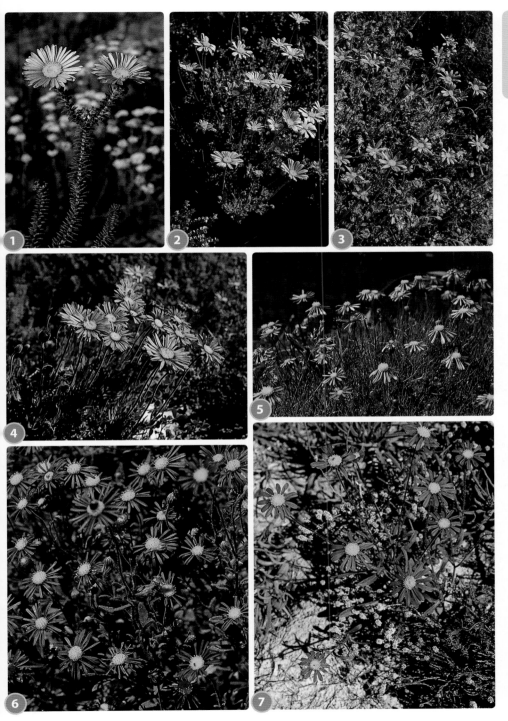

453

**1** *Felicia heterophylla*
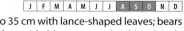
Roughly hairy annual with erect branches to 35 cm with lance-shaped leaves; bears radiate flowerheads on elongate peduncles, with blue rays and a blue (rarely yellow) disc, the ray florets without pappus bristles; the involucral bracts are in 2 series. Sandy flats and slopes in the southwestern Cape.

**2** *Felicia josephinae*
Roughly hairy annual to 15 cm, branching from the base, with lance-shaped leaves; bears radiate flowerheads on elongate peduncles, with cream-coloured rays and a small, purple disc, the ray florets without pappus bristles; the involucral bracts are in 2 series. Sandy lower slopes near Lamberts Bay.

## *Amellus* AMELLUS, GRYSASTERTJIE

Annual or perennial herbs or shrubs, *densely covered with grey hairs*. Leaves alternate, narrowly lance-shaped, sometimes toothed, *both surfaces equally grey-silky*. Flowerheads solitary on peduncles, usually radiate, rarely discoid or disciform, with 2–7 rows of hairy bracts with narrow, membranous margins; *receptacle with narrow scales*. Ray florets female, blue or purple. Disc florets fertile, 5-lobed, yellow or white. *Fruit elliptical and flattened*, hairy on the margins or throughout; *pappus of fringed scales plus a few deciduous, barbed bristles*. Winter-rainfall southern Africa: 12 spp; 5 fynbos spp.

**3** *Amellus asteroides*
Grey-silky shrublet to 40 cm with spoon- or paddle-shaped leaves; bears solitary, radiate or discoid flowerheads with mauve or white rays and a yellow disc. Coastal dunes in the southwestern Cape. *Amellus capensis* has a pappus of scales only.

**4** *Amellus tenuifolius*
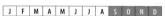
Grey-silky perennial or shrublet with slender, erect stems to 50 cm with narrow leaves; bears loose clusters of radiate flowerheads with mauve rays and a yellow disc. Sandy flats near the coast from southern Namibia to the Cape Peninsula.

## *Zyrphelis* ZYRPHELIS, PLUIMASTERTJIE

Shrublets or tufted perennials *covered with short, rough, spreading hairs and often also glandular hairs*. Leaves alternate or basal, *narrow or spoon-shaped and never toothed*. Flowerheads usually solitary on roughly hairy or glandular peduncles, radiate, with several series of narrow bracts; receptacle without scales. Ray florets fertile, white or blue (rarely yellow); *fruit elliptical and flattened*, short-haired; *pappus of deciduous, feathery bristles*. Disc florets male, 5-lobed, yellow. Southern and tropical Africa, mainly southwestern Cape: 13 spp; 11 fynbos spp.

**5** *Zyrphelis taxifolia*
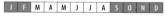
Slender, sprawling, sparsely hairy subshrub to 40 cm with needle-like leaves, minutely toothed on the margins; bears solitary, radiate flowerheads on long peduncles with blue or mauve rays, usually paler at the base, and a yellow disc. Damp sandstone slopes in the extreme southwestern Cape.

## *Polyarrhena* POLYARRHENA, WILDEASTER

Slender, often straggling shrublets. Leaves alternate, narrow to oval and usually minutely toothed, stiff, hairless or roughly hairy. Flowerheads solitary on long or short peduncles, sometimes clustered, *radiate*, with 3 rows of green bracts with narrow membranous margins; receptacle without scales. *Ray florets fertile, white above and pinkish or red beneath.* Disc florets sometimes fertile, 5-lobed, yellow. *Fruit flattened and elliptical with a thickened margin and a horny ring at the top, hairless; pappus of deciduous, barbed bristles.* Southwestern Cape: 4 spp, all fynbos.

### ① *Polyarrhena stricta*

| J | F | M | A | M | J | J | A | S | O | N | D |

Sparsely branched, roughly hairy shrublet to 30 cm with spreading, lance-shaped, roughly hairy leaves; bears several radiate flowerheads clustered at the branch tips, with white rays, purplish beneath, and a yellow disc; the involucral bracts are roughly hairy above but hairless in the lower part. Rocky sandstone slopes in fynbos in the extreme southwestern Cape. *Polyarrhena reflexa* is a straggling shrublet with triangular, recurved, toothed leaves and solitary flowerheads with hairless involucral bracts.

## *Mairia* FIRE DAISY, VUURASTER

Tufted, perennial herbs covered with thin, woolly hairs. *Leaves in a basal tuft, leathery, paddle-shaped, coarsely toothed or scalloped.* Flowerheads solitary on hairy peduncles, large, radiate, with 3–5 rows of green bracts; receptacle without scales. Ray florets female, white, pink or purple. Disc florets fertile, 5-lobed, yellow. Fruits ellipsoid and hairy; *pappus of persistent, feathery bristles,* sometimes surrounded by small, fringed scales. Southwestern Cape on sandstone slopes, flowering only after fire: 5 spp, all fynbos.

### ② *Mairia coriacea*

| J | F | M | A | M | J | J | A | S | O | N | D |

Tufted perennial to 12 cm with a basal rosette of upright, leathery, paddle-shaped leaves that are often broadly toothed at the tips and softly hairy when young, but hairless on both surfaces when mature, and with a conspicuous tuft of silky hairs at the base of the petiole; bears solitary, radiate flowerheads with pink to purple rays and a yellow disc. Rocky sandstone slopes after fire in the extreme southwestern Cape. *Mairia burchellii* has numerous, narrow, strap-shaped leaves and usually more than 1 flowerhead per stem.

### ③ *Mairia crenata*

| J | F | M | A | M | J | J | A | S | O | N | D |

Tufted perennial to 15 cm with a basal rosette of spreading, elliptical to oval, leathery leaves, with finely scalloped margins that are rolled under, softly hairy when young but hairless above when mature; bears solitary, radiate flowerheads with pink to mauve or white rays and a yellow disc. Rocky sandstone slopes and outcrops in the southwestern and southern Cape, flowering mainly after fire.

### ④ *Mairia hirsuta*

| J | F | M | A | M | J | J | A | S | O | N | D |

Short-stemmed perennial to 30 cm with thinly felted, lance-shaped leaves that are more densely hairy beneath, with slightly toothed margins that are rolled under; bears solitary, radiate flowerheads with mauve to pink rays and a yellow disc. Cool mountain slopes in the southwestern Cape, flowering after fire.

457

# DIPSACACEAE Scabious family

## *Scabiosa*  SCABIOUS, JONGMANSKNOOP

Annual or perennial herbs or shrubs, usually variously hairy. Leaves opposite, often in a basal tuft, usually variously lobed or cut. Flowers *clustered in heads* on slender stems, *with each head surrounded by 1 or 2 rows of bracts*, white or lilac, *each flower surrounded at the base by a funnel-shaped epicalyx that is expanded at the top into a membranous, saucer-like collar*; the calyx consists of 5 awns almost as long as the corolla; the corolla is funnel-shaped, hairy within and *more or less 2-lipped*, with the outermost flowers most strongly 2-lipped. Europe and Africa to Asia: ±100 spp; 3 fynbos spp. The leaves and roots have been used medicinally.

**❶ *Scabiosa africana*  Cape scabious**   J F M A M J J A S O N D

Sprawling shrublet to 1 m with large, soft-textured, velvety leaves that are toothed or cut; bears lilac flowers in heads 30–45 mm in diameter. Sheltered sandstone slopes on the Cape Peninsula.

**❷ *Scabiosa columbaria*  Bitterbos**   J F M A M J J A S O N D

Tufted perennial to 80 cm with shortly hairy leaves that are of 2 markedly different types, the lower ones paddle-shaped, toothed or incised, and the upper ones deeply cut to the midrib into slender lobes; bears white to mauve flowers in heads 15–30 mm in diameter. Widespread on rocky slopes through Africa and Eurasia.

**❸ *Scabiosa incisa***   J F M A M J J A S O N D

Straggling perennial to 80 cm with shortly hairy leaves that are deeply once- or twice-lobed; bears mauve flowers in heads 20–50 mm in diameter. Coastal sands, often on limestone, from the southwestern to the Eastern Cape.

# STILBACEAE Stilbe family

## *Retzia*  RETZIA, HEUNINGBLOM

Multi-stemmed shrublet with rod-like branches resprouting from a woody rootstock. Leaves in whorls, *long and narrow, with the margins rolled under, softly hairy when young* but more or less hairless when mature. Flowers *large, in groups of up to 3* among the upper leaves, *reddish orange with black tips*, tubular, 5-lobed and symmetrical, with *the tube 45–55 mm long and softly hairy outside*; stamens 5. Southwestern Cape in mountain fynbos: 1 sp. The flowers are pollinated by Orange-breasted Sunbirds, and the vernacular name alludes to the abundant nectar.

**❹ *Retzia capensis***   J F M A M J J A S O N D

Shrublet to 1 m with rod-like, velvety branches and whorls of 4 long, narrow leaves that are silky when young and 2-grooved beneath; bears axillary clusters of 1–3 silky, tubular, reddish-orange flowers 45–55 mm long, tipped with black. Sandstone slopes in the extreme southwestern Cape.

## Kogelbergia  KOGELBERGIA

Ericoid shrublets, single-stemmed or multi-stemmed. Leaves in whorls, narrow. Flowers small, in short, dense spikes, greyish, funnel-shaped, *5-lobed and symmetrical*, with the tube less than 12 mm long, *hairless outside* but densely fringed with a ring of hairs in the throat and the *petals densely silky on the inner surface*; stamens 4. Southwestern Cape in mountain fynbos: 2 spp, both fynbos.

**1** *Kogelbergia verticillata*

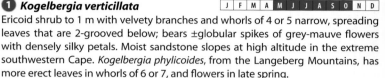

Ericoid shrub to 1 m with velvety branches and whorls of 4 or 5 narrow, spreading leaves that are 2-grooved below; bears ±globular spikes of grey-mauve flowers with densely silky petals. Moist sandstone slopes at high altitude in the extreme southwestern Cape. *Kogelbergia phylicoides*, from the Langeberg Mountains, has more erect leaves in whorls of 6 or 7, and flowers in late spring.

## Stilbe  STILBE

Ericoid shrublets, single-stemmed or multi-stemmed. Leaves in whorls, narrow. Flowers small, in short, dense spikes, white to pink, 5-lobed and *2-lipped*, with 2 erect upper lobes and 3 narrower lower lobes, with the tube less than 12 mm long, *hairless outside* but sometimes fringed with a ring of hairs in the throat; stamens 4. Southwestern Cape in fynbos: 7 spp, all fynbos.

**2** *Stilbe albiflora*

Resprouting shrublet to 1.2 m with velvety branches and whorls of 4–6 narrow, ascending to spreading leaves that are 2-grooved beneath, recurved and pointed at the tips; bears ovoid spikes of white flowers that are hairy in the throat; the calyx is firm-textured and cartilaginous. Sandstone slopes in the southwestern Cape.

**3** *Stilbe ericoides*

Resprouting, multi-stemmed shrublet to 80 cm with velvety branches and whorls of 4 narrow, ascending leaves that are 2-grooved beneath; bears ±globular spikes of pink flowers that are hairy in the throat; the calyx is thin-textured and membranous. Sandy flats or limestone hills along the coast in the southwestern Cape.

**4** *Stilbe overbergensis*

Single-stemmed shrublet to 80 cm with velvety branches and mostly with whorls of 3 narrow, ascending leaves that are 2-grooved beneath; bears ±globular spikes of pink flowers that are hairy in the throat; the calyx is thin-textured and membranous. Lower sandstone and limestone slopes on the Agulhas Plain.

**5** *Stilbe vestita*

Resprouting shrublet to 1.2 m with velvety branches and whorls of 4–6 narrow, ascending or spreading leaves that are 2-grooved beneath, recurved and pointed at the tips; bears ovoid spikes of white flowers that are hairy in the throat, with petals that are more or less silky along the margins; the calyx is firm-textured and cartilaginous. Sandstone slopes in the extreme southwestern Cape.

# LAMIACEAE                                    Mint family

## *Stachys*  WOUNDWORT, TEEBOS

Annual or perennial herbs or shrubs, variously hairy or almost hairless. Leaves narrow to broad, usually toothed. Flowers 2 to several in whorls, with the bracts mostly smaller than the leaves, usually white to purple; the *calyx is ±5-toothed*; the corolla is 2-lipped, usually with a ring of hairs near the base on the inside; the 4 stamens are arched and of 2 lengths. Mainly southern hemisphere subtropical and temperate: ±300 spp; ±3 fynbos spp. The leaves were used medicinally, hence the vernacular names.

**❶ *Stachys aethiopica*  Katbossie**   J F M A M J J A S O N D

Sprawling perennial covered with gland-tipped hairs, to 50 cm, with sparsely hairy, oval, toothed leaves; bears whorls of 2–6 white or pink to mauve flowers with darker spots, 10–15 mm long; the calyx is roughly hairy, the hairs often with glandular tips. Scrub or grassland from the southwestern Cape to Swaziland. *Stachys bolusii*, from coastal rock outcrops in the southwest, has densely hairy leaves.

## *Salvia*  SAGE, SALIE

Annual or perennial herbs or shrubs, variously hairy. Leaves entire, toothed or lobed. Flowers 2 to many in whorls with the bracts usually reduced, usually blue; the *calyx is 2-lipped* with the upper lip mostly 3-toothed and the lower lip larger and 2-toothed; the corolla is 2-lipped, with the upper lip usually longer; the *2 stamens are hinged at the elongated connective,* with the upper section longest and arching beneath the upper hood, and the lower section sterile. Worldwide: ±900 spp; ±10 fynbos spp. Many species are grown ornamentally; *Salvia officinalis*, from the Mediterranean, is the culinary herb, sage.

**❷ *Salvia africana-caerulea***   J F M A M J J A S O N D

**Bloublomsalie**  Grey shrub to 2 m with softly hairy, paddle-shaped, sometimes toothed leaves; bears whorls of mauve to blue or pink flowers with darker spots, 16–28 mm long; the calyx is glandular-silky and enlarges in fruit. Sandy flats and slopes in Namaqualand and the southwestern Cape.

**❸ *Salvia albicaulis***   J F M A M J J A S O N D

Loosely branched shrublet to 60 cm with white-velvety stems and leathery, paddle-shaped, coarsely toothed leaves; bears whorls of purplish flowers in panicles, 18–24 mm long; the calyx is densely silky and enlarges in fruit. Sandstone slopes in the interior mountains along the West Coast.

**❹ *Salvia chamelaeagnea***   J F M A M J J A S O N D

**Afrikaanse salie**  Grey shrub to 2 m with almost hairless, gland-dotted, paddle-shaped, sometimes toothed leaves; bears whorls of mauve to blue or pink flowers with darker spots, 16–28 mm long; the calyx is short-haired and gland-dotted, and enlarges in fruit. Sandy and granite slopes in the southwestern Cape.

**❶** *Salvia lanceolata* **Rooisalie**　J F M A M J J A S O N D

Aromatic, grey shrub to 2 m with paddle-shaped, sometimes toothed, grey-haired leaves; mostly bears pairs of dull rose to grey-blue flowers 25–35 mm long, with the upper lip ±17 mm long; the bracts are deciduous and the calyx is short-haired and gland-dotted, and enlarges in fruit. Mainly coastal, in fynbos on deep, acidic sands and rocky outcrops, in Namaqualand and the southwestern Cape.

**❷** *Salvia africana-lutea*　J F M A M J J A S O N D

**Bruinsalie, strandsalie**　Aromatic, grey shrub to 2 m with paddle-shaped, sometimes toothed, grey-haired leaves; mostly bears pairs of golden-brown flowers 30–50 mm long, with the upper lip ±25 mm long; the calyx is short-haired and gland-dotted, and enlarges in fruit. Coastal scrub on neutral or alkaline sands from Namaqualand to the Eastern Cape.

## *Ballota*　HOREHOUND, KATTEKRUIE

Hairy perennials or shrublets. Leaves often quilted, toothed. Purple flowers in dense whorls with the bracts similar to the leaves; the *calyx is hairy on the inside* as well as on the outside and regularly or irregularly *10- to 20-toothed,* with the teeth spreading and often sharply pointed or awned; the corolla is 2-lipped, with a ring of hairs in the throat; the 4 stamens are arched and of 2 lengths. Mostly Mediterranean and Eurasian, with 1 species in southern Africa: ±33 spp; 1 fynbos sp. Infusions or tinctures of the leaves of *Ballota africana* were used medicinally as a sedative. The vernacular name, kattekruie, is derived from the European catnip, *Nepeta cataria*.

**❸** *Ballota africana*　J F M A M J J A S O N D

Aromatic, soft-textured, greyish shrublet to 1.2 m with softly hairy, heart-shaped leaves with toothed margins; bears dense whorls of pink to purple flowers 10–15 mm long. Rocky or disturbed places in southern Africa.

## *Leonotis*　MINARET FLOWER, WILDEDAGGA

Robust annuals or perennials with strongly 4-angled and -grooved stems. Leaves scalloped or bluntly toothed. Orange flowers in dense whorls with the bracts similar to the leaves; the calyx is 8- to 10-toothed with the teeth usually stiff and sharply pointed, sometimes the upper lobe largest; the corolla is usually orange and 2-lipped, with fringes of hair inside, and the upper lip is 10–30 mm long; the 4 stamens are arched and of 2 lengths. Tropical and southern Africa: ±10 spp; 2 fynbos spp. The conspicuous flowers are adapted to pollination by sunbirds; the dried leaves were used medicinally but are not known to be narcotic, or even tolerable, as a tobacco substitute.

**❹** *Leonotis leonurus*　J F M A M J J A S O N D

Roughly hairy shrub to 2 m with narrowly lance-shaped, toothed leaves; bears whorls of velvety orange flowers 40–50 mm long, with the lower lobes curled back; the calyx is ±equally toothed. Forest margins, rough grassland and roadsides from the southwestern Cape to Gauteng. *Leonotis ocymifolia* has distinctly petiolate, oval, toothed leaves and a 2-lipped calyx.

465

# UTRICULARIACEAE    Bladderwort family

## Utricularia   BLADDERWORT

Small perennial or annual, *insectivorous herbs*, often with branching stolons, sometimes aquatic. Leaves solitary or in clusters, often withered at flowering in the terrestrial species; some *developing into minute, bladderlike traps*. Flowers mostly in racemes, 2-lipped, usually white to lilac or yellow; the *calyx is 2-lipped*, with the lower lip shortly forked; the upper lip of the corolla is small and 2- or 3-lobed, and the lower is much larger and spurred or sac-like at the base. Wordwide but mainly tropical and subtropical: ±180 spp; 1 fynbos sp.

**❶** *Utricularia bisquamata*    J F M A M J J A S O N D

Delicate annual herb to 12 cm with small, narrow leaves at the base; bears thin, wiry racemes of 2-lipped, white to lilac or, rarely, yellowish flowers, with a smooth, yellow palate at the base of the lower lip, varying greatly in size. Boggy, acidic sandstone soils throughout southern Africa.

# OROBANCHACEAE    Broomrape family

## *Alectra*   YELLOW WITCHWEED, VERFBLOMMETJIE

Annual or perennial herbs, hemiparasitic on roots. Leaves opposite or alternate, lance-shaped to oval, usually toothed, sometimes scale-like. Flowers solitary in the axils, usually forming spikes, *yellow to orange with darker veins*; calyx 5-lobed to nearly halfway; *corolla bell-shaped*, slightly oblique, 5-lobed to nearly halfway; *stamens 4, in 2 unequal or nearly equal pairs*, with the anthers 2-celled and cohering in pairs. Asia and Africa: ±40 spp; 3 fynbos spp. The vernacular name, verfblommetjie, refers to the early use of the rootstock as the source of an orange-yellow dye used for colouring fabric.

**❷** *Alectra sessiliflora*    J F M A M J J A S O N D

Hemiparasitic perennial to 25 cm with spreading, lance-shaped leaves that are coarsely toothed below and longer than the flower buds; bears spikes of yellow to orange flowers; the stamens are in 2 very unequal pairs with hairless filaments. Damp flats and lower slopes from the southwestern Cape to tropical Africa.

## *Hyobanche*  SCARLET BROOMRAPE, KATNAELS, WOLWEKOS

Annual or perennial herbs, parasitic on roots. *Leaves reduced to scales and lacking chlorophyll*, usually red. Flowers large, solitary in the axils, forming dense, often head-like, spikes, pink, red or dark maroon; calyx 5-lobed and usually 2-lipped; corolla tubular, 3-*lobed and hooded*; stamens 4 in 2 unequal or nearly equal pairs, with *only 1 anther lobe*. Southern Africa, mainly in the south: 7 spp; 4 fynbos spp. The origin of the vernacular name wolwekos is unknown but may allude to the resemblance of the plants to scraps of fresh carrion.

**❸** *Hyobanche glabrata*    J F M A M J J A S O N D

Root parasite with scale-like leaves; bears sparsely hairy, scarlet or red flowers; the floral tube is ±cylindrical and the stamens protrude beyond it. Clay slopes and flats in Namaqualand and the southwestern Cape.

### ❶ *Hyobanche sanguinea*

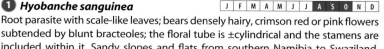

Root parasite with scale-like leaves; bears densely hairy, crimson red or pink flowers subtended by blunt bracteoles; the floral tube is ±cylindrical and the stamens are included within it. Sandy slopes and flats from southern Namibia to Swaziland. *Hyobanche rubra*, from the southern Cape coast, is similar but is dark red.

### ❷ *Hyobanche atropurpurea*

Root parasite with scale-like leaves; bears yeast-scented, dark purple to blackish flowers subtended by pointed bracteoles; the floral tube is swollen and the stamens are included within it. Rocky sandstone slopes in the interior mountains of the West Coast.

## *Harveya*  INKFLOWER, INKBLOM

Annual or perennial herbs, parasitic on roots. *Leaves reduced to scales and lacking chlorophyll,* usually yellowish. Flowers usually large, solitary in the axils, forming spikes or racemes, pink, red, white or yellow; calyx 5-lobed to more than halfway, sometimes weakly 2-lipped; corolla bell- to salver-shaped, *5-lobed and slightly oblique to 2-lipped*; stamens 4 in 2 unequal or nearly equal pairs, *with 1 anther lobe sterile and the fertile one often hooked*. Africa and the Mascarenes: ±35 spp; 9 fynbos spp. The plants turn black on drying and were used by early colonists as a source of writing ink, whence the vernacular name.

▸ **FLOWERS ORANGE OR RED**

### ❸ *Harveya bolusii*  Rooi-inkblom

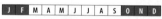

Parasitic perennial to 25 cm; bears a dense raceme of narrowly funnel-shaped, red to orange flowers 25–35 mm long, with a yellow throat and short petals; the calyx is lobed to nearly halfway. Sandstone slopes in the southwestern and southern Cape. *Harveya bodkinii*, from the mountains along the interior West Coast, has larger, cylindrical flowers.

### ❹ *Harveya squamosa*

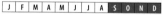

Parasitic perennial to 15 cm; bears a long spike of sessile, tubular, orange flowers 35–45 mm long, with a yellow throat and short petals; the calyx is shortly lobed and 2-lipped. Deep sandy soils, mostly coastal, in the southwestern Cape.

▸ **FLOWERS PURPLE TO PINK, WHITE OR PALE YELLOW**

### ❺ *Harveya capensis*  Witinkblom

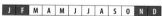

Slender, parasitic perennial to 40 cm; bears a loose raceme of sharply curved, narrowly funnel-shaped, white flowers 25–40 mm long, with a yellow, keyhole-shaped throat, and scented at night; the calyx is shortly lobed. Rocky sandstone slopes and flats in the southwestern and southern Cape. *Harveya stenosiphon*, from the mountains of the southern coast, has brilliant scarlet flowers.

### ❻ *Harveya purpurea*

(=*Harveya tubulosa*) **Persinkblom** Parasitic perennial to 15 cm; bears short or loose racemes of fragrant, broadly funnel-shaped, pale yellow or white to pink flowers 25–35 mm long, with yellow blotches in the throat; the calyx is lobed more than halfway. Sandstone slopes from the southwestern Cape to KwaZulu-Natal.

469

**❶ *Harveya pauciflora***

(=*Harveya coccinea*) Parasitic perennial to 60 cm; bears a raceme of tubular, purple flowers 20–30 mm long, with a white throat and upper petals that project forwards; the calyx is lobed to one-third. Rocky mountain slopes from the Cape Peninsula to the Eastern Cape.

# SCROPHULARIACEAE — Sutera family

▸ **FLOWERS SESSILE IN DENSE SPIKES WITH EACH CALYX JOINED TO THE SUBTENDING BRACT**

## *Dischisma* FALSE SLUGWORT

Annual or perennial herbs or shrublets. Leaves all alternate or the lower ones opposite, mostly narrow and toothed, rarely broad. Flowers *sessile in dense spikes*, white; *calyx 2-lobed, joined to the subtending bract; corolla 1-lipped with a funnel-shaped tube, split down the front* and expanded above into a 4-lobed upper lip; stamens 4 in unequal pairs inserted at different levels; *ovary with 1 ovule per chamber*. Western seaboard of southern Africa: 11 spp; 10 fynbos spp.

**❷ *Dischisma ciliatum***

J F M A M J J A S O N D

Sprawling perennial to 40 cm with narrow to elliptical, spreading, toothed leaves; bears elongate spikes of unscented or fragrant white flowers, subtended by densely hairy bracts. Rocky slopes and flats in the southwestern and southern Cape.

**❸ *Dischisma spicatum***

J F M A M J J A S O N D

Erect, hairy, annual herb to 30 cm with ascending branches and narrow, spreading, sparsely toothed leaves; bears elongate spikes of white flowers, subtended by hairy bracts. Sandy flats in Namaqualand and along the West Coast as far south as Piketberg.

## *Hebenstretia* SLUGWORT, SLAKBLOM

Annual or perennial herbs or shrublets. Leaves all alternate or the lower ones opposite, sometimes with axillary tufts, mostly narrow and toothed, rarely broad. Flowers *sessile in dense spikes*, white, usually with an orange fleck at the base of the petals; *calyx boat-shaped, sometimes notched, joined to the subtending bract; corolla 1-lipped with a funnel-shaped tube, split down the front* and expanded above into a 4-lobed upper lip; stamens 4 in unequal pairs inserted at different levels; *ovary with 1 ovule per chamber*. Southern and tropical Africa: ±40 spp; 12 fynbos spp.

▸ **PERENNIALS OR SHRUBLETS**

**❹ *Hebenstretia cordata***

J F M A M J J A S O N D

Shrublet with ±erect branches to 30 cm and overlapping, heart-shaped leaves; bears short, dense spikes of white flowers with ±sessile anthers. Coastal dunes from Namaqualand to the Eastern Cape.

**❺ *Hebenstretia robusta***

J F M A M J J A S O N D

Shrublet with erect branches and spreading, narrow, slightly toothed leaves; bears elongate spikes of honey-scented white flowers with orange to red marks and ±sessile anthers. Rocky sandstone soils in Namaqualand and the southwestern to Eastern Cape.

## ▶ ANNUAL HERBS

**1 Hebenstretia dentata**

J F M A M J **J A S O** N D

Erect, sparsely hairy annual herb with ascending branches to 40 cm and narrow, toothed leaves; bears spikes of white flowers with orange marks and ±sessile anthers. Rocky, sandstone soils in Namaqualand and the southwestern Cape.

**2 Hebenstretia repens**

J F M A M J **J A S O** N D

Sprawling annual to 45 cm with branches that turn up at the ends and narrow, sparsely toothed leaves; bears spikes of white flowers with stalked anthers. Sandy flats and slopes in Namaqualand and the southwestern Cape.

## *Microdon*   MICRODON, KATSTERTBOS

Heath-like shrublets, without short-shoots. Leaves alternate, narrow to rounded, often overlapping. Flowers *sessile in dense spikes*, greenish to brown or white and then usually with an orange patch; calyx cup-shaped with 5 short lobes, *hairless, joined to the subtending bract*; corolla 5-lobed and somewhat 2-lipped; stamens 2 or 4 in unequal pairs with 1 pair protruding beyond the tube; *ovary 1-chambered* through abortion of the second chamber, *with a single ovule*. Winter-rainfall South Africa: 7 spp; 6 fynbos spp.

**3 Microdon capitatus**

J F M A M J J A S **O N D**

Ericoid shrublet to 60 cm with tufts of short, needle-like leaves; bears dense, ovoid heads of white flowers with an orange throat, subtended by large, heart-shaped bracts; 4 stamens. Rocky, sandstone slopes in the southwestern Cape. *Microdon orbicularis* has narrowly elliptical leaves and large, papery bracts; *M. parviflorus* has overlapping, oval leaves and elongate spikes of flowers.

**4 Microdon dubius**

J **F M A M J J A S O N D**

Densely leafy shrublet with wand-like stems to 70 cm and narrow leaves; bears long spikes of yellow flowers, often with maroon to brown petals, sharply scented at night, subtended by oval, keeled bracts that are less than half as long as the flowers; 2 stamens. Rocky, sandstone slopes in Namaqualand and the southwestern Cape. *Microdon nitidus*, from the Cape Peninsula, has compact spikes of creamy white flowers, subtended by shining bracts more than half as long as the flowers.

## *Pseudoselago*   POWDERPUFF

Annual or perennial herbs, usually with *winged stems*. Leaves opposite, usually becoming alternate above, usually toothed. Flowers small, sessile, in spikes that are usually grouped into rounded or flat-topped clusters, white or mauve, sometimes with an orange patch; calyx 5-lobed, *joined to the subtending bract*; corolla tubular, 5-lobed and 2-lipped; stamens 4, in unequal pairs; *ovary with 1 ovule per chamber*. Winter-rainfall South Africa: 28 spp, all fynbos.

## ▶ FLORAL TUBE NARROWLY CYLINDRICAL, WIDENING ABRUPTLY ABOVE

**5 Pseudoselago subglabra**

J F M A M J J A S **O N D**

Annual herb to 80 cm with narrow, sometimes toothed, leaves; bears compact clusters of tubular, white or mauve flowers with an orange patch in the throat, with 2 upper petals. Damp, sandy slopes in the mountains of the southwestern Cape.

## ▶ FLORAL TUBE FUNNEL-SHAPED, FLARING GRADUALLY UPWARDS

**❶ *Pseudoselago peninsulae***  `J F M A M J J A S O N D`

Short-lived perennial to 40 cm, covered with gland-tipped hairs, with leaves toothed in the upper part only and continuing down the stems in narrow wings; bears crowded clusters of funnel-shaped white flowers with 2 upper petals. Shaded, rocky slopes on the Cape Peninsula. *Pseudoselago violacea*, from the mountains along the West Coast, has the leaves toothed to the base and mauve flowers.

**❷ *Pseudoselago serrata***  `J F M A M J J A S O N D`

Stout, leafy perennial to 40 cm with closely overlapping, oval leaves that are sparsely toothed, with the tips curved over, and that continue down the stem in narrow wings; bears dense, flat-topped clusters of funnel-shaped mauve flowers with 2 upper petals. Mountain slopes in the extreme southwestern Cape. *Pseudoselago pulchra*, from the coastal mountains around Hermanus, has closely toothed leaves that are not curved at the tips.

**❸ *Pseudoselago spuria***  `J F M A M J J A S O N D`

Sparsely hairy perennial with rod-like stems to 75 cm and narrow leaves that are toothed above, often with axillary tufts, and that continue down the stem in narrow wings; bears loose clusters of funnel-shaped mauve flowers with 2 upper petals. Mountain slopes in the extreme southwestern Cape.

## *Selago*   BITTER BUSH, AARBOSSIE

Shrublets or perennial (rarely annual) herbs with hairy stems. Leaves usually *alternate, clustered on short-shoots*, narrow and sometimes toothed. Flowers small, almost sessile, in spikes or racemes that are often aggregated into clusters, white or mauve to blue; calyx cup-shaped and 5-lobed, *joined to the subtending bract*; corolla funnel-shaped, 5-lobed and usually mostly 2-lipped; stamens 4 in pairs, *concealed within the upper lip; ovary with 1 ovule per chamber*. Southern Africa, mainly in the more arid parts: ±190 spp; ±100 fynbos spp. The vernacular name, aarbossie, refers to the alleged preference of the shrubs for situations overlying arterial water.

**❹ *Selago glabrata***  `J F M A M J J A S O N D`

Densely leafy shrublet with slender branches to 35 cm and tufts of narrow leaves; bears small white flowers in dense spikes arranged in narrow panicles; the calyx is unequally divided, with the upper 2 lobes larger. Stony slopes in renosterveld and karroid scrub from Namaqualand to the Little Karoo.

**❺ *Selago corymbosa***  `J F M A M J J A S O N D`

Densely leafy shrublet to 60 cm with stiff, spreading hairs on branches and tufts of needle-like leaves with the margins rolled under; bears small, white flowers in short spikes, arranged in rounded panicles; the calyx is equally and bluntly 5-toothed. Stony slopes and flats from the southwestern to the Eastern Cape.

**❶ *Selago glutinosa***

Dwarf, erect shrublet to 60 cm with glutinous, leathery, needle- or sausage-like leaves 5–15 mm long; bears fragrant, white flowers in dense cylindrical spikes, with shining, golden hairs. Rocky sandstone and granite slopes in arid fynbos in Namaqualand and the southwestern Cape. *Selago dregeana*, from the northern Cedarberg Mountains, has finer leaves and all 4 stamens equally protruding; *S. hispida*, from the interior mountains along the West Coast, has roughly hairy leaves that are more or less curved back.

## *Zaluzianskya* DRUMSTICKS, VERFBLOMMETJIE

Annual or perennial herbs with hairy stems. Leaves opposite but the upper ones often alternate, usually variously toothed. Flowers almost sessile in elongate or head-like spikes, either open during the day and then variously coloured, or nocturnal and then white with dull red reverse; calyx 2-lipped, *strongly 5-ribbed and pleated*; corolla nearly equally 5-lobed with the lobes often notched or forked, tubular, often with a ring of hairs in the mouth; stamens 4 in 2 unequal pairs or reduced to 2; *stigma tongue-like with 2 marginal strips of hairs*. Southern Africa, mainly the Western Cape: 55 spp; 17 fynbos spp. The annual species are concentrated in the southwest while the perennial species occur mostly in eastern South Africa. The vernacular name, verfblommetjie, refers to the use of the flowers of certain species as a source of dye.

**❷ *Zaluzianskya villosa***

Annual herb to 30 cm with the stems densely covered in down-facing hairs, and with densely hairy, rather blunt, lance-shaped leaves; bears white to mauve flowers with a yellow or red star in the centre, in crowded spikes that elongate in fruit, with deeply notched petals and a tube 10–25 mm long, enclosing 2 stamens. Sandy flats along the coast in the southwestern Cape. *Zaluzianskya affinis*, from north of Saldanha, has sharper, almost hairless leaves.

▸ FLOWERS STALKED, SOLITARY OR CLUSTERED IN THE LEAF AXILS
▸ ▸ SHRUBLETS WITH PARTLY WOODY STEMS; FLOWERS ±EQUALLY 5-LOBED

## *Freylinia* BELLBUSH, KLOKKIESBOS

Shrubs or shrublets. Leaves opposite, whorled or scattered, sometimes toothed in the upper half, often crisped or undulate on the margins. Flowers solitary or in clusters, funnel-shaped or cylindrical, white to pink or purple; calyx cup-shaped, 5-lobed; *corolla equally 5-lobed* with the tube longer than the petals; stamens 4, in unequal pairs, with *parallel anther lobes*. Southern and central Africa: 8 spp, all fynbos.

**❸ *Freylinia lanceolata***

**Heuningklokkiesbos** Small tree, 2–4(6) m, with narrow, hairless or short-haired leaves 40–120 mm long, the margins lightly rolled under; bears densely branched panicles of honey-scented, cream to yellow flowers 10–15 mm long, fading orange to brown; the style is 6–10 mm long. Stream banks, often on sandstone, in Namaqualand and the southwestern to Eastern Cape.

**❶ Freylinia undulata**

J F M A **M** **J** **J** **A** **S** O N D

Erect, stiffly branched shrub to 2 m with oval, hairless or sparsely hairy leaves 5–15 mm long, that are often minutely crisped or undulate; bears loose, narrow racemes of drooping white to purple flowers 15–20 mm long; the style is 10–15 mm long. Shale slopes along the southern coast. *Freylinia helmei*, from steep shale slopes near Bot River, has narrower leaves and flowers 25–27 mm long with the styles 15–17 mm long.

## Oftia   OFTIA

Shrubs or shrublets with sprawling, leafy stems. Leaves mostly opposite, closely toothed, with the margins *more or less rolled under*. Flowers solitary in the upper axils, white; calyx 5-lobed; *corolla more or less equally 5-lobed, with the tube longer than the petals*; stamens 4, *equal*, with *parallel anther lobes. Fruit a small, fleshy drupe.* Winter-rainfall parts of South Africa: 3 spp; 2 fynbos spp.

**❷ Oftia africana**

J F **M** **A** **M** **J** **J** **A** **S** O N D

Sprawling, roughly hairy shrublet with trailing branches to 1 m and toothed, lance-shaped leaves 10–40 mm long; bears fragrant, white flowers in the upper axils. Rocky sandstone and granite slopes in the southwestern and Eastern Cape. *Oftia glabra*, from the Little Karoo, is more erect with smaller leaves 7–12 mm long; *O. revoluta*, from Namaqualand, has narrower leaves with the margins rolled under.

## Teedia   TEEDIA

Dwarf shrubs or woody perennials growing in rock cracks. Leaves opposite, finely toothed. Flowers solitary or in few-flowered clusters in the upper axils, *pink or mauve*; calyx 5-lobed; *corolla ±equally 5-lobed, with the tube longer than the petals*; stamens 4, in unequal pairs, with *parallel anther lobes. Fruit a small, fleshy berry or drupe.* Southern Africa: 2 spp, both fynbos.

**❸ Teedia lucida**

**J** F M A M **J** **J** **A** S O N D

Sprawling, hairless shrublet to 1.2 m with glossy, finely toothed, elliptical leaves with winged petioles; bears mauve flowers. Rock crevices in the mountains from Namaqualand to eastern Zimbabwe. *Teedia pubescens*, from the southern and southwestern Cape, has densely hairy stems.

## Chaenostoma   SKUNK BUSH, STINKBOSSIE

Shrublets or woody perennials (rarely annuals), often aromatic or foetid. Leaves usually opposite, variously shaped, usually toothed. Flowers mostly solitary in the leaf axils, sometimes in racemes, *mostly white, pink or mauve to blue*, with a yellow throat; calyx 5-lobed and ±2-lipped; *corolla ±equally 5-lobed*; stamens 4, in unequal pairs, all or only the lower 2 *protruding from the tube*. Southern and tropical Africa, mainly South Africa: 49 spp; 30 fynbos spp. The genus *Chaenostoma* has recently been resurrected to accommodate all but 3 of the erstwhile species of *Sutera*, reflecting their closer relationship to the species of *Manulea*.

▸ **ALL 4 STAMENS PROTRUDING**

**❹ Chaenostoma caeruleum**

J F M A M **J** **J** **A** **S** O N D

(=*Sutera caerulea*) Erect perennial to 1 m, covered with gland-tipped hairs, and with lance-shaped, usually sparsely toothed leaves; bears long racemes of mauve or violet flowers with a shortly funnel-shaped yellow tube 3–5 mm long; all 4 stamens protrude. Stony soils in scrub throughout the southwestern and southern Cape.

## ▶ ONLY THE LOWER 2 STAMENS PROTRUDING

**1** *Chaenostoma hispidum*

J F M A M J J A S O N D

(=*Sutera hispida*) Shrublet covered with rough, gland-tipped hairs, with stiffly hairy, erect or sprawling branches to 50 cm and coarsely toothed, oval to elliptical leaves; bears axillary pairs of pink to mauve flowers with a yellow throat and narrowly funnel-shaped tube 8–12 mm long; only the lower 2 stamens protrude. Rocky sandstone or limestone outcrops in the southwestern Cape.

**2** *Chaenostoma revolutum*

J F M A M J J A S O N D

(=*Sutera revoluta*) Shrublet with gland-tipped hairs and unwinged stems to 60 cm and narrow leaves with the margins rolled under; bears racemes of white, pink or mauve flowers with a yellow throat and funnel-shaped tube 5–13 mm long; only the lower 2 stamens protrude. Stony, shale slopes in the southwestern and southern Cape.

**3** *Chaenostoma uncinatum*

J F M A M J J A S O N D

(=*Sutera uncinata*) Shrublet covered with gland-tipped hairs, with narrowly winged stems to 60 cm and narrow, mostly untoothed leaves, the margins sometimes rolled under; bears racemes or narrow panicles of pink to purple flowers with a yellow throat and narrowly funnel-shaped tube 10–19 mm long; only the lower 2 stamens protrude. Sandy or rocky places in scrub throughout the southwestern Cape.

## *Jamesbrittenia*   JAMESBRITTENIA

Shrublets, woody perennials or annual herbs, usually glandular and foetid. Leaves usually opposite, variously shaped, usually toothed. Flowers solitary in the leaf axils to form racemes, often mauve to blue, with a yellow throat; calyx 5-lobed; *corolla ±equally 5-lobed, with a slender, cylindrical tube that widens abruptly near the top;* stamens 4, in unequal pairs, *the upper 2 extending down the inside of the tube bent and abruptly widened.* Mainly central and southern Africa, with 1 species extending to India; 83 spp; 12 fynbos spp. The yellow- to purple-flowered *Jamesbrittenia atropurpurea* was used as a substitute for saffron in medicine and dyeing.

**4** *Jamesbrittenia albomarginata*

J F M A M J J A S O N D

Dwarf shrublet covered with gland-tipped hairs, to 40 cm, with small leaves ±3 mm long, that are often toothed above; bears orange to maroon flowers edged with white, with a tube 12–18 mm long. In scrub on coastal limestone flats and dunes on the Agulhas Plain.

**5** *Jamesbrittenia tenuifolia*

J F M A M J J A S O N D

Shrublet covered with gland-tipped hairs, to 60 cm, with narrow leaves 2–10(25) mm long, that have 2–6 teeth or lobes at the tips; bears purple to blue, rarely white to pink, flowers, with a tube 8–14 mm long. In scrub on sandy and rocky slopes and dunes along the southern Cape coast.

**6** *Jamesbrittenia stellata*

J F M A M J J A S O N D

Shrublet covered with gland-tipped hairs, to 40 cm, with small, lance-shaped leaves mostly 2–10 mm long; bears white or pink flowers with a wedge-shaped yellow to red patch at the base of each petal, with a tube 10–15 mm long. Sheltered places on coastal limestone cliffs on the Agulhas Plain.

481

**❶** *Jamesbrittenia calciphila*

Gnarled, very twiggy shrublet covered with gland-tipped hairs, to 45 cm, with minute, rounded, almost granular leaves, mostly 1–2 mm long, crowded on short-shoots; bears pink to blue, rarely white, flowers with a wedge-shaped yellow to red patch at the base of each petal, and a tube 9–11 mm long. Coastal, limestone rocks and cliffs on the Agulhas Plain. *Jamesbrittenia aspalathoides*, from east of Swellendam, has narrower leaves.

▶ ▶ ANNUAL OR PERENNIAL HERBS WITH SOFT STEMS; FLOWERS ±EQUALLY LOBED, WITHOUT POCKETS OR SPURS

## *Phyllopodium*   CAPEWORT, OPSLAG

Small annual or perennial herbs, all or some of the *hairs on the stems without glands, usually pointing downwards*. Leaves opposite below becoming alternate above, mostly elliptical and often toothed. Flowers in elongate or head-like racemes, white to lilac, sometimes with an orange or yellow patch; calyx 5-lobed and nearly 2-lipped, *joined to the subtending bract*; corolla 5-lobed and 2-lipped, cylindrical or funnel-shaped; stamens usually 4 in unequal pairs, rarely 2, *the upper 2 extending down the inside of the tube as ridges; stigma tongue-like with 2 marginal strips of hairs*. Namibia and South Africa, mostly in the Northern and Western Cape: 26 spp; 20 fynbos spp. The name, opslag, is a general term for young growths appearing after the first rains on lands that have been cleared or burned, and refers to the seedlings of various annual herbs.

**❷** *Phyllopodium cephalophorum*

Hairy annual herb to 30 cm with lance-shaped, lightly toothed leaves; bears crowded heads of mauve, pink or white flowers arranged in branched clusters. Sandy flats below 300 m, in southern Namaqualand and along the West Coast.

**❸** *Phyllopodium phyllopodioides*

Hairy annual to 25 cm with lance-shaped, lightly toothed leaves; bears crowded heads of mauve or rarely white flowers arranged in rounded clusters; outer bracts oval or lance-shaped, shaggy towards the base. Sandy flats below 300 m, in the southwestern Cape.

**❹** *Phyllopdium capillare*

Annual herb with gland-tipped hairs, to 26 cm, with elliptical to lance-shaped, lightly toothed leaves; bears compact heads of small white flowers on leafless stems; outer bracts oblong to elliptical, minutely hairy with shaggy margins. Sandy or stony places below 120 m, along the West Coast.

## *Polycarena*   CAPE PHLOX

Small annual or perennial herbs, with *spreading, glandular hairs on the stems*. Leaves opposite below becoming alternate above, mostly narrow and obscurely toothed. Flowers in elongate or head-like racemes, white or yellowish to lilac, sometimes with an orange or yellow patch; calyx 5-lobed and nearly 2-lipped, *joined to the subtending bract*; corolla 5-lobed and 2-lipped, cylindrical or funnel-shaped; stamens usually 4 in unequal pairs, rarely 2, *the upper 2 extending down the inside of the tube as ridges; stigma tongue-like, with 2 marginal strips of hairs*. Northern and Western Cape: 17 spp; 14 fynbos spp.

### ❶ *Polycarena lilacina*

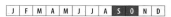

Annual herb covered with short, gland-tipped hairs, to 28 cm, with narrow, often toothed leaves; bears white to pale mauve flowers, with a yellow patch at the base of the upper petals, in heads that are arranged in flat-topped clusters, with a hairy tube 13–16 mm long. Sandy places, below 200 m, along the West Coast.

### ❷ *Polycarena gilioides*

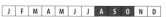

Annual herb covered with gland-tipped hairs, to 20 cm, with lance-shaped, smooth or toothed leaves; bears few-flowered clusters of white or cream flowers flushed purple on the outside, with an orange patch below the upper petals, and a hairy tube 8–10(20) mm long. Sandy soils along the interior West Coast. *Polycarena capensis* has more than 10 flowers per cluster.

### ❸ *Polycarena batteniana*

Annual herb covered with gland-tipped hairs, to 18 cm, with lance-shaped, obscurely toothed leaves; bears heads of cream to white flowers, with a yellow patch at the base of the upper petals, with an almost hairless tube 10–17 mm long. Sandy slopes in the mountains in Namaqualand and on the northern mountains of the Western Cape.

## *Lyperia*  LYPERIA

Perennial or annual herbs, usually glandular, *with narrowly winged stems*. Leaves usually opposite, variously shaped, usually toothed. Flowers solitary in the leaf axils to form racemes, greenish, or white to mauve with a yellow throat; calyx 5-lobed; *corolla ±equally 5-lobed, with a slender, cylindrical tube that widens abruptly near the top*; stamens 4, in unequal pairs, *the upper 2 extending down the inside of the tube as hairy wings or ridges*. Winter-rainfall South Africa: 6 spp, all fynbos. The flowers of most species are fragrant at night and adapted to pollination by moths.

### ❹ *Lyperia lychnidea*

Perennial covered with gland-tipped hairs, to 1 m, the leaves mostly in axillary tufts, shortly toothed above; bears racemes of greenish to yellow flowers that are clove-scented at night, with a slender tube 23–28 mm long; 4 fertile stamens. Coastal sands in scrub along the western and southern Cape coasts.

### ❺ *Lyperia tristis*

Annual herb covered with gland-tipped hairs, to 60 cm, with leaves that are sometimes toothed; bears racemes of whitish to yellow or brown flowers that are clove-scented at night, with a slender tube 20–29 mm long; 4 fertile stamens. Sandy, gravelly or stony ground, often in scrub, from Namibia to the Eastern Cape.

## *Manulea*  MANULEA, VINGERTJIES

Annual or perennial herbs, usually hairy. Leaves usually opposite, sometimes basal, variously toothed or untoothed. Flowers in racemes or various compound inflorescences, white or greenish yellow to red or brown; calyx 3-lobed and 2-lipped; corolla equally 5-lobed or 2-lipped, usually tubular; stamens usually 4 in unequal pairs, with the upper pair arising well within the tube, *all enclosed within the tube; stigma tongue-like with 2 marginal strips of hairs*. Southern and south tropical Africa, but mainly the Western Cape: 74 spp; 40 fynbos spp. Most of the species with dull-coloured flowers are adapted to pollination by moths and are delightfully fragrant at night.

485

## ▶ FLOWERS IN HEAD-LIKE RACEMES, CREAMY WHITE WITH BROAD PETALS

**❶ _Manulea corymbosa_**

J F M A M J **J A S O N** D

Annual herb covered with gland-tipped hairs, to 45 cm, the toothed leaves crowded at the base; bears crowded, head-like racemes of creamy white flowers with an orange centre and rounded petals, and a tube 8–12 mm long, with the stamens attached in the outer third and the stigma projecting slightly beyond the mouth; the calyx is 2-lipped with each sepal pouched at the base. Sandy flats along the West Coast. _Manulea adenocalyx_, from further north, has weakly pouched sepals that are not conspicuously fringed.

**❷ _Manulea altissima_**

J F M A M J **J A S** O N D

Foetid, short-lived perennial covered with gland-tipped hairs, to 1 m, the obscurely toothed leaves crowded at the base; bears head-like racemes of scented, white flowers with a yellowish centre and rounded petals, and a tube 8–10 mm long, with the stamens attached near the middle and the stigma hidden within. Deep, sandy soils in Namaqualand and along the West Coast.

## ▶ FLOWERS IN SLENDER RACEMES, ORANGE TO BROWN WITH NARROW, LONGITUDINALLY ROLLED PETALS

**❸ _Manulea cheiranthus_**

J F M A M J **J A S O N** D

Annual covered with gland-tipped hairs, to 30 cm, with coarsely toothed leaves; bears racemes of ochre to brown, 2-lipped flowers with longitudinally rolled, almost thread-like, petals and a tube 3–5 mm long, with the stamens attached in the outer third. Sandy and rocky slopes and flats in the southwestern and southern Cape.

**❹ _Manulea turritis_**

J **F M A M J J A** S O N D

Softly hairy perennial to 1 m with doubly toothed leaves; bears loosely arranged cymules of brownish-yellow to reddish flowers with narrow, longitudinally rolled petals and a tube 7–9 mm long, with the stamens attached in the outer third. Rocky, sandstone slopes in sheltered places in the West Coast interior.

**❺ _Manulea rubra_**

J F M **A M J J A S O N** D

Almost hairless perennial to 70 cm with smooth leaves crowded at the base; bears loosely arranged cymes of reddish-brown flowers with narrow, longitudinally rolled petals and a tube 8–9 mm long, with the stamens attached in the outer third; throat with 3–5 longitudinal bands of hairs. Sandy, coastal flats along the West Coast.

**❻ _Manulea tomentosa_**

J F M A M J J **A S O N** D

Perennial to 60 cm covered with grey hairs, and with toothed leaves; bears crowded cymes of orange to brown flowers with narrow, longitudinally rolled petals and a tube 7–10 mm long, with the stamens attached in the outer third; throat with 3–5 longitudinal bands of hairs. Coastal sands in the southwestern Cape. _Manulea caledonica_, from the Agulhas Plain, has the lower part of the stem covered with club-shaped (not pointed) hairs; _M. leiostachys_, from the interior mountains of the West Coast, lacks the hairy bands in the throat.

▶ ▶ **ANNUAL OR PERENNIAL HERBS WITH SOFT STEMS; FLOWERS STRONGLY 2-LIPPED WITH 1 OR MORE POCKETS OR SPURS**

## *Nemesia*  **NEMESIA, LEEUBEKKIE**

Annual or perennial herbs. Leaves opposite, variously toothed. Flowers solitary in the axils or in loose, leafy racemes, combinations of white, yellow, orange, pink or blue; calyx 5-lobed; corolla 5-lobed and strongly *2-lipped, snapdragon-like with the lower lip bulging upwards at the base and usually with 2 velvety swellings*, with *a very short tube extended into a single pouch or spur*; stamens 4 in 2 unequal pairs twisted around one another. Southern Africa, mainly temperate and winter-rainfall parts: ±60 spp; ±25 fynbos spp. Selections of *Nemesia strumosa* and *N. affinis* are popular garden annuals.

▶ **SHORT-LIVED PERENNIALS OR SOFT SHRUBLETS; LEAVES MOSTLY 3–5-VEINED FROM THE BASE; FLOWERS WHITE**

**❶ *Nemesia macrocarpa***

| J | F | M | A | M | J | J | A | S | O | N | D |

Short-lived perennial to 40 cm with oval, toothed leaves that are 3–5-veined from the base; bears small, nearly equally 2-lipped, white to pale pink flowers crowded in the upper axils, with a raised velvety palate in the throat and a short spur 2 mm long; the capsules are slightly longer than wide. Sheltered rocky slopes and forest margins in the southwestern and southern Cape. *Nemesia acuminata* and *N. petiolina* have longer, sometimes trailing, inflorescences and fruits that are respectively triangular, or distinctly longer than wide.

▶ **ANNUAL HERBS OR SHORT-LIVED PERENNIALS; LEAVES MOSTLY WITH A SINGLE VEIN FROM THE BASE; FLOWERS VARIOUSLY COLOURED**

**❷ *Nemesia bicornis***

| J | F | M | A | M | J | J | A | S | O | N | D |

Annual herb to 80 cm, loosely branching above, with narrowly lance-shaped, toothed to lobed leaves; bears branched racemes of white to pale lilac flowers with grey veins, and 4 velvety swellings in the throat, with a 4 mm-long spur, slightly swollen at the tip, and narrowly oblong upper petals; the capsules are triangular. Coastal sands in Namaqualand and the southwestern Cape.

**❸ *Nemesia affinis***

| J | F | M | A | M | J | J | A | S | O | N | D |

Annual herb to 30 cm, with elliptical to lance-shaped, toothed leaves; bears racemes of white, blue, yellow, or sometimes red flowers, with a lower lip that has a raised, cream to yellow palate, bearing 2 velvety swellings, with a spur 3–5 mm long and oblong upper petals; the capsules are as long as to slightly longer than wide. Sandy and granite slopes and flats from southern Namibia to the Eastern Cape.

**❹ *Nemesia cheiranthus***

| J | F | M | A | M | J | J | A | S | O | N | D |

Annual herb to 40 cm, with lance-shaped, lightly toothed leaves; bears racemes of white flowers, sometimes marked with purple, with a yellow lower lip that has a slightly raised palate bearing 2 velvety swellings, with a spur 3–5 mm long, and long, slender upper petals; the capsules are as long as wide. Mainly sandy slopes and flats in Namaqualand and the interior West Coast.

### 1 Nemesia barbata

J F M A M J J A S O N D

Annual herb to 30 cm with oval, toothed leaves; bears compact racemes of white to cream flowers with a blue to blackish lower lip bearing a raised, hairy palate, with a short, blunt spur up to 2 mm long and small, rounded upper petals; the capsules are longer than wide. Sandy flats and slopes, often after fire, in Namaqualand and the southwestern Cape.

### 2 Nemesia strumosa

J F M A M J J A S O N D

Annual herb to 40 cm with narrowly lance-shaped, lightly toothed leaves; bears rounded racemes of white, cream, pink, mauve, or sometimes red, flowers that are mottled brown and coarsely hairy in the throat, with a sac-like lower lip and rounded upper petals; the fruits are longer than wide. Sandy flats, often in sandveld, along the West Coast.

### 3 Nemesia bodkinii

J F M A M J J A S O N D

Short-lived perennial to 20 cm with elliptical to lance-shaped, toothed leaves that have the margins rolled under; bears a few purple to blackish flowers that are velvety in the throat with a sac-like lower lip and rounded upper petals; the fruits are longer than wide. Sandstone slopes in the interior mountains along the West Coast, flowering mainly after fire.

## Diascia   TWINSPUR, PENSIES

Annual or perennial herbs. Leaves basal or opposite, with the upper ones sometimes alternate, usually toothed or lobed and hairless. Flowers solitary in the axils on long pedicels or in racemes, mostly *pink to purple*, rarely orange or yellow, with a darker centre and *bright yellow windows*; calyx 5-lobed; corolla cup-shaped, 5-lobed and 2-lipped with 4 small upper petals and 1 large lower one, with a *very short tube extended into 2 pouches or spurs*; stamens 4 in 2 unequal pairs twisted around one another. Southern Africa, mainly the temperate and winter-rainfall parts: ±70 spp; ±30 fynbos spp. Some of the perennial species from the eastern Drakensberg Mountains are popular garden plants; the intricate flowers are pollinated by specialised oil-collecting bees that utilise the floral oils secreted by glands contained in the flower spurs. The Afrikaans vernacular name is a 17th century corruption of the English 'pansy'.

▸ **FLOWERS WITH SPURS 5–25 MM LONG**

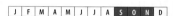

### 4 Diascia longicornis

J F M A M J J A S O N D

Annual herb to 32 cm with elliptical leaves that are toothed or deeply incised along the margins; bears reddish or white flowers 9–19 mm in diameter, with a deep magenta centre and a large and small yellow spot below each upper petal lobe; the spurs turn upwards or project downwards and are 4–18 mm long. Loamy soil in renosterveld along the West Coast. *Diascia whiteheadii*, from the mountains along the West Coast, has 1–4 small yellow spots below each upper petal lobe, and diverging spurs 18–22 mm long.

▸ **FLOWERS WITH SHALLOW SACS UP TO 5 MM DEEP**

### 5 Diascia capensis

J F M A M J J A S O N D

Erect or sprawling annual herb to 35 cm with deeply lobed leaves; bears greyish-violet flowers 12–23 mm in diameter, with a dark magenta centre and 2 yellow sacs; the stamens are borne on a yellow swelling and arch sharply downwards. Mainly coastal sandveld in the southwestern Cape. *Diascia arenicola*, from the West Coast north of Piketberg, has 2 of the stamens straight or upcurved.

491

**❶ *Diascia collina***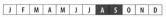

Sprawling annual herb to 20 cm with elliptical to oblong leaves that are deeply lobed or divided; bears greyish-magenta flowers 13–20 mm in diameter, with a dark magenta centre and yellow sacs 4–5 mm long; the stamens are borne on a yellow swelling and the lower filaments have a prominent swelling at the bend; the pollen is orange. Strandveld in sandy loam around Saldanha Bay. *Diascia pusilla*, from north of Saldanha, has smaller flowers 9–13 mm in diameter, with shorter sacs 2 mm long.

**❷ *Diascia diffusa***

Annual herb to 30 cm with oval to elliptical leaves that are lightly toothed to deeply lobed; bears reddish-lilac flowers 12–24 mm in diameter, with a dark red or purplish centre and 2 yellow sacs 1–2 mm deep; the stamens are borne on a yellow swelling and have hairy filaments that project forwards and downwards, with a swollen branch on each of the lower ones. Sand or loam in fynbos and renosterveld along the West Coast south of Piketberg. *Diascia appendiculata*, from between Piketberg and Citrusdal, has smaller flowers with very shallow sacs less than 1 mm deep and smooth stamen filaments; *D. occidentalis*, from coastal sandveld between Lambert's Bay and Elands Bay, also has smaller flowers 10–13 mm in diameter, with sacs 2–3 mm long.

## *Hemimeris*   HEMIMERIS, GEELGESIGGIES

Annual herbs. Leaves opposite, with the upper ones sometimes alternate, usually toothed or lobed. Flowers solitary in the axils on long pedicels or in dense, flat-topped racemes, *bright yellow with dark spots in the centre*; calyx 5-lobed; corolla cup-shaped, *4-lobed and 2-lipped* with the lower lip larger, with *a very short tube extended into 2 pouches or spurs; stamens 2*, sharply bent. The flowers are pollinated by specialised oil-collecting bees that utilise the floral oils secreted by glands contained in the flower spurs. Winter-rainfall parts of South Africa: 5 spp; 4 fynbos spp.

**❸ *Hemimeris racemosa*** 

Annual herb, 3–50 cm, with oval, toothed or lobed leaves; bears yellow flowers 7–13 mm long, with 2 spurs 1.5–3 mm long. Coastal and inland sand and clay soils from Namaqualand to the Eastern Cape. *Hemimeris centrodes* has longer spurs, 3–6 mm long; *H. gracilis* has smaller flowers, 5–8 mm long, with spurs 4–5 mm long.

**❹ *Hemimeris sabulosa*** 

Annual herb, 3–50 cm, with lobed or toothed leaves; bears yellow flowers 9–12 mm long, with 2 sacs 1–2 mm deep and with lateral pockets folded over the stamens. Sandy, coastal flats in Namaqualand and the southwestern Cape.

# INDEX TO SCIENTIFIC NAMES

CAPITAL LETTERS denote families
**Bold** denotes genera
***Bold italics*** denotes alternative generic names
*Italics* denotes alternative species names

**501**

# INDEX TO COMMON NAMES

CAPITAL LETTERS denote families

**See illustrated glossary on front endpaper for additional terms**

**actinomorphic** radially symmetrical; capable of division into two equal parts along more than one axis

**annual** plant that germinates from seed, flowers, produces new seeds, and dies within a single season, typically having fine, fibrous roots

**apical** of the tip or apex

**attenuate** tapering gradually to a point

**awn** stiff bristle, often present on the fruits of grasses

**axil** the upper angle between a stem and an attached leaf or branch; **axillary** of structures in this position

**basal** of the base

**basifixed** of an anther attached at its base to the filament

**boss** protuberance or swelling

**bract** leaf-like organ subtending a flower or inflorescence; **bracteate** bearing bracts

**bracteole** small, second-order bract

**calcareous** containing or resembling calcium carbonate; chalky

**callus** wart-like outgrowth

**carpel** single element or segment of an ovary containing ovules

**caudex** persistent, underground woody stem of some perennial plants

**cauline** arising from the stem

**cladode** modified, flattened or needle-like branchlets resembling leaves

**compound** comprised of several individual units

**coppice** to resprout from near the base

**corm** underground storage structure formed from a short, swollen stem; **cormous** of plants with a corm

**cyathium** modified inflorescence of *Euphorbia* species resembling a single flower

**dehiscent** opening spontaneously to shed seeds or pollen

**dichotomy** division into two equal parts; **dichotomously** divided in this manner

**digitate** completely divided to a central point, like the fingers

**disciform** of daisy flowerheads with several peripheral rows of tubular, female florets surrounding the funnel-shaped, bisexual disc-florets (see also p.378)

**discoid** button-like, of daisy flowerheads with only funnel-shaped, bisexual florets (see also p.378)

**ellipsoid** rugby ball-shaped

**epicalyx** series of small, sepal-like bracts forming a calyx-like whorl beneath the true calyx

**epiphyte** plant that grows on another plant but is not parasitic on it

**equisetum** genus of primitive land plants, commonly known as horsetails

**ericoid** small, stiff, needle-like leaves with the margins rolled under, as in many *Erica* species; shrubs with such leaves

**filiform** thread-like

**flowerhead** head-like inflorescence containing a number of individual small flowers or florets

**foliolate** comprising separate leaflets

**funicle** thread-like stalk attaching an ovule or seed to the wall of the ovary

**geophyte** perennial plant with underground storage organs that propagates by means of buds below the soil surface

**glaucous** covered with a grey, waxy or powdery bloom

**glume** dry, chaffy bracts of the flower spikes in grasses, restios and sedges

**gynostegium** complex structure comprising joined male and female reproductive organs in members of the Orchid and Milkweed families

**heterostylous** having styles of different lengths in different flowers

**imbricate** overlapping

**imparipinnate** of compound leaves having an uneven number of leaflets, with a terminal leaflet